Using EViews

For *Principles of Econometrics, Fourth Edition*

Using EViews

For *Principles of Econometrics, Fourth Edition*

WILLIAM E. GRIFFITHS
University of Melbourne

R. CARTER HILL
Louisiana State University

GUAY C. LIM
University of Melbourne

JOHN WILEY & SONS, INC
New York / Chichester / Weinheim / Brisbane / Singapore / Toronto

Bill Griffiths dedicates this work to Jill, David and Wendy Griffiths

Carter Hill dedicates this work to his wife, Melissa Waters

Guay Lim dedicates this work to Tony Meagher

VICE PRESIDENT AND EXECUTIVE PUBLISHER   George Hoffman
ASSISTANT EDITOR   Emily McGee
PRODUCTION MANAGER   Micheline Frederick

This book was set in Times New Roman by the authors and printed and bound by Bind-Rite Graphics. The cover was printed by Bind-Rite Graphics

This book is printed on acid-free paper.   ∞

ISBN 9781118032077

Printed in the United States of America

10 9 8 7 6 5 4 3 2

PREFACE

This book is a supplement to *Principles of Econometrics, 4th Edition* by R. Carter Hill, William E. Griffiths and Guay C. Lim (Wiley, 2011), hereinafter *POE4*. It is designed for students to learn the econometric software package EViews at the same time as they are using *POE4* to learn econometrics. It is not a substitute for *POE4*, nor is it a stand-alone computer manual. It is a companion to the textbook, showing how to do all the examples in *POE4* using EViews Version 7. For most students, econometrics only has real meaning after they are able to use it to analyze data sets, interpret results, and draw conclusions. EViews is an ideal vehicle for achieving these objectives. Others who wish to learn and practice econometrics, such as instructors and researchers, will also benefit from using this book in conjunction with *POE4*.

EViews is a very powerful and user-friendly program that is ideally suited for classroom use. You can find further details at the website **http://www.eviews.com**. The registration key that accompanies this book entitles you to download the Student Version of EViews 7 from this website. While the Student Version is perfectly adequate for handling most of the examples and exercises in POE4, it does have some limitations. A precise statement of these limitations relative to the capabilities of the full version of EViews is provided on the next page. Note that, unless you want to save a workfile, the Student Version will handle large data sets without any problems. Also, saving is often possible after deleting objects that are no longer relevant. Many students will, of course, have access to the full version of EViews in computer laboratories on campus.

The EViews workfiles for all the examples in *POE4*, and corresponding text definition files of the form **.def*, can be found at **http://www.wiley.com/college/hill**. These data sets are also available at **http://principlesofeconometrics.com/poe4/poe4.htm**, along with errata for this book and for *POE4*.

With the exception of Chapter 1, the chapters in this book parallel the chapters in *POE4*. Thus, if you seek help for the examples in Chapter 11 of *POE4*, check Chapter 11 in this book. However, within a chapter, the section numbers in *POE4* do not necessarily correspond to the sections in this EViews supplement.

We welcome comments on this book and suggestions for improvement. We would like to acknowledge the valuable assistance of David Lilien, Glenn Sueyoshi, and Gareth Thomas from Quantitative Micro Software, the company that develops and distributes EViews. Of course, David, Glenn, Gareth and EViews are not responsible for any blunders that we may have committed.

William E. Griffiths
Department of Economics
University of Melbourne
Vic 3010
Australia
wegrif@unimelb.edu.au

R. Carter Hill
Economics Department
Louisiana State University
Baton Rouge, LA 70803
eohill@lsu.edu

Guay C. Lim
Melbourne Institute for Applied
Economic and Social Research
University of Melbourne
Vic 3010
Australia
g.lim@unimelb.edu.au

The Student Version of EViews 7

The EViews Student Version allows students to analyze datasets whose size is limited only by available computer memory. Instead of imposing hard limits on the size of datasets, the Student Version places "soft" capacity restrictions on the amount of data (1,500 observations per series, 15,000 total observations, 60 objects) that may be saved or exported. Students may, without restriction, work with larger amounts of data, but workfiles that exceed the soft limits may not be saved nor the data exported.

The Student Version is also restricted to interactive use since programming capabilities and batch-mode processing are not supported. Notable excluded features are X11, X12, and Tramo/Seats X-11 seasonal adjustment, solving model objects with more than 10 equations, storing EViews objects to databases, database autosearch, and redirection of print output to text or RTF files.

Lastly, the EViews Student Version license restricts use to a single machine by a single user. The user must be a currently enrolled student or currently employed faculty member. Note specifically that the restriction of the license to a single user implies that the Student Version is not licensed for use on public-access computers. The continued use of the Student Version beyond a 14-day grace period requires product activation/registration. Product activation takes seconds to perform using our automatic registration feature (for internet-connected computers). Registration may also be performed manually after obtaining a registration key via web browser or by contacting IHS EViews by telephone. In addition, the Student Version License will expire two (2) years after first use, and the Student Version will no longer run two years after the first activation.

BRIEF CONTENTS

CONTENTS

CHAPTER 1

Introduction to EViews 7.1

CHAPTER OUTLINE

1.1 USING EVIEWS FOR PRINCIPLES OF ECONOMETRICS, 4E

This manual is a supplement to the textbook *Principles of Econometrics, 4th edition*, by Hill, Griffiths and Lim (John Wiley & Sons, Inc., 2011). It is not in itself an econometrics book, nor is it a complete computer manual. Rather it is a step-by-step guide to using EViews 7.1 for the empirical examples in *Principles of Econometrics, 4th edition*, which we will abbreviate as *POE4*. We imagine you sitting at a computer with your *POE4* text and *Using EViews for Principles of Econometrics, 4th edition* open, following along with the manual to replicate the

1

examples in *POE4*. Before you can do this you must install EViews and obtain the EViews "*workfiles*," which are documents that contain the actual data.

1.1.1 Installing EViews 7.1

EViews 7.1 is distributed on a single CD-ROM. Its contents are:

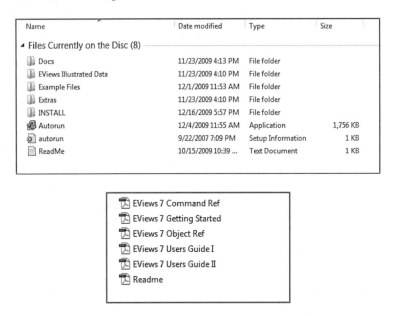

Within the Docs folder is a booklet called "EViews 7 Getting Started." It describes the installation and registration process. EViews is a Windows-based program. First close all other applications, then insert the CD into your computer's drive and wait until the setup program launches. If the CD does not spin-up on its own, navigate to the CD drive using Windows Explorer, and click on the Setup icon (AUTORUN.EXE).

1.1.2 Checking for updates

Once installed you should visit www.eviews.com and check the "**download**" link. There you will find any updates for your software. Alternatively, once EViews is installed set EViews to automatically update.

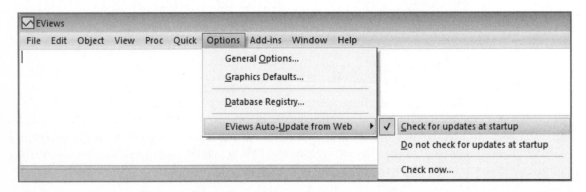

1.1.3 Obtaining data workfiles

The **EViews data workfiles** (with extension *.wf1) and other resources for *POE4* can be found at www.wiley.com/college/hill[1]. Find the link "Online resources for students." The *POE4* workfiles can be downloaded in a compressed format, saved to a subdirectory (we use c:\data\eviews), and then expanded. In addition to the EViews workfiles, there are **data definition** files (*.def) that describe the variables and show some summary statistics. The definition files are simple text files that can be opened with utilities like Notepad or Wordpad, or using a word processor. These files should be downloaded as well. Individual EViews workfiles, definition files, and other resources can be obtained from the author website www.principlesofeconometrics.com.

1.2 STARTING EVIEWS

To launch EViews, double-click the EViews 7 icon on the desktop, if one is present. It should resemble

Alternatively, select EViews 7 from the Windows Start Menu. When EViews opens you are presented with the following screen:

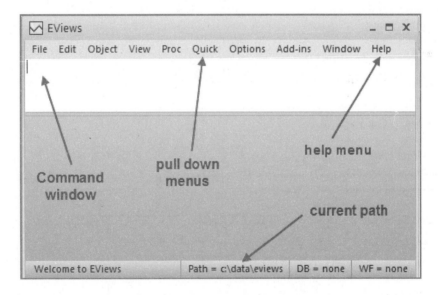

Across the top are **Drop Down Menus** that make implementing EViews procedures quite simple. Below the menu items is the **Command window**. It can be used as an alternative to the menus, once you become familiar with basic commands and syntax. Across the bottom is the **Current Path** for reading data and saving files. To change this, double-click path name and browse for a new folder. The EViews **Help Menu** is going to become a close friend.

---

[1] There are a number of books listed by authors named Hill. *POE4* will be one of them.

1.3 THE HELP SYSTEM

Click **Help** on the EViews menu:

The resulting menu is

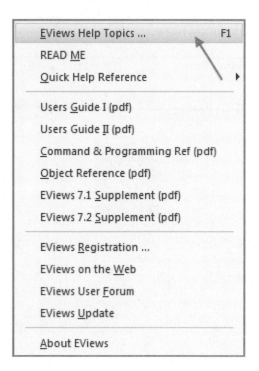

1.3.1 EViews help topics

First, click on **EViews Help Topics**. Select **User's Guide/EViews Fundamentals**. It opens a list of chapters that can take you through specifics of working with EViews. These guides will be a useful reference after you have progressed further through *Using EViews for POE4*.

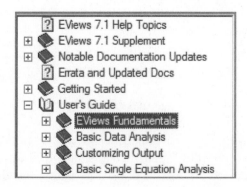

1.3.2 The read me file

On the **Help menu**, select **READ ME**. This opens a PDF file with the latest installation notes and errata.

Some basic questions about EViews 7 are answered by clicking **Help/EViews Help Topics/ User's Guide/EViews Fundamentals/Introduction**.

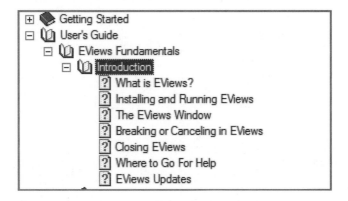

1.3.3 Quick help reference

Select **Quick Help Reference**. You find another menu. Select **Function Reference**.

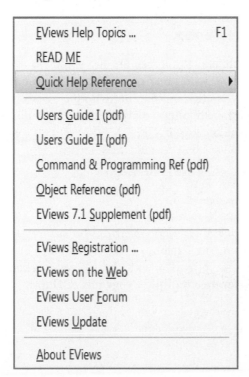
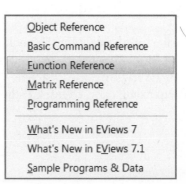

EViews has many, many functions available for easy use.

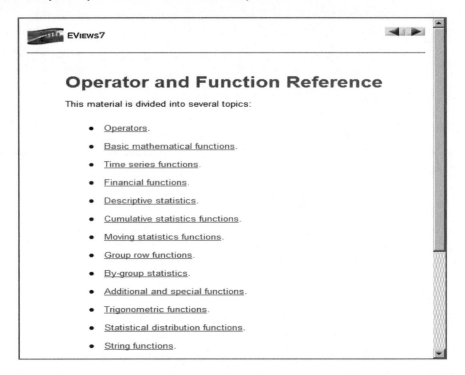

You should just take a moment to examine the **Operators** (basic addition, multiplication, etc.) and the **Basic mathematical functions** (square roots, logarithms, absolute value, etc.). This **Function Reference** help is one that you will use very frequently, and to which we will refer a great deal.

1.3.4 User's guides and command reference

The User's Guide I, User's Guide II and Command Reference are the complete documentation for the full version of EViews 7. While these are good rainy-day reading, we do not necessarily suggest you search them for information until you are more familiar with the workings of EViews 7. This book, *Using EViews for POE4*, is an effort to guide you through the essentials of EViews 7 that are needed to replicate the examples in the book *POE4*.

1.4 USING A WORKFILE

As noted earlier, all the data for the book *Principles of Econometrics, 4th edition* is provided as EViews **workfiles**. These will be used starting in Chapter 2. To illustrate some aspects of working with EViews we use a sample data set provided with the software called *demo.wf1*. Under the Help menu, choose **Quick Help Reference/Sample Programs & Data:**

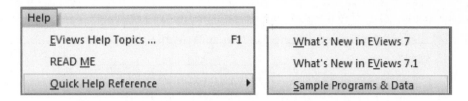

From among the choices select **EViews 7 Manual Data:**

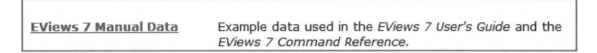

In the list of topics open the folder for Chapter 2:

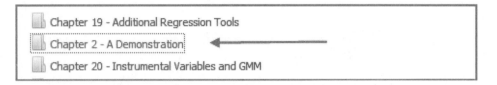

There you will find *demo.wf1*.

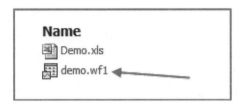

Double-clicking the icon for *demo.wf1* will open it with EViews. However it has some additional objects created during the EViews demonstration. The plain EViews workfile *demo.wf1* can be found at www.principlesofeconometrics.com/eviews.htm. The contents of this workfile are described in the definition file *demo.def*, which is a simple text file found at www.principlesofeconometrics.com/def.htm.

```
demo.def
        Obs: 180 households 1952.1 - 1996.4

        year            year
        qtr             quarter
        gdp             gross domestic product
        pr              price level index
        m1              money supply
        rs              short term interest rate


     Variable |      Obs        Mean    Std. Dev.       Min         Max
   -----------+--------------------------------------------------------
         year |      180        1974     13.0234        1952        1996
          qtr |      180         2.5     1.121153          1           4
          gdp |      180     632.419     564.2441      87.875    1948.225
           pr |      180    .5141061      .303483    .1975607    1.110511
           m1 |      180    445.0064     344.8315     126.537     1219.42
           rs |      180    5.412928     2.908939    .8143333    15.08733
```

1.4.1 Opening a workfile

Open the workfile called *demo* by clicking **File/Open/Workfile.**

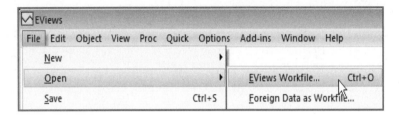

Navigate to where you have stored your EViews workfiles, then select *demo* and click on **Open**.

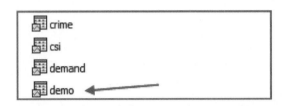

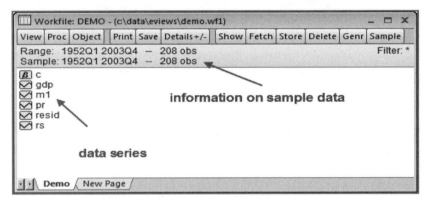

Located on the left side are data series that are indicated by the icon ☑. EViews calls the elements of the workfile **objects**. As you will discover, there are many types of objects that EViews can save into the workfile—not only series but tables, graphs, equations, and so on. As Richard Startz says, an object is a little "thingie" that computer programmers talk about. Each little icon "thingie" in the workfile is an object.

In this workfile the data series, or variables, are:

* *GDP*—gross domestic product
* *M1*—money supply
* *PR*—price level (index)
* *RS*—short term interest rate

The series **resid** and the icon labeled *β* are always present in EViews workfiles (even new ones with no data) and their use will be explained later. Across the top of the workfile are various buttons that initiate tasks in EViews, and these too will be explained later.

Below the buttons is **Range: 1952:1 2003:4**, which indicates that the 208 observations on the variables included run from 1952, Quarter 1, to 2003, Quarter 4. **Sample: 1952:1 2003:4** denotes the data observations EViews will use in calculations. Many times we will choose for analysis less than the full range of observations that are available, so **Sample** will differ from **Range**.

1.4.2 Examing a single series

It is a good idea each time you open a workfile to look at one or more series just to verify that the data are what you expect. First, select one series:

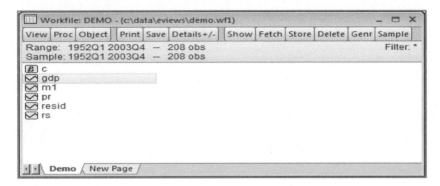

Double-click in the blue area, which will reveal a spreadsheet view of the data.

In the upper left hand corner is a button labeled **View:**

This opens a drop-down menu with a number of choices. Select **Descriptive Statistics & Tests/ Histogram and Stats**.

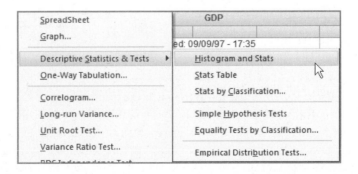

The result is

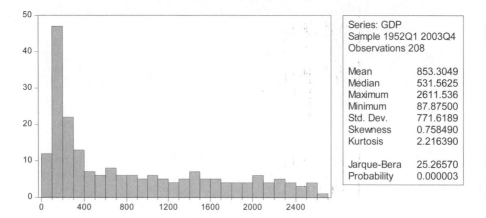

This histogram is shown with various summary statistics on the side.
　　Click on **View** again. Select **Graph**.

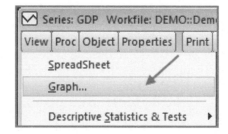

There you will see many options. The default graph type is a **Basic Graph** with the **Line & Symbol** plotted. Select **OK**.

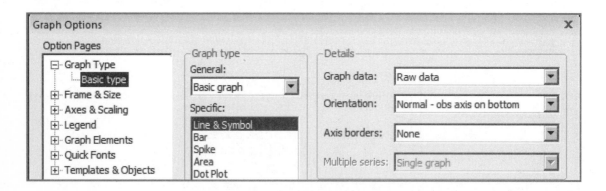

The result is a line graph. The dates are on the horizontal axis and *GDP* on the vertical axis.

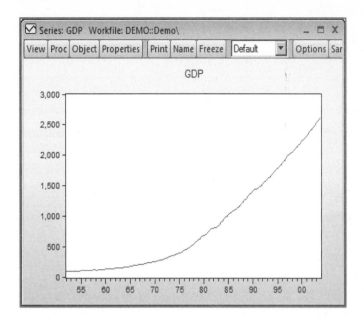

1.4.3 Changing the sample

If you wish to view the graph or summary statistics for a different sample period, click on the **Sample** button. This feature works the same in all EViews windows.

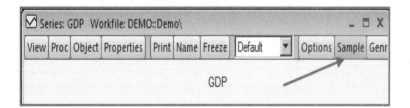

In the dialog box that opens change the sample to 1995q1 to 2003q4, then click **OK**.

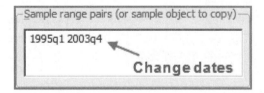

The resulting graph shows that *GDP* rose constantly during this period.

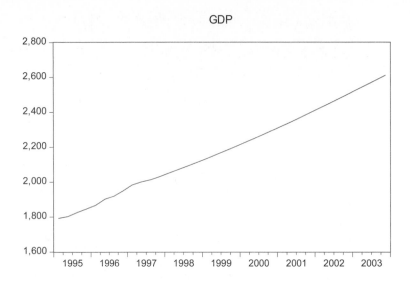

1.4.4 Copying a graph into a document

Select **View/Descriptive Statistics & Tests/Histogram and Stats**. You will now find the summary statistics and histogram of *GDP* for the period 1995:1 to 2003:4. These results can be printed by selecting the **Print** button.

You may prefer to copy the results into a word processor for later editing and combining results. How can results be taken from EViews into a document? Click inside the histogram:

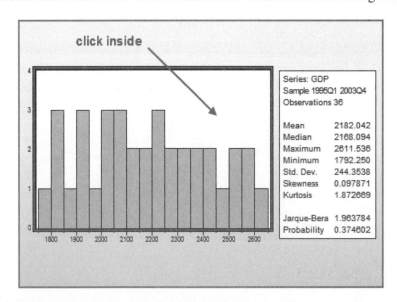

While holding down the **Ctrl** key, press **C** (which we will denote as **Ctrl+C**). This is the Windows keystroke combination for **Copy**.

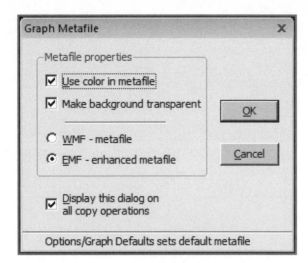

In the resulting dialog box you can make some choices, then click **OK**. This copies the graph into the Windows clipboard (memory). Open a document in your word processor and enter **Ctrl+V,** which will **Paste** the figure into your document.

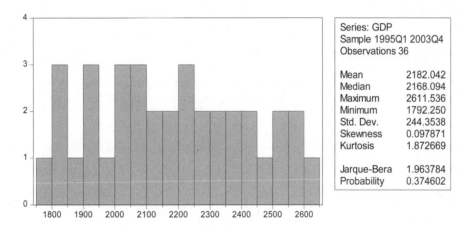

Close the graph we have been working on by clicking the **X** in the upper right-hand corner of the *GDP* screen:

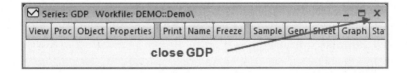

1.5 EXAMINING SEVERAL SERIES

Rather than examining one series at a time, we can view several. In the workfile window select the series *M1* and then while holding down the **Ctrl**-key select the *PR* series. Double-click inside the blue area to open what is called a **Group** of variables.

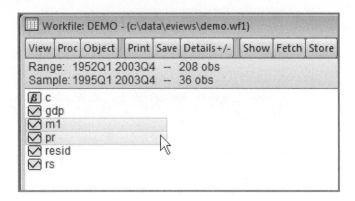

Click on **Open Group**.

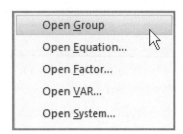

A spreadsheet view of the data will open.

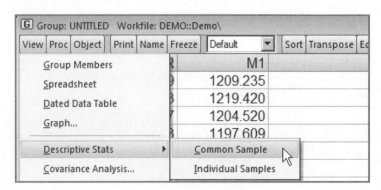

Note that the series begins in 1995:1 because we changed the **Sample** range in Section 1.4.3.

1.5.1 Summary statistics for several series

From the spreadsheet we can again examine the data by selecting the **View** button. Select **Descriptive Stats/Common Sample**.

The result is that a table of summary statistics is created for the two series (variables) in the group.

	PR	M1
Mean	1.168378	1332.789
Median	1.161996	1336.818
Maximum	1.281105	1499.480
Minimum	1.069409	1195.807
Std. Dev.	0.062083	101.9551
Skewness	0.186926	0.070017
Kurtosis	1.900155	1.579282

1.5.2 Freezing a result

These results can be "saved" several ways. Select the **Freeze** button. This actually saves an image of the table. In the new image window, select the **Name** button. Enter a name for this image, which EViews calls an **Object**. The name should be relatively short and cannot contain any spaces. Underscores "_" can be used to separate words to make recognition easier.

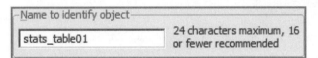

Click **OK**, then close the **Object** by clicking on the X. Check back in the workfile and you will now see a new entry, which is the table you have created.

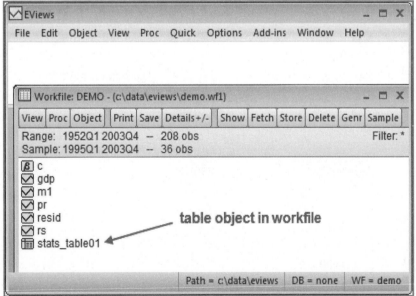

The table can be recalled at any time by double-clicking the **Table icon:**

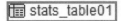

1.5.3 Copying and pasting a table

To copy these into a document directly, highlight the table of results (drag the mouse while holding down its left button) and enter **Ctrl+C**. In the resulting box click the **Formatted** radio button, check the box **Include header information**, and click **OK**. This copies the table to the Windows clipboard, which then can be pasted (**Ctrl+V**) into an open document.

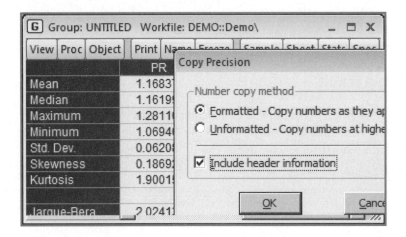

	M1	PR
Mean	1332.789	1.168378
Median	1336.818	1.161996
Maximum	1499.480	1.281105
Minimum	1195.807	1.069409
Std. Dev.	101.9551	0.062083
Skewness	0.070017	0.186926
Kurtosis	1.579282	1.900155
Jarque-Bera	3.057073	2.024137
Probability	0.216853	0.363466
Sum	47980.40	42.06160
Sum Sq. Dev.	363819.2	0.134901
Observations	36	36

This same method can be used for any table in EViews. For example, if you open the saved table **STATS_TABLE01** you can highlight the results, then copy and paste as we have done here.

1.5.4 Plotting two series

Return to the spreadsheet view of the two series *M1* and *PR*. Select **View/Graph**. In the resulting dialog box, select **Multiple graphs** in the **Multiple series** menu.

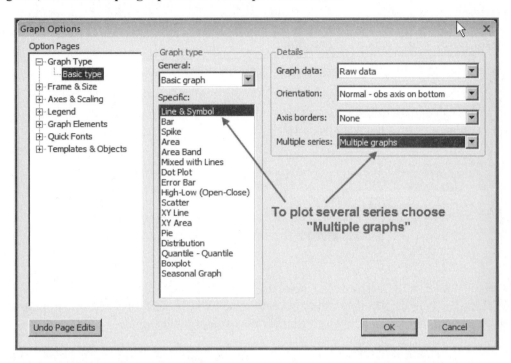

Click **OK** to obtain two plots of the series.

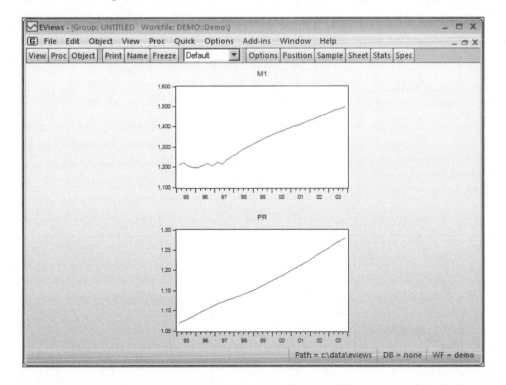

We can **Freeze** this picture, then assign it a **Name** for future reference.

1.5.5 A scatter diagram

A scatter diagram is a plot of data points with one variable on one axis and the other variable on the other axis. In the **Group** screen click **View/Graph**. For **Specific Graph type**, select **Scatter.**

Click **OK**. Copy the graph by clicking inside the graph area and entering **Ctrl+C** to copy, then paste into a document using **Ctrl+V**. Recall that we are still operating with the sample from 1995:1 to 2003:4, which is only 36 data points.

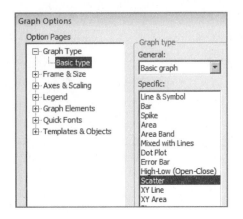

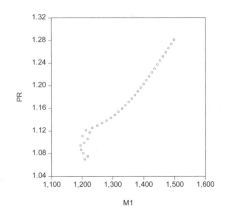

The variable *M1* is on the horizontal axis because it is the first series in the spreadsheet view.

Clicking the **X** in the Group window reveals some choices. The Group, consisting of the two series *M1* and *PR*, can be saved by selecting **Name** and assigning a name.

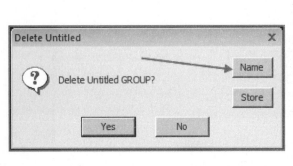

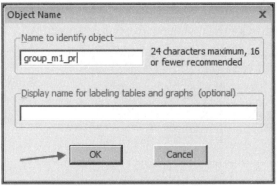

In the workfile window you will find a new object for this group.

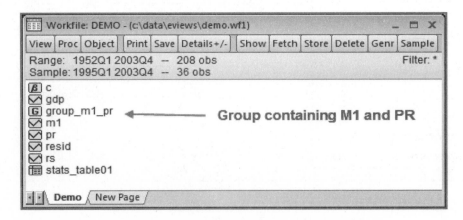

1.6 USING THE QUICK MENU

The spreadsheet view of the data is very powerful. Another key tool is the **Quick** menu on the EViews 7.1 workfile menu.

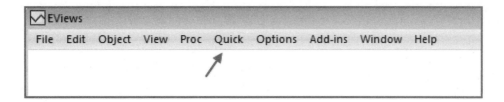

The options shown are

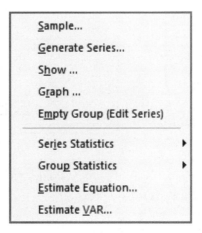

1.6.1 Changing the sample

By selecting **Sample** from this menu we can change the range of sample observations. Change the sample to 1952:1 to 2003:4 and click **OK**.

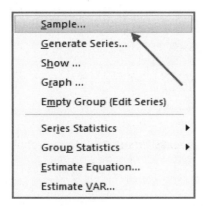
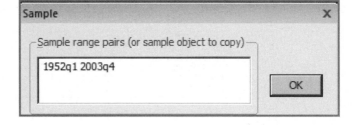

1.6.2 Generating a new series

In each problem we may wish to create new series from the existing series. For example, we can create the natural logarithm of the series *M1*. Select **Quick/Generate Series**. In the resulting dialog box type in the equation **log_m1=log(m1)**, then click **OK**. A new series will appear in the workfile. The function **log** creates the natural logarithm. All logarithms used in *Principles of Econometrics* are natural logs.

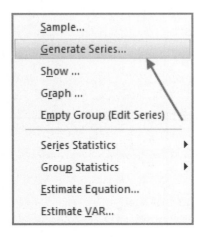
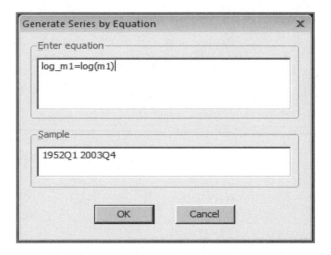

Alternatively, we can generate a new series by selecting the **Genr** button on the workfile menu. This will open the same **Generate Series** dialog box.

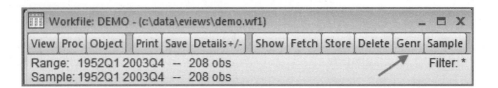

A third option is perhaps the simplest. Type into the EViews **Command window**

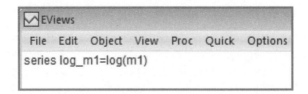

Then press **Enter**. Once a few basic commands are learned, a great deal of pointing-and-clicking can be avoided.

1.6.3 Plotting using Quick/Graph

We can create graphs from the spreadsheet view, but we can also use **Quick/Graph**.

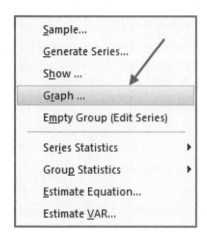 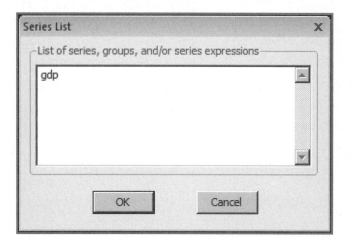

This will open the **Graph options** window. For a basic graph click **OK**.

If you enter two series into the **Series List** window then the **Graph options** window will have an additional option. Here we will plot the two series in a single graph.

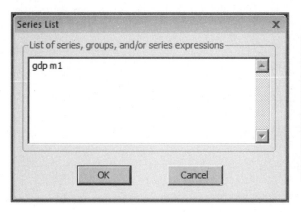 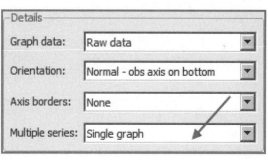

Click **OK**. The resulting graph shows the two series plots in a single window. In EViews the curves are in two different colors, but this will not show in a black and white document. The programmers at EViews have thought of this problem. Click inside the graph and enter **Ctrl+C** to copy. In the **Graph Metafile** box that opens, uncheck the box "**Use color in metafile**." Click **OK**.

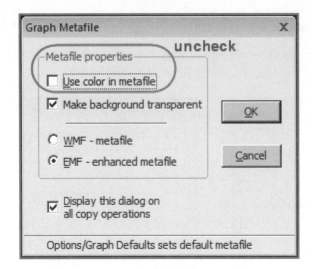

In your document enter **Ctrl+V** to paste the black and white graph.

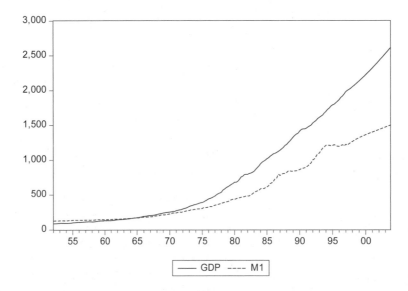

Now the graph lines show up as solid for *GDP* and broken for *M1* so that the difference can be viewed.

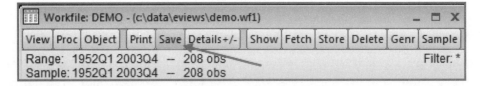

To save the graph, click **Name** and enter the name **GDP_M1_PLOT**. Click **OK**. Close the graph by clicking "**X**". You will find an icon in the workfile window.

gdp_m1_plot

If you double-click this icon, up will pop the graph you have created.

1.6.4 Saving your workfile

Now that you have put lots of work into creating new variables, plots, and so on, you can **Save** what you have done. On the workfile menu select the **Save** button

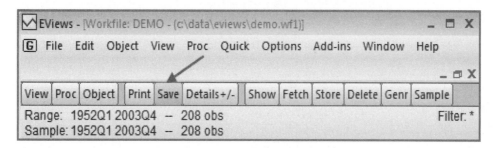

In the following window, if you click **OK** then all the objects you have created will be saved into the workfile **demo.wf1**. You may wish to save these results using a different name, so that the original data workfile is not changed. To save the workfile, select **File/Save As** on the main EViews menu:

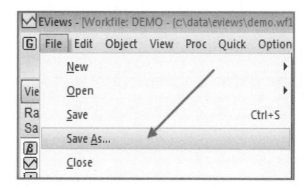

We will use the name **demo_ch1.wf1** for this workfile. Enter this and click **OK**. You will presented with some options. Use the default of **Double precision** and click **OK**.

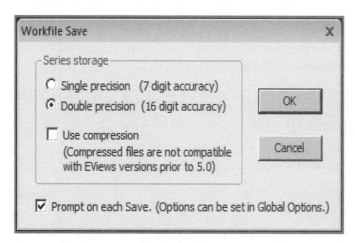

You will note that the workfile name has changed.

1.6.5 Opening an empty group

The ability to enter data manually is an important one. In Section 1.8 we show several ways you might enter data into EViews. Select **Quick/Empty Group (Edit Series)** from the EViews menu.

A spreadsheet opens in which you can enter new data. The default name for a new series is *SER01* that we will change. As you enter a number, press **Enter** to move to the next cell. You can add new data in as many columns as you like.

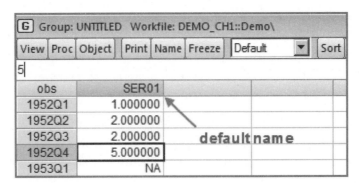

When you have finished entering the data you wish, click the **X** in the upper right corner of the active window. You will be asked if you want to "**Delete Untitled GROUP?**" Select **Yes**. In the workfile *demo_ch1.wf1* you will now find the new series labeled

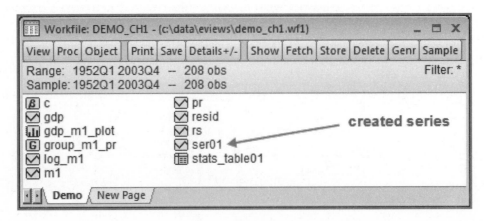

To change this name, select the series (by clicking) then **right-click** in the shaded area. A box will open in which you can enter a new name for the "object," which in this case is a data series. Press **OK.**

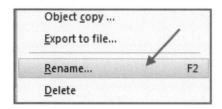

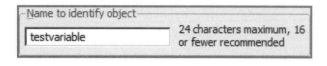

You can go through these same steps to delete an unwanted variable, such as the one we have just created. Select the series *TESTVARIABLE* in the workfile, and right-click. Select **Delete**. In the resulting window you will be asked to confirm the deletion. Select **Yes.**

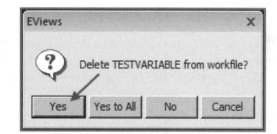

More than one series or objects can be selected for deletion by selecting one, then hold down the **Ctrl**-key while selecting others. To delete all these selected objects, **right-click** in the blue area, and repeat the steps above.

1.6.6 Quick/Series statistics

The next item on the EViews Quick menu is **Series Statistics**. Select **Quick/Series Statistics/Histogram and Stats:**

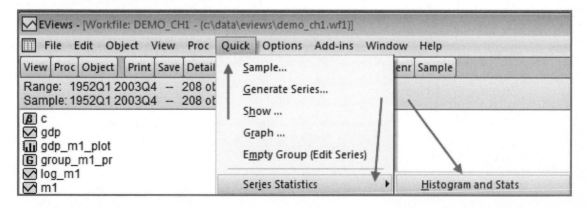

In the resulting window you can enter the name of the series (one) for which you desire the summary statistics. Then select **OK**.

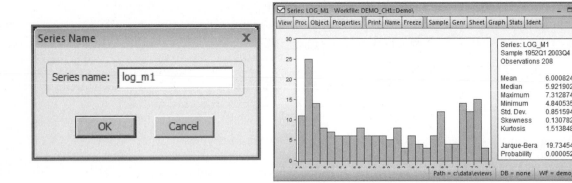

1.6.7 Quick/Group statistics

We can obtain summary statistics for a Group of series by choosing **Quick/Group Statistics**.

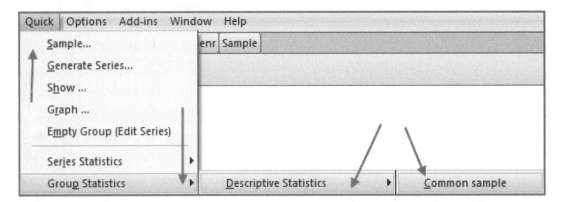

Enter the series names into the box and press **OK**. This will create the summary statistics table we have seen before. You can **Name** this group, or **Freeze** the table, or copy and paste using **Ctrl+C** and **Ctrl+V**.

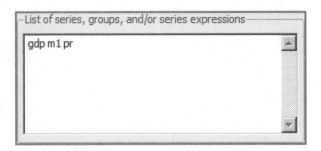

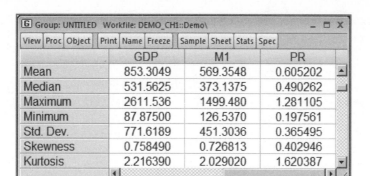

	GDP	M1	PR
Mean	853.3049	569.3548	0.605202
Median	531.5625	373.1375	0.490262
Maximum	2611.536	1499.480	1.281105
Minimum	87.87500	126.5370	0.197561
Std. Dev.	771.6189	451.3036	0.365495
Skewness	0.758490	0.726813	0.402946
Kurtosis	2.216390	2.029020	1.620387

Another option under **Quick/Group Statistics** is **Correlations**.

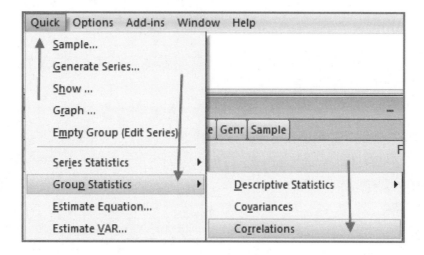

Enter the names of series for which the sample correlations are desired and click **OK**.

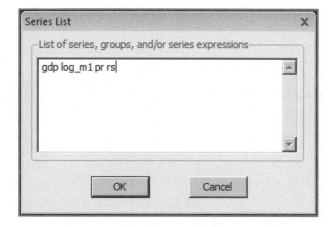

The sample correlations are arranged in an array, or matrix, format.

G Group: UNTITLED Workfile: DEMO_CH1::Demo\				
View Proc Object Print Name Freeze Sample Sheet Stats Spec				
Correlation				
	GDP	LOG_M1	PR	RS
GDP	1.000000	0.959003	0.986551	0.168504
LOG_M1	0.959003	1.000000	0.987383	0.346364
PR	0.986551	0.987383	1.000000	0.268010
RS	0.168504	0.346364	0.268010	1.000000

1.7 USING EVIEWS FUNCTIONS

Now we will explore the use of some EViews functions. Select **Help/Quick Help Reference/ Function Reference**.

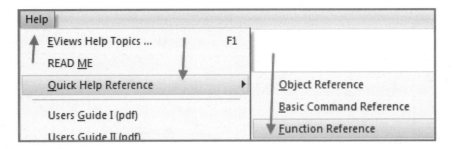

1.7.1 Descriptive statistics functions

Select **Descriptive Statistics** from the list of material links.

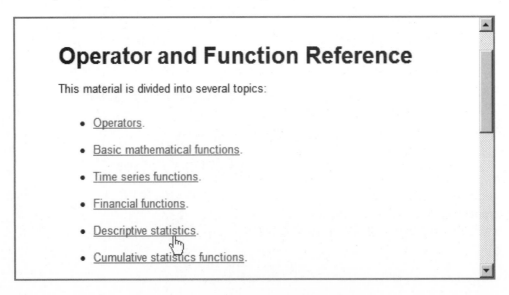

Some of the descriptive statistics functions listed there are on the next page.

In this table of functions you will note that these functions begin with the "**@**" symbol. Also, these functions return a single number, which is called a **scalar**. In the commands the variables, or series, are called **x** and **y**. The bracket notation "[,s]" is optional and we will not use it. These functions are used by typing commands into the **Command window** and pressing **Enter**. For example, to compute the sample mean of *GDP,* type

scalar gdpbar = @mean(gdp)

The Command window looks like this.

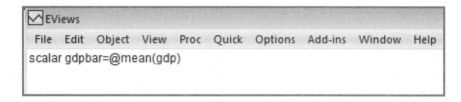

At the bottom of the EViews screen you will note the message

GDPBAR successfully computed

In the workfile window the new object is denoted with "#", which indicates a scalar.

gdpbar

We called the sample mean **GDPBAR** because sample means are often denoted by symbols like $\bar{x}$ which is pronounced "x-bar." In the "text-messaging" world in which you live, simple but meaningful names will occur to you naturally.

To view this scalar object double-click on it: it opens in a spreadsheet view.

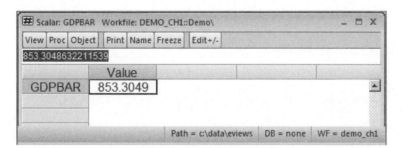

The sample mean of *GDP* during the sample period is 853.305.

Scalars you have created can be used in further calculations. For example, enter the following commands by typing them into the Command window and pressing **Enter:**

scalar t = @obs(gdp)
scalar gdpse = @stdev(gdp)
scalar z = (gdpbar-800)/(gdpse/@sqrt(t))

Selected Descriptive Statistics Functions in EViews 7.1

Function	Name	Description
`@cor(x,y[,s])`	correlation	the correlation between X and Y.
`@covs(x,y[,s])`	sample covariance	the covariance between X and Y (division by n−1).
`@inner(x,y[,s])`	inner product	the inner product of X and Y.
`@kurt(x[,s])`	kurtosis	kurtosis of values in X.
`@mae(x,y[,s])`	mean absolute error	the mean of the absolute value of the difference between X and Y.
`@mape(x,y[,s])`	mean absolute percentage error	100 multiplied by the mean of the absolute difference between X and Y, divided by Y.
`@max(x[,s])`	maximum	maximum of the values in X.
`@mean(x[,s])`	mean	average of the values in X.
`@median(x[,s])`	median	computes the median of the X (uses the average of middle two observations if the number of observations is even).
`@min(x[,s])`	minimum	minimum of the values in X.
`@prod(x[,s])`	product	the product of the elements of X (note this function is prone to numerical overflows).
`@obs(x[,s])`	number of observations	the number of non-missing observations for X in the current sample.
`@rmse(x,y[,s])`	root mean square error	the square root of the mean of the squared difference between X and Y.
`@skew(x[,s])`	skewness	skewness of values in X.
`@stdev(x[,s])`	standard deviation	square root of the unbiased sample variance (sum-of-squared residuals divided by n−1).
`@sum(x[,s])`	sum	the sum of X.
`@sumsq(x[,s])`	sum-of-squares	sum of the squares of X.
`@theil(x,y[,s])`	Theil inequality coefficient	the root mean square error divided by the sum of the square roots of the means of X squared and Y squared.
`@vars(x[,s])`	sample variance	sample variance of the values in X (division by n−1).

1.7.2 Using a storage vector

The creation of scalars leads to inclusion of additional objects into the workfile, and the scalars cannot be viewed simultaneously. One solution is to create a storage vector into which these scalars can be placed.

On the EViews menu bar select **Object/New Object**. In the resulting dialog box select **Matrix-Vector-Coef** and enter an object name, say **DEMO**. Click **OK**.

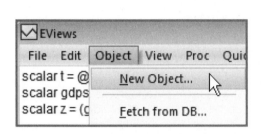 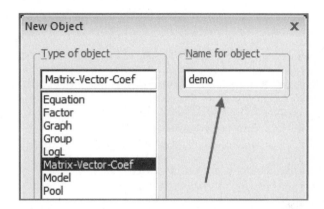

A dialog box will open asking what type of "new matrix" you want. To create a storage vector (an array) with 10 rows, select the radio button **Vector**, enter 10 for Rows, and click **OK**.

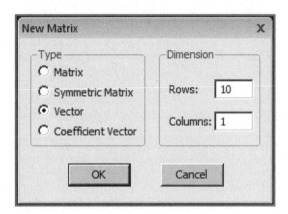

A spreadsheet will open with rows labeled R1 to R10. Now enter into the Command window the command

    demo(1) = @mean(gdp)

When you press **Enter** the value in row R1 will change to 853.3049, the sample mean of GDP.

File	Edit	Object	View	Proc	Quick	Options	Add-ins	Windo

scalar gdpbar = @mean(gdp)
demo(1) = @mean(gdp)

Workfile: DEMO_CH1 - (c:\d

View	Proc	Object		Print	Save

Range: 1952Q1 2003Q4 --
Sample: 1952Q1 2003Q4 --

ⓑ c
⊞ corr_table01
⧉ demo ⟵

Vector: DEMO   Workfile: DEMO_CH

View	Proc	Object		Print	Name	Free

	C1	
		Last update
R1	853.3049	
R2	0.000000	
R3	0.000000	

Now enter the series of commands, pressing **Enter** after each.

> **demo(2)=@obs(gdp)**
> **demo(3)=@stdev(gdp)**
> **demo(4)=(gdpbar-800)/(gdpse/@sqrt(t))**

Each time a command is entered a new item shows in the vector. Note that in the last command could be included the previously calculated members of the vector **demo.** That is,

> **demo(4) = (@mean(gdp)-800) / (@demo(3)/@sqrt(demo(2)))**

Vector: DEMO   Workfile: DEMO_CH1::Demo\   _ ☐ X

View	Proc	Object		Print	Name	Freeze		Edit+/-	Label+/-		Sheet

DEMO

	C1			
R1	853.3049			
R2	208.0000			
R3	771.6189			
R4	0.996313			
R5				

The advantage of this approach is that the contents of this table can be copied and pasted into a document for easy presentation. Highlight the contents, enter **Ctrl+C**. Choose the **Formatted** radio button and **OK**.

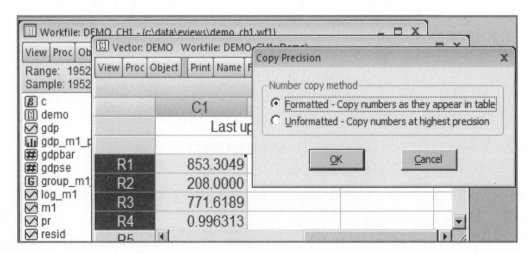

In an open document enter **Ctrl+V** to paste the table of results.

R1	853.3049
R2	208.0000
R3	771.6189
R4	0.996313

You can now edit as you would any table.

Demo vector	
GDP mean	853.3049
T sample size	208.0000
GDP Std Dev	771.6189
Z statistic	0.996313

We created many tables in the book *Principles of Econometrics* using this method.

To keep our workfile tidy, delete the scalar and vector objects that have no further use. Click the vector object **DEMO** and then while holding down the **Ctrl**-key, click on the scalars. Right-click in the blue-shaded area and select **Delete**.

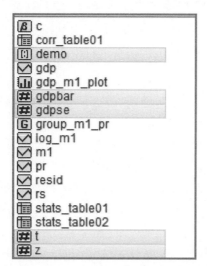
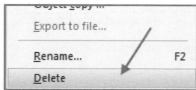

If you feel confident you can choose **Yes to All:**

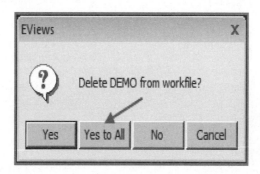

1.7.3 Basic arithmetic operations

The basic arithmetic operations can be viewed at **Help/Quick Help Reference/Function Reference:**

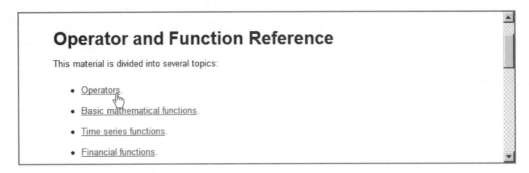

The list of operators is given on the next page. These operators can be used when working with series, as in an operation to generate a new series, *RATIO1*, defined as 3 times the ratio of *GDP* to *M1*:

series ratio1 = 3*(gdp/m1)

Basic Arithmetic Operations

Expression	Operator	Description
+	add	x+y adds the contents of X and Y.
−	subtract	x-y subtracts the contents of Y from X.
*	multiply	x*y multiplies the contents of X by Y.
/	divide	x/y divides the contents of X by Y.
^	raise to the power	x^y raises X to the power of Y.
>	greater than	x>y takes the value 1 if X exceeds Y, and 0 otherwise.
<	less than	x<y takes the value 1 if Y exceeds X, and 0 otherwise.
=	equal to	x=y takes the value 1 if X and Y are equal, and 0 otherwise.
<>	not equal to	x<>y takes the value 1 if X and Y are not equal, and 0 if they are equal.
<=	less than or equal to	x<=y takes the value 1 if X does not exceed Y, and 0 otherwise.
>=	greater than or equal to	x>=y takes the value 1 if Y does not exceed X, and 0 otherwise.

1.7.4 Basic math functions

The basic math functions can be viewed at **Help/Quick Help Reference/Function Reference.**

Operator and Function Reference

This material is divided into several topics:

- Operators.

- Basic mathematical functions.

- Time series functions.

- Financial functions.

Some of these functions are listed below. Note that common ones like the absolute value (**abs**), the exponential function (**exp**), the natural logarithm (**log**), and the square root (**sqr**) can be used with or without the **@** sign.

Selected Basic Math Functions

Name	Function	Examples/Description
`@abs(x)`, `abs(x)`	absolute value	@abs(-3)=3.
`@exp(x)`, `exp(x)`	exponential, e^x	@exp(1)=2.71813.
`@fact(x)`	factorial, $x!$	@fact(3)=6, @fact(0)=1.
`@inv(x)`	reciprocal, 1/x	inv(2)=0.5.
`@mod(x,y)`	floating-point remainder	returns the remainder of x/y with the same sign as x. If y=0 the result is 0.
`@log(x)`, `log(x)`	natural logarithm, $\log_e(x)$	@log(2)=0.693..., log(@exp(1))=1.
`@round(x)`	round to the nearest integer	@round(-97.5)=-98, @round(3.5)=4.
`@sqrt(x)`, `sqr(x)`	square root	@sqrt(9)=3.

1.8 CREATING WORKFILES

If you are fortunate enough to have your data in the form of an EViews workfile, then you can simply open that file and proceed with the various commands that we describe in the following chapters. The EViews workfile can be opened in one of three ways: (1) by using **File/Open/Workfile** as described in Section 4.1.1, (2) by double-clicking the icon of the file name, or (3) by selecting the file and, holding the left-mouse button, dragging it to the EViews icon on the desktop.

Suppose, however, that you need to collect your data, and the data are available in another format, such as an Excel file or a text file. How do you create an EViews workfile that contains the required data? We begin to answer this question by exploring how to download data from the Internet into an Excel file; then we examine ways of creating an EViews workfile from an Excel file or a text file.

1.8.1 Obtaining data from the Internet

Getting data for economic research is much easier today than it was years ago. Before the Internet, hours would be spent in libraries, looking for and copying data by hand. Now we have access to rich data sources that are a few clicks away.

Suppose you are interested in analyzing the GDP of the United States. As suggested in *POE4*, the website **Resources for Economists** contains a wide variety of data, and in particular the macro data we seek.

Websites are continually updated and improved. We will guide you through an example, but be prepared for differences from what we show here.

First, open up the website: http://www.aeaweb.org/rfe/:

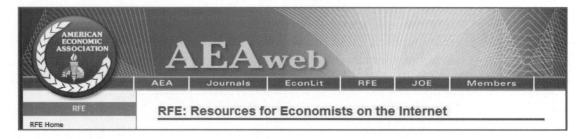

Select the **Data** option, and then select **U.S. Macro and Regional Data**.

- Introduction
- Data
- Dictionaries, Glossaries, & Encyclopedias

Data

- U.S. Macro and Regional Data
- Other U.S. Data
- World and Non-U.S. Data
- Finance and Financial Markets
- Journal Data and Program Archives

This will open up a range of sub-data categories. For the example considered here, select the **Bureau of Economic Analysis (BEA)-National Income and Produce Accounts** to get data on GDP.

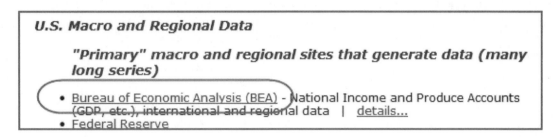

From the screen below, select the **Gross Domestic Product** option.

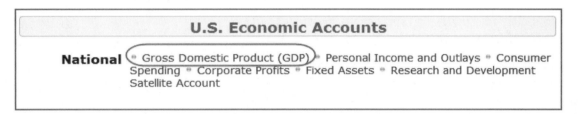

Most websites allow you to download data conveniently in Excel format.

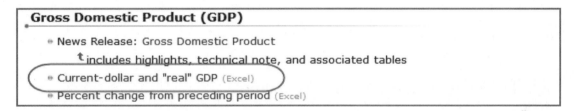

Select the Excel option and a dialog box will open. **Save** the data as *gdplev.xls*.

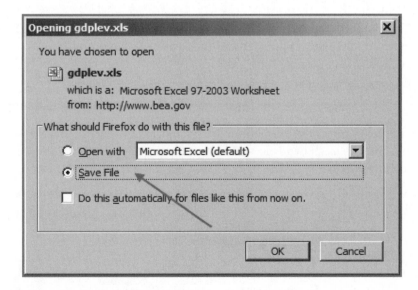

Once the file has been downloaded we can open the file; a sample of the data in Excel format is shown below.

	A	B	C	D	E	F	G	H
1			Current-Dollar and "Real" Gross Domestic Product					
2								
3		Annual				Quarterly		
4						(Seasonally adjusted annual rates)		
5								
6		GDP in billions of current dollars	GDP in billions of chained 2005 dollars			GDP in billions of current dollars	GDP in billions of chained 2005 dollars	
7								
8								
9	1929	103.6	977.0		1947q1	237.2	1,772.2	
10	1930	91.2	892.8		1947q2	240.4	1,769.5	
11	1931	76.5	834.9		1947q3	244.5	1,768.0	
12	1932	58.7	725.8		1947q4	254.3	1,794.8	
13	1933	56.4	716.4		1948q1	260.3	1,823.4	

gdplev [Compatibility Mode]

Sheet1

Let us now create the desired EViews file by importing the annual data (1929-2010) for nominal GDP (column B, first observation in cell B9) and real GDP (column C, first observation in cell C9) into an EViews workfile.

1.8.2 Importing an Excel file: drag and drop

EViews makes it very easy to import data from a variety of formats. For example, Excel 97-2003 and text (ASCII) files can be imported by "dragging and dropping."

Remark: EViews imports Excel 97-2003 files, ending in *.xls*, with no difficultly. If, however, you have a newer Excel file, ending in *.xlsx*, then you may have problems. The solution is to open the *.xlsx* file and save it under the older format before importing.

Excel 97-2003 Workbook

Highlight the file to be imported and hold down the left-mouse button. If EViews is open, drag the file icon into EViews as shown below. If EViews is not open, you can drag the file icon onto the EViews icon on the desktop.

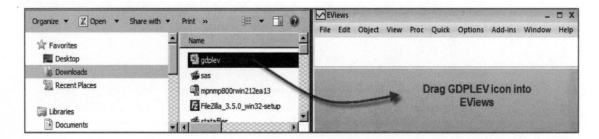

Then there will be a series of confirmatory screens. Usually the default settings are fine and we just click **Next.** In the screen shot below we have edited the image a bit, cutting out some of the data lines to make it smaller.

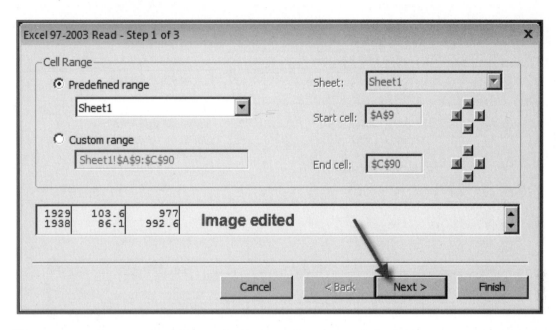

In Step 2 we have an opportunity to give the series names.

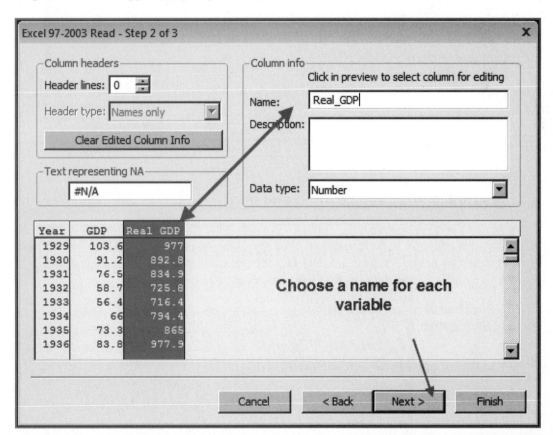

In Step 3 we can define the basic structure of the workfile, which in this case is **Dated** with a **regular annual frequency**, with the **start date** of 1929.

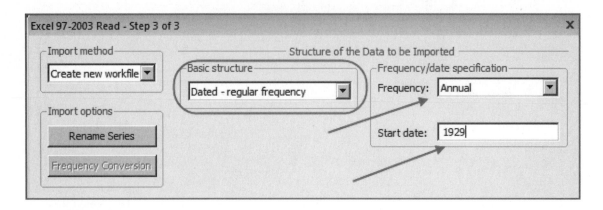

Click **Finish** and there you have it.

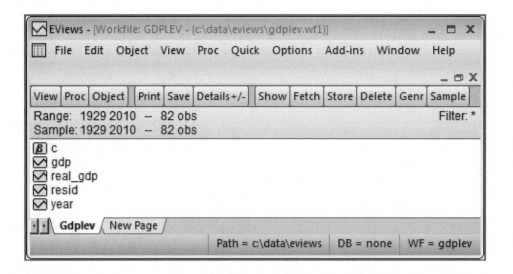

1.8.3 Importing a text data file: drag and drop

EViews supports the "drag-and-drop" approach for a number of different software formats. Let's give it a try using an ASCII, or text format, data file. The data files for *POE4* in text format are located at http://www.principlesofeconometrics.com/poe4/poe4dat.htm. These files have a *.dat extension. We will use *food.dat*. The first few observations are:

```
115.22      3.69
135.98      4.39
119.34      4.75
114.96      6.03
187.05     12.47
```

Download the file from the internet, and then drag it into EViews or onto the EViews icon on the desktop. Select the file, then holding the left-mouse button, slide the mouse.

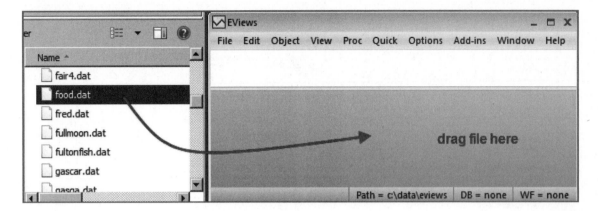

We then have a series of screens checking if the data match your expectations. In each, if all looks good, click **Next**.

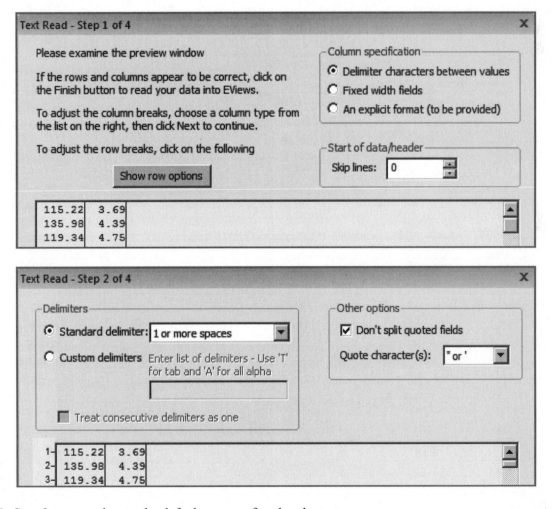

In Step 3 we can change the default names of each column.

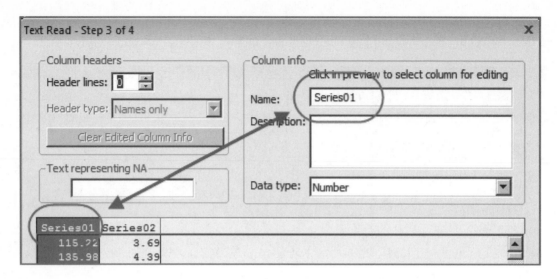

As you select each column, enter a name for that series, then highlight the next column and repeat.

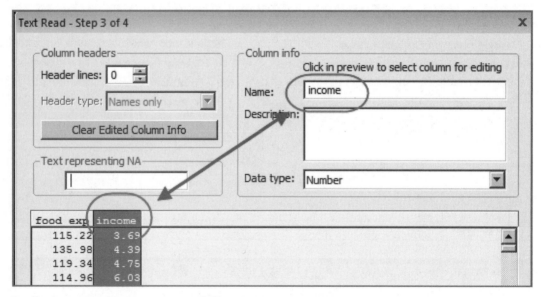

In the final step we **Create new workfile**.

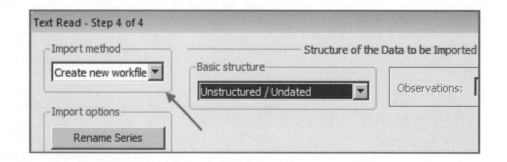

Select **Finish**. And there you have it.

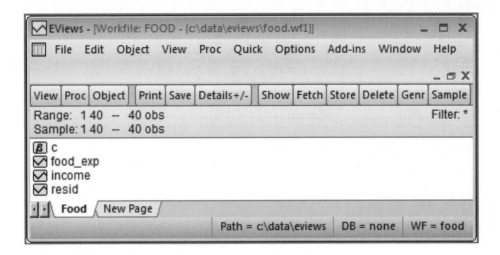

1.8.4   Importing an Excel data file using Proc/Import

Dragging and dropping is the easiest way to create an EViews workfile with data imported from another source. However, there is a longer way where you first open EViews and then use commands for importing data. In this and the next section we describe this process for Excel and text files.

To create an EViews workfile, double click on your EViews icon to open the software, then select **File/New/Workfile**. The following screen will open:

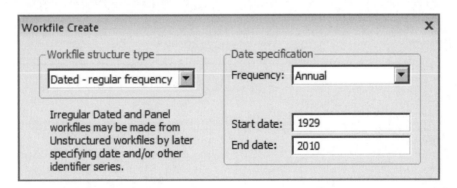

To create the workfile for annual data covering sample period **1929** to **2010**, select **Annual** from the drop-down menu in **Frequency** and type in the **Start** and **End dates**. Clicking on **OK** will create the **UNTITLED** workfile below.

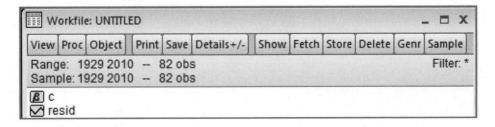

To import data select **Proc/Import/Read**.

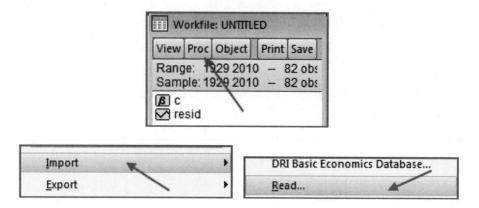

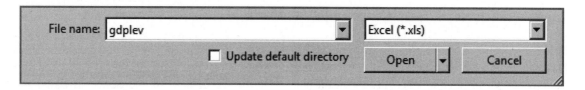

EViews will then ask you for the location of the Excel file. Open the *gdpplev.xls* file we have created:

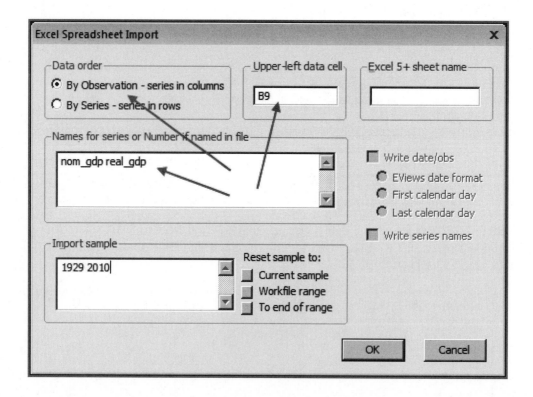

and the following screen will open:

Be sure to pick the **By observation – series in columns** option, enter the correct location of the first observation (**B9**) and type in the names of the variables – in this case *NOM_GDP* and

REAL_GDP. Clicking on **OK** will import the data from the Excel datafile to the EViews workfile. As a check, open the group *NOM_GDP* and *REAL_GDP* and you can see that we have successfully imported the data (do check this against the Excel spreadsheet shown above).

obs	NOM_GDP	REAL_GDP
1929	103.6000	977.0000
1930	91.20000	892.8000
1931	76.50000	834.9000
1932	58.70000	725.8000
1933	56.40000	716.4000
1934	66.00000	794.4000
1935	73.30000	865.0000

The final step is to **save** your workfile.

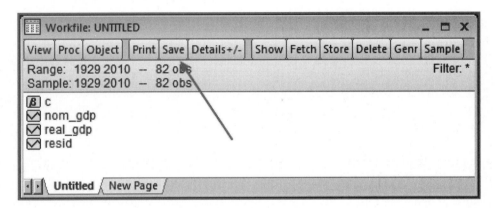

1.8.5 Importing a text data file using Proc/Import

Excel data files are a common way of handling data. However, some data also come in text form and so, for completeness, we shall consider the case of importing a text data file. As an illustration we will import an ASCII file called *food.dat*. Before trying to import the data in *food.dat*, examine the contents of the definition file *food.def*. It is an ASCII file that can be opened with NOTEPAD. The **.def* files contain variable names and descriptions. For example, open *food.def*.

```
food.def

food_exp income

  Obs:   40

  1. food_exp (y)              weekly food expenditure in $
  2. income   (x)              weekly income in $100


   variable |     Obs       Mean    Std. Dev.       Min        Max
------------+--------------------------------------------------------
   food_exp |      40   283.5735   112.6752      109.71      587.66
     income |      40   19.60475    6.847773       3.69        33.4
```

This definition file shows that there are 40 observations on two variables, *FOOD_EXP* and *INCOME*, in that order, and they are weekly food expenditure and weekly income, respectively.

To import this data, create a workfile for 40 undated observations and click **OK**. Select **File/New/Workfile** on the EViews menu.

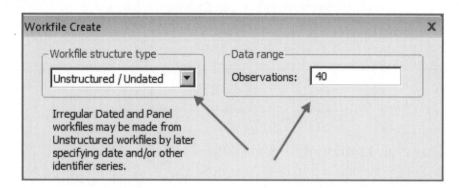

Click **Proc/Import/Read** as in the previous section, and navigate to the file *food.dat*.

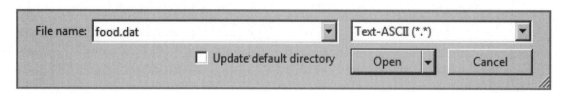

Select **Open**. A dialog box will open. And at the bottom of the dialog box, we can see the first few observations in the data file. Because the data file does not contain variable names, enter them as shown, and click **OK**.

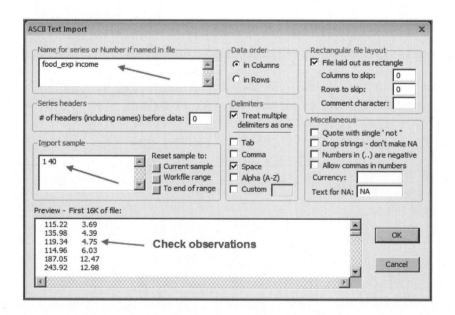

Two new series have been added, *FOOD_EXP* and *INCOME*. **Save** your file.

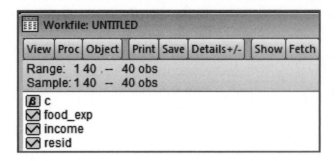

1.8.6 Adding data to an existing workfile

If you have an existing workfile containing some data, but you would like to add more data to it, you can use either the drag and drop method or the **Proc/Import** method. The procedures described in the last four sections can be used in a similar way.

1.8.7 Frequency conversions

EViews offers a range of frequencies – annual, quarterly, monthly and so on.

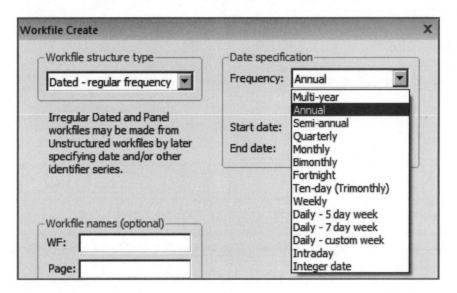

Examples of data conventions include:

- Annual: specify the year; for example, 1981, or 2007.
- Quarterly: the year, followed by a number or the quarter. Examples: 2007:3, 2007Q3.
- Monthly: the year, followed by a number or the month. Examples: 1956:11, 1956M11.
- Weekly and daily: by default, you should specify these dates as Month/Day/Year. Thus August 15, 2007 is 8/15/2007.

EViews also offers an easy way to convert from one frequency to another. Suppose we are interested in converting the annual data on GDP to their quarterly equivalents. To do so, first click on **New Page** and select **Specify by Frequency/Range**.

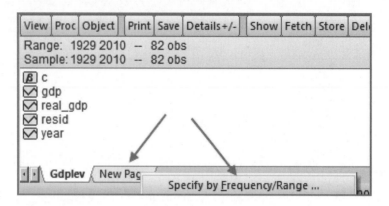

Specify the range of the quarterly data as shown.

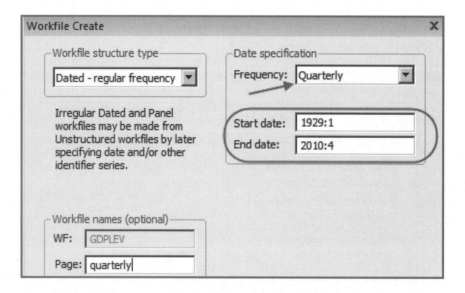

Click **OK.** The following page will open. You might like to name this page too.

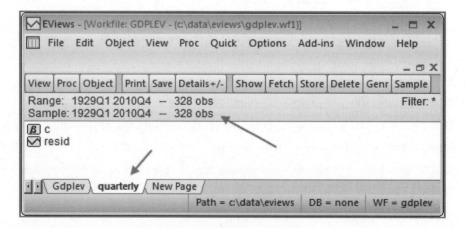

To transfer data from one frequency to another, just **right-click** on the variable on the page with the annual frequency (say *REAL_GDP*) and drag that to the bottom of the page set up for quarterly data. The screen below will open.

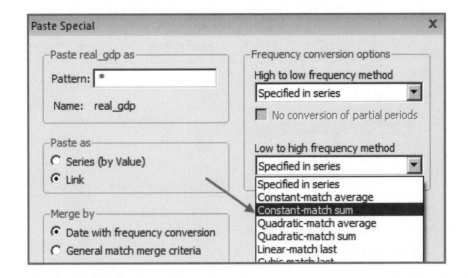

We are converting from a low to a high frequency, and in this example we are selecting the **constant-match sum** option. Clicking **OK** will create the new variable. For comparison, open the two series and you will note that the quarterly data is one-fourth of the annual.

REAL_GDP					
	Page Link: gdplev\real_gdp				
1929Q1	244.3				
1929Q2	244.3				
1929Q3	244.3				
1929Q4	244.3				
1930Q1	223.2				
1930Q2	223.2				
1930Q3	223.2				
1930Q4	223.2				
1931Q1					

1.8.8 Exporting data from EViews

There are times when you would like to export data from an EViews workfile. To illustrate, let us work with *gdplev.wf1* and export the two series. To do so, highlight the two series, then click on **Proc/Export/Write Text-Lotus-Excel.**

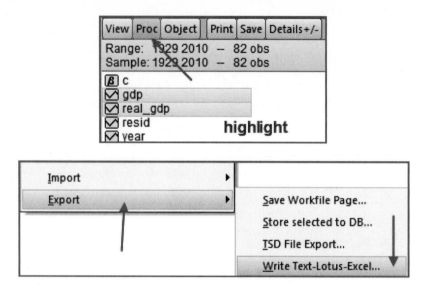

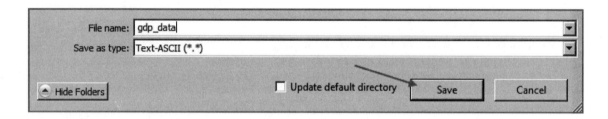

This will then open a window with the option to save as a text or Excel file.

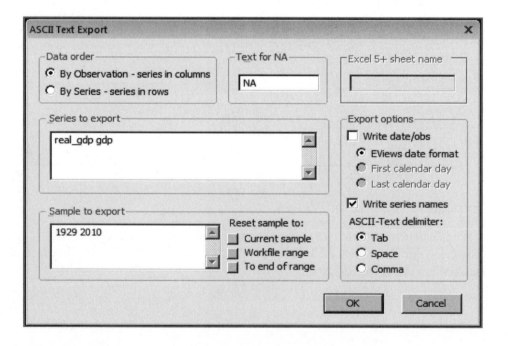

In the resulting screen you will have some choices concerning formats and delimiters.

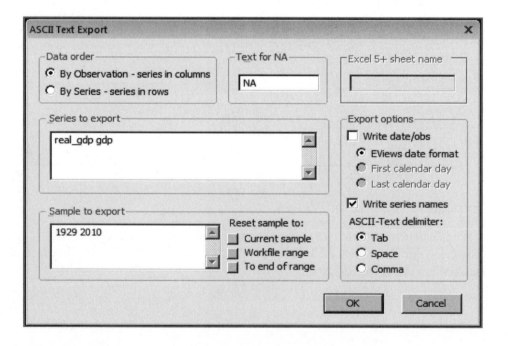

Keywords

arithmetic operators
basic graph
close series
copying a table
copying graph
correlation
Ctrl+C
Ctrl+P
Ctrl+V
data definition files
data export
data import
data range
descriptive statistics
drag and drop
EViews functions
Freeze
function reference

Generate Series
Genr
graph metafile
graph options
Group: empty
help
histogram
import Excel data
import Text data
math functions
multiple graphs
Name
Object name
open group
open series
path
quick help reference
Quick/Empty Group

Quick/Generate Series
Quick/Graph
Quick/Group Statistics
Quick/Sample
Quick/Series Statistics
Quick/Show
sample range
sample range: change
scalars
scatter diagram
series
series: delete
series: rename
spreadsheet view
vectors
workfile: open
workfile: save
workfiles

CHAPTER **2**

The Simple Linear Regression Model

In this chapter we introduce the simple linear regression model and estimate a model of weekly food expenditure. We also demonstrate the plotting capabilities of EViews and show how to use the software to calculate the income elasticity of food expenditure, and to predict food expenditure from our regression results.

2.1 OPEN THE WORKFILE

The data for the food expenditure example are contained in the workfile *food.wf1*. Locate this file and open it by selecting **File/Open/EViews Workfile**

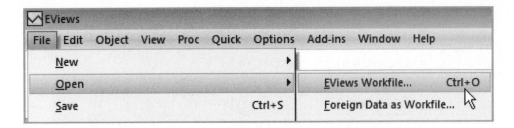

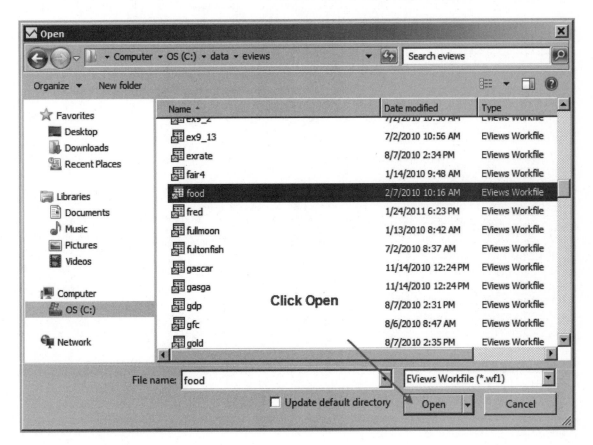

The initial workfile contains two variables *INCOME*, which is weekly household income, and *FOOD_EXP*, which is weekly household food expenditure. See the definition file ***food.def*** for the variable definitions.

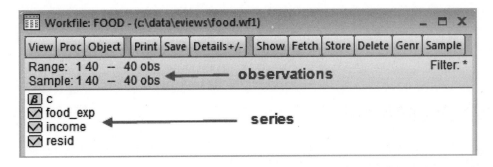

2.1.1 Examine the data

Whenever opening a new workfile it is prudent to examine the data. Select *INCOME* by clicking it, and then, while holding, the **Ctrl**-key select *FOOD_EXP*.

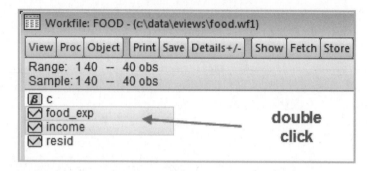

Double-click in the blue area and select **Open Group**. The data appear in a spreadsheet format, with *INCOME* first since it was selected first.

obs	FOOD_EXP	INCOME
1	115.22	3.69
2	135.98	4.39
3	119.34	4.75
4	114.96	6.03
5	187.05	12.47

2.1.2 Checking summary statistics

In the definition file *food.def* we find variable definitions and summary statistics.

```
food.def

food_exp income

  Obs:   40

  1. food_exp (y)              weekly food expenditure in $
  2. income   (x)              weekly income in $100




   Variable |     Obs       Mean     Std. Dev.       Min        Max
------------+-------------------------------------------------------
   food_exp |      40    283.5735    112.6752     109.71      587.66
     income |      40    19.60475    6.847773       3.69        33.4
```

To verify that the workfile we are using agrees, select **View/Descriptive Stats/Common Sample**.

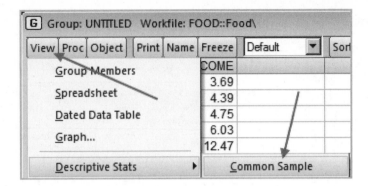

The resulting summary statistics agree with the information in the *food.def*, which assures us that we have the correct data.

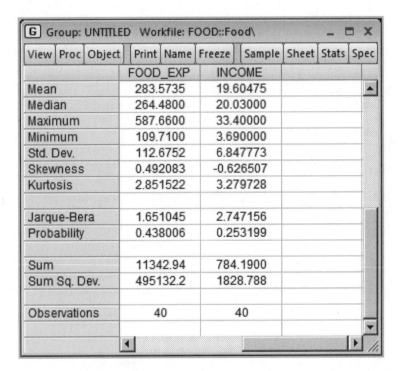

To return to the spreadsheet view, select **View/Spreadsheet.**

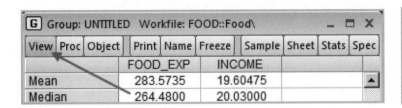

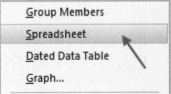

2.1.3 Saving a group

It is often useful to save a particular group of variables that are in a spreadsheet. From within the Group screen, select **Name** and then assign an **Object Name**. Click **OK**.

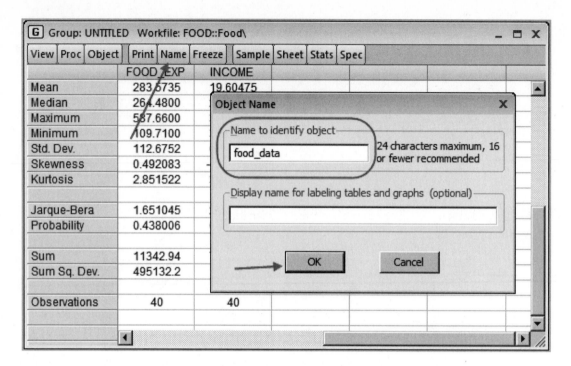

Close the spreadsheet by clicking the upper-right-hand corner.

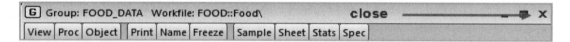

The new object in the workfile is a **Group** named **FOOD_DATA**.

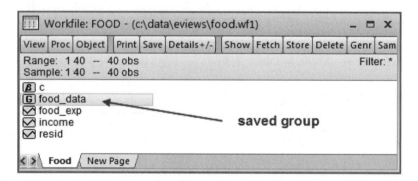

2.2 PLOTTING THE FOOD EXPENDITURE DATA

With any software there are several ways to accomplish the same task. We will make use of EViews "drop-down menus" until the basic commands become familiar. Click on **Quick/Graph**

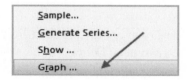

In the dialog box type the names of the variables <u>with the *x*-axis variable coming first!</u>

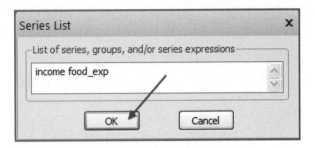

In the **Graph Options** box select **Scatter** from among the **Basic graphs**.

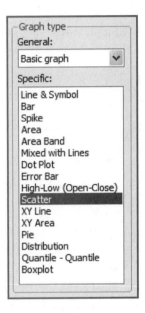

A plot appears, to which we can add labels and a title.

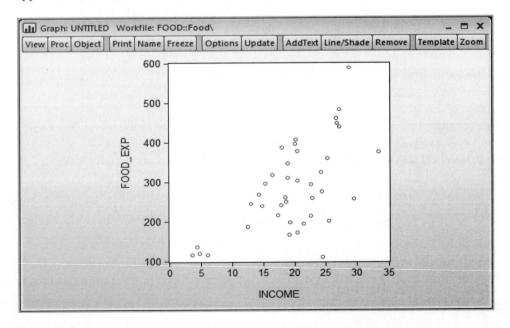

2.2.1 Enhancing the graph

While the basic graph is fine, for a written paper or report it can be improved by

- adding a title
- changing the scale on the vertical axis

These tasks are easily accomplished. To add a title, click on **AddText** on the Graph menu.

In the resulting dialog box you will be able to add a title, specify the location of the title, and use some stylistic features.

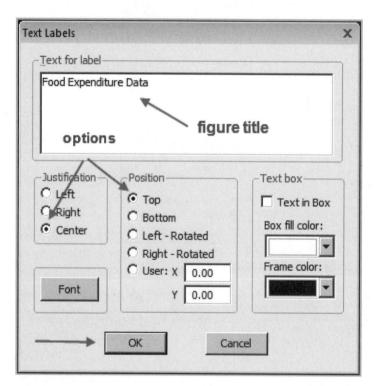

To center the title at the top, click the appropriate options and type in the title. Click **OK**.

To alter the vertical axis so that it begins at zero, click on **Options** on the Graph Menu.

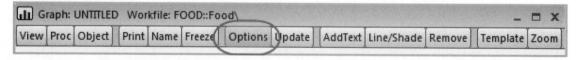

Alternatively, **double-click** inside the graph itself. Click on the **Axes/Scale** option, select the **Left Axis** from the pull-down **Edit axis** menu. Choose **User specified** in the **Left axis scale method.**

Enter 0 and 625 as the **Min** and **Max** values. Click **OK** to **return** to the graph. To make further changes, click **Apply**.

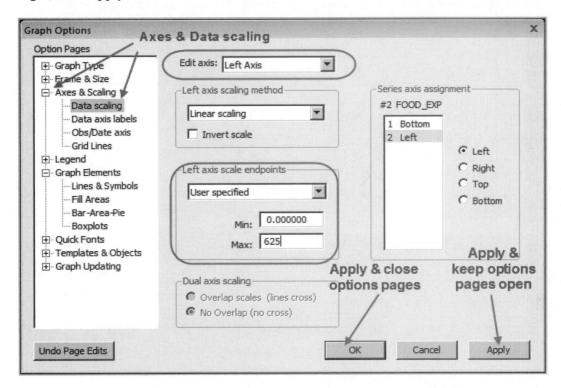

To change the "empty circles" used in the graph to "filled circles", choose **Graph Elements/ Lines & Symbols**. In the **Attributes** panel choose **Symbol/Obs label** and from the pull-down menu select the solid-looking circles. Note that other attributes can be changed as well.

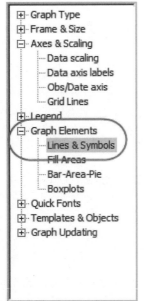

Click **OK**. The resulting graph is now

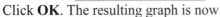

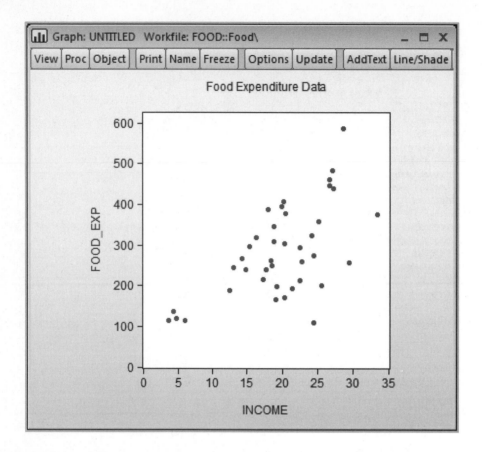

Explore the other **Graph Options** to see all the features.

2.2.2 Saving the graph in the workfile

To save the graph so that it remains in the workfile, click on **Name**, then enter a name. Note that separate words are not allowed, but separating words with an underscore is an alternative.

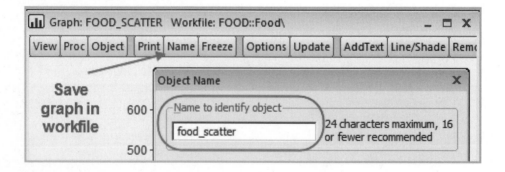

In the workfile, you will find an icon representing the graph just created:

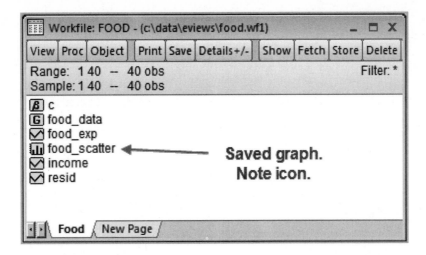

2.2.3 Copying the graph to a document

As is usual with Windows-based applications, we can copy by clicking somewhere inside the graph, to select it, then **Ctrl+C**. Or in the main window, click on **Edit/Copy**

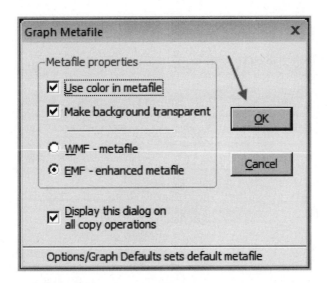

The dialog box that shows up allows you to choose the file format. Switch to your word processor and simply paste the graph (**Ctrl+V**) into the document, as we have done below.

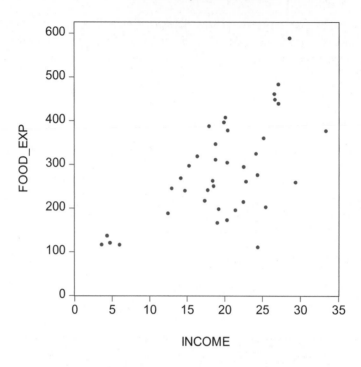

To save the graph to a disk, select the **Object** button on the Graph menu.

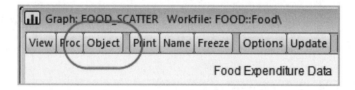

Select **View Options/Save graph to disk**. In the resulting dialog box you have several file types to choose from, and you can select a name for the graph image.

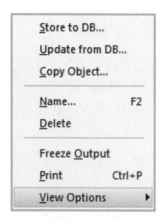

2.2.4 Saving a workfile

You may wish to save your workfile at this point. If you select the **Save** button on the workfile menu, the workfile will be saved under its current name *food.wf1*. It might be better to save this file under a new name, so that the original workfile remains untouched. Select **File/Save As** on the EViews menu.

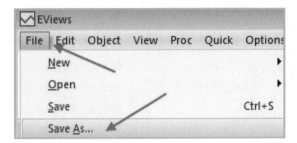

Select a simple but informative name.

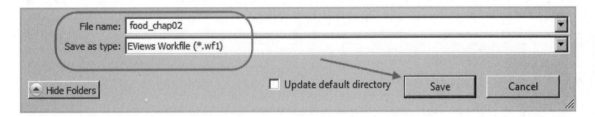

EViews will ask the precision. Choose the default.

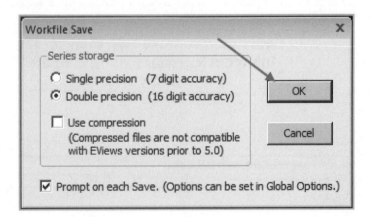

We have named it *food_chap02.wf1*. Once saved with a name, it can be re-saved using **Ctrl+S**, or by selecting **File/Save**.

2.3 ESTIMATING A SIMPLE REGRESSION

To obtain the least squares parameter estimates for the food expenditure equation, we select **Quick/Estimate Equation** from the EViews menu.

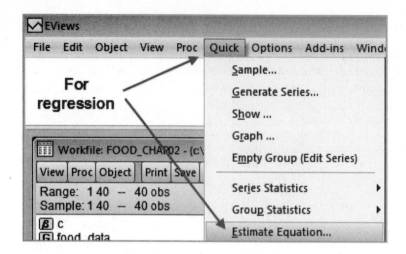

In the **Equation Specification** dialog box, type the dependent variable *FOOD_EXP* (the *y* variable) first, C (which is EViews notation for the intercept term, or constant), and then the independent variable *INCOME* (the *x* variable). Note that in the **Estimation settings** window, the **Method** is **Least Squares** and the **Sample** is **1 40**. Click **OK**.

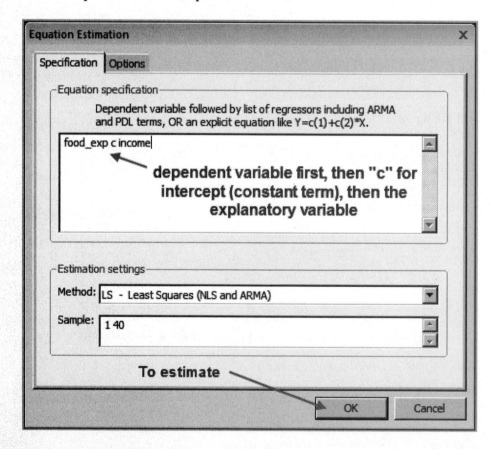

The estimated regression output appears. EViews produces an equation object in its default **Stats** view. We can name the equation object to save it permanently in our workfile by clicking on **Name** in the equation's toolbar. We have named this equation **FOOD_EQ**.

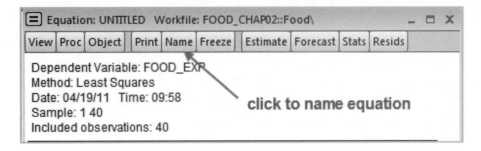

The top portion of the regression output is

Dependent Variable: FOOD_EXP
Method: Least Squares
Date: 04/19/11   Time: 09:58
Sample: 1 40
Included observations: 40

Variable	Coefficient	Std. Error	t-Statistic	Prob.
C	83.41600	43.41016	1.921578	0.0622
INCOME	10.20964	2.093264	4.877381	0.0000

Note that the estimated coefficient $b_1 = 83.41600$, the intercept in our food expenditure model, is recorded as the coefficient on the variable C. C is the EViews term for the constant in a regression model. We cannot name any of our variables C since this term is reserved exclusively for the constant or "intercept" in a regression model. In addition to $b_1 = 83.41600$, the EViews output shows that the estimated value of the slope coefficient on the variable weekly income (X) is $b_2 = 10.20964$, as reported in *POE4*, Chapter 2.3.2. The interpretation of b_2 is: for every \$100 increase in weekly income we estimate that there is about a \$10.21 increase in weekly food expenditure, holding all other factors constant.

In the workfile window, double-click on the vector object **C**. It always contains the estimated coefficients from the most recent regression.

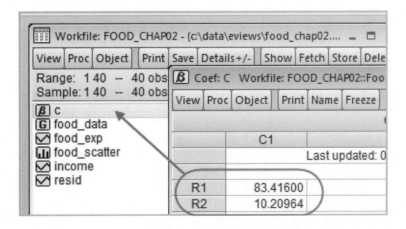

The series *RESID* always contains the least squares residuals from the most recent regression. We will return to this shortly.

2.3.1 Viewing equation representations

One EViews button that we will use often is the **View/Representations** button in a regression window:

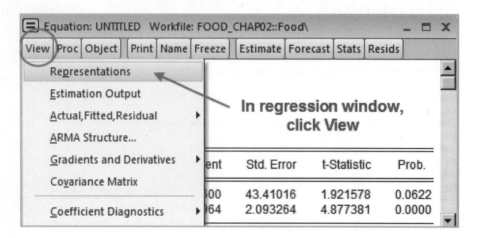

The resulting display shows three things:

- The **Estimation Command** is what can be typed into the Command window to obtain the equation results.
- The **Estimation Equation** shows the coefficients and how they are linked to the variables on the equation's right side: C(1) is the intercept and C(2) is the slope.
- The **Substituted Coefficients** displays the fitted regression line.

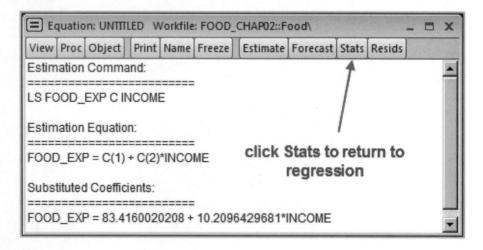

To return to the regression window click **Stats**.

2.3.2 Computing the income elasticity

As shown in equation (2.9) of *POE4*, the income elasticity is defined to be

$$\varepsilon = \frac{\Delta E(y)/E(y)}{\Delta x / x} = \frac{\Delta E(y)}{\Delta x} \cdot \frac{x}{E(y)} = \beta_2 \cdot \frac{x}{E(y)}$$

which is then implemented by replacing unknowns by estimated quantities,

$$\hat{\varepsilon} = b_2 \cdot \frac{\overline{x}}{\overline{y}} = 10.21 \times \frac{19.60}{283.57} = 0.71$$

We can use EViews as a "calculator" by simply typing into the Command window

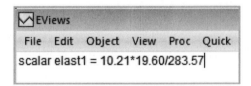

then pressing **Enter**. The word **scalar** means that the result is a single number. An icon appears in the workfile. Double-click in the shaded area:

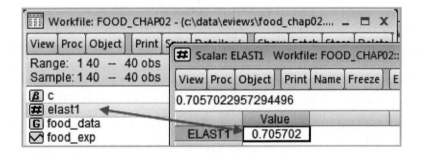

While this gives the answer, there is something to be said for using the power of EViews to simplify the calculations. EViews saves the estimates from the <u>most recent regression</u> in the workfile. They are obtained by double clicking the "*β*" icon:

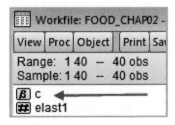

These coefficients can be accessed from the array **@coefs**. Also, EViews has functions to compute many quantities. The arithmetic mean is computed using the function **@mean**. Thus the elasticity can also be obtained by entering into the Command window

scalar elast2 = @coefs(2)*@mean(income)/@mean(food_exp)

The result is slightly different from the first computation because in the first we used "rounded-off" values of the sample means.

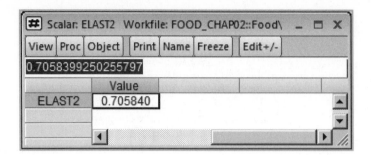

Because the array **@coefs** is not permanent, you may want to save the slope estimate as a separate quantity by entering the commands

> **scalar b2 = @coefs(2)**
> **scalar elast3 = b2*@mean(income)/@mean(food_exp)**

However, the coefficient array can always be retrieved <u>if</u> the food equation has been saved and named. Recall that we did save it with the name **FOOD_EQ**. By saving the equation we also save the coefficients, which can be retrieved from the array **FOOD_EQ.@coefs**.

> **scalar elas = food_eq.@coefs(2)*@mean(income)/@mean(food_exp)**

We have some surplus icons in our workfile now. Keep **B2** and **ELAS**. To clean out the other elasticties, highlight (hold down **Ctrl** and click each), right-click in the blue area, and select **Delete**.

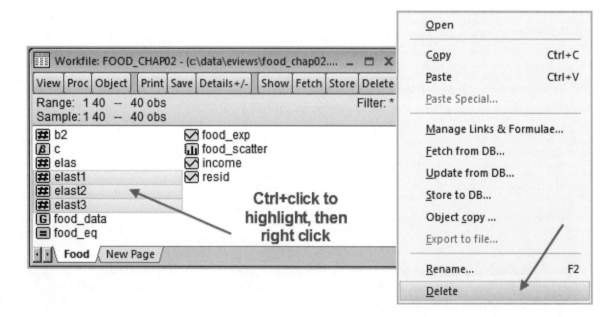

EViews will check to see if you are sure.

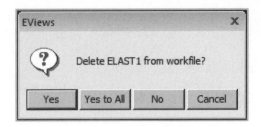

Choose **Yes to All** to delete all three objects from the workfile. **Save** the workfile, **Ctrl+S**.

2.4 PLOTTING A SIMPLE REGRESSION

Select **Quick/Graph** from the EViews menu and repeat the steps in Section 2.2 to create the scatter diagram. We will add the fitted least squares line to the graph. In the **Details** section, using the **Fit lines** drop-down menu, select **Regression Line**.

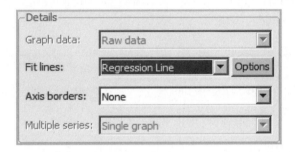

Click inside the graph, enter **Ctrl+C**, **OK**, and then paste into a document using **Ctrl+V**. The graph should look like this:

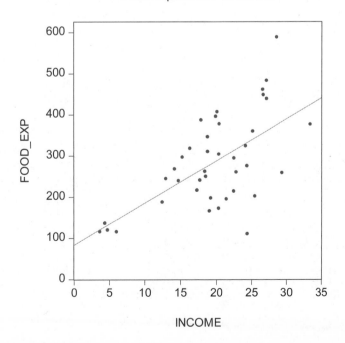

Return to EViews and in the Graph window select the **Name** button and assign a name to this object, such as **FITTED_LINE**.

2.5 PLOTTING THE LEAST SQUARES RESIDUALS

The least squares residuals are defined as

$$\hat{e}_i = y_i - \hat{y}_i = y_i - b_1 - b_2 x_i$$

As you will discover, these residuals are important for many purposes. To view the residuals, open the saved regression results in **FOOD_EQ** by double-clicking the icon.

2.5.1 Using View options

Within the equation **FOOD_EQ** window, click on **View** then **Actual, Fitted, Residual**. There you can select to view a table or several graphs.

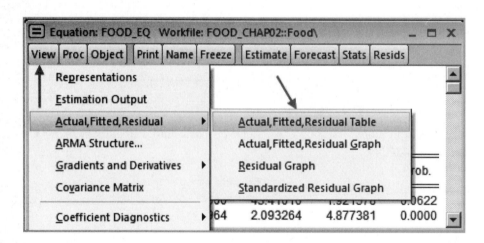

If you select **Actual, Fitted, Residual Table** you will see the values of the dependent variable y, the predicted (fitted) value of y, given by $\hat{y} = b_1 + b_2 x$, and the least squares residuals, along with a plot.

obs	Actual	Fitted	Residual	Residual Plot
1	115.220	121.090	-5.86958	
2	135.980	128.236	7.74367	
3	119.340	131.912	-12.5718	
4	114.960	144.980	-30.0201	
5	187.050	210.730	-23.6802	
6				

2.5.2 Using Resids plot

Within the object **FOOD_EQ** you can navigate by selecting buttons. Select **Resids**.

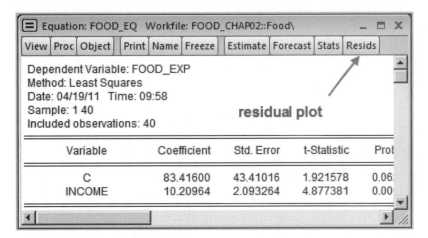

The result is a plot showing the least squares residuals (lower graph) along with the actual data (*FOOD_EXP*) and the fitted values. When using this plot, note that the horizontal axis is the **observation number** and not *INCOME*. In this workfile the data happen to be sorted by income, but note that the fitted values are not a straight line. When examining residual plots, a **lack of pattern** is consistent with the assumptions of the simple regression model.

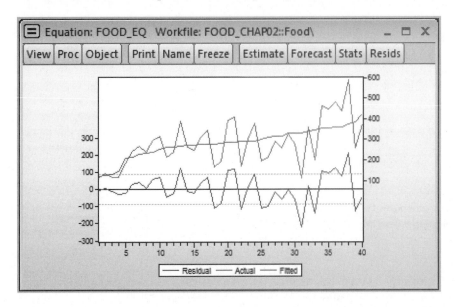

2.5.3 Using Quick/Graph

To create a graph of the residuals against income we can use the fact the EViews saves the residuals from the most recent regression in the series labeled *RESID*. Click on **Quick/Graph**. In the dialog box enter *INCOME* (*x*-axis comes first) and *RESID*.

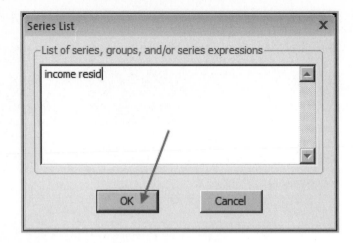

Choose the **Scatter** plot. Edit the resulting plot to add title and change symbols if desired. The resulting plot shows how the residuals relate to the values of income.

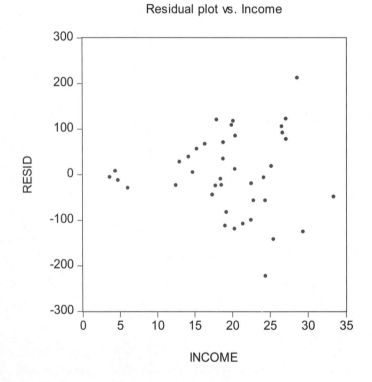

Save this plot by selecting **Name** and assigning **RESIDUAL_PLOT**.

2.5.4 Saving the residuals

To save these residuals for later use, we must **Generate** a new variable (series). In the workfile screen click **Genr** on the menu.

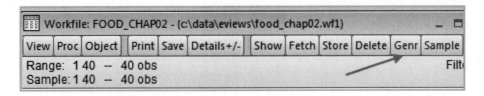

In the resulting dialog box create a new variable called *EHAT* that contains the residuals:

Generate Series by Equation   X

Enter equation

ehat = resid

Click **OK**. Alternatively, simply type into the Command window

    series ehat = resid

2.6 ESTIMATING THE VARIANCE OF THE ERROR TERM

The estimator for σ^2, the variance of the error term, is

$$\hat{\sigma}^2 = \frac{\sum \hat{e}_t^2}{N-2} = \frac{\text{Sum squared resid}}{N-2}$$

where **Sum squared resid** is the EViews name for the sum of squared residuals. The square root of the estimated error variance is called the **Standard Error of the Regression** by EViews,

$$\text{S.E. of regression} = \hat{\sigma} = \sqrt{\frac{\sum \hat{e}_t^2}{N-2}} = \sqrt{\hat{\sigma}^2}$$

Open the regression equation we have saved as **FOOD_EQ**. Below the estimation results you will find the Standard Error of the Regression and the sum of squared least squares residuals.

S.E. of regression	89.51700
Sum squared resid	304505.2

Also reported are the sample mean of the *y* values (**Mean dependent variable**):

$$\text{Mean dependent var} = \bar{y} = \sum y / N$$

The sample standard deviation of the *y* values (**S.D. dependent var**) is

$$\text{S.D. dependent var} = s_y = \sqrt{\frac{\sum (y_i - \bar{y})^2}{N-1}}$$

These are

Mean dependent var	283.5735
S.D. dependent var	112.6752

2.7 COEFFICIENT STANDARD ERRORS

The estimated error variance is used to construct the estimates of the variances and covariances of the least squares estimators as shown in *POE* equations (2.20)-(2.22). These estimated variances can be viewed from the **FOOD_EQ** regression by clicking on **View/Covariance Matrix:**

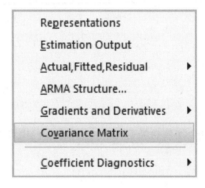

The elements are arrayed as

$$\begin{bmatrix} \widehat{\text{var}(b_1)} & \widehat{\text{cov}(b_1,b_2)} \\ \widehat{\text{cov}(b_1,b_2)} & \widehat{\text{var}(b_2)} \end{bmatrix}$$

In EViews they appear as

Coefficient Covariance Matrix		
	C	INCOME
C	1884.442	-85.90316
INCOME	-85.90316	4.381752

The highlighted value is the estimated variance of b_2. If we take the square roots of the estimated variances, we obtain the standard errors of the estimates. In the regression output these standard errors are denoted **Std. Error** and are found right next to the estimated coefficients.

Variable	Coefficient	Std. Error
C	83.41600	43.41016
INCOME	10.20964	2.093264

2.8 PREDICTION USING EVIEWS

There are several ways to create forecasts in EViews; we will illustrate two of them.

2.8.1 Using direct calculation

Open the food equation **FOOD_EQ**. Click on **View/Representations**. Select the text of the equation listed under **Substituted Coefficients**. We can choose **Edit/Copy** from the EViews menu bar, or we can simply use the keyboard shortcut **Ctrl+C** to copy the equation representation to the clipboard. Finally, we can paste the equation into the Command window.

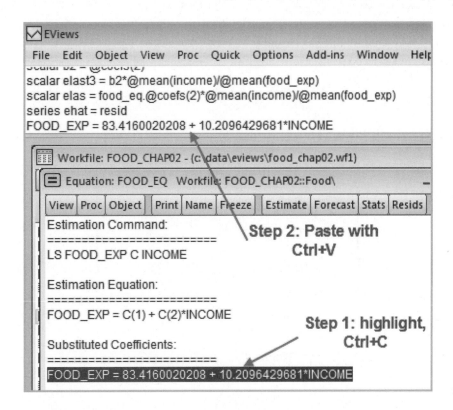

To obtain the predicted food expenditure for a household with weekly income of $2000, edit the Command window to read

scalar FOOD_EXP_HAT = 83.4160020208 + 10.2096429681*20

Press **Enter**. The resulting scalar value, both formatted and unformatted, is

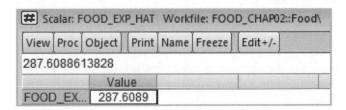

2.8.2 Forecasting

A more general, and flexible, procedure uses the power of EViews. In order to predict we must enter additional *x* observations at which we want predictions. In the main workfile window, double-click **Range**.

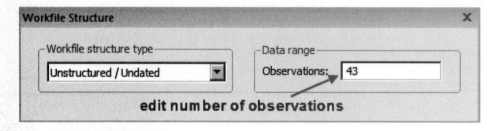

Range: 1 40 – 40 obs
Sample: 1 40 – 40 obs

This workfile has an **Unstructured/Undated** structure. Change the number of observations to 43.

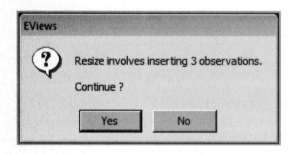

Click **OK**. EViews will check with you to confirm your action.

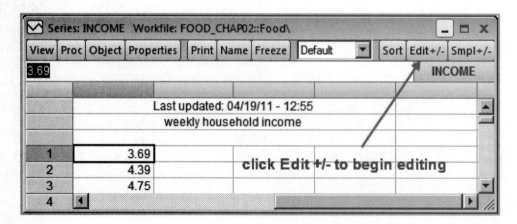

The **Sample** and **Range** will now be 43.

Range: 1 43 – 43 obs
Sample: 1 43 – 43 obs

Next, double-click on *INCOME* in the main workfile to open the series, and click the **Edit+/-** button in the series window, which puts EViews in edit mode.

Scroll to the bottom and you see NA in the cells for observations 41-43. Click the cell for observation 41 and enter 20. Enter 25 and 30 in cells 42 and 43, respectively. <u>When you are done, click the **Edit**+/- button again to turn off the edit mode.</u>

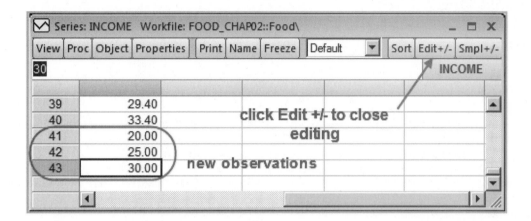

Now we have three extra *INCOME* observations that do not have *FOOD_EXP* observations. When we do a regression EViews will toss out the missing observations, but it will use the extra *INCOME* values when creating a forecast.

To forecast, first re-estimate the model with the original data. (This step is not actually necessary, but we want to illustrate a point.) Click on **Quick/Estimate Equation**. Enter the equation. Note in the dialog box that the **Sample** is 1 to 43.

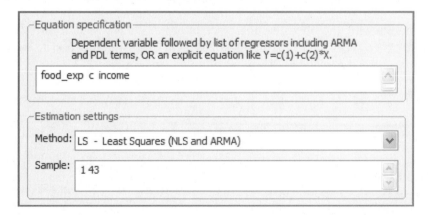

The estimation results are the same, and EViews tells us that the **Included observations** are 40 **after adjustments**. The three observations with no values for *FOOD_EXP* were discarded.

To forecast with the estimated model, click on the **Forecast** button in the equation window.

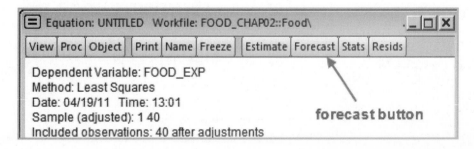

The **Forecast** dialog box appears. EViews automatically assigns the name **FOOD_EXPF** to the forecast series, so if you want a different name enter it. The **Forecast sample** is 1 to 43. Predictions will be constructed for the 40 samples values and for the 3 new values of *INCOME*. For now, ignore the other options. Click **OK**.

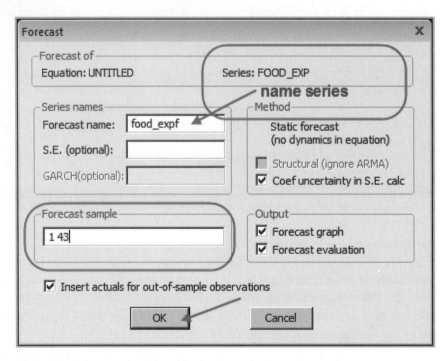

A graph appears showing the fitted line for observations 41-43 along with lines labeled ±2 S.E. We will discuss these later. To see the fitted values themselves, in the workfile window, double-click on the series named *FOOD_EXPF* and scroll to the bottom.

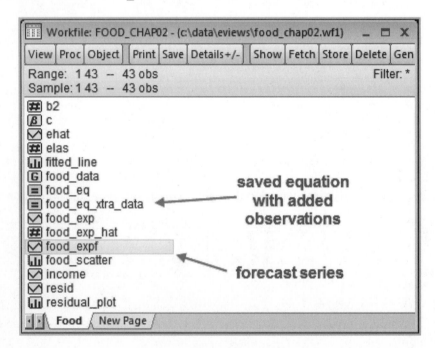

The three forecast values corresponding to incomes 20, 25 and 30 are in cells 41, 42 and 43. The value in cell 41 is 287.6089, which is the same predicted value obtained earlier in Chapter 2.3.3b.

While this approach is somewhat more laborious, by using it we can generate forecasts for many observations at once. More importantly, using EViews to forecast will make other options available to us that simple calculations will not.

2.9 ESTIMATING A NONLINEAR RELATIONSHIP

Consider a model from real estate economics in which the price (*PRICE*) of a house is related to the house size measured in square feet (*SQFT*). Open the EViews workfile *br.wf1*. Save it with a new name, such as *br_chap02.wf1*.

2.9.1 Fitting a quadratic model

A **quadratic** model for house prices includes the **squared** value of *SQFT*, giving

$$PRICE = \alpha_1 + \alpha_2 SQFT^2 + e$$

This is a simple regression model $y = \alpha_1 + \alpha_2 x + e$, with $y = PRICE$ and $x = SQRT^2$. Models with transformed variables are easily estimated in EViews using variable transformations inserted directly in the equation specification. Select **Quick/Estimate Equation** from the EViews menu. In the dialog box enter the equation using $SQFT^2$ to represent the quadratic term.

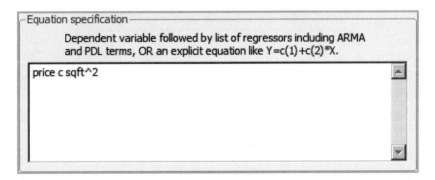

The resulting estimates are:

Sample: 1 1080
Included observations: 1080

Variable	Coefficient	Std. Error	t-Statistic	Prob.
C	55776.57	2890.441	19.29690	0.0000
SQFT^2	0.015421	0.000313	49.25420	0.0000

It is useful now to begin doing the least squares estimation using the Command window approach. The quadratic model estimated above can also be implemented by entering into the Command window

> **ls price c sqft^2**

Alternatively, the equation can be estimated and named **QUADRATIC** with one command using

> **equation quadratic.ls price c sqft^2**

2.9.2 Interpreting the quadratic model

EViews can compute the slope and elasticity at any point using the same approach as in Section 2.3.2. The slope of the fitted line is also known as the **marginal effect** in economics. It is given by

$$\frac{d\left(\widehat{PRICE}\right)}{dSQFT} = 2\hat{\alpha}_2 SQFT$$

where $\hat{\alpha}_2 = 0.015421$ is the least squares estimate of the parameter α_2 that is attached to the variable **SQFT^2** from the regression output. To compute this value we can choose a particular house size, say $SQFT = 2000$. This scalar can be calculated within EViews using the saved coefficients **@coefs**, following estimation of the regression equation. So that we can create a few predicted values, first create a new **Object**. From the EViews menu choose **Object/New Object**. In the **New Object** dialog box, choose **Matrix-Vector-Coef** and assign a name: **dydx_q** is representative for the slope of the quadratic model.

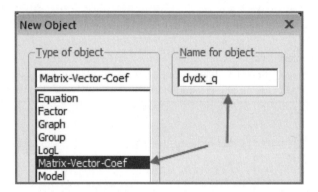

We will compute marginal effects for three house sizes, 2000, 4000, and 6000 square feet. So choose a vector with three rows and one column.

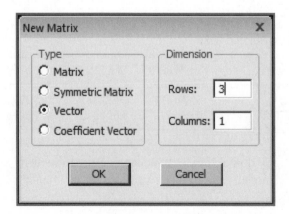

Click **OK** to open the **Vector**. In the Command window enter, one after the other,

dydx_q(1) = 2*@coefs(2)*2000
dydx_q(2) = 2*@coefs(2)*4000
dydx_q(3) = 2*@coefs(2)*6000

Note that Command window entries are simple text, and can be copied and pasted, or edited directly to produce new commands. That is, after typing the first command, highlight it, then copy and paste it into a new Command window below the previous. Or, even more simply, edit the first command by replacing (1) with (2) and 2000 with 4000, then press **Enter**. The resulting vector is now

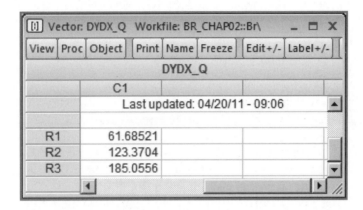

While those are the answers, it is nice to "dress them up" a bit. In the Vector, highlight the numbers and copy using **Ctrl + C**.

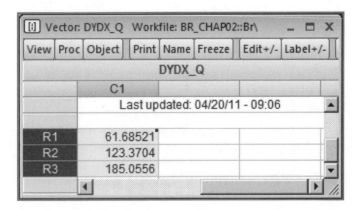

Select the formatted option, then paste the table into word processing software. Edit the table to make it presentable.

Marginal Effect of an Additional Square Foot of Living Space	
Square feet	Predicted change in price
2000	61.68521
4000	123.3704
6000	185.0556

Alternatively, the average of the marginal effects for the entire sample can be created. That is,

$$AME = \frac{1}{N}\sum_{i=1}^{N} ME_i = \frac{1}{N}\sum_{i=1}^{N} 2\hat{\alpha}_2 SQFT_i$$

Create the series $2\hat{\alpha}_2 SQFT_i$ using

series me = 2*@coefs(2)*sqft

Compute the summary statistics for this series.

		ME			
Mean	Mean	71.73798			
Median	Median	67.43735			
Maximum	Maximum	243.5640			
Minimum	Minimum	20.41780			
Std. Dev.	Std. Dev.	31.09237			
Skewness					

Series: ME   Workfile: BR_CHAP02::Br\
View | Proc | Object | Properties | Print | Name | Freeze | Sample | Genr | Sheet | Graph | Stats |

The average (over all properties in the sample) estimated increase in *PRICE* for an additional square foot of living area is \$71.74. The Standard Deviation **Std. Dev.** is one measure of how much variation there is in the estimated marginal effects.

Computing the elasticity of *PRICE* with respect to house size, *SQFT*, is much the same. The elasticity of house price with respect to house size is the percentage increase in estimated price given a 1% increase in house size. Like the slope, the elasticity changes at each point. In our example,

$$\hat{\varepsilon} = \widehat{slope} \times \frac{SQFT}{PRICE} = (2\hat{\alpha}_2 SQFT) \times \frac{SQFT}{PRICE}$$

To compute an estimate we must select values for *SQFT* and *PRICE*. A common approach is to choose a point on the fitted relationship. That is, choose a value for *SQFT* and choose for price the corresponding fitted value $\widehat{PRICE}$. An efficient way to carry out the calculations is to (i) insert three additional observations into the workfile (change Range), (ii) enter 2000, 4000, and 6000 as the additional *SQFT* values, (iii) obtain fitted values from the **QUADRATIC** equation using **Forecast**, say *PRICEF_QUAD*. Then implement the command

series elas_quad = 2*@coefs(2)*(sqft^2)/pricef_quad

Open the group consisting of *SQFT*, *PRICEF_QUAD*, and *ELAS_QUAD*. The last three rows are

Group: UNTITLED   Workfile: BR_CHAP02::Br\
View | Proc | Object | Print | Name | Freeze | Default | Sort | Transpose

obs	SQFT	PRICEF_Q...	ELAS_QUAD	
1081	2000	117461.8	1.050303	
1082	4000	302517.4	1.631251	
1083	6000	610943.4	1.817408	

The average elasticity for the 1080 individuals is obtained similarly. In the group of series above, highlight the column *ELAS_QUAD*. Select **View**.

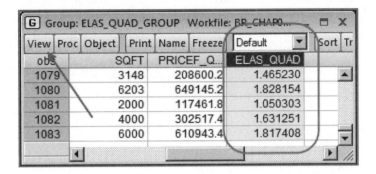

Choose **Descriptive Stats/Common Sample**.

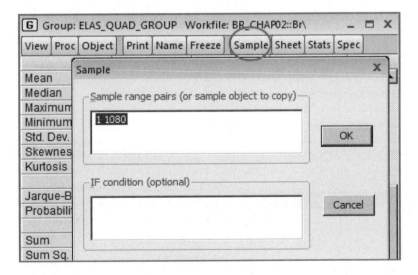

Select **Sample** and adjust the **Sample range**; click **OK**.

	SQFT	PRICEF_QUAD	ELAS_QUAD
Mean	2325.938	154863.2	1.102401
Median	2186.500	129502.8	1.138600
Maximum	7897.000	1017489.	1.890364
Minimum	662.0000	62534.86	0.216145
Std. Dev.	1008.098	102272.7	0.352835
Observations	1080	1080	1080

The average of the elasticities computed at each of the 1080 sample points is 1.1024.

2.9.3 Plotting the fitted quadratic model

How well does this equation fit the data? The plot of the quadratic fit can be accomplished by using **Quick/Graph**. In the dialog box enter

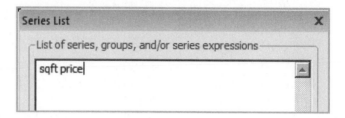

Choose the **Scatter Graph type**. Add a **Fit line**.

Click **Options** next to **Regression Line**. Choose **Power** for the **X transformations**. The default power is 2 so that no change is required. Select **Add**. Note that now we have two **Added Elements**.

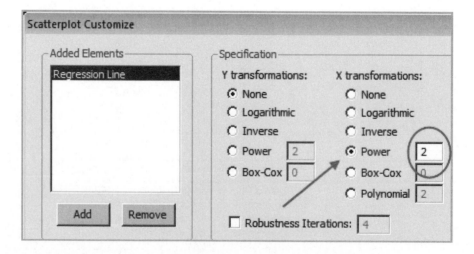

We choose to make the symbols small since there are a large number of data points:

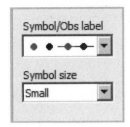

Also, we add text to the graph. Click inside the graph to highlight the border, and enter the copy short-cut **Ctrl + C**. Now you have two options. If you are creating a color document, then leave the default copy settings. If your document is not in color, a reader will not really be able to tell one fitted line from the other (except that one is curved). Remove the color option:

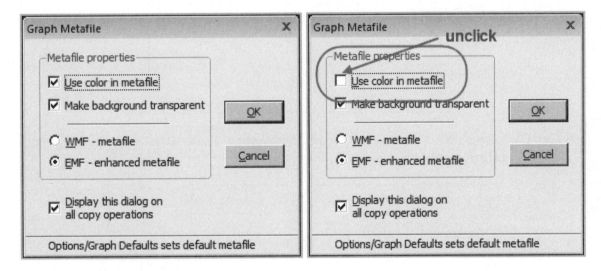

The plot with the color removed is shown below. EViews adds a legend indicating the plot.

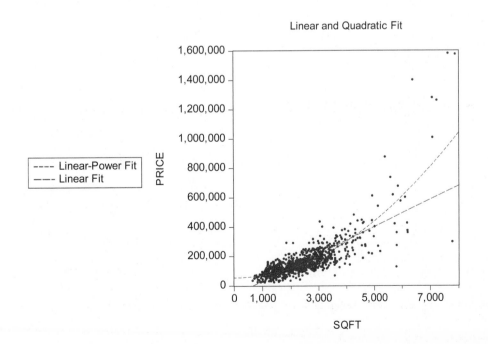

2.9.4 Estimating a log-linear model

An alternative choice for a nonlinear relationship between house price and size is the log-linear model:

$$\log\left(PRICE\right) = \gamma_1 + \gamma_2 SQFT + e$$

Logarithmically transformed dependent variables are common when the original distribution is skewed, which is frequent with economic variables like income, and housing prices. To see this, select **Quick/Graph** from the EViews menu. First, enter the variable name *PRICE*.

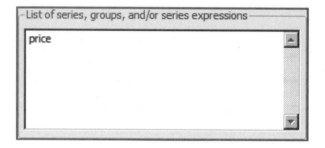

Select **OK**. Among the **Graph types** choose **Distribution**. Under **Details** the **Distribution** is identified as **Histogram**.

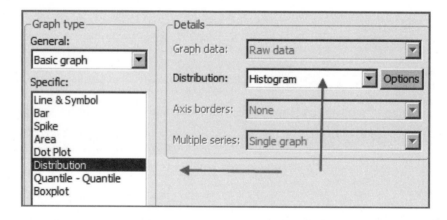

Repeat these same steps but enter **log(price)** into the series list. In EViews the function **log** is the natural logarithm.

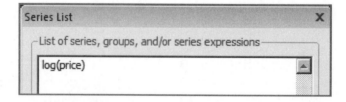

The two histograms are shown below. Notice that *PRICE* has a skewed distribution, with a long tail to the right. The distribution of *LOG(PRICE)* is much more symmetrical. If we can assume that the data are normally distributed, we will find that the statistical inference procedures of interval estimation and hypothesis testing have improved properties. These ideas will be introduced in Chapter 3.

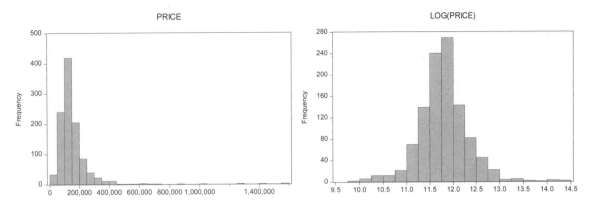

Estimation for this case uses the natural logarithmic transformation of *PRICE*. In the Command window enter

equation loglinear.ls log(price) c sqft

The resulting estimated equation is

Dependent Variable: LOG(PRICE)
Method: Least Squares
Sample: 1 1080
Included observations: 1080

Variable	Coefficient	Std. Error	t-Statistic	Prob.
C	10.83860	0.024607	440.4593	0.0000
SQFT	0.000411	9.71E-06	42.36484	0.0000

Note that the **Dependent Variable** is **LOG(PRICE).**

2.9.5 Interpreting the log-linear model

The simplest interpretation in the log-linear model is that a 1-unit increase in the explanatory variable (*SQFT*) leads to approximately a $100\hat{\gamma}_2\%$ change in the dependent variable (*PRICE*), holding all else fixed. We can say that, for a 1 square foot increase in size, we estimate a price increase of 0.04 percent. Or, perhaps more usefully, we estimate that a 100 square foot increase will increase price by approximately 4%.

The slope and elasticity in this log-linear model are

$$\frac{d\left(\widehat{PRICE}\right)}{dSQFT} = \hat{\gamma}_2 \widehat{PRICE} = 0.000411\widehat{PRICE}$$

$$\hat{\varepsilon} = \hat{\gamma}_2 SQFT = 0.000411 SQFT$$

The slope calculation requires a predicted value of *PRICE*. In the next section we see how to accomplish that.

2.9.6 Prediction in the log-linear model

To plot the fitted line we use the same steps as for the quadratic fitted line except that we apply a **Logarithmic Y transformation**.

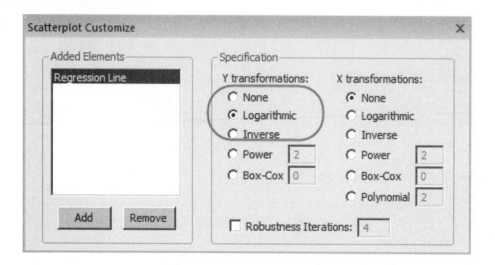

Click **Add**. We can add the quadratic fitted line as well. Click **Power**, enter "2" and click **Add**. Now we have three Added Elements.

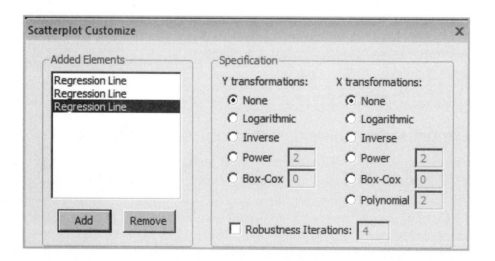

Click **OK**, then copy and paste a non-color graph. Note that we have the option of highlighting one of the **Regression Line** entries and selecting **Remove** instead of **Add**.

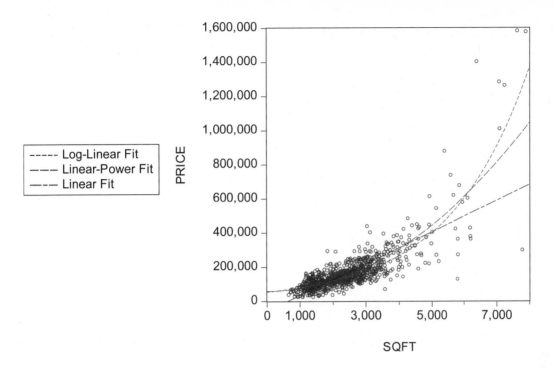

Forecasting with a log-linear model requires a little care, as the dependent variable in the model regression is *LOG(PRICE)*. From within the **LOGLINEAR** regression equation click **Forecast**.

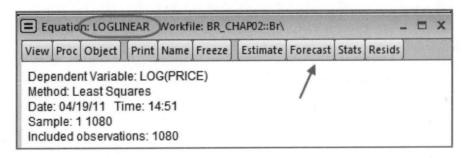

Two options are offered under **Series to forecast**.

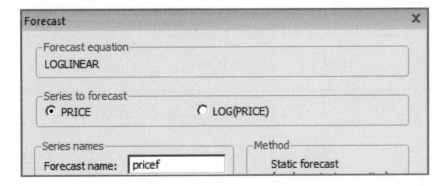

First choose the default, which is to forecast *PRICE*, generating the new series *PRICEF*. Repeat the exercise by returning to the **Stats** panel, and click **Forecast** again.

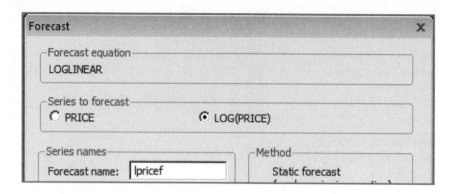

Choose the **LOG(PRICE)** radio button and give the forecast a new name, such as *LPRICEF*. This generates the fitted values

$$\widehat{\log(PRICE)} = \hat{\gamma}_1 + \hat{\gamma}_2 SQFT = 10.83860 + 0.000411 SQFT$$

where $\hat{\gamma}_1$ and $\hat{\gamma}_2$ are least squares estimates of the log-linear regression equation parameters. The predicted value of *PRICE* is obtained using the anti-logarithm, which is the exponential function

$$\widehat{PRICE} = \exp\left[\widehat{\log(PRICE)}\right]$$

In the EViews Command window we enter

    series pricehat = exp(lpricef)

Open the four series *PRICE, PRICEF, LPRICEF* and *PRICEHAT* by selecting them in order while holding down the **Ctrl** key.

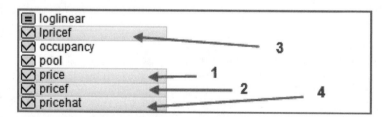

Double-click within the shaded area to open the group.

obs	PRICE	PRICEF	LPRICEF	PRICEHAT
1	66500	69102.52	11.14335	69102.52
2	66000	69102.52	11.14335	69102.52
3	68500	70509.22	11.16350	70509.22
4	102000	160036.6	11.98316	160036.6
5	54000	82266.93	11.31772	82266.93
6				

The series *PRICEF* is the same as *PRICEHAT*, so we have confirmed what EViews is doing in the forecast step with a log-linear model.

By using the predicted *PRICE*, the slope expression in Section 2.9.5 can be computed at any given house size. Alternatively, the Average Marginal Effect (AME) can be computed using

series me_llin = @coefs(2)*pricef	*ME at each observation*
coef(2) ame_llin	*Storage Vector*
ame_llin(1)=@mean(me_llin)	*Sample mean of ME*
ame_llin(2)=@stdev(me_llin)	*Std Dev of ME*

The result is

Average marginal effect of increase in house size (1 square foot) on predicted house price	
AME	61.00073
STD DEV	42.91725

2.10 REGRESSION WITH INDICATOR VARIABLES

An indicator variable is a binary (0 or 1) variable that is used to represent a non-quantitative characteristic, such as gender, race, or location. For example, in the workfile ***utown.wf1*** we have a sample of 1000 observations on house prices (*PRICE*, in thousands of dollars) in two neighborhoods. Save the file under an alternative name, such as ***utown_chap02.wf1***.

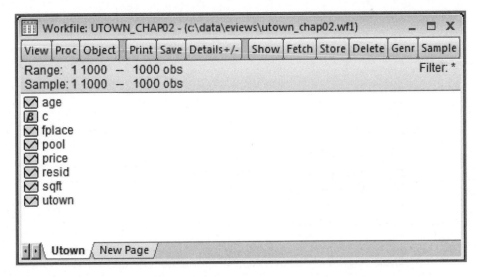

One neighborhood is near a major university and called University Town. Another similar neighborhood, called Golden Oaks, is a few miles away from the university. The indicator variable of interest is

$$UTOWN = \begin{cases} 1 & \text{house is in University Town} \\ 0 & \text{house is in Golden Oaks} \end{cases}$$

We use the **Sample** options to construct histograms for house prices in each neighborhood. Open the *PRICE* series. Click on **View/Descriptive Statistics & Tests/Histogram and Stats**. What appears is the histogram and summary statistics for the full sample of observations. Click the **Sample** button.

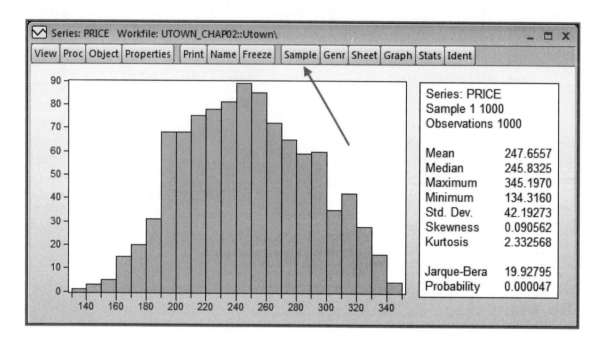

Add the **IF condition utown=1,**

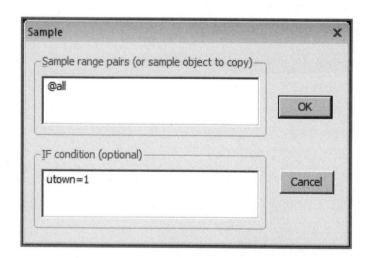

The resulting histogram is

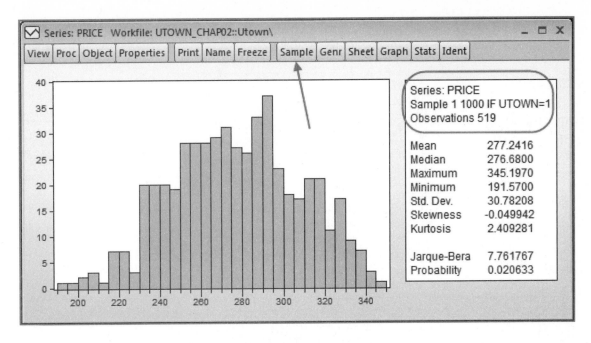

Click on **Sample** again. Change the **IF condition** to

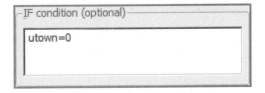

The result is

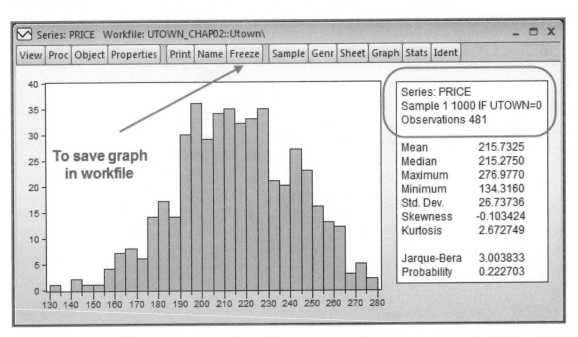

It is nice to have the two graphs in the same image. This can be achieved by selecting the two saved graphs and double-clicking in the shaded area.

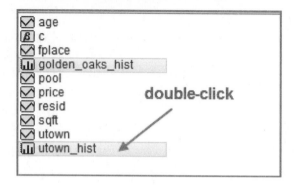

The result is

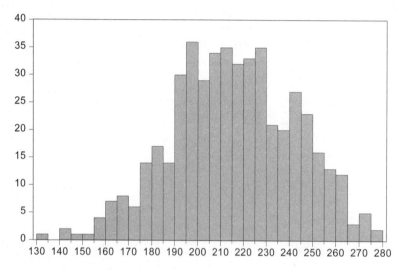

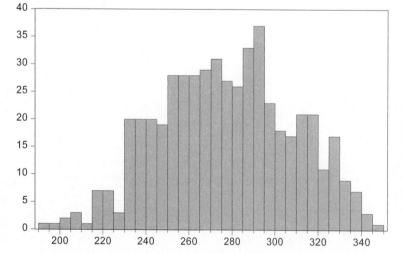

A regression model using *UTOWN* as an explanatory variable is

$$PRICE = \beta_1 + \beta_2 UTOWN + e$$

Regression using indicator variables as explanatory variables requires no special software commands. It is the interpretation that is unusual. The parameter β_2 is not a slope, because *UTOWN* is not a continuous variable. Slopes are derivatives, and derivatives are taken with respect to continuous variables. The regression function for this model is

$$E(PRICE) = \beta_1 + \beta_2 UTOWN = \begin{cases} \beta_1 + \beta_2 & \text{if } UTOWN=1 \\ \\ \beta_1 & \text{if } UTOWN=0 \end{cases}$$

Before estimating the regression we must return the sample to include all observations. Click on the **Sample** button and clear any previous condition.

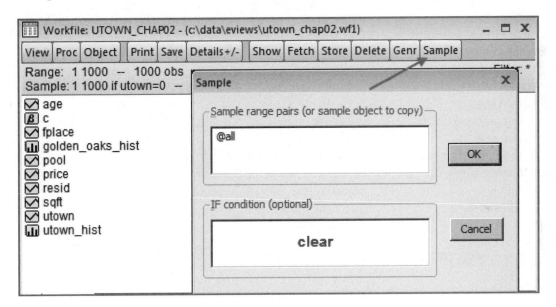

Estimate the regression using the command

equation utown_reg.ls price c utown

A portion of the output is

Dependent Variable: PRICE
Sample: 1 1000
Included observations: 1000

Variable	Coefficient	Std. Error	t-Statistic	Prob.
C	215.7325	1.318066	163.6735	0.0000
UTOWN	61.50911	1.829589	33.61908	0.0000

Note that the constant term 215.7325 is the sample mean price of houses in Golden Oaks. The coefficient of *UTOWN*, 61.50911, is the difference between the sample means of houses in University Town and Golden Oaks. The least squares estimates b_1 and b_2 in this indicator variable regression can be shown to be

$$b_1 = \overline{PRICE}_{\text{Golden Oaks}} = 215.7325$$

$$b_2 = \overline{PRICE}_{\text{University Town}} - \overline{PRICE}_{\text{Golden Oaks}} = 277.2416 - 215.7325 = 61.5091$$

where $\overline{PRICE}_{\text{Golden Oaks}}$ is the sample mean (average) price of houses in Golden Oaks and $\overline{PRICE}_{\text{University Town}}$ is the sample mean price of houses from University Town.

Keywords

average marginal effect	graph regression line	residual table
coefficient vector	graph save	residuals
covariance matrix	graph symbol pattern	S.D. dependent variable
descriptive statistics	graph title	S.E. of regression
edit +/-	group: open	sample mean
elasticity	indicator variable	sample range
equation name.ls	log	sample standard deviation
equation representations	log-linear model	scalar
equation save	marginal effect	scatter diagram
error variance	Mean dependent variable	series
estimate equation	object: Matrix-Vector-Coef	slope, regression
forecast	object: name	spreadsheet
generate series	quadratic model	standard errors
genr	quick/estimate equation	Std. Error
graph axes/scale	quick/graph	Sum of squared resid
graph copy to document	resid	workfile: open
graph options	resids	workfile: save

CHAPTER **3**

Interval Estimation and Hypothesis Testing

In this chapter we continue to work with the simple linear regression model and our model of weekly food expenditure. To begin, open the food expenditure workfile *food.wf1*. On the EViews menu choose **File/Open** and then save the file. So that the original file is not altered, save this under a new name. Select **File/Save As,** then name the file *food_chap03.wf1*. Estimate the simple regression

$$FOOD\_EXP = \beta_1 + \beta_2 INCOME + e$$

The estimation can be carried out by entering into the Command window

    ls food_exp c income

Alternatively, on the EViews menu, select **Quick/Estimate Equation**, then fill in the dialog box with the equation specification and click **OK**.

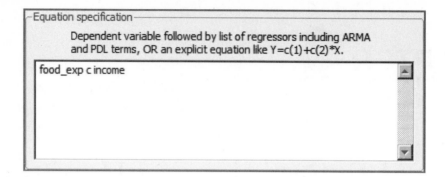

Name the resulting regression results **FOOD_EQ** by selecting the **Name** button and filling in the **Object name**.

As a third alternative, do it all in one step using the command

equation food_eq.ls food_exp c income

With this option the equation becomes an object in the workfile without opening.

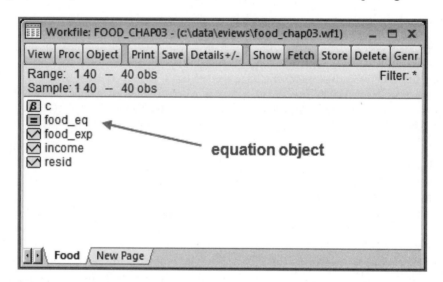

Double-click the object to open it.

3.1 INTERVAL ESTIMATION

For the regression model $y = \beta_1 + \beta_2 x + e$, and under assumptions SR1-SR6, the important result that we use in this chapter is given in equation (3.3) of *POE4*:

$$t = \frac{b_k - \beta_k}{\text{se}(b_k)} \sim t_{(N-2)} \text{ for } k = 1,2$$

Using this result, we can show that the interval $b_k \pm t_c \text{se}(b_k)$ has probability $1 - \alpha$ of containing the true but unknown parameter β_k, where the "critical value" t_c is from a t-distribution such that

$$P(t \geq t_c) = P(t \leq -t_c) = \alpha/2$$

To construct interval estimates we will use EViews' stored regression results. We will also make use of EViews built-in statistical functions. For each distribution (see **Function reference** in EViews Help) four statistical functions are provided. The two we will use are the **cumulative distribution** (CDF) and the **quantile** (Inverse CDF) functions.

For the t-distribution the CDF is given by the function **@ctdist(x,v)**. This function returns the **probability** that a t-random variable with **v** degrees of freedom falls to the left of **x**. That is,

$$@ctdist(x,v) = P\left[t_{(v)} \leq x \right]$$

The quantile function **@qtdist(p,v)** computes the **critical value** of a t-random variable with **v** degrees of freedom such that probability **p** falls to the left of it. For example, if we specify **tc=@qtdist(.975,38)**, then

$$P\left[t_{(38)} \leq t_c \right] = .975$$

To construct the interval estimates we require the least squares estimates b_k and their standard errors $\text{se}(b_k)$. After each regression model is estimated, the coefficients and standard errors are saved in the arrays **@coefs** and **@stderrs**. However, they are saved only until the next regression is run, at which time they are replaced. If you have named the regression results, as we have (**FOOD_EQ**), then the coefficients are saved as well, with the names **food_eq.@coefs** and **food_eq.@stderrs**, respectively.

3.1.1 Constructing the interval estimate

Since we have estimated only one regression we can use the simple form for the saved results. Thus **@coefs(2)** = b_2 and **@stderrs(2)** = $\text{se}(b_2)$. To generate the 95% confidence interval $\left[b_2 - t_c \text{se}(b_2), b_2 + t_c \text{se}(b_2) \right]$ enter the following commands in the EViews Command window, pressing the **<Enter>** key after each:

```
scalar tc = @qtdist(.975,38)
scalar b2 = @coefs(2)
scalar seb2 = @stderrs(2)
scalar b2_lb = b2 - tc*seb2
scalar b2_ub = b2 + tc*seb2
```

These scalar values show up in the workfile with the symbol #. For example, the value of the lower bound of the interval estimate is

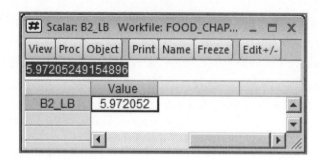

3.1.2 Using a coefficient vector

While the above approach works perfectly fine, it may be nicer for report writing to store the interval estimates in an array and construct a table. On the main EViews Menu select **Objects/New Object:**

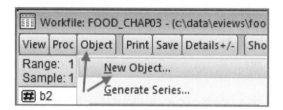

We will create a **Matrix-Vector-Coef** named **INT_EST:**

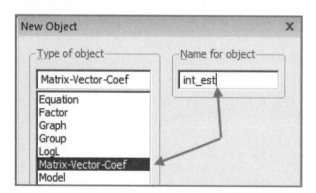

It will be a **Coefficient Vector** that has two rows and one column:

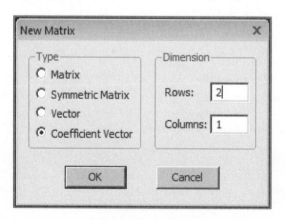

Click **OK**, and the empty array appears. Instead of all that pointing and clicking, you can simply enter on the Command window

coef(2) int_est

Now, enter the commands

int_est(1) = @coefs(2) - @qtdist(.975,38)*@stderrs(2)
int_est(2) = @coefs(2) + @qtdist(.975,38)*@stderrs(2)

Here we have used the EViews saved results directly rather than create scalars for each element. The vector we created is

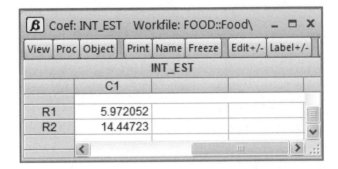

Click on **Freeze** and then **Name**. We use the name **B2_INTERVAL_ESTIMATE**; it looks like:

The advantage of this approach is that the contents can be highlighted, copied (**Ctrl+C**), and pasted (**Ctrl+V**) into a document. The resulting table can be edited as you like.

95% Interval Estimate for Beta 2	
lower bound	5.972052
upper bound	14.44723

3.1.3 Using EViews command cinterval

In the **FOOD_EQ** regression output click **View:**

Select **Coefficient Diagnostics/Confidence Intervals**.

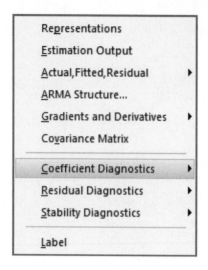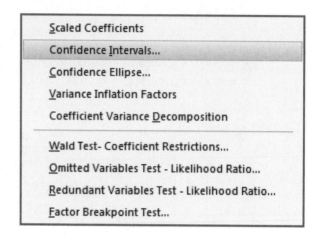

The resulting dialog box default is to construct 90, 95 and 99% interval estimates. To obtain just a 95% interval estimate use

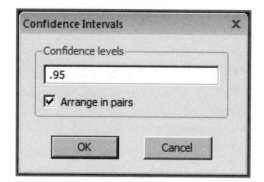

Click **OK** to obtain

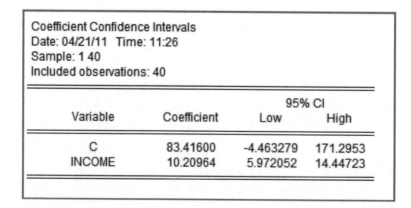

The same result can be obtained from the Command window using

food_eq.cinterval .95

3.2 RIGHT-TAIL TESTS

3.2.1 Test of significance

To test the null hypothesis that $\beta_2 = 0$ against the alternative that it is positive (> 0), as described in Chapter 3.4.1a of *POE4*, requires us to find the critical value, construct the t-statistic, and determine the p-value.

- If we choose the $\alpha = .05$ level of significance, then the critical value is the 95th percentile of the $t_{(38)}$ distribution.
- The t-statistic is the ratio of the estimate b_2 over its standard error, se(b_2).
- The p-value is the area to the <u>right</u> of the calculated t-statistic (since it is a right-tail test). This value is one minus the cumulative probability to the left of the t-statistic.

The simplest set of commands is (do not type the comments in *italic* font):

```
scalar tc95 = @qtdist(.95,38)          t-critical right tail
scalar tstat = b2/seb2                 t-statistic
scalar pval = 1 - @ctdist(tstat,38)    right-tail p-value
```

Alternatively, use the vector approach outlined in the previous section:

```
coef(10) t1                   storage vector
t1(1) = b2                    estimate
t1(2) = seb2                  standard error
t1(3) = b2/seb2               t-statistic
t1(4) = @qtdist(.95,38)       t-critical right tail
t1(5) = 1-@ctdist( t1(3),38 ) right-tail p-value
```

Use the results of this vector to construct a table, such as

Right Tail Test of Significance	
b_2	10.20964
se(b_2)	2.093264
t-stat	4.877381
critical value	1.685954
p-value	9.73E-06

EViews computes the test statistic t for the hypothesis that each coefficient is zero and reports it in each regression output.

Variable	Coefficient	Std. Error	t-Statistic	Prob.
C	83.41600	43.41016	1.921578	0.0622
INCOME	10.20964	2.093264	4.877381	0.0000

The value **Prob.** is the p-value for a **two-tail** test of significance.

3.2.2 Test of an economic hypothesis

To test the null hypothesis that $\beta_2 \leq 5$ against the alternative $\beta_2 > 5$, the same steps are executed except for the construction of the t-statistic.

coef(10) t2	*storage vector*
t2(1) = b2	*estimate*
t2(2) = seb2	*standard error*
t2(3) = (b2-5)/seb2	*t-statistic*
t2(4) = @qtdist(.95,38)	*t-critical right tail*
t2(5) = 1-@ctdist(t2(3),38)	*right-tail p-value*

Right-Tail Test, Beta 2 = 5	
b_2	10.20964
$se(b_2)$	2.093264
t-stat	2.488766
critical value	1.685954
p-value	0.008658

Except for the reporting of the critical value and the one-tail p-value, we can use EViews to carry out this test automatically. First, in the regression output **FOOD_EQ**, click the **View** button.

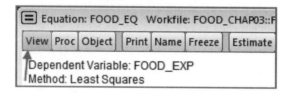

Choose **Representations**.

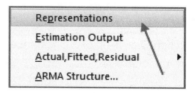

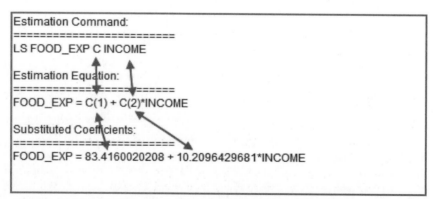

The estimates are stored in the order of the estimation command, **C(1)** for the first coefficient and **C(2)** for the second.

Then, in the regression output **FOOD_EQ**, click the **View** button again. Choose **Coefficient Diagnostics/Wald Test-Coefficient Restrictions**.

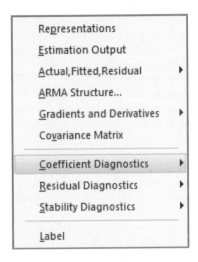
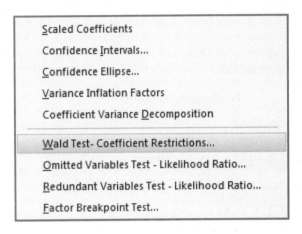

In the **Wald Test** dialog box specify the **equality** null hypothesis being tested, here $\beta_2 = 5$, using the coefficients retained by EViews.

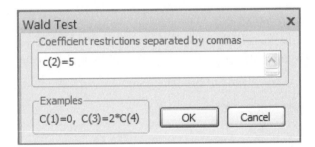

The output shows the test statistic value and the degrees of freedom. The **Probability** is the two-tail p-value. The one-tail p-value is half of this value.

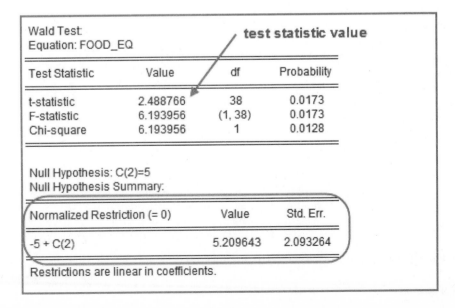

The **Null Hypothesis Summary** shows what is called the **Normalized Restriction (=0)**. This is the numerator value of the *t*-statistic

$$t = \frac{b_2 - 5}{\text{se}(b_2)}$$

The other test statistics reported will be important in the context of multiple regression.

The same result can be obtained from the Command window using

        food_eq.wald c(2)=5

3.3 LEFT-TAIL TESTS

3.3.1 Test of significance

To test the null hypothesis that $\beta_2 \geq 0$ against the alternative that it is negative (< 0) requires us to find the critical value, construct the *t*-statistic, and determine the *p*-value.

- If we choose the $\alpha = .05$ level of significance, then the critical value is the 5th percentile of the $t_{(38)}$ distribution.
- The *t*- statistic is the ratio of the estimate b_2 over its standard error, se(b_2).
- The *p*-value is the area to the <u>left</u> of the calculated *t*-statistic (since it is a left-tail test). This value is given by the cumulative probability to the left of the *t*-statistic.

The simplest set of commands is (do not type the comments in italic font)

scalar tc05 = @qtdist(.05,38)	*t-critical left tail*
scalar tstat = b2/seb2	*t-statistic*
scalar pval = @ctdist(tstat,38)	*left-tail p-value*

Alternatively,

coef(10) t3	*storage vector*
t3(1) = b2	*estimate*
t3(2) = seb2	*standard error*
t3(3) = b2/seb2	*t-statistic*
t3(4) = @qtdist(.05,38)	*t-critical left tail*
t3(5) = @ctdist(t3(3),38)	*left-tail p-value*

yielding

Left-Tail Test of Significance	
b_2	10.20964
se(b_2)	2.093264
t-stat	4.877381
critical value	-1.685954
p-value	0.999990

Note that we fail to reject the null hypothesis in this case, as expected.

3.3.2 Test of an economic hypothesis

To test the null hypothesis that $\beta_2 \geq 12$ against the alternative that $\beta_2 < 12$, we use the same steps as above except for the construction of the t-statistic:

coef(10) t4	*storage vector*
t4(1) = b2	*estimate*
t4(2) = seb2	*standard error*
t4(3) = (b2-12)/seb2	*t-statistic*
t4(4) = @qtdist(.05,38)	*t-critical left tail*
t4(5) = @ctdist(t4(3),38)	*left-tail p-value*

yielding,

Left-Tail Test that Beta 2 ≥ 12	
b_2	10.20964
$se(b_2)$	2.093264
t-stat	-0.855295
critical value	-1.685954
p-value	0.198874

The t-statistic value $-.855$ does not fall in the rejection region and the p-value is about .20, and thus we fail to reject this null hypothesis.

Using the Wald test dialog box we specify the test as

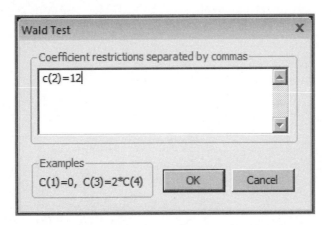

The output shows the value of the test statistic and the two-tail p-value.

Wald Test:			
Equation: FOOD_EQ			
Test Statistic	**Value**	**df**	**Probability**
t-statistic	-0.855295	38	0.3977

The same result can be obtained from the Command window using

food_eq.wald c(2)=12

3.4 TWO-TAIL TESTS

3.4.1 Test of significance

For the two-tail test of the null hypothesis that $\beta_2 = 0$ against the alternative that $\beta_2 \neq 0$, we require the same test elements:

- If we choose the $\alpha = .05$ level of significance, then the right-tail critical value is the 97.5-percentile of the $t_{(38)}$ distribution and the left tail critical value is the 2.5-percentile.
- The t-statistic is the ratio of the estimate b_2 over its standard error, $se(b_2)$.
- The p-value is the area to the <u>left</u> of minus the absolute value of the calculated t-statistic, <u>plus</u> the area to the right of the absolute value of the calculated test statistic (since it is a two-tail test). This value is given by the cumulative probability to the left of the value $-|t\text{-statistic}|$, plus 1 – the cumulative probability to the right of $|t\text{-statistic}|$.

A simple set of commands is (do not type the comments in *italic* font):

```
scalar tc975 = @qtdist(.975,38)        t-critical right tail
scalar tc025 = @qtdist(.025,38)        t-critical left tail
scalar tstat = b2/seb2                 t-statistic
scalar leftpval = @ctdist(-abs(tstat),38)   left-tail p-value
scalar rightpval = 1-@ctdist(abs(tstat),38) right-tail p-value
scalar pval2 = leftpval+rightpval      two-tail p-value
```

The two-tail p-value is

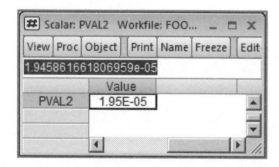

The test is carried out by EViews each time a regression model is estimated. If we examine **FOOD_EQ**, in the column labeled **t-statistic** is the ratio of the **Coefficient** to **Std. Error**. The column labeled **Prob.** contains the two-tail p-value for the test of significance. Note that the very small p-value is rounded to zero (to 4 places). For practical purposes this is enough, since levels of significance below .001 are hardly ever used.

Variable	Coefficient	Std. Error	t-Statistic	Prob.
C	83.41600	43.41016	1.921578	0.0622
INCOME	10.20964	2.093264	4.877381	0.0000

To use the coefficient vector approach, type the commands

coef(10) t5	*storage vector*
t5(1) = b2	*estimate*
t5(2) = seb2	*standard error*
t5(3) = b2/seb2	*t-statistic*
t5(4) = @qtdist(.025,38)	*t-critical left-tail*
t5(5) = @qtdist(.975,38)	*t-critical right-tail*
t5(6) = @ctdist(-abs(t5(3)),38)	*left-tail p-value portion*
t5(7) = 1 - @ctdist(abs(t5(3)),38)	*right-tail p-value portion*
t5(8) = t5(6) + t5(7)	*two-tail p-value*

The result is as follows. Here we have copied the results from EViews at the highest precision to show that the *p*-value works out to be the same as reported above.

Two-Tail Test that Beta 2 = 0	
b_2	10.2096429681
se(b_2)	2.09326353144
t-stat	4.87738061395
left critical value	-2.02439416391
right critical value	2.02439416391
left portion p-value	9.72930830907e-06
right portion p-value	9.72930830911e-06
Two-tail p-value	1.94586166182e-05

3.4.2 Test of an economic hypothesis

To test the null hypothesis that $\beta_2 = 12.5$ against the alternative $\beta_2 \neq 12.5$, the steps are the same as those above, except for the construction of the *t*-statistic. The results follow the commands.

coef(10) t6	*storage vector*
t6(1) = b2	*estimate*
t6(2) = seb2	*standard error*
t6(3) = (b2-12.5)/seb2	*t-statistic*
t6(4) = @qtdist(.025,38)	*t-critical left tail*
t6(5) = @qtdist(.975,38)	*t-critical right tail*
t6(6) = @ctdist(-abs(t6(3)),38)	*left-tail p-value portion*
t6(7) = 1 - @ctdist(abs(t6(3)),38)	*right-tail p-value portion*
t6(8) = t6(6) + t6(7)	*two-tail p-value*

Two-Tail Test that Beta 2 = 12.5	
b_2	10.20964
se(b_2)	2.093264
t-stat	-1.094156
left critical value	-2.024394
right critical value	2.024394
left portion p-value	0.140387
right portion p-value	0.140387
Two-tail p-value	0.280774

Using the Wald test, specify the null hypothesis as **C(2) = 12.5**. The test result shows the t-statistic value and the two-tail p-value.

Wald Test: Equation: FOOD_EQ			
Test Statistic	Value	df	Probability
t-statistic	-1.094156	38	0.2808

The same result can be obtained from the Command window using

       food_eq.wald c(2)=12.5

3.5 LINEAR COMBINATIONS OF PARAMETERS

3.5.1 Hypothesis tests

A more **general linear hypothesis** involves both parameters and may be stated as

$$H_0 : c_1\beta_1 + c_2\beta_2 = c_0$$

where c_0, c_1 and c_2 are specified constants. The alternative hypothesis for the null hypothesis might be

    (i) $H_1 : c_1\beta_1 + c_2\beta_2 \neq c_0$ leading to a two-tail t-test;

    (ii) $H_1 : c_1\beta_1 + c_2\beta_2 > c_0$ leading to a right-tail t-test; [Null may be $H_0 : c_1\beta_1 + c_2\beta_2 \leq c_0$]

    (iii) $H_1 : c_1\beta_1 + c_2\beta_2 < c_0$ leading to a left-tail t-test. [Null may be $H_0 : c_1\beta_1 + c_2\beta_2 \geq c_0$]

The test of the hypothesis uses the t-statistic

$$t = \frac{(c_1 b_1 + c_2 b_2) - c_0}{\text{se}(c_1 b_1 + c_2 b_2)} \sim t_{(N-2)}$$

The standard error of $(c_1 b_1 + c_2 b_2)$ is the square root of the estimated variance:

$$\text{se}(c_1 b_1 + c_2 b_2) = \sqrt{\widehat{\text{var}[c_1 b_1 + c_2 b_2]}}$$

where $\widehat{\text{var}[c_1 b_1 + c_2 b_2]} = c_1^2 \widehat{\text{var}(b_1)} + c_2^2 \widehat{\text{var}(b_2)} + 2c_1 c_2 \widehat{\text{cov}(b_1, b_2)}$.

    As an example, consider the null and alternative hypotheses

$$H_0 : \beta_1 + \beta_2 20 \leq 250 \qquad\qquad H_1 : \beta_1 + \beta_2 20 > 250$$

The required estimated variances and covariance are saved by EViews after a regression is estimated. In the estimated equation **FOOD_EQ**, select **View** and then **Covariance Matrix:**

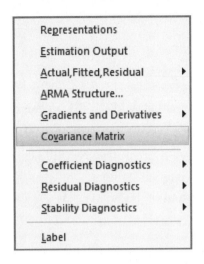
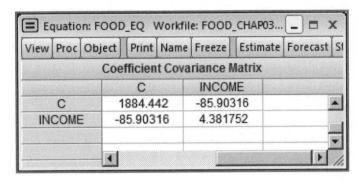

With these values the standard error and the test statistic value can be computed.

The Wald test dialog box can be used to compute the test statistic and standard error in one easy step. In the regression output **FOOD_EQ** select **View** and **Coefficient Diagnostics/Wald Test-Coefficient Restrictions**. In the **Wald Test** dialog box enter **C(1) + 20*C(2) = 250**.

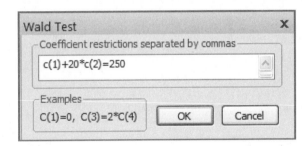

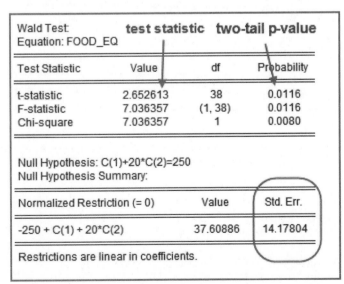

The **Normalized Restriction (=0)** is the value $b_1 + b_2 20 - 250 = 37.60886$.

From the Command window we obtain the same result using

```
food_eq.wald c(1)+20*c(2)=250
```

3.5.2 Interval estimates

A $100(1-\alpha)\%$ interval estimate of $c_1\beta_1 + c_2\beta_2$ is $(c_1b_1 + c_2b_2) \pm t_c \text{se}(c_1b_1 + c_2b_2)$, where the t-critical value is the $100(1-\alpha/2)$-percentile from the t-distribution with $N-2$ degrees of freedom. We can "trick" EViews into computing $(c_1b_1 + c_2b_2)$ and $\text{se}(c_1b_1 + c_2b_2)$ by formulating the pseudo-null hypothesis $c_1\beta_1 + c_2\beta_2 = 0$ and letting the **Wald Test** feature (following a regression) do the work. For example, to compute a 95% interval estimate for $\beta_1 + \beta_2 20$ formulate the null hypothesis **C(1)+20*C(2)=0**. The resulting output of the Wald test is

Null Hypothesis: C(1)+20*C(2)=0
Null Hypothesis Summary:

Normalized Restriction (= 0)	Value	Std. Err.
C(1) + 20*C(2)	287.6089	14.17804

Restrictions are linear in coefficients.

For a 95% interval estimate, enter the commands for the lower and upper bounds as

```
coef(2) lc
lc(1) = 287.6089-@qtdist(.975,38)*14.17804
lc(2) = 287.6089+@qtdist(.975,38)*14.17804
```

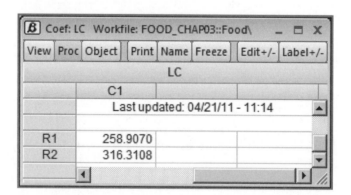

3.6 EVIEWS PROGRAMS

The purpose of this volume is not to teach EViews programming, but rather how to use the beautifully simple point-and-click user interface. That being said, there is merit in pointing out the power of EViews programming. During the EViews session, when commands are entered in the Command window, a record is kept. The list continues each time a command is issued.

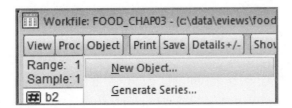

These commands can be copied and pasted into another document. Sometimes saving the commands can save a great deal of work later on. One way to save them is to select **File/Save As:**

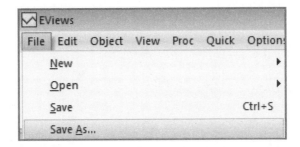

Choose **Save Command Log:**

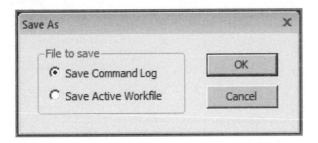

Choose a directory and a file name. The default format is as a text file.

A second option is to save the Command Log as a text object in the workfile. Select **Object/New Object:**

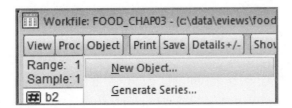

Choose a **Text** object and assign a **Name**.

Highlight all the commands in the Command window, and then paste them into the **Text** object. The series of commands can be edited, cleaned up, and comments can even be added. In EViews, lines that begin with an apostrophe (') are comments. Then, if nothing else, there is a permanent record that is an object in the workfile.

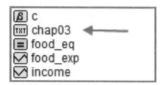

The final option, which opens a world of new possibilities, is to create an **EViews program**. In the EViews menu choose **File/New/Program:**

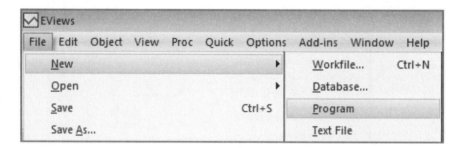

The window that opens is also a text file. Copy the commands into this window and SaveAs *chap03.prg*. EViews recognizes the extension **.prg* as a program file. This list of commands can then be executed all at once, as a batch, using the **Run** command. To the list of commands add a **program** statement. Note that comments show up in an alternate color. We can open the necessary data workfile using **load**. For example,

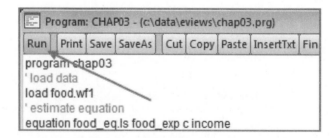

Some EViews commands, like **cinterval** and **wald**, do not create objects in the workfile. They can be saved in this programming approach using **freeze(name)**. For example,

```
' automatic interval estimate
freeze(ci95) food_eq.cinterval .95
```

Once the program file is constructed, it can be executed once EViews as opened using **File/Run:**

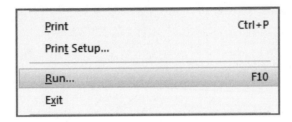

In the resulting dialog box enter the program name and choose either the slow or the fast version of the execution.

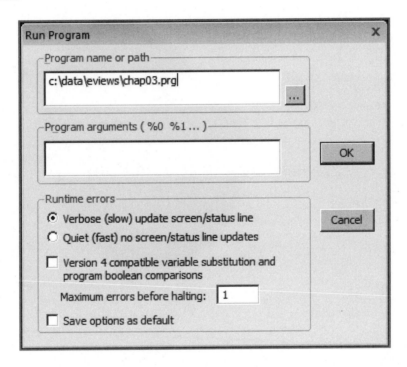

The listing of ***chap03.prg*** is given at the end of this Chapter and also at www.principlesofeconometrics.com.

Keywords

@coefs	freeze	program
@ctdist	hypothesis test	p-value
@qtdist	hypothesis test: left-tail	scalar
@stderrs	hypothesis test: one-tail	significance test
abs	hypothesis test: right-tail	t-distribution CDF
absolute value	hypothesis test: two-tail	t-distribution critical value
cinterval	interval estimation	t-statistic
coefficient vector	load	Wald
critical value	Prob.	

Chap03.prg

```
program chap03
' load data
load food.wf1
' estimate equation
equation food_eq.ls food_exp c income
' interval estimate
scalar tc = @qtdist(.975,38)
scalar b2 = @coefs(2)
scalar seb2 = @stderrs(2)
scalar b2_lb = b2 - tc*seb2
scalar b2_ub = b2 + tc*seb2
' use vector
coef(2) int_est
int_est(1) = @coefs(2) - @qtdist(.975,38)*@stderrs(2)
int_est(2) = @coefs(2) + @qtdist(.975,38)*@stderrs(2)
scalar tc95 = @qtdist(.95,38)
scalar tstat = b2/seb2
scalar pval = 1 - @ctdist(tstat,38)
' automatic interval estimate
freeze(ci95) food_eq.cinterval .95
' hypothesis test b2=0
coef(10) t1
t1(1) = b2
t1(2) = seb2
t1(3) = b2/seb2
t1(4) = @qtdist(.95,38)
t1(5) = 1-@ctdist( t1(3),38 )
' right tail test b2=5
coef(10) t2
t2(1) = b2
t2(2) = seb2
t2(3) = (b2-5)/seb2
t2(4) = @qtdist(.95,38)
t2(5) = 1-@ctdist( t2(3),38 )
freeze(test1) food_eq.wald c(2)=5
' left tail test b2=0
scalar tc05 = @qtdist(.05,38)
scalar tstat = b2/seb2
scalar pval = @ctdist(tstat,38)
' use vector
coef(10) t3
t3(1) = b2
t3(2) = seb2
t3(3) = b2/seb2
t3(4) = @qtdist(.05,38)
t3(5) = @ctdist( t3(3),38 )
' left tail test b2=12
coef(10) t4
t4(1) = b2
t4(2) = seb2
t4(3) = (b2-12)/seb2
t4(4) = @qtdist(.05,38)
t4(5) = @ctdist( t4(3),38 )
' two tail pvalue
scalar tc975 = @qtdist(.975,38)
scalar tc025 = @qtdist(.025,38)
scalar tstat = b2/seb2
scalar leftpval = @ctdist(-abs(tstat),38)
scalar rightpval = 1-@ctdist(abs(tstat),38)
```

```
scalar pval2 = leftpval+rightpval
' use vector
coef(10) t5
t5(1) = b2
t5(2) = seb2
t5(3) = b2/seb2
t5(4) = @qtdist(.025,38)
t5(5) = @qtdist(.975,38)
t5(6) = @ctdist(-abs(t5(3)),38)
t5(7) = 1 - @ctdist(abs(t5(3)),38)
t5(8) = t5(6) + t5(7)
' two tail test b2=12.5
coef(10) t6
t6(1) = b2
t6(2) = seb2
t6(3) = (b2-12.5)/seb2
t6(4) = @qtdist(.025,38)
t6(5) = @qtdist(.975,38)
t6(6) = @ctdist(-abs(t6(3)),38)
t6(7) = 1 - @ctdist(abs(t6(3)),38)
t6(8) = t6(6) + t6(7)
' test linear combination
freeze(test2) food_eq.wald c(1)+20*c(2)=250
' interval estimate linear combination
coef(2) lc
lc(1) = 287.6089-@qtdist(.975,38)*14.17804
lc(2) = 287.6089+@qtdist(.975,38)*14.17804
```

CHAPTER **4**

Prediction, Goodness-of-Fit, and Modeling Issues

4.1 PREDICTION IN THE FOOD EXPENDITURE MODEL

In this chapter we continue to work with the simple linear regression model and our model of weekly food expenditure. To begin, open workfile *food.wf1*. On the EViews menu choose **File/Open** and then save the file. So that the original file is not altered, save it under a new name. Select **File/Save As,** then name the file *food_chap04.wf1*. Estimate the simple regression

$$FOOD\_EXP = \beta_1 + \beta_2 INCOME + e$$

On the EViews menu select **Quick/Estimate Equation**, then fill in the dialog box with the equation specification and click **OK**.

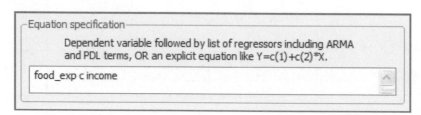

Name the resulting regression results **FOOD_EQ** by selecting the **Name** button and filling in the **Object name**.

Alternatively, the estimation can be carried out by entering into the Command window

> **equation food_eq.ls food_exp c income**

4.1.1 A simple prediction procedure

In Chapter 2.8 of this manual we illustrated a simple procedure for obtaining the predicted value of food expenditure for a household with income of $2,000 per week. We also showed that EViews can be used to generate forecasts automatically, both for the sample values and for new *INCOME* observations that we append to the workfile by increasing its range. If you need to review those steps, do so now.

What we can add now that we did not have before is the standard error of the forecasted value. The estimated variance of the forecast error is

$$\widehat{\text{var}(f)} = \hat{\sigma}^2 \left[1 + \frac{1}{N} + \frac{(x_0 - \bar{x})^2}{\sum (x_i - \bar{x})^2} \right]$$

A convenient form for calculation in the simple regression model is

$$\widehat{\text{var}(f)} = \hat{\sigma}^2 + \frac{\hat{\sigma}^2}{N} + (x_0 - \bar{x})^2 \widehat{\text{var}(b_2)}$$

Open the food equation **FOOD_EQ**. Click on **View/Representations**. Select the text of the equation listed under **Substituted Coefficients**. We can choose **Edit/Copy** from the EViews menubar, or we can simply use the keyboard shortcut **Ctrl+C** to copy the equation representation to the clipboard. Finally, we can paste the equation into the Command window.

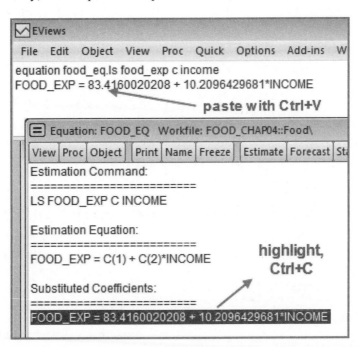

To obtain the predicted food expenditure for a household with weekly income of $2000, edit the Command window to read

scalar food_exp_hat = 83.4160020208 + 10.2096429681*20

Press **Enter**. The resulting scalar value is

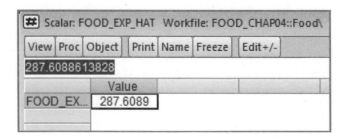

The prediction interval requires the critical value from the $t_{(38)}$ distribution. For a 95% prediction interval, the required critical value t_c is the 97.5 percentile, which is obtained as

scalar tc = @qtdist(.975,38)

The prediction interval is obtained by entering the following commands (do not type the comments in *italic* font):

scalar sig2 = (@se)^2	*@se = std error of regression*
scalar n = @regobs	*@regobs = N*
scalar varb2 = (@stderrs(2))^2	*@stderrs = std. errors of b*
scalar xbar = @mean(income)	*@mean = sample mean*
scalar varf = sig2 + sig2/n + ((20-xbar)^2)*varb2	*^2 raises to power 2*
scalar sef = @sqrt(varf)	*@sqrt = square root*
coef(2) int_est	*create vector*
int_est(1) = food_exp_hat - tc*sef	*lower bound of interval*
int_est(2) = food_exp_hat + tc*sef	*upper bound of interval*

The resulting prediction interval values are:

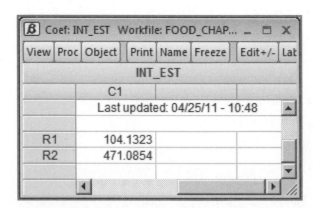

These results are correct, but obtaining a prediction interval this way each time would be tedious. Now we use the power of EViews.

4.1.2 Prediction using EViews

The above procedure for computing a prediction interval works for the simple regression model. EViews makes computing standard errors of forecasts simple. In Chapter 2.8.2 of this manual we extended the range of the workfile and entered three new observations for *INCOME* = 20, 25 and 30. Follow those same steps again to insert the same three observation values. The steps are:

- Double-click on **Range** in the main workfile window.
- Change the number of observations to 43 and click **OK**.
- Double-click on *INCOME* in the main workfile to open the series.
- Click **Edit+/-** to open edit mode.
- Enter 20, 25 and 30 in cells 41-43.
- Click **Edit+/-** to close edit mode.

In the **FOOD_EQ** window click on **Forecast:**

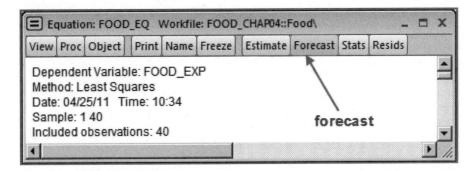

In the dialog box that opens, enter names for the **Forecast** and the **S.E.,** which is for the standard error of the forecast. Make sure the forecast sample is set to 1-43 and click **OK**.

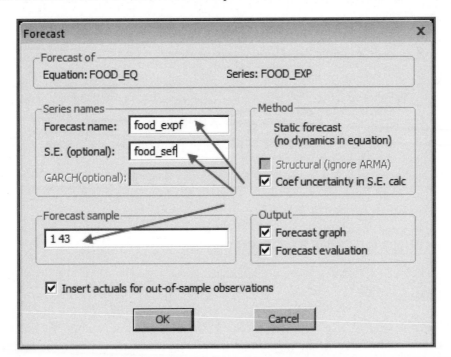

The resulting window shows the predicted values and a 95% prediction interval for the observations in their given order. For cross-sectional observations this is not so useful. We will come back to it later.

Enter the following commands into the Command window, or use the **Genr** button to open a dialog box in which the new series can be defined:

       series food_exp_ub = food_expf + tc*food_sef
       series food_exp_lb = food_expf - tc*food_sef

Create a group by clicking on *INCOME, FOOD_SEF, FOOD_EXP_LB, FOOD_EXPF, FOOD_EXP_UB*. To do this, click each one while holding down **Ctrl**. Right-click in the shaded area and select **Open/ as Group**.

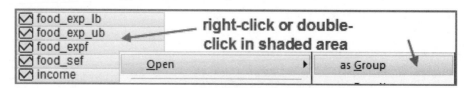

Click on **Name** and call this group **FOOD_PREDICTIONS**.

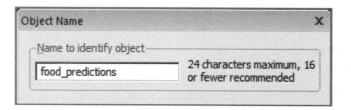

Scroll to the bottom to see the standard error of the forecast and prediction intervals for the specified values of income. Note that the values for *INCOME* = 20 are as we constructed manually.

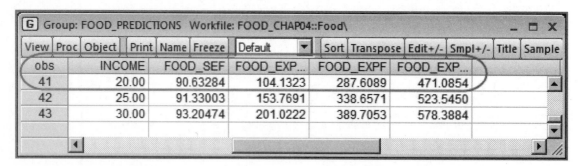

obs	INCOME	FOOD_SEF	FOOD_EXP...	FOOD_EXPF	FOOD_EXP...
41	20.00	90.63284	104.1323	287.6089	471.0854
42	25.00	91.33003	153.7691	338.6571	523.5450
43	30.00	93.20474	201.0222	389.7053	578.3884

4.2 MEASURING GOODNESS-OF-FIT

4.2.1 Calculating R^2

The usual $R^2 = 1 - SSE/SST$ is reported in the EViews regression output. In the **FOOD_EQ** window it is reported just below the regression coefficients.

Variable	Coefficient	Std. Error	t-Statistic	Prob.
C	83.41600	43.41016	1.921578	0.0622
INCOME	10.20964	2.093264	4.877381	0.0000
R-squared	0.385002	Mean dependent var		283.5735
Adjusted R-squared	0.368818	S.D. dependent var		112.6752
S.E. of regression	89.51700	Akaike info criterion		11.87544
Sum squared resid	304505.2	Schwarz criterion		11.95988

The elements required to compute it in this window are shown as well. The sum of squared least squares residuals (*SSE*) is given by

Sum squared resid   304505.2

The total sum of squares (*SST*) can be obtained from

S.D. dependent var   112.6752

Recall that the sample standard deviation of the *y* values (**S.D. dependent var**) is

$$\text{S.D. dependent var} = s_y = \sqrt{\frac{\sum(y_i - \bar{y})^2}{N-1}}$$

Thus if we square this value and multiply by $N - 1$, we have the total sum of squares. That is,

$$SST = \sum(y_i - \bar{y})^2 = (N-1)s_y^2$$

You can do this by hand, or recall that after a regression model is estimated many useful items are saved by EViews, including

    @sddep   *standard deviation of the dependent variable*
    @ssr   *sum of squared residuals*

Then, to calculate R^2 use the commands

```
scalar sst = (N-1)*(@sddep)^2
scalar r2 = 1-@ssr/sst
```

The value *N* has already been calculated as

```
scalar n = @regobs
```

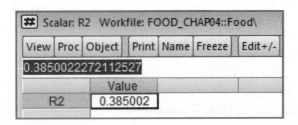

4.2.2 Correlation analysis

In the simple regression model we can compute R^2 as the square of the correlation between X and Y or the square of the correlation between Y and its predicted values. The EViews function **@cor** computes the correlation between two variables:

scalar r2_xy=(@cor(income,food_exp))^2
scalar r2_yyhat = (@cor(food_exp, food_expf))^2

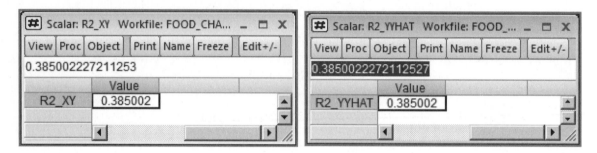

These calculations were carried out with the Range and Sample each set to 1 to 43 from our work with prediction in Section 4.1.2 above. However, because there are no values for *FOOD_EXP* for observations 41 to 43 (NA appears), EViews discarded observations 41-43 in the calculations.

4.3 MODELING ISSUES

4.3.1 The effects of scaling the data

Changing the scale of variables in EViews is very simple. **Generate** new variables that have been redefined to suit you. To illustrate, suppose we measure *INCOME* in $ rather than in 100$ increments. On the EViews menu choose **Quick/Estimate Equation** and fill in the dialog box as

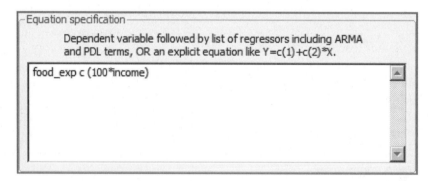

Click **OK**. Alternatively, to estimate the equation and give it a name, in the Command window enter

equation dollar_food_eq.ls food_exp c (100*income)

This illustrates a very useful feature of EViews. The regression commands allow variables to be transformed directly, including powers, logarithms and scaling. The partial result (on the next page) shows that the coefficient on income has changed, as has its standard error. Everything else in this regression is the same as in earlier estimations of the food expenditure equation.

Dependent Variable: FOOD_EXP
Method: Least Squares
Sample (adjusted): 1 40
Included observations: 40 after adjustments

Variable	Coefficient	Std. Error	t-Statistic	Prob.
C	83.41600	43.41016	1.921578	0.0622
100*INCOME	0.102096	0.020933	4.877381	0.0000
R-squared	0.385002	Mean dependent var		283.5735

4.3.2 The linear-log model

The linear-log model transforms the x variable but not the y variable: $y = \beta_1 + \beta_2 \ln(x) + e$. In this model a 1% increase in x leads to an estimated $\beta_2/100$ unit change in y. In the food expenditure model the estimation command is

equation linlog.ls food_exp c log(income)

The resulting regression output is:

Dependent Variable: FOOD_EXP

Variable	Coefficient	Std. Error	t-Statistic	Prob.
C	-97.18642	84.23744	-1.153720	0.2558
LOG(INCOME)	132.1658	28.80461	4.588357	0.0000
R-squared	0.356510	Mean dependent var		283.5735
Adjusted R-squared	0.339577	S.D. dependent var		112.6752
S.E. of regression	91.56711	Akaike info criterion		11.92073
Sum squared resid	318612.4	Schwarz criterion		12.00517
Log likelihood	-236.4146	Hannan-Quinn criter.		11.95126
F-statistic	21.05302	Durbin-Watson stat		1.836580
Prob(F-statistic)	0.000048			

We would interpret the results by saying that a 1% increase in income leads to about a \$1.32 increase in weekly food expenditure.

To see how this model fits the data, create a scatter plot that includes the fitted regression line. Select **Quick/Graph**. Into the dialog box enter **income** (the x-variable) and **food_exp** (the y-variable. Add a regression fit to the scatter diagram; in the **options** menu choose

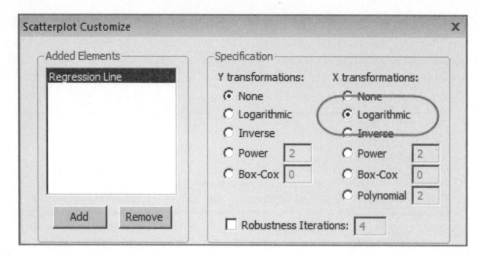

Click **OK** twice, then edit the graph by changing the scale of the vertical axis and adding a title, as done previously in Chapter 2.2.1. The linear-log model has a slope that decreases as income rises—it increases at a decreasing rate, and this may be more relevant than the linear model for an expenditure model such as the food expenditure example.

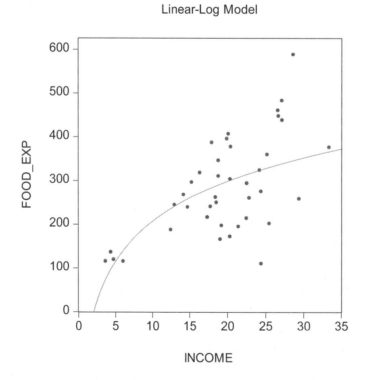

4.3.3 Residual plots

Each time a regression is estimated, a certain number of regression diagnostics should be carried out. It is through the residuals of the fitted model that we may detect problems in a model's specification. After estimation, EViews saves the least squares residuals in the **resid** object. Plot these residuals against the *x*-variable and the predicted *y*-variable. Within the linear-log regression window select **Forecast:**

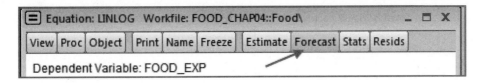

Name the series to be generated:

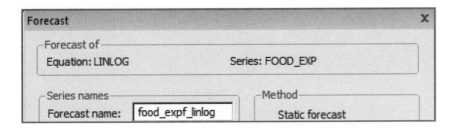

In the figures below these plots show distinct nonrandom patterns, indicating to us that there may be specification issues to resolve. The left-hand figure indicates increasing residual variation as income increases. The right-hand figure shows greater variation as the predicted food expenditure becomes larger. Both are symptoms of heteroskedasticity.

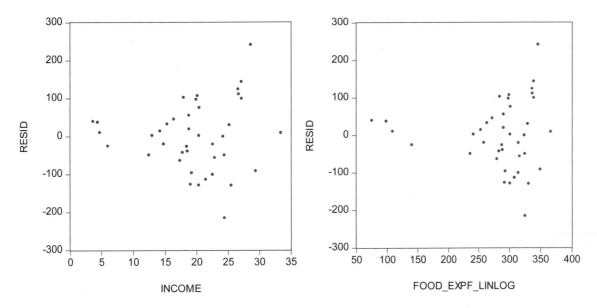

4.3.4 Are the regression errors normally distributed?

One aspect of the error that we can examine is whether the errors appear normally distributed. EViews reports diagnostics for the residuals each time a model is estimated. For example, in the **FOOD_EQ** window, select **View/Residual Diagnostics/Histogram-Normality Test:**

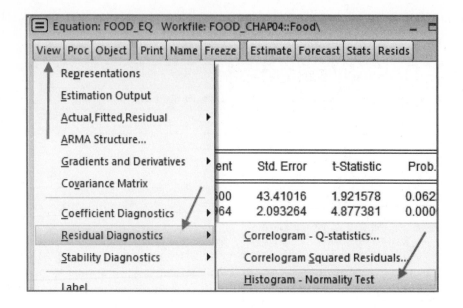

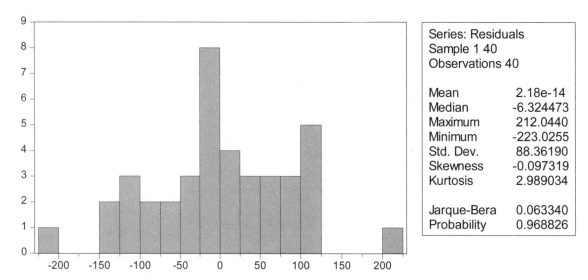

A **Histogram** is produced along with other summary measures. The **Mean** of the residuals is always zero for a regression that includes an intercept term. In the histogram we are looking for a general "Bell-shape", and a value of the **Jarque-Bera** test statistic with a large p-value. This test is valid in large samples, so what it tells us in a sample of size $N = 40$ is questionable. The test statistic has a $\chi^2_{(2)}$ distribution under the null hypothesis that the **Skewness** is zero and **Kurtosis** is three, which are the measures for a normal distribution. The critical value for the chi-square distribution is obtained by typing into the Command window

```
scalar chisq_95 = @qchisq(.95,2)
```

which produces the scalar value

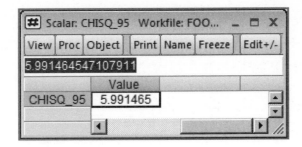

Save your workfile and close it, since we are moving to another example.

4.3.5 A wheat production example

Open the workfile *wa_wheat.wf1* by selecting on the EViews menu **File/Open/EViews Workfile**. Locate *wa_wheat.wf1* and click **OK**. It contains 48 annual observations on the variables *NORTHAMPTON*, *CHAPMAN*, *MULLEWA*, *GREENOUGH* and *TIME*. The first four variables are average annual wheat yields in shires of Western Australia. See the definition file *wa-wheat.def*. These are annual data from 1950 to 1997.

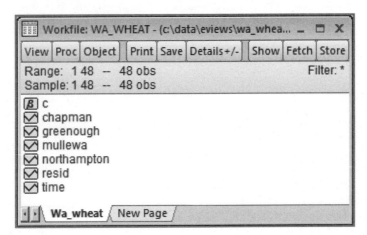

Before working with the data, double-click on **Range**. This will reveal the **Workfile structure**. When this file was created the annual nature of the data and time span was not used.

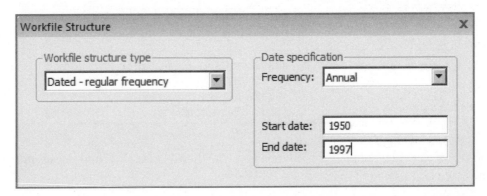

In the **Date specification** choose an **Annual** frequency with **Start date** 1950 and **End date** 1997, then click **OK**.

This will not have any impact on the actual results we obtain, but it is good to take advantage of the time series features of EViews. The resulting workfile is now

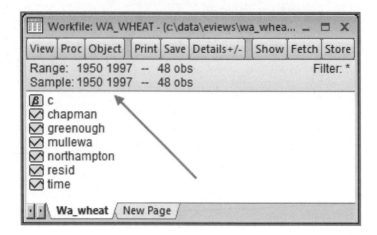

Save this workfile with a new name. Select **File/Save As** to open a dialog box. We will call it **wheat_chap04**. Estimate the linear regression of yield in *GREENOUGH* shire on *TIME* by entering

equation linear.ls greenough c time

Alternatively, use the usual **Quick/Estimate Equation** dialog box, and then name the result.

```
 Equation: LINEAR   Workfile: WHEAT_CHAP04::Wa_wheat\         _  □  X
 View Proc Object   Print Name Freeze  Estimate Forecast Stats Resids

 Dependent Variable: GREENOUGH
 Method: Least Squares
 Date: 04/27/11  Time: 09:27
 Sample: 1950 1997
 Included observations: 48
```

Variable	Coefficient	Std. Error	t-Statistic	Prob.
C	0.637778	0.064131	9.944999	0.0000
TIME	0.021032	0.002279	9.230452	0.0000

R-squared	0.649394	Mean dependent var	1.153060
Adjusted R-squared	0.641772	S.D. dependent var	0.365387
S.E. of regression	0.218692	Akaike info criterion	-0.161529
Sum squared resid	2.200009	Schwarz criterion	-0.083562

In the EViews workfile, double-click on **Resids**. Then choose **Actual, Fitted, Residual/Residual Graph**.

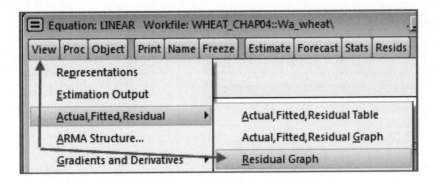

The default is a line graph, as shown on the left. Double-click inside and change the **Attributes** to **Symbol only**. This produces the figure on the right, which is Figure 4.12 in *POE4*.

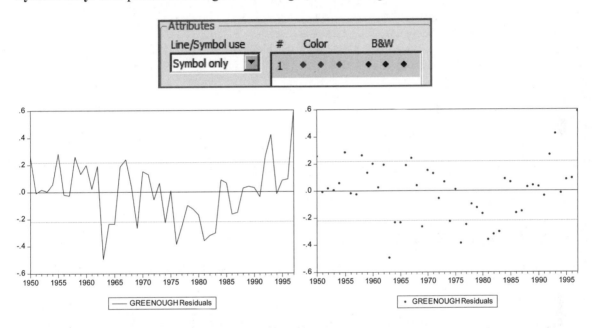

To generate the cubic equation results described in the text, enter the command (or use drop-down boxes)

equation cubic.ls greenough c (time/100)^3

Variable	Coefficient	Std. Error	t-Statistic	Prob.
C	0.874117	0.035631	24.53270	0.0000
(TIME/100)^3	9.681516	0.822355	11.77292	0.0000
R-squared	0.750815	Mean dependent var		1.153060
Adjusted R-squared	0.745398	S.D. dependent var		0.365387
S.E. of regression	0.184368	Akaike info criterion		-0.502997
Sum squared resid	1.563604	Schwarz criterion		-0.425030

An alternative to the cubic specification is the log-linear model, as discussed in Chapter 4.5.1 in *POE4*. Enter the equation estimation command

equation loglin.ls log(greenough) c time

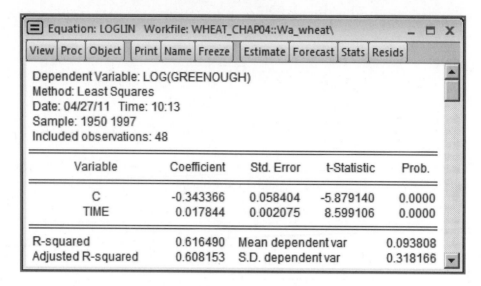

The log-linear model coefficient of *TIME* is an estimate of $\log(1+g)$ where g is the growth rate in wheat production over time. Using the approximation $\log(1+x) \cong x$, for small x, we estimate that the growth rate in wheat production is about 1.78% per year.

This workfile (*wheat_chap04.wf1*) can now be saved and closed.

4.4 THE LOG-LINEAR MODEL

To illustrate the log-linear model we will use the workfile *cps4_small.wf1*, with data definitions in *cps_small4.def*. This data file consists of 1000 observations.

Save the workfile with a new name, such as *cps4_small_chap04.wf1*. Estimate the log-linear equation using

equation lwage_eq.ls log(wage) c educ

Note that we have given the **Name LWAGE_EQ** to this equation.

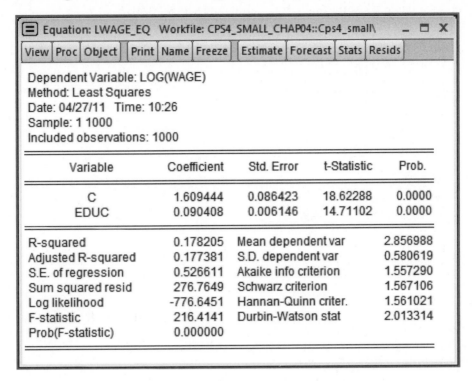

4.4.1 Prediction in the log-linear model

First we illustrate prediction with the equation **LWAGE_EQ,** in which we regressed the series *LWAGE* on *EDUC*. In the estimated equation window, click on **Forecast**.

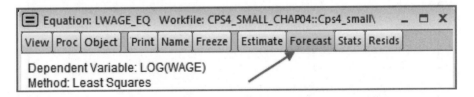

Because we have specified the equation with a logarithmic dependent variable, EViews recognizes that we may want a forecast of *WAGE* or *LOG*(*WAGE*). The default is to forecast *WAGE*. Call this series *WAGEF*.

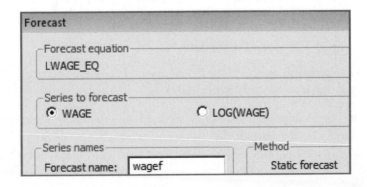

Repeat the exercise and forecast *LOG(WAGE)*. Call this forecast *LWAGEF*. Also create the standard error of the forecast for this series, calling the series *LWAGE_SEF*.

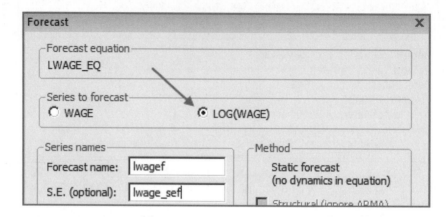

Recall that the antilogarithm for the natural log is the exponential function. That is,

$$x = \exp\left[\ln(x)\right]$$

For the purpose of understanding what EViews does when forecasting *WAGE*, create a new series called *EXP_LWAGEF* that is

    series exp_lwagef = exp(lwagef)

Now open the series *EDUC*, *WAGE*, *WAGEF* and *EXP_LWAGEF*, and examine them as a group.

obs	EDUC	WAGE	WAGEF	EXP_LWAGEF
1	16	18.70	21.24192	21.24192
2	12	11.50	14.79580	14.79580
3	16	15.04	21.24192	21.24192
4	14	25.95	17.72826	17.72826
5	12	24.03	14.79580	14.79580
6				

The series *WAGEF* and *EXP_LWAGEF* are identical. In the log-linear equation a forecast for *WAGE* is obtained using the "natural" predictor.

In large samples a more precise predictor is obtained by correcting for log-normality. To do so we multiply the natural predictor by $\exp(\hat{\sigma}^2/2)$. The value of the estimate $\hat{\sigma}$ is saved after a regression as **@se**. Thus the **corrected predictor** is

    scalar sig2 = (@se)^2
    series wagef_c = exp(lwagef)*exp(sig2/2)

A few values for the actual wage, the prediction interval, and the natural and corrected predictors are shown below. Note that the corrected predictor is always going to be larger than the natural predictor because the correction factor is always larger than one. The second row is for a person with 12 years of education, which is the calculation illustrated in *POE4*.

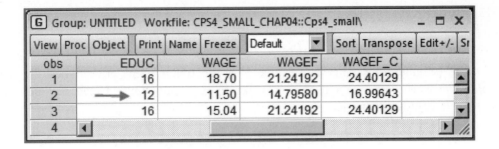

4.4.2 A prediction interval in the log-linear model

To create a prediction interval for the predicted value of *WAGE*, we first create a 95% interval for **lwagef** as the forecast plus and minus the *t*-critical value times the standard error of the forecast. Then, to convert it from logs to a numerical scale we take the antilog using the **exponential function**. The following commands create the *t*-value and the upper and lower bounds of predicted wage:

```
scalar tc = @qtdist(.975,998)
series wage_ub = exp(lwagef + tc*lwage_sef)
series wage_lb = exp(lwagef - tc*lwage_sef)
```

In repeated samples this prediction interval procedure will work 95% of the time. The example in *POE4* considers a person with 12 years of education.

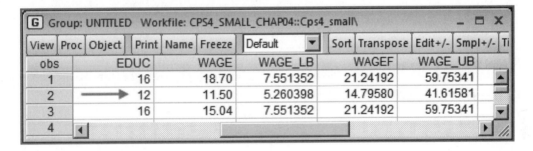

4.4.3 Generalized R^2

A generalized goodness-of-fit measure is the squared correlation between the actual value of the dependent variable and its best predictor. Using the EViews function **@cor**, we obtain

```
scalar r2g = (@cor(wage,wagef_c))^2
```

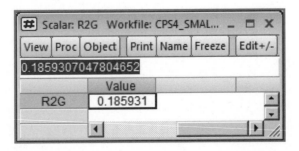

Save and close your workfile ***cps4_small_chap04.wf1***.

4.5 THE LOG-LOG MODEL

In the log-log model $\ln(y) = \beta_1 + \beta_2 \ln(x) + e$ the parameter β_2 is an elasticity. The example in *POE4* is the demand for poultry per capita as a function of real price. Open the workfile ***newbroiler.wf1***. Save it under a new name, say ***newbroiler_chap04.wf1***. Create a scatter diagram. Select **Quick/Graph** and list price (**p**) first, and quantity (**q**) second.

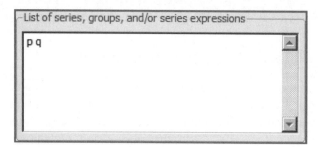

Choose **Scatter** and then augment it with a fitted regression line using the options

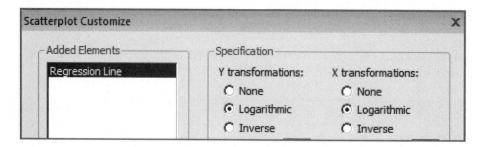

The resulting fitted line, shown below, displays the nonlinear relationship associated with a constant-elasticity demand function.

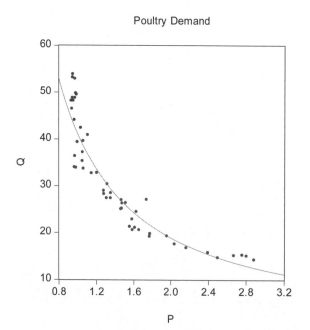

The fitted line above is based on the **natural predictor**, as discussed on page 157 of *POE4*. As an exercise develop the **corrected predictor**. You will find these two predictors very similar in this cases because the correction factor is nearly one. Estimate the log-log model using

equation loglog.ls log(q) c log(p)

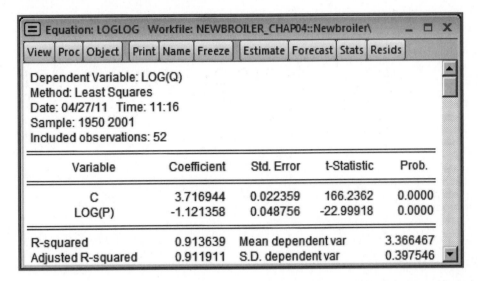

The generalized R^2, R_g^2, can be obtained as shown on the bottom of page 157 in *POE4*. The calculation will be similar to that in Section 4.4.3 in this manual.

Keywords

@cor
@qchisq
@qtdist
@regobs
@se
@sddep
@ssr
cubic equation
data range
data sample
data scaling
elasticity

equation eqname.ls
exponential function
forecast
forecast standard error
generalized R^2
goodness-of-fit
histogram
Jarque-Bera test
linear-log model
log function
log-linear model
log-log model

ls
normality test
prediction
prediction interval
prediction: corrected
prediction: log-linear model
prediction: natural
residual plot
R^2
workfile structure

CHAPTER **5**

The Multiple Regression Model

In the simple linear regression model the average value of a dependent variable is modeled as a linear function of a constant and a single explanatory variable. The multiple linear regression model expands the number of explanatory variables. As such, it is a simple but important extension that makes linear regression quite powerful.

The example used in this chapter is a model of sales for Big Andy's Burger Barn. Big Andy's sales revenue depends on the prices charged for hamburgers, fries, shakes, and so on, and on the level of advertising. The prices charged in a given city are collected together into a weighted price index that is denoted by $P = PRICE$ and measured in dollars. Monthly sales revenue for a given city is denoted by $S = SALES$ and measured in $1,000 units. Advertising expenditure for each city $A = ADVERT$ is also measured in thousands of dollars. The model includes two explanatory variables and a constant and is written as

$$SALES = E(SALES) + e = \beta_1 + \beta_2 PRICE + \beta_3 ADVERT + e$$

In this chapter we use EViews to (1) estimate this model, (2) obtain forecasts from the model, (3) examine the covariance matrix and standard errors of the estimates, and (4) compute confidence intervals and hypothesis test values for each of the coefficients and functions of the coefficients.

While performing these tasks, we reinforce some of the EViews steps described in earlier chapters as well as introduce some new ones. Reference will be made to where the results can be found in *Principles of Econometrics*, 4th edition (*POE4*).

5.1 THE WORKFILE: SOME PRELIMINARIES

Observations on *SALES*, *PRICE* and *ADVERT* for 75 cities are available in the file ***andy.wf1***. Select **File/Open/EViews Workfile.** Note that the keystroke combination **Ctrl+O** is the equivalent. The following screen appears:

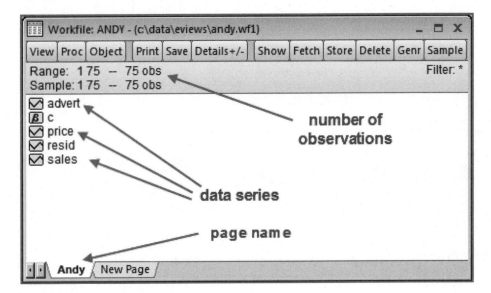

Note that the **range** and **sample** are set at 75 observations. And note the location of the data series in the workfile. The other objects **C** and **RESID** appear automatically in all EViews workfiles. We explain them as they become needed.

5.1.1 Naming the page

It is possible to use a number of "pages" within the same EViews file. We will rarely use this option because most problems can fit neatly within the one page. Note that the default name for the workfile page is **Andy**. To change this, right-click the page name, then fill in a new page name and select **OK**.

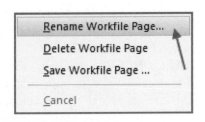

You can also reach this point from your workfile toolbar **Proc/Rename Current Page:**

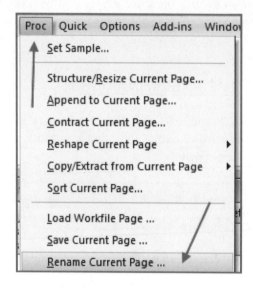

After choosing the name **Andys_Burgers**, your workfile will appear as

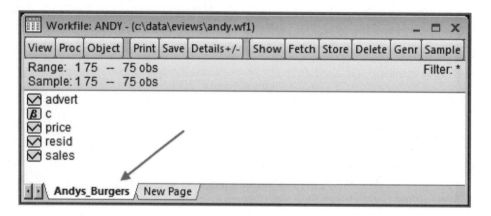

At this point it is prudent to save the workfile under a new name, such as *andy_chap05.wf1*.

5.1.2 Creating objects: a group

The data on each of the variables *SALES*, *PRICE* and *ADVERT* can be examined one at a time or as a group, as described in Chapters 1 and 2. We will create a **group** and then check the data and summary statistics to make sure they match those in Table 5.1 on page 171 of *POE4*. In Chapters 1 and 2 we created a group by (1) highlighting the series to be included in the group, (2) double-clicking the highlighted area, and (3) selecting **Open Group**. To extend your knowledge of EViews, we now describe another way. This new way is more cumbersome, but it will help you understand the more general concept of an **object** and how objects are created.

A group is one of many types of objects that can be created by EViews. The concept of an object is a bit vague, but you can think of it as anything that gets stored in your workfile. As Richard Startz says in *EViews Illustrated* [QMS, 2007, p.5], "object is a computer science buzz word meaning 'thingie'."

To see a list of possible objects, select **Object/New Object** from the workfile toolbar.

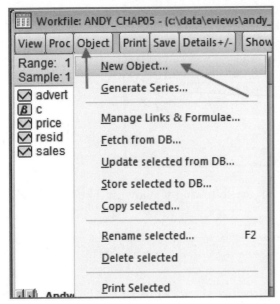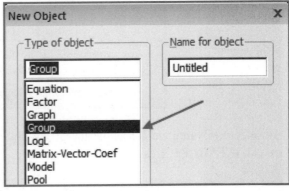

A long list of possible objects appears. We will encounter many of these objects (but not all) as we proceed through the book. One that you encountered in the earlier chapters is **Matrix-Vector-Coef**. Only the top few are displayed in the above screen shot. At present we select **Group** as the relevant object, and then click **OK**. We have left **Name for object** as **Untitled**. We will name it later. In the following window that appears, we type the names of the series to be included in the group, and then click **OK**.

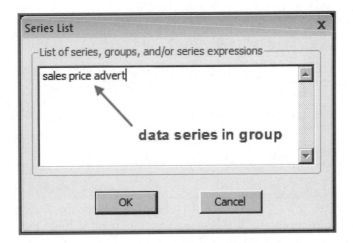

The following screen appears. Note that the first five observations are the same as those in Table 5.1 on page 171 of *POE4*. The last three observations can be checked by scrolling down.

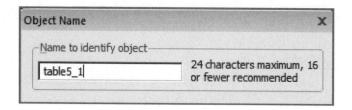

By selecting **Name** we can name the group object in the following window. In line with *POE4*, we call it **TABLE5_1**.

One of the advantages of creating a group of variables is that we can view a variety of information on the collection of variables in that group. The list of observations that we checked against Table 5.1 is one type of information; it is called the **spreadsheet** view of the group. Another useful view is the **Descriptive Stats** view giving summary statistics that can be checked against those that appear in the lower panel of Table 5.1. To obtain this view we open the group and then select **View/Descriptive Stats/Common Sample**.

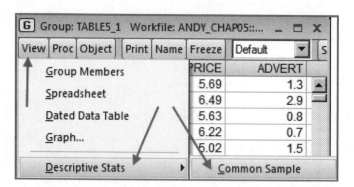

The summary statistics appear in the following window. In addition to the sample **mean, median, maximum, minimum,** and **standard deviation** for each series, the table presents **skewness** and **kurtosis** measures (see page 702 in *POE4*), the value of the **Jarque-Bera statistic** for testing whether a series is normally distributed and its corresponding *p*-value (see page 148 of *POE4*), and the **sum** $\sum x_i$ and **sum of squared deviations** $\sum (x_i - \overline{x})^2$ for each of the series. Stop and check to see if you know how to obtain the standard deviation values from the sum of squared deviations.

After viewing the descriptive statistics, the table can be saved by selecting **Freeze:**

Then **Name** the resulting **Table** as an image

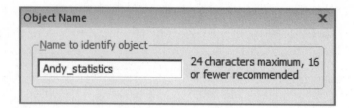

Then **ANDY_STATISTICS** appears as an object in the workfile.

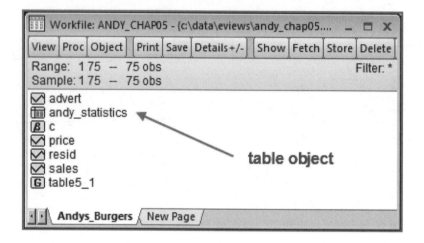

5.2 ESTIMATING A MULTIPLE REGRESSION MODEL

The steps for estimating a multiple regression model are a natural extension of those for estimating a simple regression. We will consider two alternative ways. One is using the **Quick** menu considered in earlier chapters. The other is via the **Object** menu that we used in the previous section to define a **group.**

5.2.1 Using the Quick menu

To use the Quick menu for estimating an equation, go to the upper EViews window and select **Quick/Estimate Equation**.

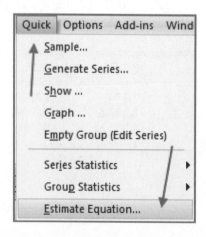

An **Equation Estimation** window appears. We add to it in the following way:

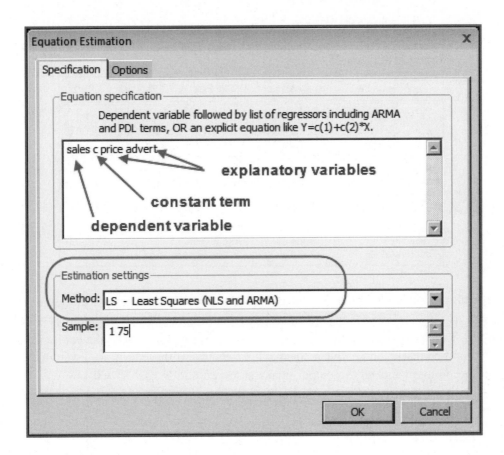

The **Equation Specification** dialog box is where you tell EViews what model you would like to estimate. Our equation is

$$SALES = \beta_1 + \beta_2 PRICE + \beta_3 ADVERT + e$$

The dependent variable *SALES* is inserted first, followed by the constant *C* and the explanatory variables *PRICE* and *ADVERT*. Under **Estimation settings** in the lower half of the window, you can choose the estimation **Method** and the **Sample** observations to be used for estimation. The **least-squares** method is the one we want, and is the one that is automatically used unless another one is selected. A **sample** of **1 75** means that all observations in our sample are being used to estimate the equation. Clicking **OK** yields the regression output.

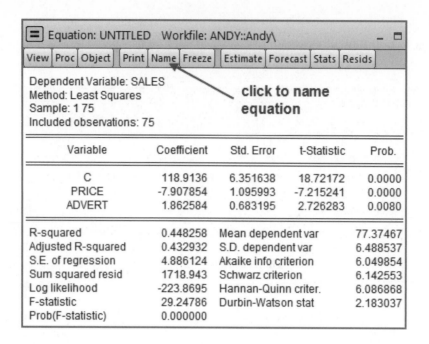

Compare this output with Table 5.2 on page 175 of *POE4*. Least squares estimates of the coefficients β_1, β_2 and β_3 appear in the column **Coefficient**; their standard errors are in the column **Std. Error**; *t*-values for testing a zero null hypothesis for each of the coefficients appear in the column **t-Statistic**; and *p*-values for two-tail versions of these tests are given in the column **Prob.** In the bottom panel in the output, make sure you can locate $R^2 = 0.4483$, $\hat{\sigma}_y = 6.4885$, $SSE = \sum \hat{e}_i^2 = 1718.943$ and the estimated standard deviation of the error term $\hat{\sigma} = 4.8861$. Also, you should make sure you know how to compute (a) $\hat{\sigma}$ from the value of SSE (page 177 of *POE4*) and (b) R^2 from SSE and $\hat{\sigma}_y$ (page 198 of *POE4*).

5.2.2 Using the Object menu

The same results can be obtained by direct creation of the relevant equation object. To proceed in this way, select **Object/New Object** from the workfile toolbar. In the resulting **New Object** window, select **Equation** as the **Type of object**.

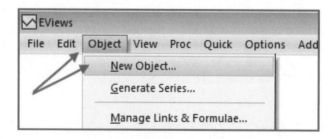

Then name the object (we chose **BURGER_EQN**) and click **OK**.

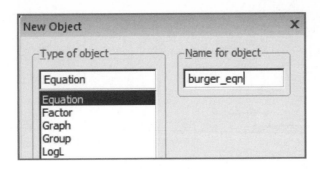

The **Equation Estimation** window will appear. It can be filled in as described earlier. Clicking **OK** yields the same regression output that we illustrated earlier using the Quick menu.

After closing the output window, check the EViews workfile and note that, since you opened the workfile, two new objects have been added. These objects are the group of variables **TABLE5_1** and the estimated equation **BURGER_EQN**. To reopen one of these objects, highlight it, and then double-click:

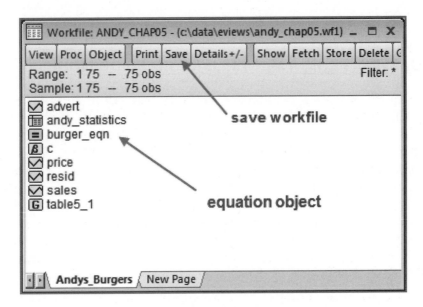

To ensure the estimated equation and the group of variables are retained for future use, click **save**. If you wish to save the file under another name, go to the upper EViews toolbar and select **File/Save As**.

5.2.3 Using the equation Command

The same results can be obtained using the EViews **equation** command. Into the Command window enter

equation andy_eq.ls sales c price advert

With this approach the regression results do not open in a new window, but the equation object **ANDY_EQ** appears in the workfile.

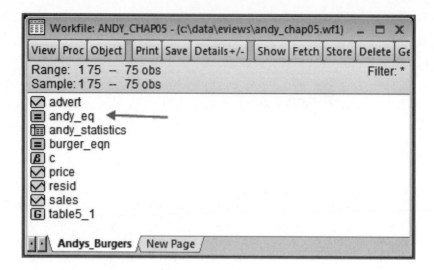

Double-click to open the regression window.

5.3 FORECASTING FROM A MULTIPLE REGRESSION MODEL

Using EViews to obtain forecasts was considered extensively in Chapter 4 for both linear and log-linear models. Those procedures carry over directly to the multiple regression model. In this section we reinforce those procedures by showing how EViews can be used to forecast (or predict) hamburger sales revenue for $PRICE = 5.5$ and $ADVERT = 1.2$, as done on page 176 of *POE4*. Two preliminary explanatory remarks are in order. First, note that we are using the terms "forecast" and "predict" interchangeably; neither has any special significance. Second, the steps we follow do not mimic exactly those in Chapter 4. The variations are deliberate. They are designed to expose you to more of the features of EViews. As in Chapter 4, we consider a simple forecasting procedure and one using EViews' special forecasting capabilities. While the simple one is ideal for obtaining a single static forecast, it is not convenient for obtaining a forecast of standard error, and it less than ideal for dynamic forecasting, a topic considered in Chapter 9.

5.3.1 A simple forecasting procedure

After you use EViews to estimate a regression model, the estimated coefficients are stored in the object **C** that appears in your workfile. You can check this fact out by highlighting **C** and double-clicking it. A spreadsheet will appear with the estimates stored in a column called **C1**. In further commands that you might supply to EViews, the three values in that column can be used by referring to them as C(1), C(2), and C(3), respectively. That is, in terms of notation used in *POE4*, the least squares estimates are

$$b_1 = C(1) \qquad b_2 = C(2) \qquad b_3 = C(3)$$

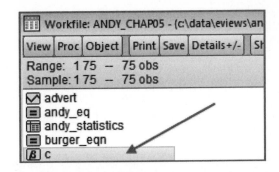

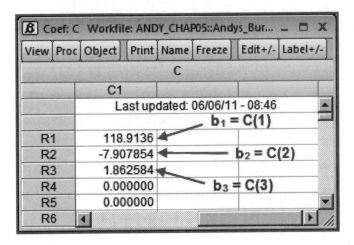

Our objective is to get EViews to perform the calculation

$$\widehat{SALES} = b_1 + b_2 \times 5.5 + b_3 \times 1.2$$

The corresponding EViews command is

scalar sales_f = c(1) + c(2)*5.5 + c(3)*1.2

The first word **scalar** tells EViews that we are computing a scalar object (a single number) to be stored in the workfile. The second word **sales_f** is the name we are giving to that scalar object, which is our predicted value. The right side of the equation performs the calculation. Type the command and press Enter. A message will appear at the bottom of the EViews window saying **SALES_F successfully computed.**

A word of warning: The values C(1), C(2), and C(3) will always be the coefficient estimates for the model most recently estimated. If you have only estimated one equation, there will be no confusion. However, if you have estimated another model, successfully or not, the values will change. Make sure you are using the correct ones.

You have now calculated the forecast. How do you read off the answer? Go to the **SALES_F** object in your workfile and double-click it.

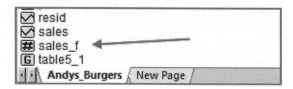

A spreadsheet appears with the forecast, first with lots of digits and in the spreadsheet rounded to five decimals:

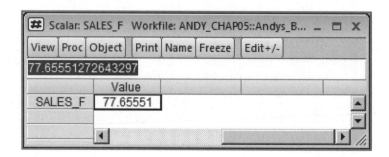

5.3.2 Using the Forecast option

To use EViews automatic **Forecast** command to produce out-of-sample forecasts, it is necessary to extend the size of the workfile to accommodate the observations for which we want forecasts. To do so you select, from the workfile toolbar, **Proc/Structure/Resize Current Page**.

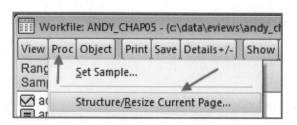

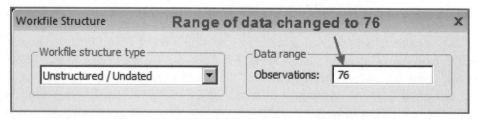

Alternatively, simply double-click the **Range** shown in the workfile.

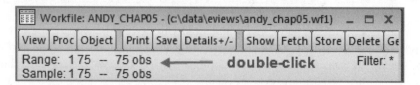

EViews will ask you whether you are sure you wish to make this change.

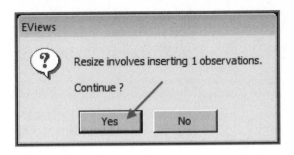

Notice that both the range and the sample in the workfile have changed from **1 75** to **1 76**. The next task is to insert the values *PRICE* = 5.5 and *ADVERT* = 1.2 for which we want to make the forecast. We insert these values at observation 76. To do so, we begin by opening the *PRICE* spreadsheet by double-clicking on this series in the workfile.

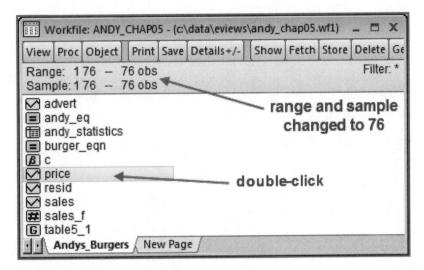

The lower portion of the *PRICE* spreadsheet appears below. Notice how EViews responded to your request to extend the range from 75 to 76. It did not have an observation for observation 76 so it specified this observation as **NA**, short for "not available". To replace **NA** with **5.5**, click on **Edit +/ -**, and change the spreadsheet.

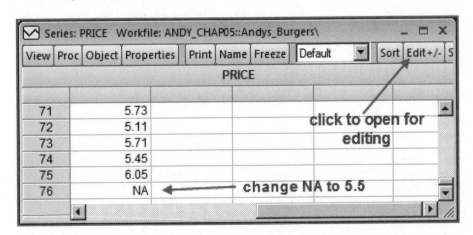

Click on **Edit +/ -** again after you have made the change.

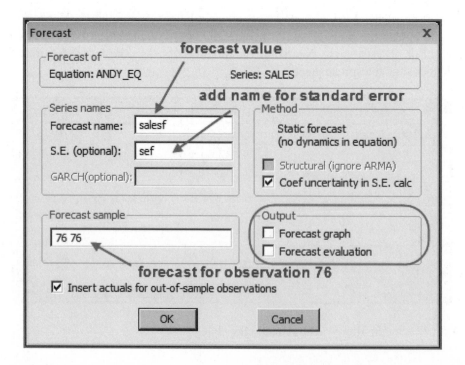

Similar steps are followed for the *ADVERT* spreadsheet to insert the value 1.2.

Now you are ready to compute the forecast. Go to your workfile and open the equation **ANDY_EQ** by double-clicking on it. Then click on the **Forecast** button in the toolbar. Before doing so, note that the number of observations used to estimate the equation is still 75. We are using the first 75 observations to estimate an equation that is then used to forecast sales for observation 76. Increasing the range of observations in a workfile does not change equations in the workfile that have already been estimated with fewer observations.

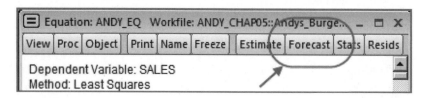

The following forecast dialog box appears. Let us consider the various items in this box.

Series names: The forecasts and their standard errors will appear in the workfile under the names *SALESF* and *SEF*, respectively. The forecast standard error is computed using the formula on page 244 of *POE4*. This formula includes what EViews calls **Coef uncertainty in S.E. calculation**. In this particular case, not including this uncertainty would mean the forecast standard error is the same as the standard deviation of the error term.

Forecast sample: We have chosen to forecast for just observation 76. We could have defined the **forecast sample** as **1 76**, in which case EViews would produce both the in-sample forecasts as well as the out-of-sample forecast.

Method: There are no **dynamics** in the equation because we do not have time series observations with lagged variables. These issues are considered in Chapter 9.

Output: At this point we are not concerned with a **Forecast graph** or a **Forecast evaluation**.

Insert actuals for out-of-sample observations: A tick in this box asks EViews to insert actual values for *SALES* for the observations that lie outside your **Forecast sample** – in this case that is observations 1 to 75.

After clicking **OK** and closing the equation, you will be returned to the workfile where you will discover that *SALESF* and *SEF* appear as two new series in the workfile.

On opening these series by double-clicking on them, you will further discover that the forecast and its standard error appear at observation 76. The other values for *SALESF* at observations 1 to 75 are the actual sample values. For *SEF* the other values are **NA** because we did not ask for within-sample forecasts.

obs	SALESF	SEF
74	81.30000	NA
75	75.00000	NA
76	77.65551	4.942008

The forecast and its standard error are $\widehat{SALES} = 77.6555$ and $\mathrm{se}(f) = 4.942$. These values can be used to compute a forecast interval as $\widehat{SALES} \pm t_{(1-\alpha/2,\,72)} \times \mathrm{se}(f)$.

5.4 INTERVAL ESTIMATION

After obtaining least squares estimates of an equation, we can proceed to use it for forecasting as we have done in the preceding section. In addition, we may be interested in obtaining interval estimates that reflect the precision of our estimates, or testing hypotheses about the unknown coefficients. The covariance matrix of the least squares estimates is a useful tool for these purposes, and one we will return to in Chapter 6. We begin by explaining how it can be viewed.

5.4.1 The least squares covariance matrix

To examine the least squares covariance matrix, go to the object **ANDY_EQ** in your workfile and open it by double clicking. Select **View/Covariance Matrix** from the toolbar and drop-down menu. The covariance matrix of the least-squares estimates will appear.

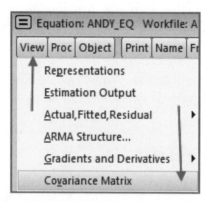

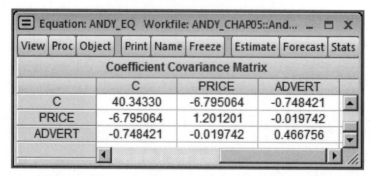

Check these values against those on p. 179 of *POE4*. Also note the relationship between the variances that appear on the diagonal of the covariance matrix and the standard errors. For example,

$$\text{cov}(b_2, b_3) = -0.74842 \qquad \text{se}(b_2) = \sqrt{\widehat{\text{var}(b_2)}} = \sqrt{1.201201} = 1.09599$$

5.4.2 Computing interval estimates

A $100(1-\alpha)\%$ confidence interval for one of the unknown parameters, say β_k, is given by

$$b_k \pm t_{(1-\alpha/2,\, N-K)} \times \text{se}(b_k)$$

Thus, to get EViews to compute a confidence interval, we need to locate values for b_k, $\text{se}(b_k)$ and $t_{(1-\alpha/2, N-K)}$, and then do the calculations. As we noted earlier in this chapter, the least squares estimates b_k will be stored in the object **C** in the workfile. Alternatively, they are stored in the array **@coefs** that was used for computing interval estimates in Chapter 3. That is, **C** = **@coefs**. If we are interested in one particular b_k, say b_2, then C(2) = **@coefs(2)** = -7.907854. Similarly, the standard errors are stored in the array **@stderrs**, so that **@stderrs(2)** = 1.09599. Note that **C**, **@coefs**, and **@stderrs** will contain values from the most recently estimated equation. If you are in doubt about their contents, quickly re-estimate the equation of interest. The remaining value that is required is $t_{(1-\alpha/2, N-K)}$. It can be found using the EViews function **@qtdist(p,v)** where **p** is equal to $1-\alpha/2$ and **v** is the number of degrees of freedom, in this case $N-K = 75-3 = 72$. Putting all these ingredients together, upper and lower bounds for 95% and interval estimates for β_2 and β_3 can be found from the following sequence of commands:

```
scalar tc = @qtdist(0.975,72)
scalar beta2_low = c(2) - tc*@stderrs(2)
scalar beta2_up = c(2) + tc*@stderrs(2)
scalar beta3_low = c(3) - tc*@stderrs(3)
scalar beta3_up = c(3) + tc*@stderrs(3)
```

These commands are entered, one at a time, in the EViews Command window. Each command is executed after you push the **enter** key. The answers are stored as scalars marked by ⊞ in the workfile.

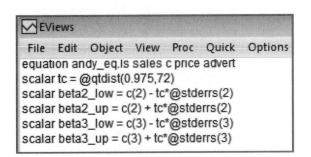 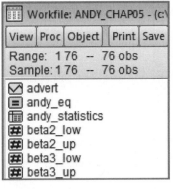

To view the upper and lower bounds of the interval estimates, double-click each of the scalars in the workfile. For example, the lower and upper bounds of the 95% interval estimate for β_2 are

	Value
BETA2_LOW	-10.09268
BETA2_UP	-5.723032

You will discover that these interval estimates coincide with those on page 182 of *POE4*.

It will not surprise you that EViews has the capability of automatically generating interval estimates. In the **ANDY_EQ** regression window select **View/Coefficient Diagnostics/ Confidence Intervals**.

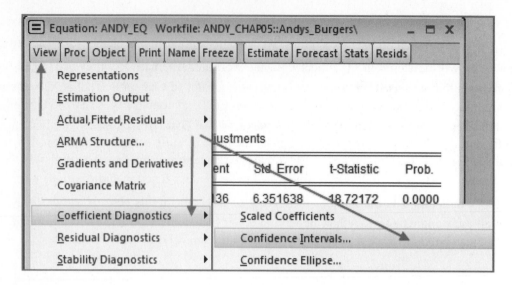

In the resulting dialog box. choose the desired level of confidence, or more than one. Those for a 95% level of confidence are:

		95% CI	
Variable	Coefficient	Low	High
C	118.9136	106.2519	131.5754
PRICE	-7.907854	-10.09268	-5.723032
ADVERT	1.862584	0.500659	3.224510

Coefficient Confidence Intervals

To obtain 95% and 90% interval estimates using **cinterval** in the Command window, we write

    andy_eq.cinterval .95 .9

5.4.3 Interval estimates for linear combinations of coefficients

Chapter 5.4.2 of *POE4* discusses interval estimates for linear combinations of regression coefficients. As an example, consider the linear combination

$$\lambda = -0.4\beta_2 + 0.8\beta_3$$

Why this might be interesting is discussed in *POE4*, pp. 183-184. The point estimate of the linear combination is

$$\hat{\lambda} = -0.4b_2 + 0.8b_3$$

An interval estimate for this quantity is

$$\hat{\lambda} \pm t_c \text{se}\left(\hat{\lambda}\right)$$

where t_c is the $t_{(1-\alpha/2, N-K)}$ percentile of the t-distribution. The difficult (tedious) component of the calculation is the standard error of $\hat{\lambda}$. This becomes less tedious by using the EViews Wald test to compute it for us. In the **ANDY_EQ** regression window select **View/Coefficient Diagnostics/ Wald Test-Coefficient Restrictions**.

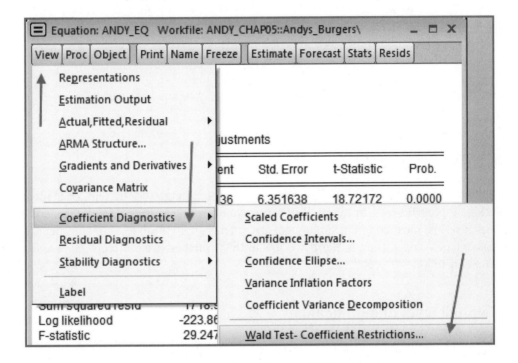

Into the dialog box, enter

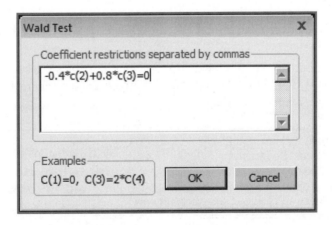

The equation is posed as a hypothesis test or coefficient restriction, which is not what we really want, but the method produces both the estimate and the standard error:

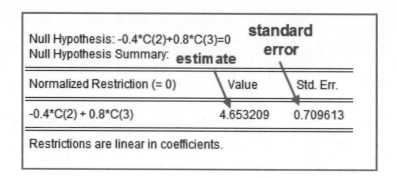

The interval estimate lower and upper bounds can then be computed as scalars.

5.5 HYPOTHESIS TESTING

In this chapter we are concerned with hypothesis tests on a single coefficient, or a single linear combinations of coefficients, in the multiple regression model. More complex tests are deferred until Chapter 6. The most common single-coefficient tests are two-tail tests of significance where, in the context of Andy's Burger Barn, we are testing whether price affects sales and whether advertising expenditure affects sales.

5.5.1 Two-tail tests of significance

Two-tail tests of significance for the effect of price and the effect of advertising are considered on pages 185-186 in *POE4*. The hypotheses for these tests are

$H_0 : \beta_2 = 0$ (no price effect) $H_1 : \beta_2 \neq 0$ (there is a price effect)

$H_0 : \beta_3 = 0$ (no advertising effect) $H_1 : \beta_3 \neq 0$ (there is an advertising effect)

Using EViews to calculate the *t*-values and *p*-values for these tests is trivial. They are automatically computed when you estimate the equation. To see where they are reported, we return to the least squares output for **ANDY_EQ**.

Dependent Variable: SALES
Method: Least Squares
Date: 06/06/11 Time: 10:40
Sample (adjusted): 1 75
Included observations: 75 after adjustments

t-values and p-values for two-tail tests of significance

Variable	Coefficient	Std. Error	t-Statistic	Prob.
C	118.9136	6.351638	18.72172	0.0000
PRICE	-7.907854	1.095993	-7.215241	0.0000
ADVERT	1.862584	0.683195	2.726283	0.0080

Do you know where these numbers come from? Consider the test for the effect of advertising. The t-value is given by $t = 1.8626/0.6832 = 2.726$. The p-value is given by

$$p\text{-value} = P\left(t_{(72)} > 2.726\right) + P\left(t_{(72)} < -2.726\right) = 2 \times P\left(t_{(72)} < -2.726\right) = 0.008044$$

We can confirm the above result by asking EViews to compute the above probability, using the command

scalar pval_advert = 2*@ctdist(-2.726,72)

The function **@ctdist(x, v)** computes the distribution function value $P\left(t_{(v)} < x\right)$. The command can be entered in the EViews Command window. If you are unsure of how to do so or how to read off the result, go back and check the earlier part of this chapter where we introduced a simple forecasting procedure, or the section where we computed interval estimates.

Knowing the p-value is sufficient information for rejecting or not rejecting H_0. In the case of advertising expenditure we reject $H_0 : \beta_3 = 0$ at a 5% significance level because the p-value of 0.0080 is less than 0.05. Suppose, however, that we wanted to make a decision about H_0 by comparing the calculated value $t = 2.726$ to a 5% critical value. How do we find that critical value? We need values t_c and $-t_c$ such that $P\left(t_{(72)} < t_c\right) = 0.975$. Table 2 inside the front cover of *POE4* is not sufficiently detailed to provide this value. It can be obtained using the EViews command

scalar tc = @qtdist(0.975,72)

The answer is $t_c = 1.993$, a value that leads us to reject $H_0 : \beta_3 = 0$ because $2.726 > 1.993$.

The p-value for testing $H_0 : \beta_2 = 0$ against $H_1 : \beta_2 \neq 0$ is given as 0.0000 in the EViews regression output. As an exercise, use EViews to show that, using more decimal places, the value is 4.424×10^{-10}.

5.5.2 A one-tail test of significance

To collect evidence on whether or not the demand for burgers is price elastic, on page 187 of *POE4* we test $H_0 : \beta_2 \geq 0$ against the alternative $H_1 : \beta_2 < 0$. In this case we are not particularly interested in the single point $\beta_2 = 0$, but, nevertheless, for testing $H_0 : \beta_2 \geq 0$ we act as if the null hypothesis is $H_0 : \beta_2 = 0$. Thus, this test can be viewed as a one-tail test of significance. The p-value for this test is $P\left(t_{(72)} < -7.215241\right) = 2.212 \times 10^{-10}$. Because the calculated value t-value $t = -7.215241$ is negative, and the rejection region is in the left tail (as suggested by the direction of the alternative hypothesis $H_1 : \beta_2 < 0$), we can compute the p-value by taking half of the p-value given in the EViews regression output. However, since half of 0.0000 is 0.0000, this example is not a very interesting one. If we considered a one-tail test for advertising of the form $H_0 : \beta_3 \leq 0$ against $H_1 : \beta_3 > 0$, we could calculate its p-value as 0.0040, half of 0.0080.

If the calculated t-value is positive, and the rejection region is the left tail (or the calculated t-value is negative, and the rejection region is the right tail), the p-value will be greater than 0.5 and is not simply half of the EViews p-value. In such instances the p-value is given by $p = 1 - p^*/2$ where p^* is the EViews supplied p-value. Do you understand why? Check it out!

What is the 5% critical value for a one-tail test? For the case of β_2 where the critical value is a negative one in the left tail of the distribution, we can obtain it using the EViews command

scalar tc1 = @qtdist(0.05,72)

The value obtained is $t_c = -1.666$. Thus, making the test decision by reference to the critical value, we reject $H_0 : \beta_2 \geq 0$ in favor of $H_1 : \beta_2 < 0$ because $-7.215 < -1.666$.

5.5.3 Testing nonzero values

One-tail test

For advertising to be effective, β_3 must be greater than 1. Thus we test $H_0 : \beta_3 \leq 1$ against $H_1 : \beta_3 > 1$. On page 188 of *POE4*, we compute the key quantities for performing this test. They are the calculated t-value

$$t = \frac{b_3 - 1}{se(b_3)} = \frac{1.8626 - 1}{0.6832} = \frac{0.8626}{0.6832} = 1.263$$

and its corresponding p-value

$$P\left(t_{(72)} > 1.263\right) = 1 - P\left(t_{(72)} \leq 1.263\right) = 0.105$$

You can compute these quantities using the following commands in the EViews Command window:

```
scalar t3 = (c(3) - 1)/@stderrs(3)
scalar pval3 = 1 - @ctdist(t3,72)
```

Two-tail test

For two-tail tests there is an easier way to get the results from EViews. You can tell EViews the hypothesis that you want to test and it will do the rest. To illustrate, we turn the recent hypothesis about the effect of advertising expenditure into a two-tail test, namely

$$H_0 : \beta_3 = 1 \qquad \text{against} \qquad H_1 : \beta_3 \neq 1$$

For testing this hypothesis, the calculated t-value is the same as before:

$$t = \frac{b_3 - 1}{se(b_3)} = \frac{1.8626 - 1}{0.6832} = \frac{0.8626}{0.6832} = 1.2626$$

The p-value will be different, however. It is

$$P\left(t_{(72)} > 1.2626\right) + P\left(t_{(72)} < 1.2626\right) = 2 \times 0.1054 = 0.2108$$

We have included more digits after the decimal so that we can match the accuracy of EViews. To get EViews to automatically compute these values, we proceed as follows. Open the equation object **ANDY_EQ** and then select **View/Coefficient Diagnostics/Wald Test-Coefficient Restrictions**.

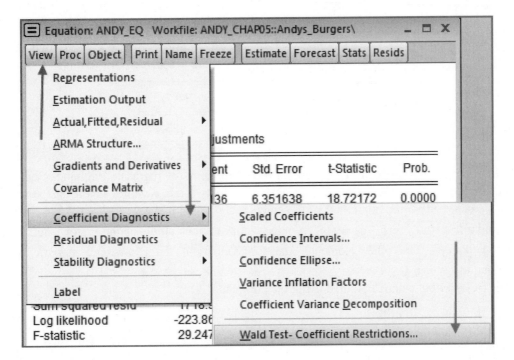

In the resulting dialog box, type in the null hypothesis using the notation $C(1) = \beta_1$, $C(2) = \beta_2$, $C(3) = \beta_3$, and so on. For the null hypothesis $H_0 : \beta_3 = 1$, we type **c(3) = 1**. Then click **OK**.

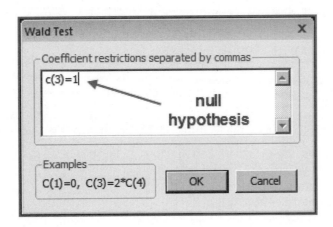

The following test results appear:

```
Wald Test:
Equation: ANDY_EQ

Test Statistic        Value         df        Probability

t-statistic          1.262573        72         0.2108
F-statistic          1.594091      (1, 72)      0.2108
Chi-square           1.594091        1          0.2067
```

t-value numerator

Null Hypothesis: C(3)=1   **t-value denominator**
Null Hypothesis Summary:

```
Normalized Restriction (= 0)      Value        Std. Err.

-1 + C(3)                       0.862584       0.683195
```

The test is called a **Wald test**. The t-test on the coefficients of regression equations belongs to this class of tests. EViews reports the t-value and the two-tail p-value. In the last row of the output we can read off the numerator of the calculated t-value, namely $b_3 - 1 = 0.8626$, as well as its standard error $se(b_3 - 1) = 0.6832$ that appears in the denominator. Of course, $se(b_3 - 1) = se(b_3)$. The other elements, the F-statistic and the Chi-square statistic, will be introduced in Chapter 6.

The same output can be obtained using the command

    andy_eq.wald c(3)=1

The result of the Wald test can be saved as a table by selecting **Freeze** and then **Name** the resulting table. That is,

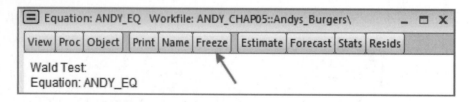

Then

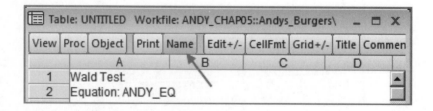

5.5.4 Testing linear combinations of coefficients

The Wald test can be used for testing hypotheses about linear combinations of coefficients. In *POE4*, pages 188-189, we test

$$H_0 : -0.2\beta_2 - 0.5\beta_3 \leq 0 \qquad H_1 : -0.2\beta_2 - 0.5\beta_3 > 0$$

In the equation **ANDY_EQ**, select **View/Coefficient Diagnostics/Wald Test-Coefficient Restrictions**. Into the dialog box enter

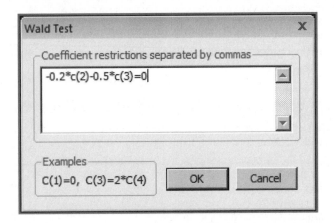

This produces the Wald test result. The reported *p*-value is for a two-tail test. The one-tail *p*-value is half 0.1092, or 0.0546, which we have rounded to 0.055 in *POE4*.

Wald Test: Equation: ANDY_EQ			tw o-ta il *p*-va lue
Test Statistic	Value	df	Probability
t-statistic	1.621705	72	0.1092

The corresponding command is

> **andy_eq.wald -0.2*c(2)-0.5*c(3)=0**

5.6 POLYNOMIAL EQUATIONS

To take into account the fact that the marginal effect of advertising is most likely a diminishing function of advertising, the squared value of advertising is added to Andy's *SALES* equation. The new specification is

$$SALES = \beta_1 + \beta_2 PRICE + \beta_3 ADVERT + \beta_4 ADVERT^2 + e$$

Adding the term $\beta_4 ADVERT^2$ to our original specification yields a model in which the response of expected revenue to a change in advertising expenditure depends on the level of advertising. Specifically, applying the polynomial derivative rule given in equation (5.20) on page 191 of *POE4*, and holding *PRICE* constant, the response of $E(SALES)$ to a change in *ADVERT* is

$$\frac{\Delta E(SALES)}{\Delta ADVERT}\bigg|_{(PRICE \text{ held constant})} = \frac{\partial E(SALES)}{\partial ADVERT} = \beta_3 + 2\beta_4 ADVERT$$

The partial derivative sign "∂" is used in place of the derivative sign "d" in *POE4* equation (5.20) because *SALES* depends on two variables, *PRICE* and *ADVERT*, and we are holding *PRICE* constant. Following the discussion on *POE4*, page 193, we expect $\beta_3 > 0$. Also, to achieve diminishing returns the response must decline as *ADVERT* increases. That is, we expect $\beta_4 < 0$.

EViews makes estimating polynomial equations quite easy. Functions of the variables are entered directly into the equation specification. The polynomial operator is "^" so that $x^p = X \wedge P$. Enter the command

equation andy_quad.ls sales c price advert advert^2

The resulting estimates are

Dependent Variable: SALES
Method: Least Squares
Sample (adjusted): 1 75
Included observations: 75 after adjustments

Variable	Coefficient	Std. Error	t-Statistic	Prob.
C	109.7190	6.799045	16.13742	0.0000
PRICE	-7.640000	1.045939	-7.304442	0.0000
ADVERT	12.15124	3.556164	3.416950	0.0011
ADVERT^2	-2.767963	0.940624	-2.942688	0.0044

The marginal effect of advertising is estimated using

$$\frac{\widehat{\partial E(SALES)}}{\partial ADVERT} = b_3 + 2b_4 ADVERT = C(3) + 2*C(4)*ADVERT$$

This linear combination of coefficients can be evaluated for any value of *ADVERT* using the estimated equation **ANDY_QUAD** and **View/Coefficient Diagnostics/Wald Test-Coefficient Restrictions**. For example, the marginal effect of advertising on *SALES* when *ADVERT* = 2 ($2000 per week) is obtained using

andy_quad.wald c(3)+2*c(4)*2=0

The marginal effect in the output is reported as 1.079. We estimate that if *ADVERT* = 2, the marginal effect of an additional $1000 of advertising expenditure is $1,079.

Null Hypothesis: C(3)+2*C(4)*2=0	**marginal effect when**	
Null Hypothesis Summary:	**ADVERT=2**	
Normalized Restriction (= 0)	Value	Std. Err.
C(3) + 4*C(4)	1.079383	0.701935

In addition to the estimated marginal effect, EViews reports the standard error of the linear combination of coefficients, which permits calculation of an interval estimate in the usual way. That is, an interval estimate is **value $\pm$ t_c std.err.**, where the t_c is the $1 - \alpha / 2$ percentile of the t-distribution with $N - K = 75 - 4 = 71$ degrees of freedom.

The Wald test also reports the t-statistic for the hypothesis that the estimated marginal effect is zero:

Wald Test: Equation: ANDY_QUAD			
Test Statistic	Value	df	Probability
t-statistic	1.537725	71	0.1286

We cannot reject the null hypothesis that the marginal effect is zero at the 5% level of significance. What does this mean? Figure 5.4 in *POE4* shows the fitted quadratic function at different levels of advertising. The marginal effect is the slope of the fitted curve. The fitted function reaches its maximum when $ADVERT = 2.19$. At that point the slope of the fitted quadratic function is zero. Since $ADVERT = 2$ is near this maximizing value, it is not surprising that we cannot reject the null hypothesis that the marginal effect is zero.

5.6.1 The optimal level of advertising

Andy's objective is not to maximize *SALES*. It is to maximize profit. The profit maximizing level of advertising is where marginal revenue (the marginal effect) is equal to marginal cost ($1, since the cost of advertising units is $1). Thus, advertising should be increased to the point where

$$\beta_3 + 2\beta_4 ADVERT_0 = 1$$

with $ADVERT_0$ denoting the optimal level of advertising. Using the least squares estimates for β_3 and β_4 a point estimate for $ADVERT_0$ is

$$\widehat{ADVERT_0} = \frac{1 - b_3}{2b_4} = \frac{1 - 12.1512}{2 \times (-2.76796)} = 2.014$$

implying the optimal monthly advertising expenditure is $2,014. To assess the reliability of this estimate we need a standard error for the estimate $(1 - b_3)/2b_4$. The standard error is obtained using the **delta method**, as explained in *POE4*, page 194. The very tedious calculation is made simple by EViews. The **Wald Test-Coefficient Restrictions** approach will compute nonlinear functions of the estimates and the standard error. Enter the command

```
andy_quad.wald (1-c(3)) / (2*c(4))=0
```

We have used parentheses to control the order of operations, so that **(1-c(3))** is divided by **(2*c(4))**. All computer languages do calculations within parentheses first. The result is

Null Hypothesis: (1-C(3))/(2*C(4))=0	**nonlinear function value and**	
Null Hypothesis Summary:	**delta method standard error**	
Normalized Restriction (= 0)	Value	Std. Err.
(1 - C(3)) / 2 / C(4)	2.014340	0.128723
Delta method computed using analytic derivatives.		

Use the delta method standard error to obtain an interval estimate or to test a hypothesis about the nonlinear function value.

5.7 SAVING COMMANDS

Throughout this chapter we have entered a number of commands in the EViews Command window. It is a good idea to save these commands so that you have a record of them when you return to your work. To do so, highlight the commands and push **Ctrl+C.** Then go to **Object/New Object** and select the object **Text**. As a name for the object, enter **CHAP05_ANDY**. After positioning the cursor within the **Text** dialog box, push **Ctrl+V**. The following **Text** object will then be stored in your workfile:

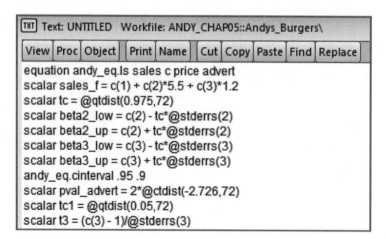

```
TXT  Text: UNTITLED   Workfile: ANDY_CHAP05::Andys_Burgers\

View  Proc  Object   Print  Name   Cut  Copy  Paste  Find  Replace

equation andy_eq.ls sales c price advert
scalar sales_f = c(1) + c(2)*5.5 + c(3)*1.2
scalar tc = @qtdist(0.975,72)
scalar beta2_low = c(2) - tc*@stderrs(2)
scalar beta2_up = c(2) + tc*@stderrs(2)
scalar beta3_low = c(3) - tc*@stderrs(3)
scalar beta3_up = c(3) + tc*@stderrs(3)
andy_eq.cinterval .95 .9
scalar pval_advert = 2*@ctdist(-2.726,72)
scalar tc1 = @qtdist(0.05,72)
scalar t3 = (c(3) - 1)/@stderrs(3)
```

Save the work file *andy_chap05.wf1* and close it.

5.8 INTERACTION VARIABLES

Interaction variables are products of explanatory variables. See the discussion in *POE4*, Chapter 5.7. To illustrate, open the workfile *pizza4.wf1*. Save it as *pizza4_chap05.wf1*. This data file contains data on 40 individuals. The variables are

PIZZA   annual pizza expenditure, $
FEMALE   =1 if female

HS	=1 if highest degree received is high school diploma
COLLEGE	=1 if highest degree received is a college diploma
GRAD	=1 if highest degree received is a post-graduate degree
INCOME	annual income in thousands of dollars
AGE	age in years

One equation of interest might be

$$PIZZA = \beta_1 + \beta_2 AGE + \beta_3 INCOME + e$$

The problem with this equation is that the marginal effects of *AGE* and *INCOME* on annual *PIZZA* expenditure are constant. That is, an increase in income of $1000 has the same effect on expected expenditure for a person who is 20 years old and a person who is 70 years old. That is a very strong and questionable assumption. If *AGE* moderates the income effect, we might specify

$$PIZZA = \beta_1 + \beta_2 AGE + \beta_3 INCOME + \beta_4 (AGE \times INCOME) + e$$

In this revised model the effects of *INCOME* and *AGE* are:

$$\partial E(PIZZA)/\partial AGE = \beta_2 + \beta_4 INCOME$$

$$\partial E(PIZZA)/\partial INCOME = \beta_3 + \beta_4 AGE$$

Including interaction variables is straightforward using EViews. The equation specification can incorporate the EViews multiplication operator "*". That is, $X \times Z = X * Z$. Enter the command

equation pizza_eq.ls pizza c age income age*income

```
Dependent Variable: PIZZA
Method: Least Squares
Date: 06/07/11  Time: 11:11
Sample: 1 40
Included observations: 40
```

Variable	Coefficient	Std. Error	t-Statistic	Prob.
C	161.4654	120.6634	1.338147	0.1892
AGE	-2.977423	3.352101	-0.888226	0.3803
INCOME	6.979905	2.822768	2.472717	0.0183
AGE*INCOME	-0.123239	0.066719	-1.847148	0.0730

The estimated marginal effect of income is

$$\overline{\partial E(PIZZA)/\partial INCOME} = b_3 + b_4 AGE = C(3) + C(4)*AGE$$

For individuals of ages 20 and 50, the marginal effects are given by

pizza_eq.wald c(3)+c(4)*20=0
pizza_eq.wald c(3)+c(4)*50=0

The results are

Null Hypothesis: C(3)+C(4)*20=0 Null Hypothesis Summary:		
Normalized Restriction (= 0)	Value	Std. Err.
C(3) + 20*C(4)	4.515118	1.520394

Null Hypothesis: C(3)+C(4)*50=0 Null Hypothesis Summary:		
Normalized Restriction (= 0)	Value	Std. Err.
C(3) + 50*C(4)	0.817938	0.709968

The marginal effect of income for the 50-year-old is much smaller than the marginal effect of income for the 20-yearold.

5.8.1 Interactions in log-linear models

The estimation of log-linear models with interaction variables is carried out in exactly the same way. Open the workfile *cps4_small.wf1* and save it as *cps4_small_chap05.wf1*. Estimate the three specifications discussed on page 197 of *POE4* using

> **equation lwage.ls log(wage) c educ exper**
> **equation lwage2.ls log(wage) c educ exper educ*exper**
> **equation lwage3.ls log(wage) c educ exper educ*exper exper^2**

5.9 GOODNESS-OF-FIT

Open the workfile *andy_chap05.wf1* that we used earlier in this chapter. Examine the saved equation **ANDY_EQ**. If you did not save it earlier, re-estimate the equation using

> **equation andy_eq.ls sales c price advert**

Below the parameter estimates are various summary measures including the $R^2 = 0.448258$.

Variable	Coefficient	Std. Error	t-Statistic	Prob.
C	118.9136	6.351638	18.72172	0.0000
PRICE	-7.907854	1.095993	-7.215241	0.0000
ADVERT	1.862584	0.683195	2.726283	0.0080
R-squared	0.448258	Mean dependent var		77.37467
Adjusted R-squared	0.432932	S.D. dependent var		6.488537

Section 5.8 in *POE4* makes the point that the usual interpretation of R^2 does not hold when the model does not include an intercept. Just to make that point further, estimate the *SALES* equation omitting the intercept, using

equation andy_noint.ls sales price advert

Variable	Coefficient	Std. Error	t-Statistic	Prob.
PRICE	12.12089	0.572860	21.15855	0.0000
ADVERT	4.068586	1.618979	2.513057	0.0142
R-squared	-2.237677	Mean dependent var		77.37467
Adjusted R-squared	-2.282029	S.D. dependent var		6.488537

Here the R^2 is negative and greater than one in absolute value. It is most definitely not the percent of the variation in *SALES* about its mean explained by the model.

5.10 MONTE CARLO SIMULATION

In a regression model with normally distributed errors and explanatory variables that are assumed nonrandom, we can derive the finite sample properties of our estimators and test statistics. We know that our estimators are unbiased, expressions for variances are exact, and, for linear functions of the coefficients, properties of hypothesis tests and interval estimates based on the *t*-distribution hold exactly in finite samples. When we move to a world where the errors are not normally distributed or the explanatory variables are random, the properties of our estimators and test statistics no longer hold exactly in finite samples. They are approximations that require a large sample to be valid. The critical question that students always ask and instructors never answer is: "How large does the sample have to be?" The reason instructors are evasive is that the answer depends on many things such as the underlying model and the distributions of the errors and the explanatory variables. What we can do to try to answer the question (under a specific set of assumptions) is to set up a Monte Carlo experiment where a large number of samples are generated and a large number of estimates obtained. We can then examine the properties of the estimates for the sample size used in the Monte Carlo experiment and change the sample size to see how the properties change.

In this Section we show how to use EViews to run the Monte Carlo experiment in Appendix 5B of *POE4* (pages 213-220). We consider just one sample size, that where $N = 40$. Begin by creating a workfile, *appendix_5b.wf1*, with 40 observations:

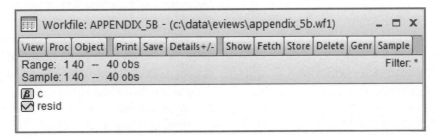

Then you need to create an Eviews **program**. To do so, go to **File/New/Program**.

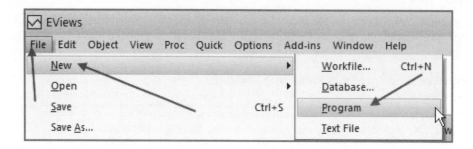

A program window will appear in which you can write your program. Although we have not yet written any commands, it is a good idea to click **Save as** to give the program file a name and store it in a convenient folder. We have named it *appendix_5B.prg*. Note that we now have two files, a workfile and a program file, named *appendix_5B.wf1* and *appendix_5B.prg*, respectively.

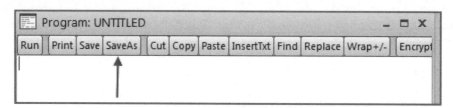

The following screen shot displays the program window with the first few commands of the program that we are about to describe. We will give you the complete program, and then explain what the commands are designed to achieve. After we have written the complete program with all its commands, we explain how to run that program.

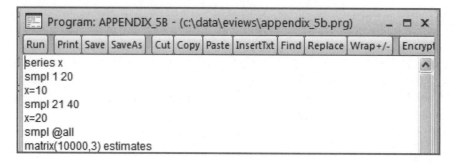

The complete set of commands in the program follows. The explanatory comments in italics on the right are not part of the program.

series x	*Create series x*
smpl 1 20	*Change sample to first 20 observations*
x=10	*Set values of x for first half of sample*
smpl 21 40	*Change sample to last 20 observations*
x=20	*Set values of x in second half of sample*
smpl @all	*Change sample back to 40 observations*
matrix(10000,3) estimates	*Create 10000x3 matrix for storing estimates*
scalar reject=0	*Create and initial reject*
scalar cover=0	*Create and initial cover*
scalar close=0	*Create and initial close*
series ey=100+10*x	*Create the expected value of y*
scalar tc95=@qtdist(0.95,38)	*Find critical t for testing*

```
scalar tc975=@qtdist(0.975,38)          Find critical t for interval estimates
for !i=1 to 10000                       Start loop for 10000 estimates
    series v=@rchisq(4)                 Generate series of χ²(4) random variates

    series e=50*(v-4)/@sqrt(8)          Generate random errors mean 0 and s.d. 50
    series y=ey+e                       Generate y from expected y and errors
    equation eq.ls y c x                Find least squares estimates
    scalar tee=(c(2)-10)/@stderrs(2)    Compute t-value for test
    scalar check=(tee>tc95)             check=1 for reject, otherwise 0
    reject=reject+check                 Increment reject by 1 if there was a rejection
    scalar upper=c(2)+tc975*@stderrs(2) Compute upper bound for interval estimate
    scalar lower=c(2)-tc975*@stderrs(2) Compute lower bound for interval estimate
    check=(10>=lower and 10<=upper)     check=1 if β₂=10 lies in interval, otherwise 0

    cover=cover+check                   Increment cover by 1 if β₂ in interval

    check=(c(2)>=9 and c(2)<=11)        check=1 if 9≤b₂≤11, otherwise 0

    close=close+check                   Increment close by 1 if 9≤b₂≤11

    estimates(!i,1)=c(1)                Store b₁ in matrix

    estimates(!i,2)=c(2)                Store b₂ in matrix

    estimates(!i,3)=@se^2               Store σ̂² in matrix
next                                    Return to beginning of loop to start next sample
reject=reject/10000                     Change reject from number to proportion
cover=cover/10000                       Change cover from number to proportion
close=close/10000                       Change close from number to proportion
```

To explain the first block of commands, note that we are considering the model

$$y_i = E(y_i \mid x_i) + e_i = \beta_1 + \beta_2 x_i + e_i = 100 + 10x_i + e_i \qquad i = 1, 2, \ldots, 40$$

where $x_i = 10$ for the first 20 observations and $x_i = 20$ for the last 20 observations. In the following commands we create the series X and assign the required values to it:

```
series x
smpl 1 20
x=10
smpl 21 40
x=20
smpl @all
```

We are going to generate 10000 samples, each of size 40, and find least squares estimates for each of those samples. We are interested in such things as the means and variances and distributions of the 10000 estimates. For that reason we need a place to store the estimates. The next command creates a (10000×3) matrix called **estimates** that we plan to use to store the estimates $(b_1, b_2, \hat{\sigma}^2)$. The estimates from the ith sample will be stored in the ith row of the matrix. The first column of the matrix will contain all the estimates for β_1, the second column all the estimates for β_2, and the third column all the estimates for $\hat{\sigma}^2$.

```
matrix(10000,3) estimates
```

We are also interested in (1) the proportion of times $H_0 : \beta_2 = 10$ is rejected in favor of the alternative $H_0 : \beta_2 > 10$ at a 5% significance level (the probability of a type I error, also known as the size of the test), (2) the proportion of times a 95% interval estimate for β_2 contains the true value $\beta_2 = 10$, and (3) the proportion of times the estimate b_2 lies in the interval (9,11). These three proportions are called **reject**, **cover** and **close**. However, in the earlier part of the program, we use **reject**, **cover** and **close** to keep track of the **number of times** (1) there is a rejection, (2) the interval contains the true parameter, and (3) the estimate is close to β_2. We convert the numbers to proportions at the very end of the program. At the beginning of the program we define **reject**, **cover** and **close** as scalars and set their initial values to zero. Later, we keep track of the number of times a condition is satisfied by adding 1 when required. The following commands define the scalars and initial them to zero:

```
scalar reject=0
scalar cover=0
scalar close=0
```

An alternative approach is to define another (10000×3) matrix that will contain ones and zeros, indicating when the conditions are satisfied and not satisfied.

The next 3 commands create the series $E(y_i \mid x_i) = 100 + 10x_i$, and define two critical *t*-values, one for the hypothesis test and one for the interval estimate:

```
series ey=100+10*x
scalar tc95=@qtdist(0.95,38)
scalar tc975=@qtdist(0.975,38)
```

We have now reached a stage where we want to generate 10000 samples and repeat a number of commands 10000 times. All the commands up to this point are performed only once. We have put them in our program, but they could equally well be placed in the Command window and executed one at a time. Commands that are to be repeated 10000 times are placed in a **loop**. Loops must be placed in a program and cannot be executed in the Command window. The command that signals the beginning of the loop is

```
for !i=1 to 10000
```

The command that signals the end of the loop is

```
next
```

Go back to the complete listing of the program and see where the loop starts and ends. All commands in between the beginning and the end of the loop are executed 10000 times, once for each value of the **loop index**, **!i**, which takes values 1 to 10000. The commands within the loop are executed for **!i=1**, then for **!i=2**, and so on up to **!i=10000**.

The first three commands within the loop generate a sample of Y values in three steps. In the first step a series V containing randomly generated $\chi^2_{(4)}$ values is created from **v=@rchisq(4)**. In the second step these values are normalized to have a mean of zero and variance of one, and then multiplied by 50 to create the series E, **e=50*(v-4)/@sqrt(8)**. Then the Y values are created by adding E to EY.

```
series v=@rchisq(4)
series e=50*(v-4)/@sqrt(8)
series y=ey+e
```

Least squares estimates are obtained by the least squares regression command

> **equation eq.ls y c x**

In the next block of commands the scalar **tee** is the t-value $t = (b_2 - 10)/\text{se}(b_2)$ used to test $H_0 : \beta_2 = 10$ against the alternative $H_0 : \beta_2 > 10$. The scalar **check** is set equal to 1 if we are rejecting H_0 and 0 otherwise. If H_0 is rejected, **reject** increases by 1, otherwise it stays the same.

> **scalar tee=(c(2)-10)/@stderrs(2)**
> **scalar check=(tee>tc95)**
> **reject=reject+check**

To check whether $\beta_2 = 10$ lies within the 95% interval estimate $b_2 \pm t_{(0.975,38)}\text{se}(b_2)$, we first compute the upper and lower bounds of the interval, **upper** and **lower**. Then **check** is set equal to 1 if 10 lies in the interval and 0 otherwise. If 10 does lie in the interval, **cover** increases by 1, otherwise it stays the same. Because **check** was previously defined as a scalar, we can omit **scalar** from the front of its command. Note also that we can use the same scalar **check** to check different things. It is reset every time we use it. Using the same name helps prevent a proliferation of objects in your workfile.

> **scalar upper=c(2)+tc975*@stderrs(2)**
> **scalar lower=c(2)-tc975*@stderrs(2)**
> **check=(10>=lower and 10<=upper)**
> **cover=cover+check**

In the next two commands we use **check** and **close** in a similar way to increase **close** by 1 if $9 \leq b_2 \leq 11$:

> **check=(c(2)>=9 and c(2)<=11)**
> **close=close+check**

The final block of commands within the loop stores the values for $(b_1, b_2, \hat{\sigma}^2)$ in the matrix **estimates**. The loop index **!i** specifies the row of the matrix where the estimates are stored:

> **estimates(!i,1)=c(1)**
> **estimates(!i,2)=c(2)**
> **estimates(!i,3)=@se^2**

At the end of the loop **reject**, **cover** and **close** will contain the number of samples where (1) H_0 was rejected, (2) the interval estimate contained the true β_2, and (3) the estimate b_2 was inside the interval $\beta_2 \pm 1$. To convert these numbers to proportions, we divide by 10000:

> **reject=reject/10000**
> **cover=cover/10000**
> **close=close/10000**

After entering all the commands into your program, click **Save** and then **Run**. Your workfile should also be open at this time.

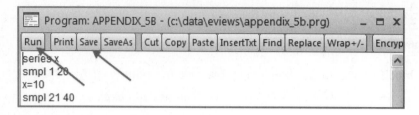

EViews will respond with the following window:

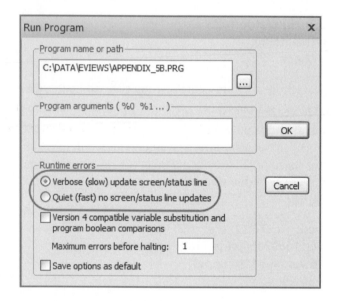

You can simply click **OK**, but first it is good to choose between **Verbose** mode and **Quiet** mode. **Verbose** mode is a good choice if you are uncertain about whether your program has errors, or if you want the reassurance that something is being computed. In this mode EViews keeps updating a "status line" with the most recent quantity calculated. **Verbose** mode is much slower than **Quiet** mode, however. If you run this program in **Verbose** mode, you can go to the bathroom and come back; it will still be running. There is no time for diversions if you choose **Quiet** mode. In this case the 10000 regressions are computed almost instantaneously.

After the program has run, your workfile will contain several extra items. Those that we are interested in are **REJECT**, **COVER**, **CLOSE** and **ESTIMATES**. The equation **EQ** will contain the estimates from the last regression where **!i=10000**. Similary, series V, E and Y will contain values from the last sample; we have not stored values from earlier samples. You may wish to delete these items to clean up your workfile.

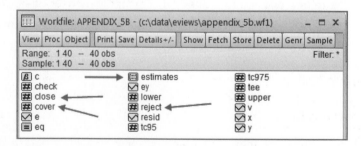

Checking the values for **REJECT**, **COVER**, **CLOSE**, we find

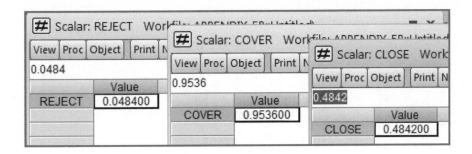

These values are similar in magnitude to those in Table 5B.1 on *POE4* page 214, but not identical. Because they are dependent on the random samples that are generated, they will be different each time that you run the program. With more and more samples, the variation will be less.

If our estimators are unbiased, the means of $\left(b_1, b_2, \hat{\sigma}^2\right)$, computed from the 10000 samples, should be close to the true values (100,10,2500). We can find those means by opening the matrix **ESTIMATES**, and choosing **View/Descriptive Stats by Column**:

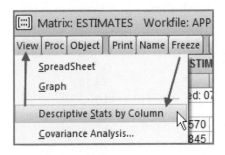

The means in the following table are in fact very close to the true values and comparable in magnitude to those in *POE4* Table 5B.1. There is considerable variation from sample to sample, however. Look at the maximum and minimum values. There are some estimates that miss the target by a long way.

	ESTIMATES		
	C1	C2	C3
Mean	99.75583	10.01221	2497.790
Median	98.58043	10.01867	2349.227
Maximum	212.5482	16.72384	8977.462
Minimum	5.862786	3.824178	452.4047
Std. Dev.	24.91974	1.573192	905.2230

To obtain histograms of the distributions of the estimates, open the matrix **ESTIMATES**, go to **View/Graph**, and fill in the resulting dialog box as

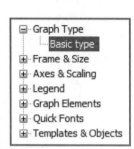
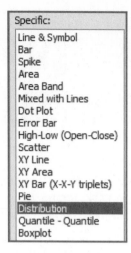
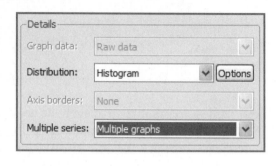

The distribution for b_2 is given below; it resembles that in Figure 5B.2 on page 215 of *POE4*.

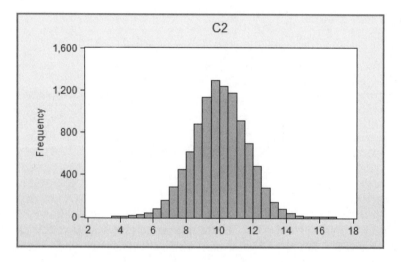

In *POE4* Appendix 5B, a further simulation is carried out to evaluate the finite sample distributions of the nonlinear functions of the coefficients $g_1 = \exp(b_2/10)$ and $g_2 = b_1/b_2$. You might like to see how you would alter the program to include these quantities. Alternatively, you could compute samples of these quantities from the matrix **ESTIMATES**. The following matrix commands will create vectors **G1** and **G2** containing the 10000 values for $g_1 = \exp(b_2/10)$ and $g_2 = b_1/b_2$.

```
vector b1 = @columnextract(estimates,1)
vector b2 = @columnextract(estimates,2)
vector g1 = @exp(b2*(1/10))
vector g2 = @ediv(b1,b2)
```

The function **@columnextract** extracts a column from a matrix and puts it in a vector. The command **g2=@ediv(b1,b2)** asks EViews to divide each element in **b1** by the corresponding element in **b2**, and to store the results in a new vector called **g2**. The following histogram for **G2** resembles that in Figure 5B.4a in *POE4*.

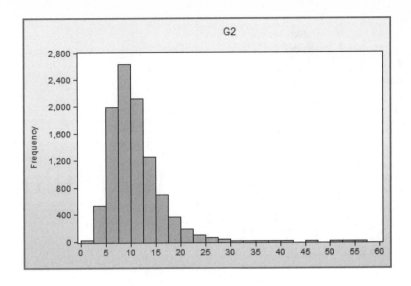

Keywords

@coefs
@columnextract
@ctdist
@ediv
@qtdist
@rchisq
@se
@stderrs
c object
cinterval
coefficient
coefficient tests
commands: saving
covariance matrix
delta method
descriptive statistics
edit +/-
equation name.ls specification
equation specification
estimate equation
for
forecast
forecast sample
forecast standard error
group: naming
group: open

hypothesis testing
interaction variables
interval estimates
least squares
linear combinations
log-linear model
loop
loop index
marginal effects
matrix
Monte Carlo
NA
name.wald specification
next
object: creating
object: equation
object: group
object: name
object: text
page: naming
page: resize
polynomials
proc
program
p-value (Prob.)

quick/estimate equation
quiet
range
range: change
regression output
R-squared
S.D. dependent variable
S.E. of regression
sample
sample: change
scalar
simulation
smpl
spreadsheet
standard errors
Std. Error
test of significance
test: nonzero value
test: one-tail
test: two-tails
t-test
t-value (t-Statistic)
verbose
Wald test
workfile

CHAPTER 6

Further Inference in the Multiple Regression Model

6.1 *F-* AND CHI-SQUARE TESTS

In Chapter 5 we saw how to use EViews to test a null hypothesis about a single coefficient or a single function or combination of coefficients in a regression model. This test can be extended. We may want to test a **joint null hypothesis** that specifies two or more restrictions on two or more coefficients. The choice of test statistic depends on whether the null hypothesis is single or joint and on whether the test is a one-tail test or a two-tail test. One-tail tests are only considered for single null hypotheses. In this case the relevant test statistic is $t_{(N-K)}$. For two-tail tests of single hypotheses, we can use either the test statistic $t_{(N-K)}$ or the statistic $F_{(1,N-K)}$. The tests from each are equivalent because $t_{(N-K)}^2 = F_{(1,N-K)}$. Another test that can be used is a **chi-square test** that uses a **chi-square statistic** with one degree of freedom $\chi_{(1)}^2$. The value of this statistic is identical to $F_{(1,N-K)}$, but the test is different because a different distribution is used to compute the *p*-value. The *F*-test is an exact finite sample test suitable when the equation errors are normally distributed. The χ^2-test is an approximate large sample test that does not require the normality assumption. For joint null hypotheses the *t*-test is no longer suitable, nor do we consider one-tail tests. The alternative hypothesis H_1 is that one or more of the restrictions in H_0 does not hold. We can use the F-test or the χ^2-test depending on whether or not we are invoking the normality assumption. The number of restrictions in H_0 gives the numerator degrees of freedom for the F-statistic and the degrees of freedom for the χ^2-statistic. The two tests are different, but the value of one statistic can be calculated from the other using the relationship $F_{(J, N-K)} = \chi^2_{(J)}/J$. All these different possibilities are summarized in the following table.

Test Statistics for Testing Coefficients in a Multiple Regression Model

Test Type	Null Hypothesis		Statistic	Relationship
	Coefficients	Restrictions		
Single H_0, 1 tail	≥ 1	1	$t_{(N-K)}$	
Single H_0, 2 tails	≥ 1	1	$t_{(N-K)}$ or $F_{(1, N-K)}$ or $\chi^2_{(1)}$	$t^2_{(N-K)} = F_{(1, N-K)} = \chi^2_{(1)}$
Joint H_0	≥ 2	$J \geq 2$	$F_{(J, N-K)}$ or $\chi^2_{(J)}$	$F_{(J, N-K)} = \chi^2_{(J)}/J$

In the first part of this chapter we use Andy's Burger Barn example to demonstrate how these various testing scenarios can be handled within EViews. Our main focus will be on F- and χ^2-tests.

The general formula for the F-value is

$$F = \frac{(SSE_R - SSE_U)/J}{SSE_U/(N-K)}$$

where SSE_R is the sum of squared errors from the model estimated assuming the restrictions in H_0 hold and SSE_U is the sum of squared errors from the unrestricted model. The corresponding χ^2-value is given by $\chi^2 = J \times F$. We can use EViews to compute F and χ^2 and their p-values automatically, or we can use EViews to compute the restricted and unrestricted models, locate SSE_R and SSE_U on the output, and then calculate F and χ^2.

6.1.1 Testing significance: a coefficient

Our first example is to test $H_0 : \beta_2 = 0$ against the alternative $H_1 : \beta_2 \neq 0$ in the model

$$SALES = \beta_1 + \beta_2 PRICE + \beta_3 ADVERT + e$$

In other words, should *PRICE* be included in the equation? We used a t-test to perform this test in Section 5.5.1; we discovered we could read the result directly from the regression output. Let us see how we can do it using F- and χ^2-tests.

Using EViews' test option

Return to the workfile *andy.wf1* and save it as *andy_chap06.wf1*. Estimate the base regression using

equation andy_eq.ls sales c price advert

Open the equation object **ANDY_EQ**. Select **View/Coefficient Diagnostics/Wald Test-Coefficient Restrictions**:

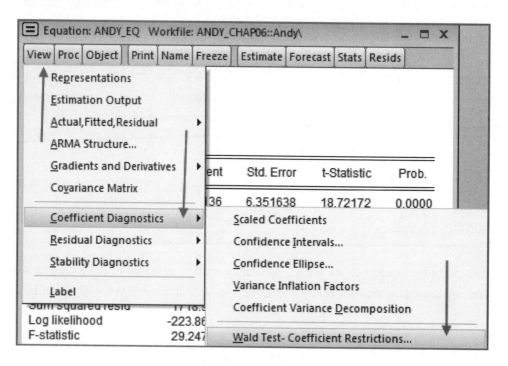

In the dialog box that appears we type the null hypothesis $H_0 : \beta_2 = 0$ as **C(2) = 0**. EViews uses the notation $C(k)$ to denote the coefficient β_k. The order of the coefficients C(1), C(2), C(3),... is the order in which they were specified in the **Equation Estimation** dialog box (and the order in which they appear in the regression output).

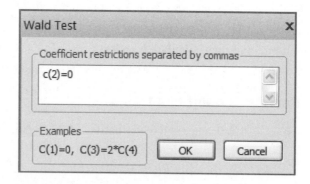

Clicking **OK** yields the output that appears below. The equivalent command is

andy_eq.wald c(2)=0

Wald Test: Equation: ANDY_EQ			
Test Statistic	Value	df	Probability
t-statistic	-7.215241	72	0.0000
F-statistic	52.05971	(1, 72)	0.0000
Chi-square	52.05971	1	0.0000

t-test statistic, F-test statistic, chi-square test statistic

Null Hypothesis: C(2)=0
Null Hypothesis Summary:

Normalized Restriction (= 0)	Value	Std. Err.
C(2)	-7.907854	1.095993

Restrictions are linear in coefficients.

b_2 $se(b_2)$

. You should note the following:

1. The test is called a **Wald test**. The t-test and F-tests on the coefficients of regression equations belong to this class of tests.

2. The **Normalized Restriction (=0)** in the bottom part of the table refers to the null hypothesis rearranged so that the right-hand side of the restriction in H_0 is zero. In this particular example no rearrangement is necessary because the right-hand side of $H_0 : \beta_2 = 0$ is already zero.

3. **Value** and **Std. Err.** of the **Normalized Restriction** refer to the estimated value of the left-hand side of the rearranged H_0 and its standard error. In this case these values are $b_2 = -7.907854$ and $se(b_2) = 1.095993$.

4. The calculated F- and χ^2-values are approximately $F = \chi^2 = 52.06$. They are identical because there is only one restriction in H_0 $(J = 1)$, and they are equal to the square of the t-value for testing this hypothesis. There is a theorem that says a $t_{(v)}$ random variable squared is equal to an $F_{(1,v)}$ random variable. In words, the square of a t random variable with v degrees of freedom is equal to an F random variable with one degree of freedom in the numerator and v degrees of freedom in the denominator. That is,

$$\left(\frac{b_2}{se(b_2)}\right)^2 = \left(\frac{-7.907854}{1.095993}\right)^2 = 52.06$$

5. The degrees of freedom (**df**) are $(1, 72)$ for the F-test and 1 for the χ^2-test.

6. The reported p-values for each of the tests are both 0.0000. Thus, we reject $H_0 : \beta_2 = 0$ at all reasonable significance levels.

Using the formula for F

To perform the test using the formula for F we need the quantities SSE_U and SSE_R. We can read $SSE_U = 1718.943$ from the regression output:

R-squared	0.448258	Mean dependent var	77.37467
Adjusted R-squared	0.432932	S.D. dependent var	6.488537
S.E. of regression	4.886124	Akaike info criterion	6.049854
Sum squared resid	1718.943	Schwarz criterion	6.142553
Log likelihood	-223.8695	Hannan-Quinn criter.	6.086868

After estimation EViews stores this quantity as **@ssr**, short for "sum of squared residuals". Since the text uses SSR for "regression sum of squares", this notation can be confusing. Be careful! We can call it something more familiar by using the EViews command

> **scalar sseu = @ssr**

To find SSE_R we estimate the model under the assumption that $H_0: \beta_2 = 0$ is true. This model is

$$SALES = \beta_1 + \beta_3 ADVERT + e$$

Use the command

> **equation andy_r.ls sales c advert**

Using EViews to estimate this model, we find $SSE_R = 2961.827$ which can be read directly from the regression output:

R-squared	0.049320	Mean dependent var	77.37467
Adjusted R-squared	0.036297	S.D. dependent var	6.488537
S.E. of regression	6.369692	Akaike info criterion	6.567284
Sum squared resid	2961.827	Schwarz criterion	6.629084
Log likelihood	-244.2731	Hannan-Quinn criter.	6.591960

To save this quantity using a convenient name, we use the EViews command

> **scalar sser = @ssr**

Then, the required F-value is given by

> **scalar fval = (sser - sseu)/(sseu/(75-3))**

A check of this calculated value shows it is the same as that obtained using EViews' test option.

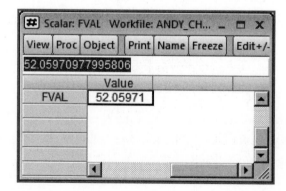

To finalize the test we need either the *p*-value or the critical value. These values can be obtained using EViews commands for the *F* distribution function and the *F* quantile function. For the *p*-value we have

scalar pval = 1 - @cfdist(fval,1,72)

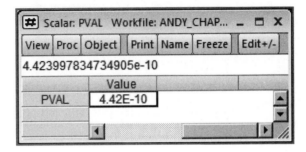

For the critical value we have

scalar fc = @qfdist(0.95,1,72)

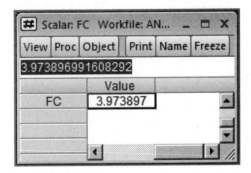

The critical value is equal to the square of the *t* critical value: $F_c = 3.9739 = t_c^2 = 1.99346^2$

What about the χ^2-test? The χ^2-value is the same as the *F*, that is, $\chi^2 = 52.06$. Its *p* and critical values can be found using the EViews commands for the χ^2 distribution function and the χ^2 quantile function:

scalar pvalchi = 1 - @cchisq(fval,1)

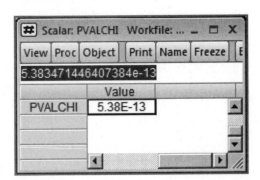

scalar chic = @qchisq(0.95,1)

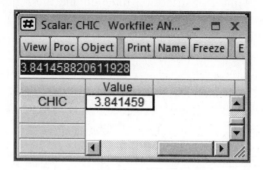

Note that the p-values from the F- and χ^2-tests are different, although the test conclusion is clearly the same.

6.1.2 Testing significance: the model

The F-test for testing the significance of a model is given special prominence in the regression output. In the context of Andy's Burger Barn the hypotheses for this test are

$$H_0 : \beta_2 = 0 \text{ and } \beta_3 = 0 \qquad H_1 : \beta_2 \neq 0 \text{ and/or } \beta_3 \neq 0$$

The null hypothesis is a joint one because there are two restrictions, $\beta_2 = 0$ and $\beta_3 = 0$. The restricted model that assumes H_0 is true is

$$SALES = \beta_1 + e$$

Estimate this restricted model using

equation andy_null.ls sales c

This model has no explanatory variables. The sum of squared errors for the restricted model is given in the regression output as

Variable	Coefficient	Std. Error	t-Statistic	Prob.
C	77.37467	0.749232	103.2720	0.0000

R-squared	0.000000	Mean dependent var	77.37467
Adjusted R-squared	0.000000	S.D. dependent var	6.488537
S.E. of regression	6.488537	Akaike info criterion	6.591195
Sum squared resid	3115.482	Schwarz criterion	6.622095
Log likelihood	-246.1698	Hannan-Quinn criter.	6.603533

Note the restricted least squares estimator for β_1 is the sample mean for *SALES*. The sum of squared residuals in this case is

$$SSE_R = \sum \left(y_i - b_1 \right)^2 = \sum \left(y_i - \overline{y} \right)^2 = SST = 3115.482$$

This quantity is also called the Total Sum of Squares, or *TSS* or *SST*. The total sum of squares for a series y is given by

$$SST = \sum (y_i - \bar{y})^2 = \sum y_i^2 - N\bar{y}^2$$

It is equal to the sum of squared deviations of *SALES* around its mean.

Testing the significance of a model is equivalent to testing whether any of the explanatory variables influences the dependent variable. The sum of squared errors for the unrestricted model is the same as before, $SSE_U = 1718.943$. Using this information, a sequence of EViews commands that computes the required F-value and its p-value are

```
scalar sst = @ssr
scalar f_model = ((sst - sseu)/2)/(sseu/(75-3))
scalar p_model = 1 - @cfdist(f_model,2,72)
```

which yields

	Value		Value
F_MODEL	29.24786	P_MODEL	5.04E-10

In practice there is no need to go through this sequence of calculations. The F- and p-values are automatically reported on the **ANDY_EQ** regression output:

R-squared	0.448258	Mean dependent var	77.37467
Adjusted R-squared	0.432932	S.D. dependent var	6.488537
S.E. of regression	4.886124	Akaike info criterion	6.049854
Sum squared resid	1718.943	Schwarz criterion	6.142553
Log likelihood	-223.8695	Hannan-Quinn criter.	6.086868
F-statistic	29.24786	Durbin-Watson stat	2.183037
Prob(F-statistic)	0.000000		

The test result can also be obtained using the command

```
andy_eq.wald c(2)=0, c(3)=0
```

Wald Test:
Equation: ANDY_EQ

Test Statistic	Value	df	Probability
F-statistic	29.24786	(2, 72)	0.0000
Chi-square	58.49572	2	0.0000

The corresponding chi-square value is given by $\chi^2 = J \times F = 2 \times 29.24786 = 58.49572$.

6.2 TESTING IN AN EXTENDED MODEL

Andy's Burger Barn model is extended to also include the square of advertising expenditure as one of the explanatory variables. The new model is

$$SALES = \beta_1 + \beta_2 PRICE + \beta_3 ADVERT + \beta_4 ADVERT^2 + e$$

Estimate this model as we did in Chapter 5 of this manual, using

equation andy_quad.ls sales c price advert advert^2

Variable	Coefficient	Std. Error	t-Statistic	Prob.
C	109.7190	6.799045	16.13742	0.0000
PRICE	-7.640000	1.045939	-7.304442	0.0000
ADVERT	12.15124	3.556164	3.416950	0.0011
ADVERT^2	-2.767963	0.940624	-2.942688	0.0044

6.2.1 Testing: a joint H_0, two coefficients

Since advertising appears twice in the equation, as $ADVERT$ and as $ADVERT^2$, to test whether advertising has an effect on sales we need to test $H_0 : \beta_3 = 0$ and $\beta_4 = 0$ against the alternative $H_1 : \beta_3 \neq 0$ and/or $\beta_4 \neq 0$. The null hypothesis is called a joint null hypothesis because it contains two restrictions. To obtain the test result, use in the regression object **ANDY_QUAD**, **View/Coefficient Diagnostics/Wald Test-Coefficient Restrictions** and test **c(3)=0, c(4)=0**. Alternatively,

andy_quad.wald c(3)=0, c(4)=0

Wald Test:
Equation: ANDY_QUAD

Test Statistic	Value	df	Probability
F-statistic	8.441360	(2, 71)	0.0005
Chi-square	16.88272	2	0.0002

Null Hypothesis: C(3)=0, C(4)=0

The above output contains the following information:

1. The calculated F- and χ^2-values for testing H_0 are $F = 8.441$ and $\chi^2 = 16.883$. Because there are two restrictions, $\chi^2 = 2 \times F$.

2. The degrees of freedom (**df**) are (2,71) for the F-test and 2 for the χ^2-test.

3. The reported p-values for F- and χ^2-tests are 0.0005 and 0.0002, respectively. Thus, we reject $H_0 : \beta_3 = 0$ and $\beta_4 = 0$ at all conventional significance levels.

6.2.2 Testing: a single H_0, two coefficients

On pages 229-230 of *POE4* both a *t*-test and an *F*-test are used to test whether $ADVERT = 1.9$ is the optimal level of advertising. We will show how EViews automatic commands can be used to perform *F*- and χ^2-tests and how, along the way, information for the *t*-test is produced. Performing the *t*-test requires one to compute the standard error for a linear function of two coefficients. We illustrate how this value can be read from the EViews test output as well as how to calculate it from the EViews coefficient covariance matrix.

The null and alternative hypotheses are

$$H_0 : \beta_3 + 3.8\beta_4 = 1 \qquad\qquad H_1 : \beta_3 + 3.8\beta_4 \neq 1$$

The Wald command is

andy_quad.wald c(3)+3.8*c(4)=1

```
Wald Test:
Equation: ANDY_QUAD

Test Statistic        Value         df        Probability

t-statistic          0.967572        71          0.3365
F-statistic          0.936195      (1, 71)       0.3365
Chi-square           0.936195        1           0.3333


Null Hypothesis: C(3)+3.8*C(4)=1
Null Hypothesis Summary:

Normalized Restriction (= 0)        Value        Std. Err.

-1 + C(3) + 3.8*C(4)               0.632976      0.654190

Restrictions are linear in coefficients.
```

To write $H_0 : \beta_3 + 3.8\beta_4 = 1$ as a **Normalized Restriction (=0)**, EViews moves 1 from the right-hand side to the left-hand side, giving the normalization $H_0 : -1 + \beta_3 + 3.8\beta_4 = 0$. **Value** is an estimate of the left-hand side, namely $-1 + b_3 + 3.8b_4 = 0.632976$. **Std. Err.** refers to $se(-1 + b_3 + 3.8b_4) = 0.65419$. It is calculated by EViews using the formula

$$se(-1 + b_3 + 3.8b_4) = \sqrt{\widehat{\text{var}(b_3 + 3.8b_4)}}$$

$$= \sqrt{\widehat{\text{var}(b_3)} + 3.8^2 \times \widehat{\text{var}(b_4)} + 2 \times 3.8 \times \widehat{\text{cov}(b_3, b_4)}}$$

The calculated *F*- and χ^2-values for testing H_0 are $F = \chi^2 = 0.9362$. They are both the same because there is only one restriction. The degrees of freedom (**df**) are (1,71) for the *F*-test and 1 for the χ^2-test. The reported *p*-values for *F*- and χ^2-tests are 0.3363 and 0.3333, respectively. Thus, we do not reject H_0 at a 5% significance level. The *p*-value for the *F*-test can be confirmed with the command

scalar pval_fopt = 1 - @cfdist(0.936195, 1,71)

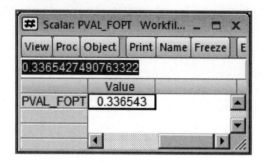

Similarly the p for the chi-square test is

scalar pval_chiopt = 1 - @cchisq(0.936195, 1)

Notice that the EViews output also gives enough information to perform a t-test manually. The required test value is given by

$$t = \frac{\textbf{Value}}{\textbf{Std. Err.}} = \frac{0.632976}{0.654190} = 0.9676$$

Because $t^2 = 0.9676^2 = 0.936 = F$, for a two-tail test there is no need to consider both t-and F-tests. Both give the same result. However, the information for the t-test is useful for one-tail tests.

Standard error for a linear function of coefficients

It is instructive to see how to compute the standard error $se(b_3 + 3.8b_4) = 0.65419$ from the least squares covariance matrix. After estimating the equation for the quadratic model and saving it as the equation object **ANDY_QUAD**, the covariance matrix for the least squares estimates is stored as a symmetric matrix called **andy_quad.@cov**. A symmetric matrix is a square array of numbers where the values above the diagonal are equal to the corresponding ones below the diagonal. If the columns are made rows and the rows are made columns, we get the same array. A covariance matrix is always symmetric because $cov(b_k, b_\ell) = cov(b_\ell, b_k)$ for any two coefficients b_ℓ and b_k. EViews refers to symmetric matrix objects as **sym**. Thus, to list the least squares covariance matrix in our workfile with the name **covb**, we use the command

sym covb = andy_quad.@cov

The command to compute $\widehat{var(b_3 + 3.8b_4)} = \widehat{var(b_3)} + 3.8^2 \times \widehat{var(b_4)} + 2 \times 3.8 \times \widehat{cov(b_3, b_4)}$ and save it in the workfile with name **var_lincom** is

scalar var_lincom = covb(3,3) + 3.8^2*covb(4,4) + 2*3.8*covb(3,4)

and the standard error, called **se_lincom**, is

scalar se_lincom = @sqrt(var_lincom)

Following these steps will give the value $se(b_3 + 3.8b_4) = 0.65419$.

Using restricted and unrestricted SSE

On page 229 in *POE4*, the *F*-value for testing the optimality of advertising expenditure is computed using SSE_U and SSE_R. As we have seen, it is more easily computed using the EViews automatic test option. Nevertheless, we will show you how the values for SSE_U and SSE_R can be obtained. The value $SSE_U = 1532.084$ is located from the output for **ANDY_QUAD**.

R-squared	0.508235	Mean dependent var	77.37467
Adjusted R-squared	0.487456	S.D. dependent var	6.488537
S.E. of regression	4.645283	Akaike info criterion	5.961440
Sum squared resid	1532.084	Schwarz criterion	6.085039
Log likelihood	-219.5540	Hannan-Quinn criter.	6.010792

The value $SSE_R = 1552.286$ is obtained by estimating the model

$$(SALES - ADVERT) = \beta_1 + \beta_2 PRICE + \beta_4 (ADVERT^2 - 3.8 \times ADVERT) + e$$

To estimate this model we use the following command:

equation andy_quad_r.ls (sales-advert) c price (advert^2-3.8*advert)

R-squared	0.480719	Mean dependent var	75.53067
Adjusted R-squared	0.466295	S.D. dependent var	6.355780
S.E. of regression	4.643224	Akaike info criterion	5.947873
Sum squared resid	1552.286	Schwarz criterion	6.040573
Log likelihood	-220.0452	Hannan-Quinn criter.	5.984887

6.2.3 Testing: a joint H_0, four coefficients

The final example of a test using the extended hamburger model is on pages 230-231 of *POE4*. Here we are concerned with testing the joint null hypothesis

$$H_0 : \beta_3 + 3.8\beta_4 = 1 \quad \text{and} \quad \beta_1 + 6\beta_2 + 1.9\beta_3 + 3.61\beta_4 = 80$$

They are entered in the **Wald Test** command:

andy_quad.wald c(3)+3.8*c(4)=1, c(1)+6*c(2)+1.9*c(3)+3.61*c(4)=80

In the output that follows, EViews has written these restrictions in the normalized formats $-1 + \beta_3 + 3.8\beta_4 = 0$ and $-80 + \beta_1 + 6\beta_2 + 1.9\beta_3 + 3.61\beta_4 = 0$. Note that the EViews output has abbreviated the latter of these two restrictions. Their estimated values and the corresponding standard errors found in the bottom part of the output are

$$-1 + b_3 + 3.8b_4 = 0.632976 \qquad \text{se}(b_3 + 3.8b_4) = 0.65419$$

$$-80 + b_1 + 6b_2 + 1.9b_3 + 3.61b_4 = -3.025963 \qquad \text{se}(b_1 + 6b_2 + 1.9b_3 + 3.61b_4) = 0.917713$$

As expected, the values for the restriction considered in the previous section have not changed. The test values $F = 5.7413$ and $\chi^2 = 11.482$, and their respective p-values of 0.0049 and 0.0032, lead to rejection of H_0 at a 5% significance level.

```
Wald Test:
Equation: ANDY_QUAD
```

Test Statistic	Value	df	Probability
F-statistic	5.741229	(2, 71)	0.0049
Chi-square	11.48246	2	0.0032

Null Hypothesis: C(3)+3.8*C(4)=1, C(1)+6*C(2)+1.9*C(3)
　　　　+3.61*C(4)=80
Null Hypothesis Summary:

Normalized Restriction (= 0)	Value	Std. Err.
-1 + C(3) + 3.8*C(4)	0.632976	0.654190
-80 + C(1) + 6*C(2) + 1.9*C(3) ...	-3.025963	0.917713

Restrictions are linear in coefficients.

6.2.4 Comparing joint and individual tests

It is sometimes difficult for students to grasp the difference between a joint test of hypotheses and individual tests of those hypotheses. In the context of Andy's Burger Barn we considered the quadratic model

$$SALES = \beta_1 + \beta_2 PRICE + \beta_3 ADVERT + \beta_4 ADVERT^2 + e$$

To test the significance of advertising we employed the joint hypothesis test for the null and alternative hypotheses:

$$H_0 : \beta_3 = 0 \text{ and } \beta_4 = 0 \quad H_1 : \beta_3 \neq 0 \text{ and/or } \beta_4 \neq 0$$

We now look at the difference between this joint hypothesis and the two individual hypotheses

$$H_0 : \beta_3 = 0 \text{ versus } H_1 : \beta_3 \neq 0 \text{ and } H_0 : \beta_4 = 0 \text{ versus } H_1 : \beta_4 \neq 0$$

One difference is of course that the joint test uses a F-test statistic, and the two individual tests are normally carried out using t-tests. But there is actually more to it than that. To explain we employ a graphical device related to interval estimation.

In the multiple regression model, using assumptions MR1-MR6 given on page 173 of *POE4*, we know that

$$t = \frac{b_k - \beta_k}{\text{se}(b_k)} \sim t_{(N-K)}$$

Using this fact, and letting $t_c = t_{(1-\alpha/2, N-K)}$ be the $1 - \alpha / 2$ percentile of the $t_{(N-K)}$ distribution, we construct the $100(1-\alpha)\%$ interval estimator

$$P\left[-t_c \le \frac{b_k - \beta_k}{\text{se}(b_k)} \le t_c\right] = P\left[b_k - t_c \text{se}(b_k) \le \beta_k \le b_k + t_c \text{se}(b_k)\right] = 1 - \alpha$$

The interval estimate is

$$\left[b_k - t_c \text{se}(b_k), b_k + t_c \text{se}(b_k)\right] \tag{6.1}$$

Similarly, we use the t-statistic to test the null hypothesis $H_0 : \beta_k = c_k$ versus $H_1 : \beta_k \ne c_k$. The test statistic is $t_k = (b_k - c_k)/\text{se}(b_k)$. We reject the null hypothesis if t_k falls in the rejection region, that is, if $t_k \ge t_{(1-\alpha/2, N-K)} = t_c$ or if $t_k \le t_{(\alpha/2, N-K)} = -t_{(1-\alpha/2, N-K)} = -t_c$. We fail to reject the null hypothesis if

$$-t_c \le \frac{b_k - c}{\text{se}(b_k)} \le t_c \Rightarrow b_k - t_c \text{se}(b_k) \le c_k \le b_k + t_c \text{se}(b_k) \tag{6.2}$$

Compare equation (6.1) to equation (6.2). Equation (6.2) shows that we will fail to reject the null hypothesis $H_0 : \beta_k = c_k$ versus the two-tail alternative $H_1 : \beta_k \ne c_k$ at the α level of significance if the hypothesized value c_k falls within the $100(1-\alpha)\%$ interval estimate given in equation (6.1). This is a handy trick, because it means you can immediately make a conclusion about a two-tail hypothesis test by seeing if the hypothesized value falls in the corresponding interval estimate. Sometimes we say "if the interval estimate **covers** the hypothesized value."

Return now to the regression object **ANDY_QUAD** and select **View/Coefficient Diagnostics/Confidence Ellipse:**

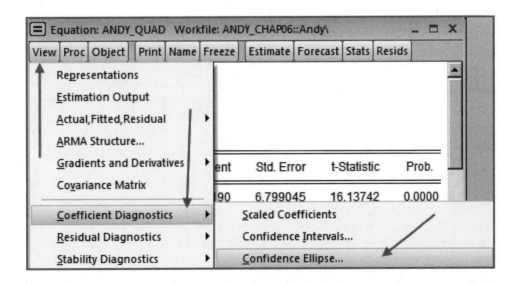

Fill in the resulting dialog box as shown on the next page:

The resulting figure is

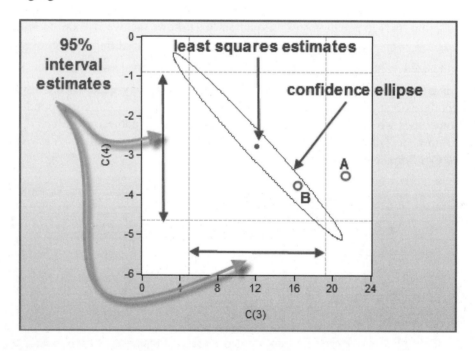

This interesting figure has a 95% interval estimate for β_3 on the horizontal axis and a 95% interval estimate for β_4 on the vertical axis. The interval estimates are shown as dotted lines. Using the figure it is easy to see, for example, that if we test β_3 equaling 8, 12, or 18 we will fail to reject at the 5% level of significance, since these values fall within the dotted lines representing the 95% interval estimate on the horizontal axis. Similarly, we see that if we test β_3 equaling 0, 4 or 20, we will reject the null hypothesis at the 5% level of significance since these values fall outside the 95% interval estimate on the horizontal axis.

The square formed by the dotted lines represents the area the two interval estimates have in common .The "dot" in the center identifies the location of the two point estimates $b_3 = C(3)$ and $b_4 = C(4)$.

The ellipse is a joint 95% confidence region. The theory behind the ellipse is advanced and involves matrix algebra; it is given in an appendix to this chapter. But the point now is that this joint confidence region works just like the individual coefficient interval estimates. The region covered by the ellipse is our 95% interval region of the parameter pair (β_3, β_4). We can use the ellipse to illustrate joint hypothesis tests. Just as in the individual interval estimates, any point "covered" by the ellipse represents a pair of values that will not be rejected in a joint F-test at the 5% level of significance. Thus, the pair of values represented by point **B** in the figure would not be rejected by a joint test. However the pair of values represented by point **A**, say a_3 on the horizontal axis and a_4 on the vertical axis, would be rejected at the 5% level using a joint test. The point **A** is a pair of values that is unlikely given our data.

On the other hand, at point **A**, if we performed individual t-tests using the 5% level of significance, we would fail to reject the hypothesis $\beta_4 = a_4$, but we would reject the hypothesis $\beta_3 = a_3$, using two-tail tests at the 5% significance level. There are many such points of disagreement between the joint test and two t-tests. The reason for the conflict is that a joint test is examining likely and unlikely **pairs** of values, while the t-test is concerned with only one coefficient at a time.

The shape of the ellipse is long and slender in this example. This has to do with the presence of collinearity between $ADVERT$ and $ADVERT^2$. We will discuss this further in Section 6.4 of this chapter.

Now you can save the workfile ***andy_chap06.wf1*** and close it. We will use it again before the end of this chapter.

6.3 MODEL SPECIFICATION

When specifying a regression model all relevant explanatory variables should be included. Here we investigate what happens (1) when we omit relevant variables or (2) include irrelevant variables. An adequate model specification also includes choosing a functional form that can account for nonlinearities in the relationship between dependent and independent variables. As an example we use the data in the workfile ***edu_inc.wf1***. Open this data file and save it as ***edu_inc_chap06.wf1***. There are 428 observations on:

FAMINC	= Family income in 2006 dollars
HEDU	= Husband's educational attainment, in years
WEDU	= Wife's educational attainment, in years
KL6	= Number of children less than 6 years old in household
XTRA_X5	= an artificially generated irrelevant variables.
XTRA_X6	= a second artificially generated irrelevant variable.

> **Remark: Early distributions of this file had variables *HE* and *WE* instead of *HEDU* and *WEDU*. To correct name, highlight, then right-click to rename.**

We consider several estimations to illustrate the consequences of omitting relevant variables and including irrelevant ones. Issue the following estimation command:

equation base.ls faminc c hedu wedu

The first estimation, **BASE**, shows the estimates

Variable	Coefficient	Std. Error	t-Statistic	Prob.
C	-5533.629	11229.53	-0.492775	0.6224
HEDU	3131.509	802.9080	3.900209	0.0001
WEDU	4522.641	1066.327	4.241328	0.0000
R-squared	0.161300	Mean dependent var		91213.00
Adjusted R-squared	0.157354	S.D. dependent var		44117.35
S.E. of regression	40497.86	Akaike info criterion		24.06287
Sum squared resid	6.97E+11	Schwarz criterion		24.09132

The coefficients of *HEDU* and *WEDU* are positive and significant as would be expected. Among the summary statistics below the estimates are:

1. The model **R-squared** is 0.1613. This measure increases when variables are added.
2. The **Adjusted R-Squared** is 0.1574. It is a goodness-of-fit type measure that imposes a "penalty" for adding additional variables, which, while reducing *SSE,* also reduces $(N-K)$, meaning that the **Adjusted R-Squared** does not necessarily increase when a variable is added. It is calculated using

$$\bar{R}^2 = 1 - \frac{SSE/(N-K)}{SST/(N-1)}$$

3. **Akaike information criterion** (AIC) is 24.06287. This value is computed using equation (6.26) in *POE4* plus the extra amount $1+\log(2\pi)$, which is constant and does not affect any judgments based on AIC. It is also a penalized goodness-of-fit measure, with the penalty taking a different form. A smaller AIC indicates a better fit:

$$AIC = \log\left(\frac{SSE}{N}\right) + \frac{2K}{N} + 1 + \log(2\pi)$$

Following estimation of the **BASE** model, compute AIC using

scalar aic_base = log(@ssr/428) + 2*3/428 + 1+ log(2*3.14159)

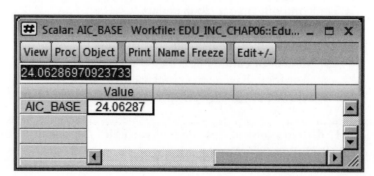

4. The Schwartz criterion (SC), also known as the Bayesian information criterion (BIC), is 24.09132. It is computed using equation (6.27) in *POE4* plus the extra amount $1 + \log(2\pi)$. It is similar to AIC in that a smaller value is preferred.

$$SC = \log\left(\frac{SSE}{N}\right) + \frac{K\log(N)}{N} + 1 + \log(2\pi)$$

Following the estimation of the **BASE** equation, compute SC using

scalar sc_base = log(@ssr/428) + 3*log(428)/428 + 1+ log(2*3.14159)

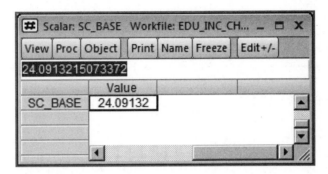

Now estimate the other three specifications discussed in *POE4* on pages 234-236. First, estimate the **BASE** model omitting *WEDU*:

equation omit_wedu.ls faminc c hedu

Variable	Coefficient	Std. Error	t-Statistic	Prob.
C	26191.27	8541.108	3.066495	0.0023
HEDU	5155.483	658.4574	7.829639	0.0000

R-squared	0.125801	Mean dependent var	91213.00
Adjusted R-squared	0.123749	S.D. dependent var	44117.35
S.E. of regression	41297.49	Akaike info criterion	24.09965
Sum squared resid	7.27E+11	Schwarz criterion	24.11862

The estimated coefficient of *HEDU* has increased because of the omission of the relevant variable *WEDU*. The bias in the estimation of the coefficient of *HEDU* is given by *POE4* equation (6.23),

$$bias\left(b_2^*\right) = E\left(b_2^*\right) - \beta_2 = \beta_3 \frac{\widehat{\operatorname{cov}}(x_2, x_3)}{\widehat{\operatorname{var}}(x_2)}$$

The direction of the bias is determined by the sign of the coefficient of the omitted variable, which we suspect is positive, and the sign of the covariance, or correlation between *HEDU* and *WEDU*, which is positive. Thus omitting *WEDU* from the equation biases the coefficient of *HEDU* upwards.

To find the correlations among the variables in the data set, select each of the variables by clicking while holding down the **Ctrl** key. Then double-click inside the shaded area, then **Open Group:**

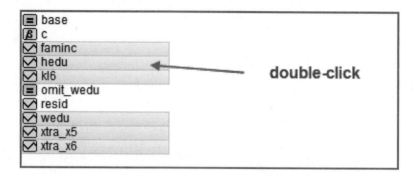

Select **View/Covariance Analysis** from the menu in the spreadsheet.

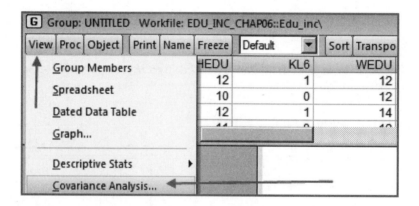

In the **Statistics** panel, un-tick **Covariance** and tick **Correlation**.

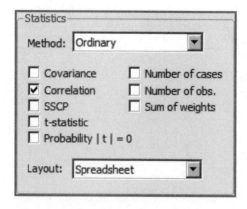

Select **OK** to produce the correlation matrix shown below. Note that the correlation between *HEDU* and *WEDU* is about 0.59, a positive correlation.

	Correlation					
	FAMINC	HEDU	KL6	WEDU	XTRA_X5	XTRA_X6
FAMINC	1.000000	0.354684	-0.071956	0.362328	0.289817	0.351366
HEDU	0.354684	1.000000	0.104877	0.594343	0.836168	0.820563
KL6	-0.071956	0.104877	1.000000	0.129340	0.148742	0.159522
WEDU	0.362328	0.594343	0.129340	1.000000	0.517798	0.799306
XTRA_X5	0.289817	0.836168	0.148742	0.517798	1.000000	0.900206
XTRA_X6	0.351366	0.820563	0.159522	0.799306	0.900206	1.000000

Now to the **BASE** model add the variable *KL6*:

equation add_kl6.ls faminc c hedu wedu kl6

Variable	Coefficient	Std. Error	t-Statistic	Prob.
C	-7755.330	11162.93	-0.694739	0.4876
HEDU	3211.526	796.7026	4.031022	0.0001
WEDU	4776.907	1061.164	4.501574	0.0000
KL6	-14310.92	5003.928	-2.859937	0.0044

R-squared	0.177173	Mean dependent var	91213.00
Adjusted R-squared	0.171351	S.D. dependent var	44117.35
S.E. of regression	40160.08	Akaike info criterion	24.04844
Sum squared resid	6.84E+11	Schwarz criterion	24.08637

Compared to the **BASE** regression, the estimates here for the effects of *HEDU* and *WEDU* have changed very little. The **BASE** regression does not suffer much from omitted variables bias because *KL6* is only weakly correlated to *HEDU* (0.10) and *WEDU* (0.13).

Finally, add the two extra irrelevant variables:

equation extra.ls faminc c hedu wedu kl6 xtra_x5 xtra_x6

Variable	Coefficient	Std. Error	t-Statistic	Prob.
C	-7558.613	11195.41	-0.675153	0.4999
HEDU	3339.792	1250.039	2.671750	0.0078
WEDU	5868.677	2278.067	2.576165	0.0103
KL6	-14200.18	5043.720	-2.815419	0.0051
XTRA_X5	888.8426	2242.491	0.396364	0.6920
XTRA_X6	-1067.186	1981.685	-0.538524	0.5905

R-squared	0.177796	Mean dependent var	91213.00
Adjusted R-squared	0.168055	S.D. dependent var	44117.35
S.E. of regression	40239.89	Akaike info criterion	24.05702
Sum squared resid	6.83E+11	Schwarz criterion	24.11393

Note that the **R-squared** has increased for this model relative to **ADD_KL6** but the **Adjusted R-squared**, **AIC**, and **SC** have gone down, indicating that the improvement in fit does not compensate for the addition of the extra variables. Also note that the extra variables are not statistically significant, but their inclusion has greatly increased the standard errors of the coefficients of *HEDU* and *WEDU*. The reason for this is collinearity, which we discuss later in this chapter.

6.3.1 RESET

The regression specification test, commonly abbreviated RESET, is designed to detect an incorrect functional form, such as when a linear relationship is fitted to curvilinear data. However it will also detect omitted variables. Thus it is a rather broad diagnostic test. It works by augmenting a model with powers, usually the 2nd, 3rd, and perhaps 4th, of the model fitted values, $\hat{y}^2, \hat{y}^3, \hat{y}^4$. In a well specified equation these extra variables should have no explanatory power. RESET includes one or more of these variables and tests their joint significance using an *F*-test, or a *t*-test if only a single power is included.

   This test is built into EViews. For example, open the regression object **OMIT_WEDU**. Then, select **View/Stability Diagnostics/Ramsey RESET test**. It is named "Ramsey RESET test" after its developer James Ramsey.

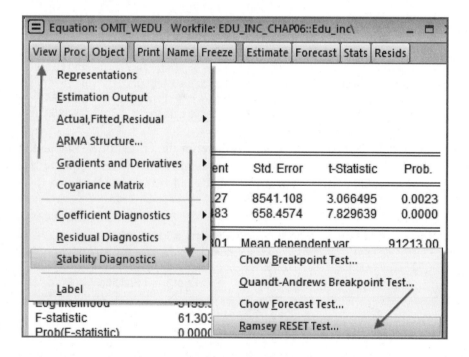

In the resulting dialog box enter the number of fitted terms: 1 for $\hat{y}^2$, 2 for $\hat{y}^2, \hat{y}^3$ and 3 for $\hat{y}^2, \hat{y}^3, \hat{y}^4$. Here we choose "2".

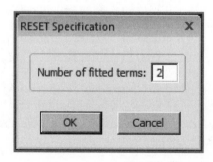

Quite a bit of output is produced, but the most relevant portion is the F-test statistic for the joint significance of $\hat{y}^2, \hat{y}^3$:

Ramsey RESET Test
Equation: OMIT_WEDU
Specification: FAMINC C HEDU
Omitted Variables: Powers of fitted values from 2 to 3

	Value	df	Probability
F-statistic	4.979882	(2, 424)	0.0073

We reject the joint insignificance of these variables based on the low p-value, and conclude that the estimated equation has some problem: an incorrect functional form and/or omitted variables. In practice, carry out the test using two, three, and four fitted terms. If a problem is detected the diagnostic test does not give any clear advice about what to do, other than to re-examine the specification.

6.4 COLLINEARITY

The consequences of collinearity are discussed in Chapter 6.4 of *POE4*. Collinearity refers to intercorrelations and/or other associations among the explanatory variables in a model. In the workfile **educ_inc_chap06.wf1** we examined the correlations among the variables in the data set. Note that *HEDU* and *WEDU* have a correlation of about 0.60. This is a pairwise association, and these two variables are said to be collinear. Most economic variables are correlated with one another to some degree, so the question will be if this pairwise correlation is strong enough to be harmful to our least squares estimation.

Also note that *XTRA_X5* is correlated with *XTRA_X6* and with *HEDU* and *WEDU*. Similarly, *XTRA_X6* is correlated with *XTRA_X5* and quite strongly with *HEDU* and *WEDU*. Correlations only measure pairwise associations, and it is not uncommon for there to be more general interrelationships among the variables, creating "multicollinearities." One way to diagnose these more general relationships is to estimate so-called **auxiliary regressions**, which have an explanatory variable as dependent variable and all other explanatory variables on the right-hand side. For example, regress *WEDU* on all remaining explanatory variables:

equation aux_wedu.ls wedu c hedu kl6 xtra_x5 xtra_x6

Variable	Coefficient	Std. Error	t-Statistic	Prob.
C	1.438114	0.228488	6.294044	0.0000
HEDU	0.115784	0.026079	4.439696	0.0000
KL6	0.070061	0.107596	0.651150	0.5153
XTRA_X5	-0.762312	0.030282	-25.17376	0.0000
XTRA_X6	0.769175	0.019756	38.93423	0.0000
R-squared	0.860094	Mean dependent var		12.65888

These results are interesting in two regards. First, the **R-squared** is 0.86, meaning that 86% of the variation in *WEDU* is explained by the remaining explanatory variables. A general rule of thumb is that if the R-squared from the auxiliary regression is above 0.80 you may have cause for concern. Second, we see specifically that *HEDU, XTRA_X5,* and *XTRA_X6* seem significantly related to *WEDU*, suggesting an intercorrelation among those variables. This means that in the regression object **EXTRA** we can expect that isolating the effect of *WEDU* on *FAMINC* may be difficult. Another reason this goodness-of-fit measure is useful is that the estimated variance of the coefficient of *WEDU* is

$$\widehat{\text{var}}\left(b_{WEDU}\right) = \frac{\hat{\sigma}^2}{\left(1 - R_{WEDU.}^2\right)\sum\left(WEDU_i - \overline{WEDU}\right)^2}$$

The first term in the denominator is 1 minus the R-squared from the auxiliary regression. This expression shows that if this R-squared were zero, then the estimated variance would depend only on the estimated error variance and the sum of squared deviations of *WEDU* about its mean, which would be the same expression as in the simple regression model. The **variance inflation factor** (VIF) measures how the presence of intercorrelations increases estimator variance from what it would be in an ideal world, in which regressors are uncorrelated.

$$\text{VIF}\left(b_{WEDU}\right) = \frac{1}{\left(1 - R_{WEDU.}^2\right)}$$

The VIF factors are available in EViews. In the regression object **EXTRA** select **View/ Coefficient Diagnostics/Variance Inflation Factors**.

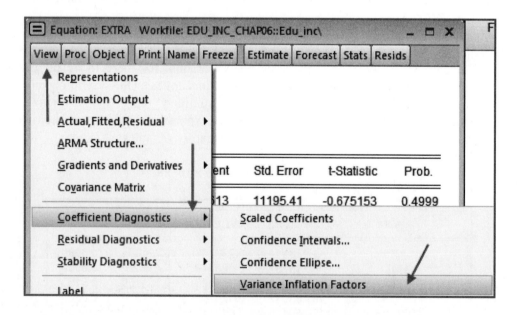

In the following output, **Centered VIF** $= \text{VIF}\left(b_{WEDU}\right) \cong 1/\left(1 - 0.860094\right) = 7.148$.

Variance Inflation Factors
Date: 06/10/11   Time: 10:12
Sample: 1 428
Included observations: 428

Variable	Coefficient Variance	Uncentered VIF	Centered VIF
C	1.25E+08	33.12915	NA
HEDU	1562598.	69.49455	3.795997
WEDU	5189590.	226.9608	7.147639
KL6	25439108	1.162572	1.030429
XTRA_X5	5028766.	225.5953	15.57809
XTRA_X6	3927077.	682.1862	26.43263

The exact calculation following estimation of the auxiliary regression is

scalar auxr2=1-@ssr/((@regobs-1)*(@sddep)^2)
scalar vif_wedu = 1/(1-auxr2)

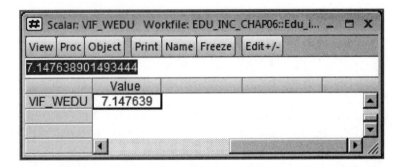

Another indication of the presence of collinearity and its consequences can be obtained by examining confidence ellipses for pairs of coefficients. In the regression object **EXTRA,** select **View/Coefficient Diagnostics/Confidence Ellipse**. In the dialog box enter

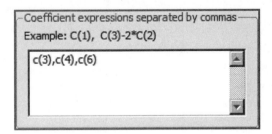

Recall that C(3) is the coefficient of *WEDU*, C(4) is the coefficient of *KL6* and C(6) is the coefficient of *XTRA_X6*.

More circular confidence ellipses result for pairs of coefficients for relatively uncorrelated variables. For example, in the following figure the coefficient C(4) is the coefficient of *KL6*, and this variable is relatively uncorrelated with the rest. However, C(6) is the coefficient of *XTRA_X6,* which is highly correlated with *WEDU*, whose coefficient is C(3). The elongated ellipse means that many pairs of values that are jointly significant will be insignificant when tested individually, which is a symptom of and a consequence of collinearity.

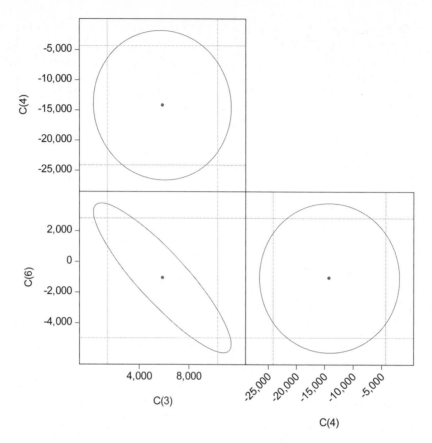

EViews offers another set of advanced collinearity diagnostics. In a regression window choose **View/Coefficient Diagnostics/Coefficient Variance Decomposition**. The analysis is a modification of that introduced in Belsley, Kuh and Welsch (1980), *Regression Diagnostics*, New York: John Wiley & Sons. The analysis of Belsley, Kuh and Welsch is discussed in Chapter 21 of *Introduction to the Theory and Practice of Econometrics, Second Edition*, by Judge et al., John Wiley & Sons, 1988.

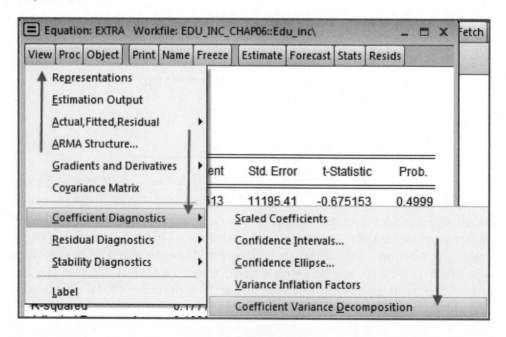

Discussions of collinearity tend to be heated and frustrating since there is little most practicing economists can do about it; we use non-experimental data, with a design not of our choosing. At the end of the day, the only thing that matters is whether estimation is sufficiently precise for the results to be usefully applied and/or interpreted. One available tool for counteracting the effects of collinearity is the use of nonsample information, discussed in the following section.

6.5 INCLUDING NONSAMPLE INFORMATION

The model used on page 231 of *POE4* to illustrate the inclusion of nonsample information is the demand for beer equation

$$\ln(Q) = \beta_1 + \beta_2 \ln(PB) + \beta_3 \ln(PL) + \beta_4 \ln(PR) + \beta_5 \ln(I) + e$$

where Q is quantity demanded, PB is the price of beer, PL is the price of liquor, PR is the price of remaining goods and services, and I is income. The data are stored in the file *beer.wf1*. The nonsample information that economic agents do not suffer from "money illusion" can be expressed as

$$\beta_4 = -\beta_2 - \beta_3 - \beta_5$$

Restricted least squares estimates of the coefficients that satisfy this restriction incorporate the nonsample information. The restriction is imposed on the model by substituting-out the parameter β_4 in the estimation equation. With EViews it is possible to simply substitute the restriction into the equation. EViews is smart enough to estimate it without you worrying about how to rearrange it. Substituting the restriction in to the equation yields

$$\ln(Q) = \beta_1 + \beta_2 \ln(PB) + \beta_3 \ln(PL) + (-\beta_2 - \beta_3 - \beta_5) \ln(PR) + \beta_5 \ln(I) + e$$

This equation can be entered as a command, or into the equation dialog box, as

```
equation rls.ls log(q)=c(1) + c(2)*log(pb) + c(3)*log(pl) +
    (-c(2)-c(3)-c(5))*log(pr)+c(5)*log(i)
```

Notice that the equation has been written in full. It is not just a list of variables. The resulting output follows. The values are consistent with those in equation (6.19) in *POE4*.

LOG(Q)=C(1) + C(2)*LOG(PB) + C(3)*LOG(PL) + (-C(2)-C(3)-C(5)) *LOG(PR)+C(5)*LOG(I)				
	Coefficient	Std. Error	t-Statistic	Prob.
C(1)	-4.797798	3.713905	-1.291847	0.2078
C(2)	-1.299386	0.165738	-7.840022	0.0000
C(3)	0.186816	0.284383	0.656916	0.5170
C(5)	0.945829	0.427047	2.214813	0.0357

The value for b_4^* can be retrieved using the command

c(4) = - c(2) - c(3) - c(5)

Checking the **C** object yields the complete set of estimates:

Last updated: 06/11/11 - 0...
-4.797798
-1.299386
0.186816
0.166742
0.945829

APPENDIX 6A THE DERIVATION OF A CONFIDENCE ELLIPSE[1]

Under assumptions MR1-MR6 we know that

$$t = \frac{b_k - \beta_k}{\text{se}(b_k)} \sim t_{(N-K)}$$

As we have mentioned several times, the square of a t-random variable has an F-distribution with one numerator degree of freedom and $N - K$ denominator degrees of freedom

$$t^2 = \left(\frac{b_k - \beta_k}{\text{se}(b_k)}\right)^2 = \frac{(b_k - \beta_k)^2}{\text{var}(b_k)} = (b_k - \beta_k)\left[\text{var}(b_k)\right]^{-1}(b_k - \beta_k) \sim F_{(1, N-K)}$$

A 95% interval estimate is obtained from the probability statement

$$\Pr\left\{\left[(b_k - \beta_k)\left[\text{var}(b_k)\right]^{-1}(b_k - \beta_k)\right] \le F_{(0.95, 1, N-K)}\right\} = 0.95$$

where $F_{(0.95, 1, N-K)}$ is the 95th percentile of the $F_{(1, N-K)}$-distribution.

A similar result holds for a pair of coefficients. To see this, let the estimated $K \times K$ coefficient covariance matrix of the least squares estimator be denoted $\hat{\mathbf{V}}$. Let v^{ij} denote the value in the ith row and jth column of the matrix inverse of $\hat{\mathbf{V}}$. Then a joint confidence interval for β_i and β_j is given by

$$\Pr\left\{\frac{1}{2}\left[(b_i - \beta_i)^2 v^{ii} + 2(b_i - \beta_i)(b_j - \beta_j)v^{ij} + (b_j - \beta_j)^2 v^{jj}\right] \le F_{(0.95, 2, N-K)}\right\} = 0.95$$

---

[1] This appendix contains advanced material.

The boundary of the joint interval estimate is an ellipse given by the equation

$$\frac{1}{2}\left[\left(b_i - \beta_i\right)^2 v^{ii} + 2\left(b_i - \beta_i\right)\left(b_j - \beta_j\right)v^{ij} + \left(b_j - \beta_j\right)^2 v^{jj}\right] = F_{(0.95, 2, N-K)}$$

For a complete exposition see Judge et al. (1988), *Introduction to the Theory and Practice of Econometrics, Second Edition,* New York: John Wiley and Sons, Chapter 6.3.

Keywords

@cchisq

@cfdist

@cov

@mean

@qchisq

@qfdist

@sqrt

@ssr

@sumsq

adjusted R^2

AIC

Akaike information criterion

Bayesian information criterion

BIC

chi-square statistic

chi-square test

collinearity

confidence ellipse

correlation matrix

covariance analysis

covariance matrix

descriptive statistics

df

equation name.ls specification

fitted terms

forecast

F-statistic

F-test

F-value

group

name.wald specification

nonsample information

normalized restriction

null hypothesis: joint

null hypothesis: single

Prob(F-statistic)

p-value (Prob.)

RESET

restricted least squares

SC

Schwartz criterion

SSE: restricted

SSE: unrestricted

stability tests

sum squared resid

sym

symmetric matrix

testing significance

variance inflation factor

VIF

Wald coefficient restrictions

Wald test

CHAPTER **7**

Using Indicator Variables

CHAPTER OUTLINE

7.1 INDICATOR VARIABLES

Indicator variables are binary 0-1 variables indicating the presence or absence of some condition. Open workfile ***utown.wf1*** containing real estate transaction data from "University Town" and rename it as ***utown_chap07.wf1***, or something similar.

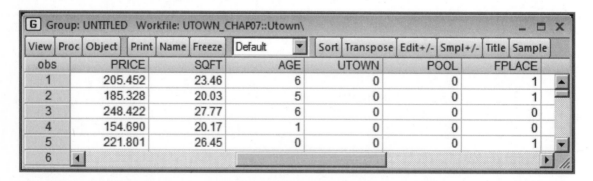

Opening a **Group** (hold **Ctrl,** click each series, double-click in blue) with the variables, we see that *PRICE*, *SQF,* and *AGE* contain the usual type of values, but the rest are 0s and 1s. These are indicator variables. They are used in a regression just like any other variables. Estimate *POE4* equation (7.7). Use **Quick/Estimate Equation** or enter the command

equation utowneq.ls price c utown sqft sqft*utown age pool fplace

206

The result is

Variable	Coefficient	Std. Error	t-Statistic	Prob.
C	24.49998	6.191721	3.956894	0.0001
UTOWN	27.45295	8.422582	3.259446	0.0012
SQFT	7.612177	0.245176	31.04775	0.0000
SQFT*UTOWN	1.299405	0.332048	3.913307	0.0001
AGE	-0.190086	0.051205	-3.712291	0.0002
POOL	4.377163	1.196692	3.657720	0.0003
FPLACE	1.649176	0.971957	1.696758	0.0901

Dependent Variable: PRICE
Method: Least Squares
Date: 05/02/11   Time: 08:45
Sample: 1 1000
Included observations: 1000

R-squared	0.870570	Mean dependent var		247.6557
Adjusted R-squared	0.869788	S.D. dependent var		42.19273

7.1.1 Creating indicator variables

Creating indicator variables is not exactly like creating any other variable. To create an indicator variable that is 1 for large houses and zero otherwise, we must decide what a large house is. The summary statistics for *SQFT* show that the median house size in the sample is 2536 square feet. Because *SQFT* is measured in 100s of square feet, this is *SQFT* = 25.36. Suppose that houses larger than this size we take to be "large." On the workfile window click the **Genr** button and enter

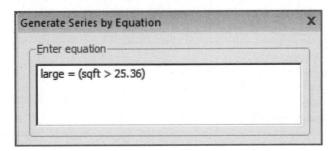

Alternatively, enter the command

    series large = (sqft > 25.36)

What this does is create a new variable, *LARGE*, that takes the value 1 if the statement **(sqft > 25.36)** is true for a particular observation and zero otherwise. Looking the first few observations, we can see that this has worked.

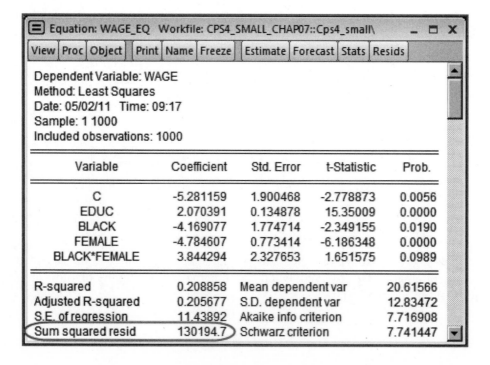

Search for **Help** on **Operators** for more information. Save the workfile as ***utown_chap07.wf1*** to maintain the original workfile, and close.

7.2 INTERACTING INDICATOR VARIABLES

To illustrate further aspects of indicator variables, open ***cps4_small.wf1***. Save the file under the name ***cps4_small_chap07.wf1***. Estimate the wage equation

$$WAGE = \beta_1 + \beta_2 EDUC + \delta_1 BLACK + \delta_2 FEMALE + \gamma \left(BLACK \times FEMALE \right) + e$$

Use **Quick/Estimate Equation** or enter the command

   equation wage_eq.ls wage c educ black female black*female

Save the regression results by naming them **WAGE_EQ**:

Equation: WAGE_EQ Workfile: CPS4_SMALL_CHAP07::Cps4_small\

Dependent Variable: WAGE
Method: Least Squares
Date: 05/02/11 Time: 09:17
Sample: 1 1000
Included observations: 1000

Variable	Coefficient	Std. Error	t-Statistic	Prob.
C	-5.281159	1.900468	-2.778873	0.0056
EDUC	2.070391	0.134878	15.35009	0.0000
BLACK	-4.169077	1.774714	-2.349155	0.0190
FEMALE	-4.784607	0.773414	-6.186348	0.0000
BLACK*FEMALE	3.844294	2.327653	1.651575	0.0989

R-squared	0.208858	Mean dependent var	20.61566
Adjusted R-squared	0.205677	S.D. dependent var	12.83472
S.E. of regression	11.43892	Akaike info criterion	7.716908
Sum squared resid	130194.7	Schwarz criterion	7.741447

We have highlighted the **Sum squared resid** for later use.

In the regression results window, select **View/Representations**. The estimation equation is

Estimation Equation:
==========================
WAGE = C(1) + C(2)*EDUC + C(3)*BLACK + C(4)*FEMALE + C(5)*BLACK*FEMALE

To test the hypothesis that neither race nor gender affects wage, we formulate the null hypothesis

$$H_0 : \delta_1 = 0, \delta_2 = 0, \gamma = 0$$

In the regression window, select **View/Coefficient Diagnostics/Wald Test – Coefficient Restrictions**. Using the equation representation, we see that it is the coefficients C(3), C(4), and C(5) that we wish to test.

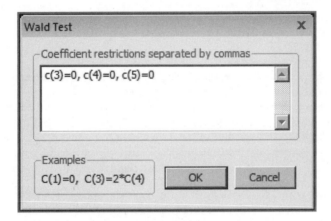

The result is

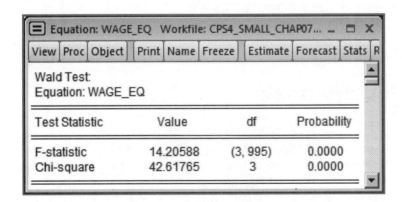

To save the test result as an object in the workfile, **Freeze** and **Name**.

Alternatively, to use the *F*-statistic directly,

$$F = \frac{(SSE_R - SSE_U)/J}{SSE_U/(N-K)}$$

we require the sum of squared least squares residuals from the unrestricted model and the model that is restricted by the null hypothesis. The *WAGE* regression **WAGE_EQ** is the unrestricted model in this case, and the SSE_U is

Sum squared resid   130194.7

To obtain the restricted model we omit the variables *BLACK*, *FEMALE* and their interaction. Use the command

equation rwage_eq.ls wage c educ

Recall that this notation assigns the name **RWAGE** to the regression object. Alternatively, use **Quick/Estimate Equation** and then assign a name. The result is

Dependent Variable: WAGE
Method: Least Squares
Date: 05/02/11   Time: 09:27
Sample: 1 1000
Included observations: 1000

Variable	Coefficient	Std. Error	t-Statistic	Prob.
C	-6.710328	1.914156	-3.505633	0.0005
EDUC	1.980288	0.136117	14.54838	0.0000

R-squared	0.174972	Mean dependent var		20.61566
Adjusted R-squared	0.174145	S.D. dependent var		12.83472
S.E. of regression	11.66376	Akaike info criterion		7.752848
Sum squared resid	135771.1	Schwarz criterion		7.762663

The "restricted" sum of squared residuals is SSE_R = 135771.1. Using these values, we can calculate F = 14.20588.

The critical value for the test comes from an *F*-distribution with three numerator degrees of freedom and 995 denominator degrees of freedom. The critical value is computed using **@qfdist**:

scalar fc = @qfdist(.99,3,995)

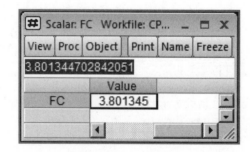

7.3 INDICATOR VARIABLES WITH SEVERAL CATEGORIES

Estimate the regression

$$WAGE = \beta_1 + \beta_2 EDUC + \delta_1 BLACK + \delta_2 FEMALE + \gamma(BLACK \times FEMALE)$$
$$+ \gamma_1 SOUTH + \gamma_2 MIDWEST + \gamma_3 WEST + e$$

On the command line enter

equation regions.ls wage c educ black female black*female south midwest west

```
Dependent Variable: WAGE
Method: Least Squares
Date: 05/02/11   Time: 09:45
Sample: 1 1000
Included observations: 1000
```

Variable	Coefficient	Std. Error	t-Statistic	Prob.
C	-4.806210	2.028691	-2.369119	0.0180
EDUC	2.071231	0.134469	15.40307	0.0000
BLACK	-3.905465	1.786258	-2.186395	0.0290
FEMALE	-4.744129	0.769838	-6.162502	0.0000
BLACK*FEMALE	3.625021	2.318375	1.563604	0.1182
SOUTH	-0.449906	1.025024	-0.438922	0.6608
MIDWEST	-2.608406	1.059644	-2.461587	0.0140
WEST	0.986633	1.059815	0.930948	0.3521

R-squared	0.218887	Mean dependent var	20.61566
Adjusted R-squared	0.213375	S.D. dependent var	12.83472
S.E. of regression	11.38336	Akaike info criterion	7.710150
Sum squared resid	128544.2	Schwarz criterion	7.749412

Select **View/Representations** in the regression window. We see that the estimation equation is

```
Estimation Equation:
=========================
WAGE = C(1) + C(2)*EDUC + C(3)*BLACK + C(4)*FEMALE + C(5)
*BLACK*FEMALE + C(6)*SOUTH + C(7)*MIDWEST + C(8)*WEST
```

Test the null hypothesis that there are no regional differences by selecting **View/Coefficient Diagnostics/Wald Test – Coefficient Restrictions**. Enter the null hypothesis that coefficients 6, 7 and 8 are zero. Alternatively, use the command

regions.wald c(6)=0, c(7)=0, c(8)=0

The result is

Wald Test: Equation: REGIONS			
Test Statistic	Value	df	Probability
F-statistic	4.245566	(3, 992)	0.0054
Chi-square	12.73670	3	0.0052

The F-statistic's p-value shows that we reject the null hypothesis of no regional differences at the 1% level of significance. The chi-square statistic is an alternative approach to the test.

To construct the F-statistic directly we need the "unrestricted" sum of squared residuals from the **REGIONS** model above. The "restricted" sum of squared errors comes from the model omitting the regional dummies. We obtained this result above in the regression **WAGE_EQ**.

7.4 TESTING THE EQUIVALENCE OF TWO REGRESSIONS

The Chow test is illustrated using ***cps4_small.wf1*** in Section 7.2.3 of *POE4*. The *WAGE* model in *POE* equation (7.10) is obtained by interacting the variable *SOUTH* with the variables *EDUC*, *BLACK*, *FEMALE* and *BLACK×FEMALE*

The estimation can be carried out using the command

```
equation chow.ls wage c educ black female black*female
        south educ*south black*south female*south black*female*south
```

The result is

Variable	Coefficient	Std. Error	t-Statistic	Prob.
C	-6.605572	2.336628	-2.826968	0.0048
EDUC	2.172554	0.166464	13.05120	0.0000
BLACK	-5.089360	2.643060	-1.925556	0.0544
FEMALE	-5.005078	0.899007	-5.567338	0.0000
BLACK*FEMALE	5.305574	3.497267	1.517063	0.1296
SOUTH	3.943910	4.048453	0.974177	0.3302
EDUC*SOUTH	-0.308541	0.285734	-1.079818	0.2805
BLACK*SOUTH	1.704396	3.633327	0.469101	0.6391
FEMALE*SOUTH	0.901120	1.772665	0.508342	0.6113
BLACK*FEMALE*SOUTH	-2.935834	4.787647	-0.613210	0.5399
R-squared	0.210135	Mean dependent var		20.61566
Adjusted R-squared	0.202955	S.D. dependent var		12.83472
S.E. of regression	11.45851	Akaike info criterion		7.725292
Sum squared resid	129984.4	Schwarz criterion		7.774369

Select **View/Representations** to see the estimation equation:

```
Estimation Equation
========================
WAGE = C(1) + C(2)*EDUC + C(3)*BLACK + C(4)*FEMALE + C(5)*BLACK*FEMALE + C(6)*SOUTH +
C(7)*EDUC*SOUTH + C(8)*BLACK*SOUTH + C(9)*FEMALE*SOUTH + C(10)*BLACK*FEMALE*SOUTH
```

To test the null hypothesis that wages for the *SOUTH* are no different from the rest of the country, select **View/Coefficient Diagnostics/Wald Test – Coefficient Restrictions**. Enter the null hypothesis that coefficients 6-10 are zero. Alternatively, enter the command

chow.wald c(6)=0, c(7)=0, c(8)=0, c(9)=0, c(10)=0

The *F*-test statistic value is

Wald Test: Equation: CHOW			
Test Statistic	Value	df	Probability
F-statistic	0.320278	(5, 990)	0.9009
Chi-square	1.601389	5	0.9011

The regression for the *SOUTH* observations is obtained by selecting **Quick/Estimate Equation**. In the dialog box enter the equation and modify the **Sample** to include observations for which *SOUTH* = 1:

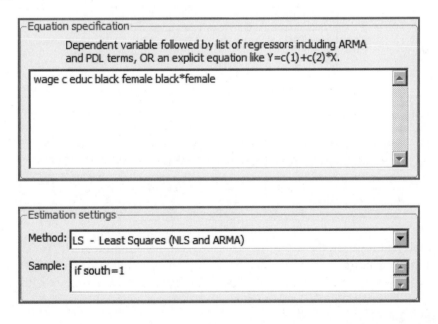

To obtain the results for the *NONSOUTH*, estimate the equation using the observations for which *SOUTH* = 0.

Sample: 1 1000 IF SOUTH=1
Included observations: 296

Variable	Coefficient	Std. Error	t-Statistic	Prob.
C	-2.661662	3.420413	-0.778170	0.4371
EDUC	1.864013	0.240268	7.758049	0.0000
BLACK	-3.384964	2.579268	-1.312374	0.1904
FEMALE	-4.103958	1.580621	-2.596421	0.0099
BLACK*FEMALE	2.369740	3.382739	0.700539	0.4842

R-squared	0.184206	Mean dependent var		20.65791
Adjusted R-squared	0.172992	S.D. dependent var		13.03583
S.E. of regression	11.85478	Akaike info criterion		7.800088
Sum squared resid	40895.95	Schwarz criterion		7.862425

Using the condition on the regression dialog box does not change the current sample in the workfile, which is convenient. There are several other ways to obtain this result that are worth noting. To change the workfile, choose **Sample** on the EViews menu:

Workfile: CPS4_SMALL_CHAP07 - (c:\data\eviews\cps4_small_chap07.wf1)

| View | Proc | Object | | Print | Save | Details+/- | | Show | Fetch | Store | Delete | Genr | Sample |

Range: 1 1000 — 1000 obs   Filter: *
Sample: 1 1000 — 1000 obs

Enter the **IF condition**

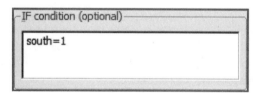

IF condition (optional)

    south=1

This changes the workfile sample:

Workfile: CPS4_SMALL_CHAP07 - (c:\data\eviews\cps4...

| View | Proc | Object | | Print | Save | Details+/- | | Show | Fetch | Store | Dele |

Range: 1 1000 — 1000 obs   Filter: *
Sample: 1 1000 if south=1 — 296 obs

Now estimation will result in the use of the 296 observations from the *SOUTH*. The sample will remain with this condition imposed until the condition is removed. Select **Sample** from the EViews menu and remove the condition. Instead of using the **Sample** dialog box, the command is

    smpl if south=1

To return the sample to its complete form, use

    smpl @all

7.5 LOG-LINEAR MODELS

Regression equations with log-transformed dependent variables are common. In EViews the function **log** creates the natural logarithm. The estimation equation can be represented as

equation log_wage.ls log(wage) c educ female

The result is

Dependent Variable: LOG(WAGE)
Method: Least Squares
Date: 05/02/11   Time: 10:51
Sample: 1 1000
Included observations: 1000

Variable	Coefficient	Std. Error	t-Statistic	Prob.
C	1.653868	0.084379	19.60057	0.0000
EDUC	0.096248	0.006037	15.94432	0.0000
FEMALE	-0.243214	0.032728	-7.431485	0.0000

The exact calculation of the effect of gender on wages looks complicated, but it is simple in EViews. Select **View/Coefficient Diagnostics/Wald Test – Coefficient Restrictions**. In EViews the **exponential** function is **exp**. To make the nonlinear calculation, enter it as a hypothesis.

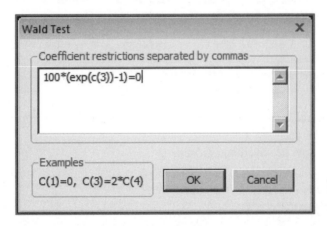

In the lower portion of the "test" result we find:

Null Hypothesis Summary:		
Normalized Restriction (= 0)	Value	Std. Err.
100 * (-1 + EXP(C(3)))	-21.58963	2.566176

Delta method computed using analytic derivatives.

The EViews command is

log_wage.wald 100*(exp(c(3))-1)=0

The calculated percentage difference in wages is −21.59% and EViews computes a standard error for this quantity by the "Delta method," which was introduced in Chapter 5.

The next example includes an interaction term

$$\ln(WAGE) = \beta_1 + \beta_2 EDUC + \beta_3 EXPER + \gamma(EDUC \times EXPER)$$

To estimate this model, the command is

equation log_wage2.ls log(wage) c educ exper educ*exper

The approximate effect of another year of experience, holding education constant and equal to a given value, is

$$100(\beta_3 + \gamma EDUC)\%$$

For a person with 16 years of education, this marginal effect is calculated using

log_wage2.wald 100*(c(3) + 16*c(4))=0

Null Hypothesis: 100*(C(3) + 16*C(4))=0		
Null Hypothesis Summary:		
Normalized Restriction (= 0)	Value	Std. Err.
100 * (C(3) + 16*C(4))	0.574639	0.174402
Restrictions are linear in coefficients.		

We see that the marginal effect of another year of experience is approximately 0.57%, holding education constant at 16 years.

This workfile can now be saved and closed.

7.6 THE LINEAR PROBABILITY MODEL

To begin, let us represent the variable indicating a choice as

$$y = \begin{cases} 1 & \text{if first alternative is chosen} \\ 0 & \text{if second alternative is chosen} \end{cases}$$

If we observe the choices that a random sample of individuals makes, then y is a random variable. If p is the probability that the first alternative is chosen, then $P[y = 1] = p$. The probability that the second alternative is chosen is $P[y = 0] = 1 - p$. The probability function for the binary indicator variable y is

$$f(y) = p^y (1-p)^{1-y}, \quad y = 0,1$$

The indicator variable y is said to follow a Bernoulli distribution. The expected value of y is $E(y) = p$ and its variance is $\text{var}(y) = p(1-p)$.

We are interested in identifying factors that might affect the probability p using a linear regression function, or in this context a **linear probability model**,

$$E(y) = p = \beta_1 + \beta_2 x_2 + \cdots + \beta_K x_K$$

Proceeding as usual, we break the observed outcome y into a systematic portion, $E(y)$, and an unpredictable random error, e, so that the econometric model is

$$y = E(y) + e = \beta_1 + \beta_2 x_2 + \cdots + \beta_K x_K + e$$

The error term for this regression model is heteroskedastic, an idea that is further explored in Chapter 8 of this manual. For the present we will apply least squares estimation.

7.6.1 A marketing example

A shopper is deciding between Coke and Pepsi brands of soda. Define the variable *COKE*:

$$COKE = \begin{cases} 1 & \text{if Coke is chosen} \\ 0 & \text{if Pepsi is chosen} \end{cases}$$

The expected value of this variable is $E(COKE) = p_{COKE} =$ probability that Coke is chosen. What factors might enter the choice decision? The relative price of Coke to Pepsi (*PRATIO*) is a potential factor. As the relative price of Coke rises we should observe a reduced probability of its choice. Other factors influencing the consumer might be the presence of store displays for these products. Let *DISP_COKE* and *DISP_PEPSI* be indicator variables taking the value 1 if the respective store display is present and 0 if it is not present. We expect that the presence of a Coke display will increase the probability of a Coke purchase, and the presence of a Pepsi display will decrease the probability of a Coke purchase.

The workfile *coke.wf1* contains "scanner" data on 1140 individuals who purchased Coke or Pepsi. Open this data file and examine the summary statistics. First open the group of variables. Note that *COKE*, *DISP_COKE* and *DISP_PEPSI* are indicator variables.

obs	COKE	PRATIO	DISP_COKE	DISP_PEPSI
1	1	1.000000	0	0
2	1	0.497207	1	0
3	1	0.631206	0	0
4	1	0.743017	0	0
5	1	1.000000	0	0
6				

Select **View/Descriptive Statistics/Common Sample**. The result is

	COKE	PRATIO	DISP_COKE	DISP_PEPSI
Mean	0.447368	1.027249	0.378947	0.364035
Median	0.000000	1.000000	0.000000	0.000000
Maximum	1.000000	2.324675	1.000000	1.000000
Minimum	0.000000	0.497207	0.000000	0.000000
Std. Dev.	0.497440	0.286608	0.485338	0.481370
Skewness	0.211702	0.836951	0.499057	0.565156
Kurtosis	1.044818	4.238597	1.249058	1.319402
Jarque-Bera	190.0954	205.9633	192.9464	194.8458
Probability	0.000000	0.000000	0.000000	0.000000
Sum	510.0000	1171.063	432.0000	415.0000
Sum Sq. Dev.	281.8421	93.56216	268.2947	263.9254
Observations	1140	1140	1140	1140

In this sample 44.7% of the customers chose Coke. Estimate the regression model using

equation linprob.ls coke c pratio disp_coke disp_pepsi

The estimated regression model is

Sample: 1 1140
Included observations: 1140

Variable	Coefficient	Std. Error	t-Statistic	Prob.
C	0.890215	0.065485	13.59421	0.0000
PRATIO	-0.400861	0.061349	-6.534067	0.0000
DISP_COKE	0.077174	0.034392	2.243970	0.0250
DISP_PEPSI	-0.165664	0.035600	-4.653517	0.0000

R-squared	0.120059	Mean dependent var		0.447368
Adjusted R-squared	0.117736	S.D. dependent var		0.497440
S.E. of regression	0.467240	Akaike info criterion		1.319557
Sum squared resid	248.0043	Schwarz criterion		1.337237

The estimated coefficients have the anticipated signs and are statistically significant.

7.6.2 Predicted probabilities

Predictions from the linear probability model are estimates of the probability of choosing Coke for a particular value of the price ratio and display variables. In the **LINPROB** regression window, select **Forecast**. Assign a name to the forecast, or use the default:

Series names	
Forecast name:	cokef
S.E. (optional):	
GARCH(optional):	

Examine the forecast values. Double-click *COKEF*.

Series: COKEF Workfile: COKE_CHAP07::Coke\   _ □ X

View Proc Object Properties   Print Name Freeze   Default

COKEF

Last updated: 05/06/11 - 10:30	
Modified: 1 1140 // linprob.fit(f=actual) cokef	

1	0.489354
2	0.768078
3	0.637189
4	0.592368
5	0.489354
6	-0.000239
7	-0.207321
8	

A problem with the linear probability model is immediately evident. Some of the predicted values, which are estimated probabilities, fall outside the interval $[0,1]$. There is no control in the linear probability model for this type of problem. In Chapter 16 we present a model called **probit** that is designed to keep predicted probabilities in the unit interval.

7.7 TREATMENT EFFECTS

If we perform a **randomized controlled experiment** by randomly assigning subjects to treatment and control groups, we ensure that the differences we observe will result from the treatment. Define the indicator variable d as

$$d_i = \begin{cases} 1 & \text{individual in treatment group} \\ 0 & \text{individual in control group} \end{cases}$$

The effect of the treatment on the outcome can be modeled as

$$y_i = \beta_1 + \beta_2 d_i + e_i, \quad i = 1,\ldots,N$$

where e_i represents the collection of other factors affecting the outcome. The regression functions for the treatment and control groups are

$$E(y_i) = \begin{cases} \beta_1 + \beta_2 & \text{if in treatment group, } d_i = 1 \\ \beta_1 & \text{if in control group, } d_i = 0 \end{cases}$$

A longitudinal experiment was conducted in Tennessee beginning in 1985 and ending in 1989. A single cohort of students was followed from kindergarten through third grade. In the experiment children were randomly assigned within schools into three types of classes: small classes with 13-17 students, regular-sized classes with 22-25 students, and regular-sized classes with a full-time teacher's aide to assist the teacher. Student scores on achievement tests were recorded as well as some information about the students, teachers, and schools. Data for the kindergarten classes is contained in the data file *star.wf1*.

Let us first compare the performance of students in small classes versus regular classes. The variable *TOTALSCORE* is the combined reading and math achievement scores; *SMALL* = 1 if the student was assigned to a small class and 0 if the student is in a regular class. The variable *AIDE* is an indicator variable that is 1 for students in regular-sized classes with a teacher and a teacher's aide. Modify the sample to exclude those observations. Do so by choosing the **Sample** condition *AIDE* = 0.

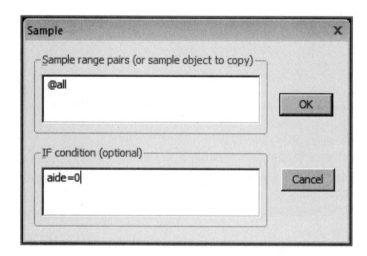

The sample size is reduced from 5786 to 3743. The remaining students were in either a small or regular-sized class. Estimate the model

$$TOTALSCORE = \beta_1 + \beta_2 SMALL + e$$

equation star.ls totalscore c small

Sample: 1 5786 IF AIDE=0
Included observations: 3743

Variable	Coefficient	Std. Error	t-Statistic	Prob.
C	918.0429	1.667157	550.6638	0.0000
SMALL	13.89899	2.446592	5.680962	0.0000

The estimated effect of being in a small class is to increase the total test score by 13.89 points, holding all else fixed.

Additional control variables can be added to the specification if there are other factors that may affect test scores. For example, add teacher's experience, *TCHEXPER*:

equation star2.ls totalscore c small tchexper

Sample: 1 5786 IF AIDE=0
Included observations: 3743

Variable	Coefficient	Std. Error	t-Statistic	Prob.
C	907.5643	2.542413	356.9696	0.0000
SMALL	13.98327	2.437332	5.737121	0.0000
TCHEXPER	1.155511	0.212276	5.443447	0.0000

In the *star* data, another factor that we might consider affecting the outcome is the school itself. The students were randomized <u>within</u> schools (conditional randomization) but not <u>across</u> schools. Some schools may be located in more wealthy school districts, allowing them to pay higher salaries, thus attracting better teachers. The students in our sample are enrolled in 79 different schools. One way to account for school effects is to include an indicator variable for each school. That is, we can introduce 78 new indicators

$$SCHOOL\_j = \begin{cases} 1 & \text{if student is in school } j \\ 0 & \text{otherwise} \end{cases}$$

This is an "intercept" indicator variable, allowing the expected total score to differ for each school. The model including these indicator variables is

$$TOTALSCORE_i = \beta_1 + \beta_2 SMALL_i + \beta_3 TCHEXPER_i + \sum_{j=2}^{79} \delta_j SCHOOL\_j_i + e_i$$

The regression function for a student in school j is

$$E(TOTALSCORE_i) = \begin{cases} (\beta_1 + \delta_j) + \beta_3 TCHEXPER_i & \text{student in regular class} \\ (\beta_1 + \delta_j + \beta_2) + \beta_3 TCHEXPER_i & \text{student in small class} \end{cases}$$

The expected score for a student in a regular class for a teacher with no experience is adjusted by the fixed amount δ_j. This **fixed effect** controls for some differences in the schools that are not accounted for in the regression model.

Another way to achieve control for school fixed-effects is to include 79 indicator variables and omit the intercept. For the base model without *TCHEXPER*, we then have

$$TOTALSCORE_i = \beta_2 SMALL_i + \sum_{j=1}^{79} \gamma_j SCHOOL\_j_i + e_i$$

The regression function is

$$E\left(TOTALSCORE_i\right) = \begin{cases} \gamma_j & \text{student in regular class} \\ \gamma_j + \beta_2 & \text{student in small class} \end{cases}$$

This particular formulation is conveniently handled in EViews using **@expand**. The **@expand** function allows you to create a group of indicator variables by expanding out one or more series into individual categories. In the *star* data we have the variable *SCHID*, which is an identifier for each school. Estimate this fixed effects model using

equation star_fe.ls totalscore small @expand(schid)

The result, in part, omitting many of the fixed effects variables, is

Dependent Variable: TOTALSCORE
Method: Least Squares
Sample: 1 5786 IF AIDE=0
Included observations: 3743

Variable	Coefficient	Std. Error	t-Statistic	Prob.
SMALL	15.99778	2.222846	7.196978	0.0000
SCHID=112038	838.7586	11.55958	72.55963	0.0000
SCHID=123056	894.2657	11.38703	78.53368	0.0000
SCHID=128068	887.0332	11.91750	74.43113	0.0000
SCHID=128076	886.1151	11.21193	79.03327	0.0000
SCHID=128079	881.0535	10.76685	81.83020	0.0000
SCHID=264945	959.1413	9.449693	101.4997	0.0000

R-squared	0.237713	Mean dependent var	924.4967
Adjusted R-squared	0.221273	S.D. dependent var	74.96196
S.E. of regression	66.15056	Akaike info criterion	11.24289
Sum squared resid	16028908	Schwarz criterion	11.37599
Log likelihood	-20961.06	Hannan-Quinn criter.	11.29023
Durbin-Watson stat	1.962306		

The estimated effect on *TOTALSCORE* of being in a small class, rather than a regular-sized class, is 15.9978 points. The 79 indicator variables, most of which we have omitted, are the school fixed effects.

A hypothesis of interest is $H_0 : \gamma_1 = \gamma_2, \gamma_2 = \gamma_3, \dots, \gamma_{78} = \gamma_{79}$ against the alternative that at least one pair of fixed effects is not equal. The unrestricted $SSE = 16028908$ from the fixed effects regression. The restricted $SSE = 20847551$ comes from the regression we named **STAR**. The F-statistic is

$$F = \frac{\left(SSE_R - SSE_U\right)/J}{SSE_U/\left(N-K\right)} = \frac{(16028908 - 20847551)/78}{20847551/(3743-80)} = 14.1177$$

This outcome is statistically significant at the 0.01 level, and we conclude that there are school differences in the data.

Other variables such as teacher experience can also be included, as in

equation star2_fe.ls totalscore small tchexper @expand(schid)

Another important question is whether students were actually randomly assigned within schools. The ability of randomized controlled experiments to estimate treatment effects depends critically on this assumption. To test this we can use the linear probability model, regressing *SMALL* against any features of the data that characterize the students. For example,

equation star_linprob.ls small c boy white_asian tchexper freelunch

```
Dependent Variable: SMALL
Method: Least Squares
Date: 05/07/11   Time: 09:10
Sample: 1 5786 IF AIDE=0
Included observations: 3743
```

Variable	Coefficient	Std. Error	t-Statistic	Prob.
C	0.466462	0.025156	18.54250	0.0000
BOY	0.001411	0.016339	0.086346	0.9312
WHITE_ASIAN	0.004406	0.019597	0.224813	0.8221
TCHEXPER	-0.000603	0.001439	-0.418768	0.6754
FREELUNCH	-0.000886	0.018193	-0.048693	0.9612

R-squared	0.000063	Mean dependent var	0.464333
Adjusted R-squared	-0.001007	S.D. dependent var	0.498793
S.E. of regression	0.499044	Akaike info criterion	1.449090
Sum squared resid	930.9297	Schwarz criterion	1.457409
Log likelihood	-2706.972	Hannan-Quinn criter.	1.452049
F-statistic	0.059022	Durbin-Watson stat	1.919152
Prob(F-statistic)	0.993555		

The results show that the overall *F*-test of significance cannot reject the null hypothesis that there is no significant relationship, and the individual *t*-values are statistically insignificant. Thus there is no evidence that the assignment was not random.

7.7.1 Natural experiments

Randomized controlled experiments are rare in economics. More common nowadays are "natural experiments." The estimator $\hat{\delta}$ defined on page 283 of *POE4* can be conveniently calculated using a simple regression. Define y_{it} to be the observed outcome for individual i in period t. Let $AFTER_t$ be an indicator variable that equals 1 in the period after the policy change ($t = 2$) and equals 0 in the period before the policy change ($t = 1$). Let $TREAT_i$ be a dummy variable that equals 1 if individual i is in the treatment group, and equals 0 if the individual is in the control (non-treatment) group. Consider the regression model, which is called a **differences-in-differences** regression,

$$y_{it} = \beta_1 + \beta_2 TREAT_i + \beta_3 AFTER_t + \delta\left(TREAT_i \times AFTER_t\right) + e_{it}$$

The regression function is

$$E\left(y_{it}\right) = \begin{cases} \beta_1 & TREAT = 0,\ AFTER = 0 \\ \beta_1 + \beta_2 & TREAT = 1,\ AFTER = 0 \\ \beta_1 + \beta_3 & TREAT = 0,\ AFTER = 1 \\ \beta_1 + \beta_2 + \beta_3 + \delta & TREAT = 1,\ AFTER = 1 \end{cases}$$

The treatment effect is captured by the coefficient δ of the interaction variable $TREAT_i \times AFTER_t$.

To illustrate, Card and Krueger (1994)[1] provide an example of a natural experiment and the differences-in-differences estimator. On April 1, 1992, New Jersey's minimum wage was increased from \$4.25 to \$5.05 per hour, while the minimum wage in Pennsylvania stayed at \$4.25 per hour. Card and Krueger collected data on 410 fast food restaurants in New Jersey (the treatment group) and eastern Pennsylvania (the control group). The "before" period is February, 1992, and the "after" period is November, 1992. Using these data, they estimate the effect of the "treatment" of raising the New Jersey minimum wage on employment at fast food restaurants in New Jersey. Their interesting finding, that there was no significant reduction in employment, sparked a great debate and much further research. In the model above we will test the null and alternative hypotheses

$$H_0 : \delta \geq 0 \quad \text{versus} \quad H_1 : \delta < 0$$

The relevant Card and Krueger data is in the data file ***njmin3.wf1***. The relevant variables are

NJ	= 1 if New Jersey
$D01$	= 1 if after New Jersey minimum wage increase
D_NJ	= $NJ \times D01$ interaction
FTE	= full time-equivalent employees

Estimate the model

equation did.ls fte c nj d01 d01*nj

Sample: 1 820
Included observations: 794

Variable	Coefficient	Std. Error	t-Statistic	Prob.
C	23.33117	1.071870	21.76679	0.0000
NJ	-2.891761	1.193524	-2.422877	0.0156
D01	-2.165584	1.515853	-1.428625	0.1535
D01*NJ	2.753606	1.688409	1.630888	0.1033

---

[1] David Card and Alan Krueger (1994), "Minimum Wages and Employment: A Case Study of the Fast Food Industry in New Jersey and Pennsylvania," *The American Economic Review*, 84, 316-361. We thank David Card for letting us use the data.

Because not all restaurants were observed in both periods, the number of observations used for estimation, 794, is less than the sample size of 820. The null hypothesis $H_0 : \delta \geq 0$ cannot be rejected using the relevant **left-tail test.**

Using panel data, we can control for **unobserved individual-specific characteristics**. There are characteristics of the restaurants that we do not observe. Some restaurants will have preferred locations, some may have superior managers, and so on. These unobserved individual specific characteristics are included in the error term of the differences-in-differences regression. Let c_i denote any unobserved characteristics of individual restaurant i that do not change over time. Adding c_i to the model, we have

$$FTE_{it} = \beta_1 + \beta_2 NJ_i + \beta_3 D_t + \delta(NJ_i \times D_t) + c_i + e_{it}$$

Whatever c_i might be, it contaminates this regression model. A solution is at hand *if* we have a panel of data. If we have $T = 2$ repeat observations we can *eliminate* c_i by analyzing the changes in *FTE* from period 1 to period 2. Recall that $D_t = 0$ in period 1, so $D_1 = 0$; and $D_t = 1$ in period 2, so $D_2 = 1$. Subtract the observation for $t = 1$ from that for $t = 2$:

$$FTE_{i2} = \beta_1 + \beta_2 NJ_i + \beta_3 1 + \delta(NJ_i \times 1) + c_i + e_{i2}$$

$$- \quad FTE_{i1} = \beta_1 + \beta_2 NJ_i + \beta_3 0 + \delta(NJ_i \times 0) + c_i + e_{i1}$$

$$\Delta FTE_i = \beta_3 + \delta NJ_i + \Delta e_i$$

where $\Delta FTE_i = FTE_{i2} - FTE_{i1}$ and $\Delta e_i = e_{i2} - e_{i1}$. Using the **differenced data**, the regression model of interest becomes

$$\Delta FTE_i = \beta_3 + \delta NJ_i + \Delta e_i$$

In the workfile ***njmin3.wf1***, the variable *DEMP* is the change in employment for those restaurants observed in both periods. Using only the observations for time period 2 (the differences are repeated in the data file), estimate the equation

```
smpl if d01=1
equation diff.ls demp c nj
```

Sample: 1 820 IF D01=1				
Included observations: 384				
Variable	Coefficient	Std. Error	t-Statistic	Prob.
C	-2.283333	1.035507	-2.205038	0.0280
NJ	2.750000	1.154355	2.382282	0.0177

The estimate of the treatment effect is very similar to that from the differences-in-differences regression. Much more will be said about panel data in Chapter 15 of this manual.

Keywords

@expand

@qfdist

@trend

Chow test

coefficient vector

delta method

differenced data

differences-in-differences

dummy variables

equation name.ls

estimation equation

exponential function

fixed effects

forecast

if condition

indicator variables

interactions

linear probability model

log function

log-linear

marginal effect

natural experiments

nonlinear hypothesis

operators

panel data

representations

sample range

series

smpl

smpl @all

treatment effects

unobserved effect

Wald test

CHAPTER **8**

Heteroskedasticity

CHAPTER OUTLINE

8.1 EXAMINING RESIDUALS

In this chapter we return to the example considered in Chapters 2 to 4 where weekly expenditure on food was related to income. Data in the file *food.wf1* were used to find the following least squares estimates:

Dependent Variable: FOOD_EXP
Method: Least Squares
Sample: 1 40
Included observations: 40

Variable	Coefficient	Std. Error	t-Statistic	Prob.
C	83.41600	43.41016	1.921578	0.0622
INCOME	10.20964	2.093264	4.877381	0.0000

We are now concerned with whether the error variance for this equation is likely to vary over observations, a characteristic called heteroskedasticity. To carry out a preliminary investigation of this question, we examine the least squares residuals. If they increase with increasing income, that suggests that the error variance increases with income.

8.1.1 Plot against observation number

There are a variety of ways in which EViews can be used to examine least squares residuals. We begin by checking the obvious ones. After estimating the equation and naming it **ls_eqn**, go to **View/Actual, Fitted, Residual**. At that point you will see a menu with the following options:

> **Actual, Fitted, Residual Table**
> **Actual, Fitted, Residual Graph**
> **Residual Graph**
> **Standardized Residual Graph**

Check each of these options to get a feel for the different ways in which they convey information. As you might expect from the names of the options, each alternative presents information on one or more of the series **actual, fitted,** and **residual**. In terms of the names of the series in your workfile,

$$\textbf{actual} = FOOD\_EXP$$

$$\textbf{fitted} = \widehat{FOOD\_EXP} = b_1 + b_2 INCOME$$

$$\textbf{resid} = \hat{e} = FOOD\_EXP - \widehat{FOOD\_EXP}$$

The **Standardized Residual Graph** is a graph of $\hat{e}/\hat{\sigma}$; the residuals have been standardized (made free of units of measurement) by dividing by the estimated standard deviation of the error term.

In each case the series are graphed against the observation number. As an example, consider the **Residual Graph** selected in the following way:

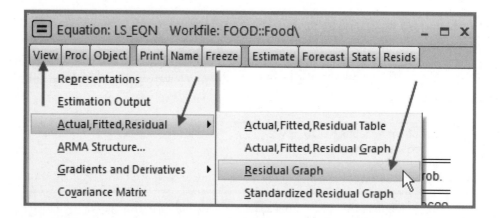

In the residual graph that follows, it is clear that the absolute magnitude of the residuals has a tendency to be larger as the observation number gets larger. The reason such is the case is that the observations are ordered according to increasing values of *INCOME*, and the absolute magnitude of the residuals increases as *INCOME* increases. Given it is this latter relationship that we are really interested in, it is preferable to graph the residuals against income. Nevertheless, residual graphs like the one below are important for examining which observations are not well captured by the estimated model (outliers) and, in the case of time series data, for discerning patterns in the residuals. To help you assess which observations could be viewed as outliers, dotted lines are drawn at points one standard deviation ($\hat{\sigma} = 89.517$) either side of zero.

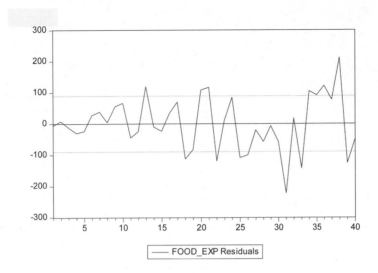

8.1.2 Plot against an explanatory variable

To graph the residuals against income we begin by naming the residuals and the fitted values:

series ehat = resid

series foodhat = food_exp – ehat

Recall that these commands can be executed by typing them in the EViews Command window or by clicking on **Genr** and writing the equation to generate the series in the resulting box. Illustrations of these two alternatives are:

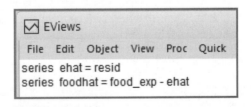

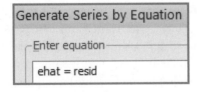

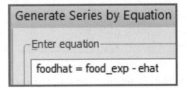

Returning to our task of graphing the residuals, we create a **graph object** by going to **Object/ New Object** and selecting **Graph**. As a name for the graph, we chose **EHAT_ON_INCOME**.

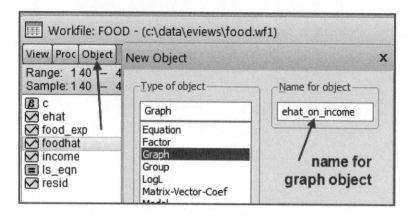

After clicking **OK**, you will be asked for the series that you want to graph. The one that is to go on the *x*-axis comes first:

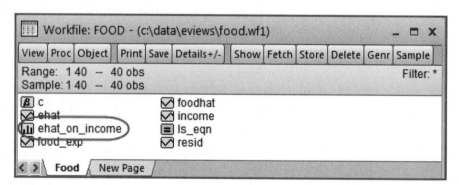

After clicking **OK** one more time, a graph object will appear in your workfile:

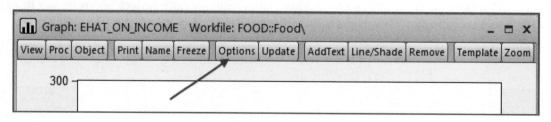

Double-clicking on this object will open it. Be careful, however. It may not look like what you expected! Unless told otherwise, EViews will assume you want both *INCOME* and *EHAT* graphed against the observation number. You need to tell EViews to change the graph so that *INCOME* is on the *x*-axis and *EHAT* is on the *y*-axis. Also, given that income is not measured in equally spaced intervals, dots are preferred to a line graph. With these factors in mind, open the graph and select **Options**.

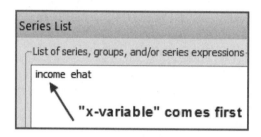

Then select **Graph Type/Scatter**, click **Apply**, and click **OK**.

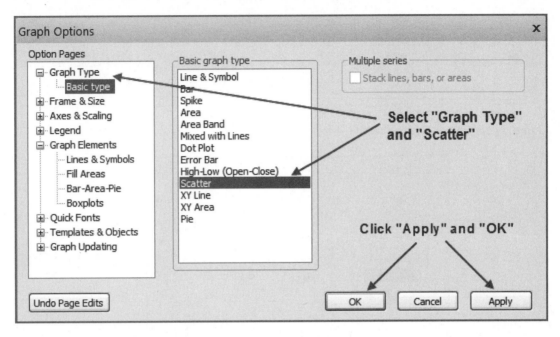

A nice-looking scatter plot will appear. You can make it look even nicer by making the dots more distinct and by drawing a horizontal line at zero. To make the dots more distinct, return again to **Options**. Select **Graph Elements/Lines & Symbols**. Then choose from the drop-down menus for **Symbol/Obs label** and **Symbol size**. We have chosen the large rounded diamond-shaped symbols with colored interiors. Click **Apply** and **OK**.

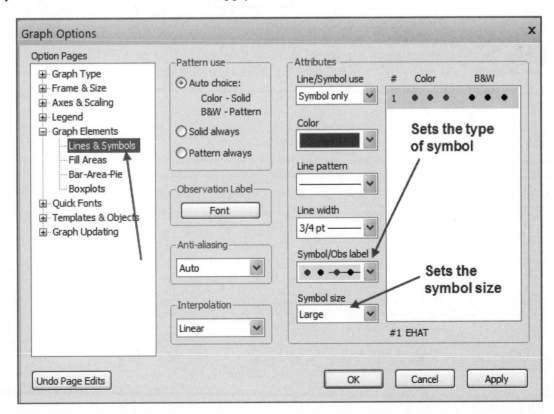

To draw a horizontal line at zero, go to **Line/Shade.**

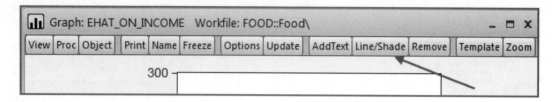

Fill in the resulting dialog box as follows:

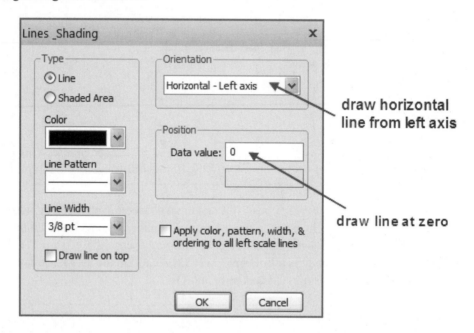

draw horizontal
line from left axis

draw line at zero

Clicking **OK** gives the required graph that appears as Figure 8.3 on page 303 of *Principles of Econometrics 4th edition* (*POE4*). Notice how the absolute magnitude of the residuals is larger for larger values of income, an indication of heteroskedasticity.

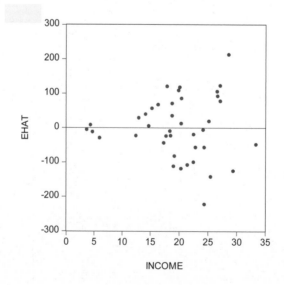

8.1.3 Plot of least squares line

Another way to illustrate the dependence of the magnitude of the residuals on *INCOME* is to plot *FOOD_EXP* and the least squares estimated line against *INCOME*, as is displayed in Figure 8.2 on page 301 of *POE4*. One way to reproduce this figure was considered in Section 2.4 of this manual. Here we consider an alternative way. Select **Object/New Object/Graph** and give the graph a name, say **FIGURE_8_2**:

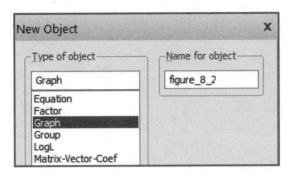

The relevant three variables for the graph are *INCOME*, *FOOD_EXP* and *FOODHAT*, with *FOODHAT* being required to draw the least-squares estimated line. The *x*-axis variable *INCOME* is listed first.

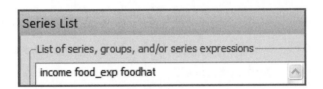

After clicking **OK**, a graph will appear in your workfile. Several adjustments are needed to this graph to convert it to the one we want. The process is slightly complicated because we want a line graph for *FOODHAT*, but we want dots or symbols for *FOOD_EXP*. The strategy that we adopt is to ask for line graphs first, and then change the one for *FOOD_EXP* to dots. With these points in mind, open the graph object **FIGURE_8_2** and select **Options/Graph Type/XY Line**. Click **Apply**.

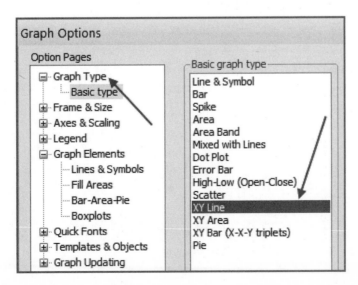

Then select **Graph Elements/Lines & Symbols**. The snapshot below shows you how you change the line for *FOOD_EXP* to dots (symbols). No changes are needed for series #2, *FOODHAT*. It is already represented by the required line. Click **Apply**. Click **OK**.

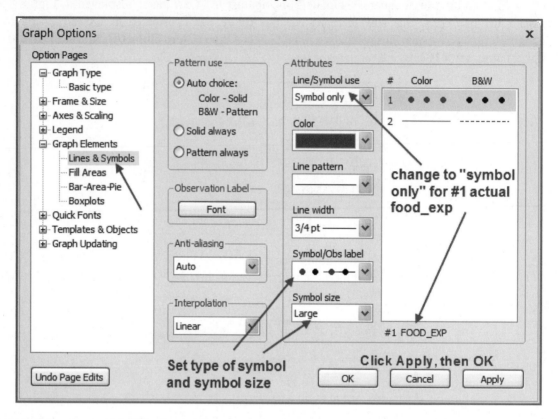

The graph object **FIGURE_8_2** will now appear as follows. Compare it with Figure 8.2 in *POE4*. Other changes can be made. We could label the line, and we could change the **legend** that at present appears in a box on the left of the graph. We suggest you experiment with these options.

For labeling, select the button AddText. For changing the legend, go to **Options/ Legend**. You can also cut and paste it into a document using **Ctrl+C** followed by **Ctrl+V**.

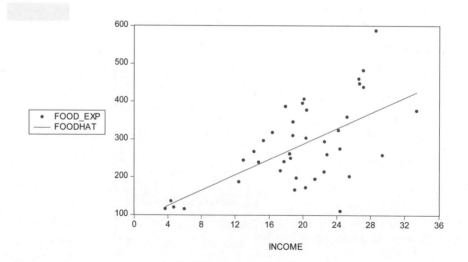

8.2 TESTING FOR HETEROSKEDASTICITY

Examining the residuals is an informal method for detecting heteroskedasticity. A more formal way of proceeding is to carry out a statistical test. We examine three possible tests: the Breusch-Pagan test, the White test and the Goldfeld-Quandt test. The Breusch-Pagan and White tests both belong to a class of tests known as Lagrange multiplier tests that are considered in Section 8.2.2 of *POE4*.

8.2.1 Lagrange multiplier tests

Lagrange multiplier tests for heteroskedasticity are based on an estimated variance function of the form

$$\hat{e}^2 = \alpha_1 + \alpha_2 z_2 + \alpha_3 z_3 + \cdots + \alpha_S z_S + v$$

where $\hat{e}^2$ are the squared least-squares residuals and $z_2, z_3, \ldots, z_S$ are the variance equation regressors. EViews has the capability to automatically compute test statistic values for these tests as well as their corresponding *p*-values. To locate this facility, open the least-squares estimated equation and then select **View/Residual Diagnostics/Heteroskedasticity Tests**.

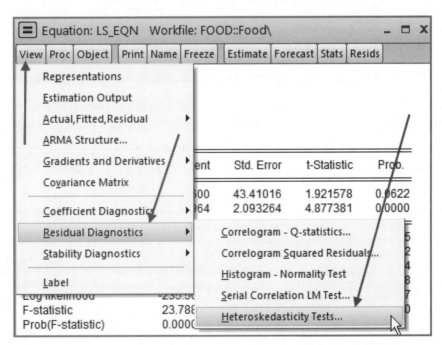

A large number of possibilities – more than you have ever dreamed of – will appear. In line with pages 303-306 of *POE4*, we will consider just two, the Breusch-Pagan test and the White test. We will also indicate where values for the tests described in Appendix 8B of *POE4* can be found. The other options are **Harvey,** where a variance function with dependent variable equal to the log of the squares of the least squares residuals is considered, **Glejser,** where the absolute value of the least squares residuals is the dependent variable, and **ARCH**, a test considered in Chapter 14. The **Custom Test Wizard** that appears at the bottom of the menu can be used to guide your choices from these options, but it is not essential.

Breusch-Pagan test

The Breusch-Pagan test (also called Breusch-Pagan-Godfrey test to recognize that Godfrey independently derived the test at about the same time as Breusch and Pagan) can be selected from the **Heteroskedasticity Tests** dialog box as indicated below. You have the option of selecting the "*z*-variables". If you do nothing, EViews will automatically insert those in the mean regression equation. For future reference, inserting *INCOME* and $INCOME^2$ leads to the White test, which will be considered next.

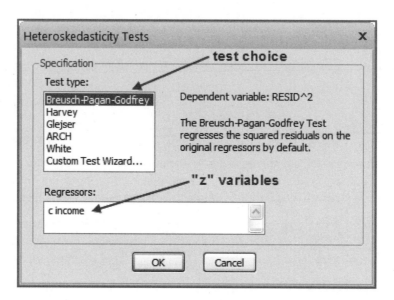

Clicking **OK** gives the following output. The value of the chi-square statistic considered on page 306 of *POE4* is $\chi^2 = N \times R^2 = 40 \times 0.1846 = 7.38$. Its corresponding *p*-value is 0.0066, leading to rejection of H_0 at a 5% significance level. The screen shot below shows where these values can be located on the output. Values for another two tests statistics also appear. If you are curious about where these values come from, please read *POE4*, Appendix 8B.

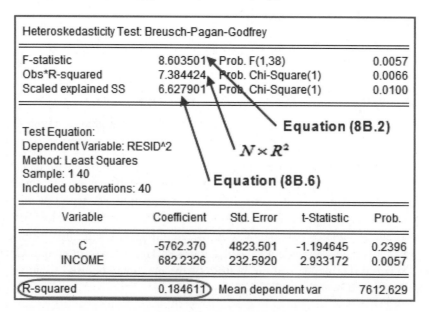

Using equations (8B.2) and (8B.6) on *POE4* pages 332-333, we can get the values of the other two tests given in the EViews output:

$$F = \frac{(SST - SSE)/(S-1)}{SSE/(N-S)} = \frac{(4.61075 \times 10^9 - 3.75956 \times 10^9)/1}{3.75956 \times 10^9/38} = 8.6035$$

$$\chi^2 = \frac{SST - SSE}{2\hat{\sigma}_e^4} = \frac{4.61075 \times 10^9 - 3.75956 \times 10^9}{2 \times 89.517^4} = 6.628$$

White test

The White test is the Breusch-Pagan test with the z-variables chosen to be the x-variables and their squares, and possibly their cross-products. In our example there is only one x-variable, namely $x = INCOME$, and so the z-variables are $INCOME$ and $INCOME^2$; there are no possible cross-product terms. In this case, if you do not tick the **Include White cross terms** box, the test will omit $INCOME$ and only use $INCOME^2$. Select **White** and click **OK**.

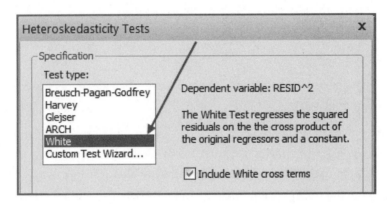

The output is given below. The value of the chi-square statistic considered in *POE4* is $\chi^2 = N \times R^2 = 40 \times 0.18888 = 7.555$. Its corresponding p-value is 0.0229, leading to rejection of H_0 at a 5% significance level. Can you see where these values are located on the output?

Heteroskedasticity Test: White

F-statistic	4.307884	Prob. F(2,37)		0.0208
Obs*R-squared	7.555079	Prob. Chi-Square(2)		0.0229
Scaled explained SS	6.781072	Prob. Chi-Square(2)		0.0337

Equation (8B.2)

Test Equation:
Dependent Variable: RESID^2
Method: Least Squares
Sample: 1 40
Included observations: 40

$N \times R^2$

Equation (8B.6)

Variable	Coefficient	Std. Error	t-Statistic	Prob.
C	-2908.783	8100.109	-0.359104	0.7216
INCOME	291.7457	915.8462	0.318553	0.7519
INCOME^2	11.16529	25.30953	0.441150	0.6617

R-squared	0.188877	Mean dependent var	7612.629

The values of the other two test statistics on the output come from equations (8B.2) and (8B.6) in *POE4* Appendix 8B. After some detective work, you will discover they are calculated as

$$F = \frac{(SST - SSE)/(S-1)}{SSE/(N-S)} = \frac{(4.61075 \times 10^9 - 3.73989 \times 10^9)/2}{3.73989 \times 10^9/37} = 4.308$$

$$\chi^2 = \frac{SST - SSE}{2\hat{\sigma}_e^4} = \frac{4.61075 \times 10^9 - 3.73989 \times 10^9}{2 \times 89.517^4} = 6.781$$

8.2.2 The Goldfeld-Quandt test

The statistic for the Goldfeld-Quandt test is the ratio of error variance estimates from two subsamples of the observations. If those estimates are $\hat{\sigma}_1^2$ and $\hat{\sigma}_2^2$, obtained from subsample regressions with $(N_1 - K_1)$ and $(N_2 - K_2)$ degrees of freedom, respectively, then, under the null hypothesis $H_0 : \sigma_1^2 = \sigma_2^2$, the test statistic is

$$F = \frac{\hat{\sigma}_2^2}{\hat{\sigma}_1^2} \sim F_{(N_2 - K_2, \, N_1 - K_1)}$$

If the alternative hypothesis is $H_1 : \sigma_1^2 \neq \sigma_2^2$, and a 5% significance level is used, the test is a two-tail one with critical values $F_{(0.975, \, N_2 - K_2, \, N_1 - K_1)}$ and $F_{(0.025, \, N_2 - K_2, \, N_1 - K_1)}$. For a 5% one-tail test with $H_1 : \sigma_2^2 > \sigma_1^2$, the critical value is $F_{(0.95, \, N_2 - K_2, \, N_1 - K_1)}$. For $H_1 : \sigma_2^2 < \sigma_1^2$, the numerator and denominator and degrees of freedom for the test can be reversed, or the critical value $F_{(0.05, \, N_2 - K_2, \, N_1 - K_1)}$ can be used. We consider application of this test to a wage equation on pages 307-8 of *POE4* and to the food expenditure equation on *POE4* page 309.

The wage equation

For the wage equation, we use data from the file ***cps2.wf1*** to estimate the equation

$$WAGE = \beta_1 + \beta_2 EDUC + \beta_3 EXPER + \beta_4 METRO + e$$

We are hypothesizing that *WAGE* depends on education (*EDUC*), experience (*EXPER*), and whether a worker lives in a metropolitan area (*METRO* $=1$ for metropolitan area, *METRO* $=0$ for rural area). We begin by finding the least squares estimates of this equation given in *POE4*, equation (8.19). No new EViews features are required for this estimation, but we report the output and then the window that produced that output for completeness.

Dependent Variable: WAGE
Method: Least Squares
Sample: 1 1000
Included observations: 1000

Variable	Coefficient	Std. Error	t-Statistic	Prob.
C	-9.913984	1.075663	-9.216631	0.0000
EDUC	1.233964	0.069961	17.63782	0.0000
EXPER	0.133244	0.015232	8.747835	0.0000
METRO	1.524104	0.431091	3.535459	0.0004

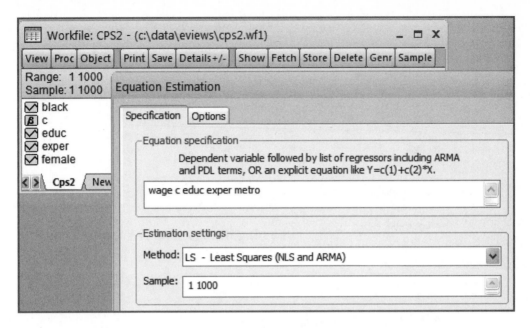

We are hypothesizing that the variance of wages for metropolitan workers could be different from that for rural workers. Thus, in the context of this example, the two variances are $\sigma_2^2 = \sigma_M^2$ and $\sigma_1^2 = \sigma_R^2$, with σ_M^2 denoting the variance of *METRO* wages and σ_R^2 denoting the variance of *RURAL* wages. The hypotheses are

$$H_0 : \sigma_R^2 = \sigma_M^2 \qquad\qquad H_1 : \sigma_R^2 \neq \sigma_M^2$$

To find estimates of σ_M^2 and σ_R^2, we estimate two separate equations, one for metropolitan workers given by

$$WAGE_{Mi} = \beta_{M1} + \beta_2 EDUC_{Mi} + \beta_3 EXPER_{Mi} + e_{Mi} \qquad i = 1,2,\ldots,N_M$$

and one for rural workers given by

$$WAGE_{Ri} = \beta_{R1} + \beta_2 EDUC_{Ri} + \beta_3 EXPER_{Ri} + e_{Ri} \qquad i = 1,2,\ldots,N_R$$

where N_M and N_R are the numbers of metropolitan workers in the sample and the number of rural workers in the sample, respectively.

Estimating the metropolitan wage equation

To estimate the wage equation for metropolitan workers, we use EViews to restrict the sample to the relevant observations. We change the sample by going to the **Estimation settings** box and specifying

> **sample 1 1000 if metro = 1**

This instruction tells EViews to consider all 1000 observations, but to restrict estimation to those where **metro = 1**.

The estimation window and the results follow. Notice that EViews reminds you about the sample you have chosen and it also tells you how many observations satisfy the restriction that you imposed. We have 808 metropolitan observations. Of particular interest are the standard deviation and variance of the error term, $\hat{\sigma}_M = 5.641$ and $\hat{\sigma}_M^2 = 31.824$. The value $\hat{\sigma}_M = 5.641$ is stored temporarily as **@se**; we can save it as **SE_METRO** using the command

```
scalar  se_metro = @se
```

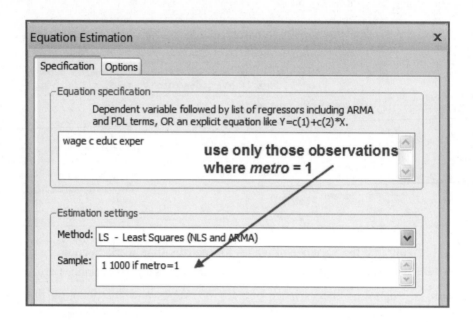

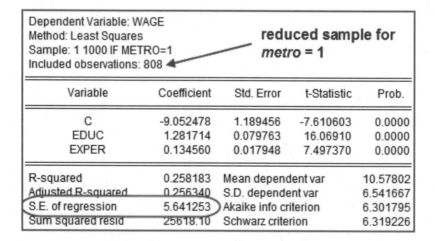

Estimating the rural wage equation

The same steps are followed for the rural observations, but in this case we restrict the sample to those observations where **metro = 0**. The results below show that there are 192 rural observations. The standard deviation and variance of the error term are, respectively, $\hat{\sigma}_R = 3.904$ and $\hat{\sigma}_R^2 = 15.243$. We save the value for $\hat{\sigma}_R$ using the command

```
scalar  se_rural = @se
```

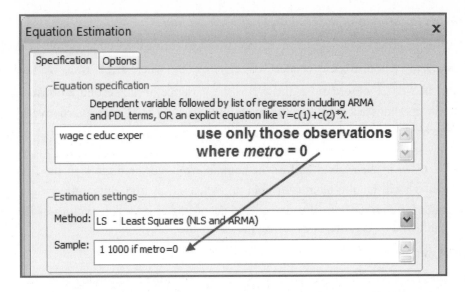

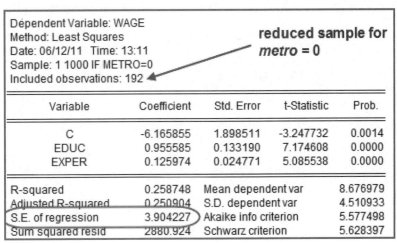

Testing the error variances from the wage equations

Having estimated the error variances for the rural and metropolitan wage equations, we are now in a position to test $H_0 : \sigma_R^2 = \sigma_M^2$ against the alternative $H_1 : \sigma_R^2 \neq \sigma_M^2$. The F-value is

$$F = \frac{\hat{\sigma}_M^2}{\hat{\sigma}_R^2} = \frac{31.824}{15.243} = 2.09$$

Given that $\hat{\sigma}_M$ and $\hat{\sigma}_R$ were earlier saved as **SE_METRO** and **SE_RURAL**, respectively, the F-value, and its 5% upper and lower critical values $F_{Uc} = 1.26$ and $F_{Lc} = 0.81$, can be computed from the commands below. Note that $N_M - K_M = 805$ and that $N_R - K_R = 189$.

```
scalar f_val = (se_metro)^2/(se_rural)^2
scalar fcrit_up = @qfdist(0.975,805,189)
scalar fcrit_low = @qfdist(0.025,805,189)
```

Testing the error variance in the food expenditure equation

For the food expenditure example there are no two well defined subsamples for σ_1^2 and σ_2^2. For convenience, and to improve our chances of rejecting H_0 when H_1 is true, we take σ_1^2 as the variance for the first 20 observations and σ_2^2 as the variance of the second 20 observations, after sorting the observations according to the magnitude of *INCOME*. Our alternative hypothesis is that σ_i^2 increases as *INCOME* increases; σ_1^2 and σ_2^2 are not actual variances, but devices to aid the testing procedure. Sorting the observations according to the values of *INCOME* means that values of *INCOME* in the second half of the sample are larger than those in the first half of the sample. Thus, $\hat{\sigma}_2^2$ will tend to be greater than $\hat{\sigma}_1^2$ when H_1 is true, but similar when H_0 is true. The observations in *food.wf1* are already ordered according to increasing values of *INCOME*, but, if they were not, you can reorder them using the command

    sort income

This command reorders all series in your workfile according the magnitude of *INCOME*.

To use the first 20 observations to estimate σ_1^2, we restrict the **Sample** as follows:

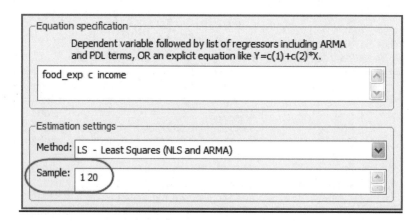

The value $\hat{\sigma}_1^2 = (59.78939)^2 = 3574.8$ is obtained by squaring the value of **S.E. of regression** in the resulting output. We give it the name **SIG1_SQ**.

    scalar sig1_sq = @se^2

A similar exercise is followed for the second half of the sample.

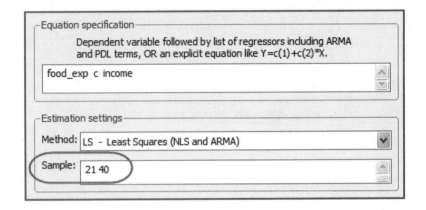

Dependent Variable: FOOD_EXP
Method: Least Squares
Sample: 21 40 ◄─────────── **second half of sample**
Included observations: 20

Variable	Coefficient	Std. Error	t-Statistic	Prob.
C	-24.91465	184.9249	-0.134729	0.8943
INCOME	14.26400	7.425093	1.921054	0.0707

R-squared	0.170142	Mean dependent var	326.9640
Adjusted R-squared	0.124038	S.D. dependent var	121.4566
S.E. of regression	113.6747	Akaike info criterion	12.39920

The variance estimate $\hat{\sigma}_2^2 = (113.6747)^2 = 12921.9$ can be obtained with the following command:

> **scalar sig2_sq = @se^2**

Then, the following two commands yield the F-value, $F = \hat{\sigma}_2^2 / \hat{\sigma}_1^2 = 1291.9/3574.8 = 3.61$, as well as the 5% critical value, $F_{(0.95,18,18)} = 2.22$:

> **scalar f_val = sig2_sq/sig1_sq**
> **scalar f_crit = @qfdist(0.95, 18, 18)**

8.3 HETEROSKEDASTICITY-CONSISTENT STANDARD ERRORS

One option for correcting conventional least-squares interval estimates and hypothesis tests that are no longer correct under heteroskedasticity is to use what are known as White's heteroskedasticity-consistent standard errors. These standard errors are obtained in EViews by choosing an estimation option. In the **Equation Estimation** box, click on the **Options** tab. In the **Options** dialog box, the relevant "sub-box" is the one entitled **Coefficient covariance matrix**. Select **White**. We have also ticked the degrees of freedom adjustment box, **d.f. Adjustment**, in line with *POE4* equation (8.25). Click **OK**.

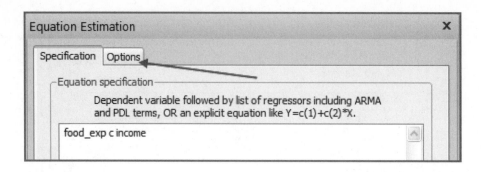

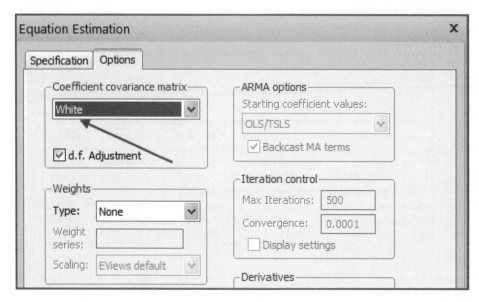

In the output that follows there is a note telling you that the standard errors and covariance are the heteroskedasticity-consistent ones. By "covariance", it means the whole covariance matrix for the estimated coefficients. The standard errors are the square roots of the diagonal elements of this matrix. All test outcomes computed from this new object, including the **Wald tests** considered extensively in Chapter 6, will use the new covariance matrix. The least squares estimates remain the same.

Dependent Variable: FOOD_EXP
Method: Least Squares
Sample: 1 40
Included observations: 40
White heteroskedasticity-consistent standard errors & covariance

Variable	Coefficient	Std. Error	t-Statistic	Prob.
C	83.41600	27.46375	3.037313	0.0043
INCOME	10.20964	1.809077	5.643565	0.0000

To find 95% interval estimates for β_1 and β_2 using the White standard errors, go to the estimation output, and then select **View/Coefficient Diagnostics/Confidence Intervals**, and put 0.95 in the resulting **Confidence Intervals** dialog box.

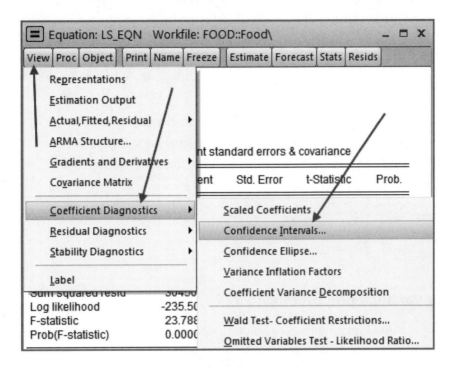

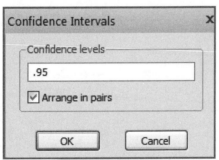

The output gives the 95% interval estimates (27.82, 139.01) for β_1 and (6.55, 13.87) for β_2

Coefficient Confidence Intervals
Sample: 1 40
Included observations: 40

| | | 95% CI | |
Variable	Coefficient	Low	High
C	83.41600	27.81855	139.0135
INCOME	10.20964	6.547359	13.87193

8.4 GENERALIZED LEAST SQUARES ESTIMATION

When the errors are heteroskedastic, the minimum variance unbiased estimator for the regression coefficients is the generalized least squares (GLS) estimator. To appreciate the nature of this estimator, let the error variance for the ith observation be given by σ_i^2. The GLS estimator is obtained by applying least squares to the transformed model:

$$\left(\frac{y_i}{\sigma_i}\right) = \beta_1\left(\frac{1}{\sigma_i}\right) + \beta_2\left(\frac{x_{i2}}{\sigma_i}\right) + \cdots + \beta_K\left(\frac{x_{iK}}{\sigma_i}\right) + \left(\frac{e_i}{\sigma_i}\right)$$

Each observation is weighted by $(1/\sigma_i)$, the inverse of the standard deviation of the error. For this reason, the GLS estimator is often called **weighted least squares**. We show how to obtain GLS or weighted least squares estimates for three different assumptions about σ_i^2:

1. $\sigma_i^2 = \sigma^2 x_i$

2. $\sigma_i^2 = \sigma_M^2$ or σ_R^2

3. $\sigma_i^2 = \sigma^2 x_i^\gamma$

8.4.1 Error variance proportional to *x*

Returning to the food expenditure equation $y_i = \beta_1 + \beta_2 x_i + e_i$, where $y = FOOD\_EXP$ and $x_i = INCOME$, we assume that the error variance is given by

$$\sigma_i^2 = \sigma^2 x_i = \sigma^2 INCOME_i$$

The transformed model becomes

$$\left(\frac{y_i}{\sqrt{x_i}}\right) = \beta_1\left(\frac{1}{\sqrt{x_i}}\right) + \beta_2\frac{x_i}{\sqrt{x_i}} + \frac{e_i}{\sqrt{x_i}}$$

or

$$\left(\frac{FOOD\_EXP_i}{\sqrt{INCOME_i}}\right) = \beta_1\left(\frac{1}{\sqrt{INCOME_i}}\right) + \beta_2\frac{INCOME_i}{\sqrt{INCOME_i}} + \frac{e_i}{\sqrt{INCOME_i}}$$

We consider a short way and a long way to compute the weighted least squares (GLS) estimator.

A short way

Weighted least squares is another **Equation Estimation** option, so our starting point is the same as that for the White standard errors:

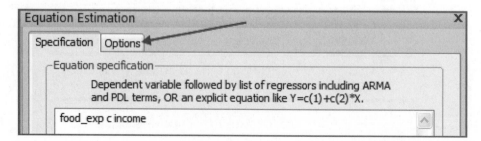

One of the options in the **Options** dialog box is the **Weights**. There are three things to specify in the **Weights** box: **Type**, **Weight series** and **Scaling**.

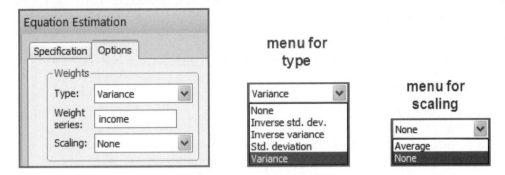

Type refers to the series that is entered in the **Weight series** box below it. In our case we entered *INCOME*. Since we are assuming the error variance is proportional to income, $\sigma_i^2 = \sigma^2 INCOME_i$, we choose **Variance** from the **Type** menu. The other types could also be used. In the context of this example, where we continue to assume $\sigma_i^2 = \sigma^2 INCOME_i$, they would be entered in the following way. Note that **sqr** is EViews' function for square root.

Type	Weight series
Inverse standard deviation	$1/\mathrm{sqr}(INCOME)$
Inverse variance	$1/INCOME$
Standard deviation	$\mathrm{sqr}(INCOME)$
Variance	$INCOME$

There are two options for **Scaling** – **Average** and **None**. We have chosen the less complicated option, which is **None**. In this case EViews defines a weight as $w_i = 1/INCOME_i$ and finds transformed variables as

$$y_i^* = \sqrt{w_i}\, y_i \qquad x_{i1}^* = \sqrt{w_i} \qquad x_{i2}^* = \sqrt{w_i}\, x_{i2}$$

If **Average** is chosen, the variables are transformed by multiplying by $\sqrt{w_i^*}$, where

$$w_i^* = \frac{w_i}{\overline{w}} = \frac{w_i}{\dfrac{1}{N}\sum_{i=1}^{N} w_i} = \frac{1/INCOME_i}{\dfrac{1}{N}\sum_{i=1}^{N}\left(1/INCOME_i\right)}$$

Since $N^{-1}\sum_{i=1}^{N}\left(1/INCOME_i\right)$ is constant for all observations i, the type of scaling has no effect on the GLS estimates, their standard errors, t and p-values. However, it does change the sum of squared errors and the estimate for σ^2 obtained using the transformed variables. To see how the specification for σ^2 changes, note that we can write

$$\mathrm{var}(e_i) = \sigma^2 INCOME_i = \frac{\sigma^2}{w_i} = \frac{\sigma^2}{\overline{w}}\frac{\overline{w}}{w_i} = \frac{\sigma_*^2}{w_i^*}$$

With average scaling we estimate $\sigma_*^2 = \sigma^2/\overline{w}$; with no scaling we estimate σ^2.

The weighted least squares (GLS) estimates follow. They are those given in equation (8.32) of *POE4*. Note that EViews tells you the weighting series and type of scaling that have been used. EViews also gives a set of weighted statistics and a set of unweighted statistics. The weighted statistics are calculated using the transformed variables. The unweighted statistics use the original variables.

Dependent Variable: FOOD_EXP
Method: Least Squares
Sample: 1 40
Included observations: 40
Weighting series: INCOME
Weight type: Variance (no scaling)

Variable	Coefficient	Std. Error	t-Statistic	Prob.
C	78.68408	23.78872	3.307621	0.0021
INCOME	10.45101	1.385891	7.541002	0.0000

Weighted Statistics

R-squared	0.599438	Mean dependent var	64.71431
Adjusted R-squared	0.588897	S.D. dependent var	18.78239
S.E. of regression	18.75006	Akaike info criterion	8.748977
Sum squared resid	13359.45	Schwarz criterion	8.833421
Log likelihood	-172.9795	Hannan-Quinn criter.	8.779509
F-statistic	56.86672	Durbin-Watson stat	1.905701
Prob(F-statistic)	0.000000	Weighted mean dep.	235.7496

Unweighted Statistics

R-squared	0.384787	Mean dependent var	283.5735
Adjusted R-squared	0.368597	S.D. dependent var	112.6752
S.E. of regression	89.53266	Sum squared resid	304611.7
Durbin-Watson stat	1.892377		

The 95% confidence interval given on page 313 of *POE4* can be obtained by selecting **View/ Coefficient Diagnostics/Confidence Intervals**.

Coefficient Confidence Intervals
Sample: 1 40
Included observations: 40

Variable	Coefficient	95% CI Low	High
C	78.68408	30.52633	126.8418
INCOME	10.45101	7.645419	13.25660

A long way

The long way to obtain weighted least squares estimates is to transform each of your variables by dividing by $\sqrt{INCOME}$ as described on page 312 of *POE4*, and to then apply least squares without the weights. The variables can be transformed by creating new series, or by dividing each variable by $\sqrt{INCOME}$ in the equation specification. If you choose to create new series, the following commands are suitable:

```
series  wt = 1/income
series  swt = sqr(wt)
series  ystar = food_exp*swt
series  x1star = swt
series  x2star = income*swt
```

Enter these new series in the **Equation specification** box:

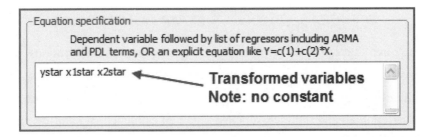

Click **OK**. Observe that the resulting estimates are the same as those we obtained the short way. In the summary statistics beneath the estimates, the value for R^2 is different. Since there is no unambiguous, unique definition of R^2 in GLS models or in models with no constant term, we suggest avoiding the use of R^2 in these situations.

Dependent Variable: YSTAR
Method: Least Squares
Sample: 1 40
Included observations: 40

Variable	Coefficient	Std. Error	t-Statistic	Prob.
X1STAR	78.68408	23.78872	3.307621	0.0021
X2STAR	10.45101	1.385891	7.541002	0.0000

R-squared	0.028993	Mean dependent var	64.71431
Adjusted R-squared	0.003440	S.D. dependent var	18.78239
S.E. of regression	18.75006	Akaike info criterion	8.748977
Sum squared resid	13359.45	Schwarz criterion	8.833421
Log likelihood	-172.9795	Hannan-Quinn criter.	8.779509
Durbin-Watson stat	1.905701		

An alternative way that avoids the need to define new series is to transform the variables within the **Equation specification**, as illustrated below. Try it. Check your output.

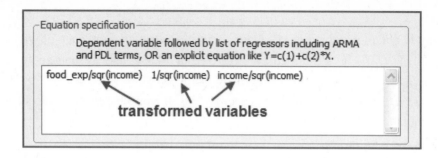

8.4.2 Grouped data: two error variances

In this section we consider a case where the observations are divided into two groups, and the error variance is different for each of the groups. We use data from the file *cps2.wf1* to estimate the equation

$$WAGE = \beta_1 + \beta_2 EDUC + \beta_3 EXPER + \beta_4 METRO + e$$

under the assumption that the error variance from the metropolitan observations σ_M^2 is different from the error variance for the rural observations σ_R^2. Recall that, in Section 8.2.2, we showed that the Goldfeld-Quandt test rejects the hypothesis $H_0 : \sigma_M^2 = \sigma_R^2$. We estimated separate equations for metropolitan and rural workers and obtained estimates $\hat{\sigma}_M$ and $\hat{\sigma}_R$ that we saved as **SE_METRO** and **SE_RURAL**, respectively.

To obtain GLS estimates of the equation, we get EViews to estimate a transformed model where the variables are divided by $\hat{\sigma}_M$ for the metropolitan observations and by $\hat{\sigma}_R$ for the rural observations. We create the following series to use in the **Weight series** box:

series stdevn = metro*se_metro + (1-metro)*se_rural

The series *STDEVN* is equal to $\hat{\sigma}_M$ for the metropolitan observations and $\hat{\sigma}_R$ for the rural observations. The equation specification is

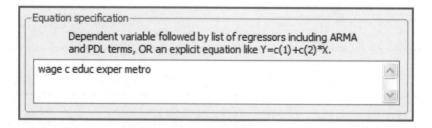

The **Weights** dialog box found under **Options** is filled out as follows:

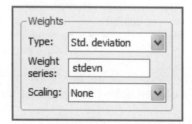

The following results can be checked against those on page 315 of *POE4*:

Dependent Variable: WAGE
Method: Least Squares
Sample: 1 1000
Included observations: 1000
Weighting series: STDEVN
Weight type: Standard deviation (no scaling)

Variable	Coefficient	Std. Error	t-Statistic	Prob.
C	-9.398362	1.019673	-9.217038	0.0000
EDUC	1.195721	0.068508	17.45375	0.0000
EXPER	0.132209	0.014549	9.087448	0.0000
METRO	1.538803	0.346286	4.443740	0.0000

8.4.3 GLS with an unkown variance function

For this Section, we return to the food expenditure example. The heteroskedastic assumption made in Section 8.4.1 ($\sigma_i^2 = \sigma^2 x_i$) can be viewed as a special case of the more general assumption $\sigma_i^2 = \sigma^2 x_i^\gamma$ where γ is an unknown parameter. Under this more general assumption γ must be estimated before we can proceed with weighted or generalized least squares estimation. In line with Section 8.5 of *POE4*, we first estimate σ^2 and γ and then proceed to generalized least squares estimation.

Variance function estimates and predictions

The equation for estimating σ^2 and γ is written as

$$\ln(\hat{e}_i^2) = \alpha_1 + \alpha_2 \ln(x_i) + v_i$$

where $\hat{e}_i$ are the least squares residuals, $\alpha_1 = \ln(\sigma^2)$ and $\alpha_2 = \gamma$. Recognizing that the $\hat{e}_i$ were previously saved in the workfile ***food.wf1*** under the name *EHAT* and that $x_i = INCOME$, least squares estimates for α_1 and α_2 are obtained using the following **Equation specification**:

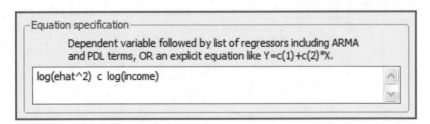

Output for the estimated equation $\widehat{\ln(\hat{e}_i^2)} = \hat{\alpha}_1 + \hat{\alpha}_2 \ln(INCOME_i)$ appears at the top of the next page; $\hat{\alpha}_1 = 0.937796$ and $\hat{\alpha}_2 = 2.329239$. To proceed to generalized least squares estimation, we need the exponential of the predictions from this equation, $\hat{\sigma}_i^2 = \exp(\hat{\alpha}_1 + \hat{\alpha}_2 \ln(INCOME_i))$ or their square roots $\hat{\sigma}_i$. It is instructive to consider two ways of computing them.

Dependent Variable: LOG(EHAT^2)
Method: Least Squares
Sample: 1 40
Included observations: 40

Variable	Coefficient	Std. Error	t-Statistic	Prob.
C	0.937796	1.583106	0.592377	0.5571
LOG(INCOME)	2.329239	0.541336	4.302761	0.0001

The first way to compute the predictions $\hat{\sigma}_i^2 = \exp\left(\hat{\alpha}_1 + \hat{\alpha}_2 \ln(INCOME_i)\right)$ and their square roots is using the commands

> **series sig2hat = exp(c(1) + c(2)*log(income))**
> **series sighat = @sqrt(sig2hat)**

If the variance equation is the most recently estimated regression, then $C(1) = \hat{\alpha}_1$ and $C(2) = \hat{\alpha}_2$.

An alternative way of obtaining $\hat{\sigma}_i =$ **sighat** is to use the **forecast** option. In the window displaying the output from estimating the variance equation, click on [Forecast]. In the resulting forecast window, you will see two possible series that can be forecast, **EHAT** and **LOG(EHAT^2)**. This choice arises because the dependent variable in the **Equation specification** was written as $\log(\hat{e}^2)$, a transformation of the series $\hat{e}$. EViews is giving you the option of forecasting the original series $\hat{e}$ or its transformed version $q = \log(\hat{e}^2)$. If you had defined the variable $q = \log(\hat{e}^2)$ via a **series** command and then specified your dependent variable as q, there would be no choice; EViews would assume you want to forecast q. Writing the transformation as part of the equation specification is what leads to the choice.

Now consider the two options. If you click **LOG(EHAT^2)**, EViews will give you the forecasts $\hat{q}_i = \ln(\hat{\sigma}_i^2)$. If you click **EHAT**, it will invert the transformation given in the **Equation specification** and give you the forecasts $\hat{\sigma}_i = \sqrt{\exp(\hat{q}_i)}$. Since it is convenient to use $\hat{\sigma}_i$ to transform the variables in the generalized least squares procedure, we choose **EHAT**. We call the forecast series *SIGHAT*.

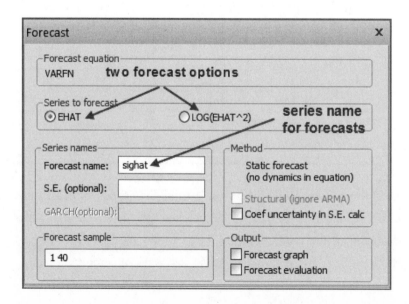

GLS estimates

To obtain the generalized least squares estimates in equation (8.47) on page 318 of *POE4*, we use EViews weighted least squares option, with **Weight Type** given by **Std. deviation** and **Weight series** given by $\hat{\sigma}_i = SIGHAT$. The **Equation specification,** the **Weights** dialog box, and the resulting output follow.

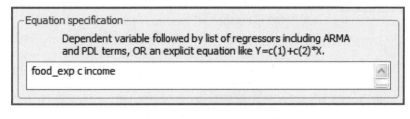

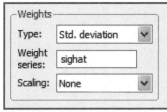

Dependent Variable: FOOD_EXP
Method: Least Squares
Sample: 1 40
Included observations: 40
Weighting series: SIGHAT
Weight type: Standard deviation (no scaling)

Variable	Coefficient	Std. Error	t-Statistic	Prob.
C	76.05379	9.713489	7.829709	0.0000
INCOME	10.63349	0.971514	10.94528	0.0000

8.5 THE LINEAR PROBABILITY MODEL

In Section 8.6 of *POE4* we consider a linear probability model where the choice of purchasing either Coke $(COKE = 1)$ or Pepsi $(COKE = 0)$ depends on the relative price of Coke to Pepsi $(PRATIO)$ and whether store displays were present $(DISP\_COKE = 1$ if a display was present for Coke, 0 otherwise; $DISP\_PEPSI = 1$ if a display was present for Pepsi; 0 otherwise). Data are in the file ***coke.wf1***. Table 8.1 on page 320 of *POE4* contains four sets of results. Those for least squares and for least squares with robust standard errors can be obtained using EViews procedures that we have already discussed. Thus, we focus on the last two columns in the Table: GLS estimates where least squares predicted probabilities that are outside the (0,1) interval have been truncated to 0.01 or 0.99, and GLS estimates that ignore observations where least squares predicted probabilities are outside the (0,1) interval.

Suppose that you have obtained least squares estimates using the following **Equation Specification**:

Equation specification

Dependent variable followed by list of regressors including ARMA and PDL terms, OR an explicit equation like Y=c(1)+c(2)*X.

coke c pratio disp_coke disp_pepsi

Estimation settings

Method: LS - Least Squares (NLS and ARMA)

Sample: 1 1140

From the least squares estimates, go to [Forecast] to obtain the predictions $\hat{p} = PHAT$.

Forecast	X

Forecast of

Equation: LS   Series: COKE

Series names

Forecast name: PHAT

S.E. (optional):

GARCH(optional):

Method

Static forecast
(no dynamics in equation)

☐ Structural (ignore ARMA)
☐ Coef uncertainty in S.E. calc

Forecast sample

1 1140

Output

☐ Forecast graph
☐ Forecast evaluation

Having found the values for $\hat{p}$, we need to check how many of them are less than or equal to zero and how many are greater than or equal to one. We can do so by creating indicator variables that are equal to one for the offending observations:

```
series  plt0 = (phat <= 0)
series  pgt1 = (phat >= 1)
```

These commands assign a value of 1 to the series if the statement in parentheses is true and 0 otherwise. Thus, **plt0** will be equal to 1 when $\hat{p} \le 0$ and equal to 0 when $\hat{p} > 0$. Similarly, **pgt1** will be equal to 1 when $\hat{p} \ge 1$ and equal to 0 when $\hat{p} < 1$. The following two commands compute the number of observations for which $\hat{p} \le 0$ and the number of observations for which $\hat{p} \ge 1$:

```
scalar  nlt0 = @sum(plt0)
scalar  ngt1 = @sum(pgt1)
```

We find 16 observations where $\hat{p} \le 0$ and no observations where $\hat{p} \ge 1$:

	Value
NLT0	16.00000

	Value
NGT1	0.000000

For the first set of GLS estimates, we need to truncate the non-positive values of $\hat{p}$ to 0.01. The following command creates a new series **ptrun** along these lines:

series ptrun = (1-plt0)*phat + plt0*0.01

Then, recalling that the variance of the error term in the linear probability model is $p_i(1-p_i)$, we fill in the **Weights** dialog box as follows:

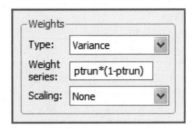

The output agrees with that in the third column in Table 8.1 in *POE4*.

Dependent Variable: COKE
Method: Least Squares
Sample: 1 1140
Included observations: 1140
Weighting series: PTRUN*(1-PTRUN)
Weight type: Variance (no scaling)

Variable	Coefficient	Std. Error	t-Statistic	Prob.
C	0.650522	0.056847	11.44337	0.0000
PRATIO	-0.165240	0.044370	-3.724125	0.0002
DISP_COKE	0.093987	0.039874	2.357123	0.0186
DISP_PEPSI	-0.131423	0.035404	-3.712115	0.0002

For the second set of GLS estimates, we omit those observations where $\hat{p} \le 0$. Thus, we have

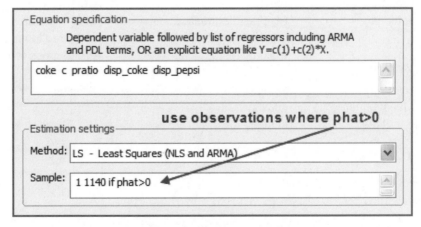

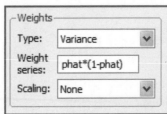

The output corresponding to the last column in Table 8.1 is

Dependent Variable: COKE
Method: Least Squares
Sample: 1 1140 IF PHAT>0
Included observations: 1124
Weighting series: PHAT*(1-PHAT)
Weight type: Variance (no scaling)

Variable	Coefficient	Std. Error	t-Statistic	Prob.
C	0.879501	0.059389	14.80928	0.0000
PRATIO	-0.385885	0.052704	-7.321738	0.0000
DISP_COKE	0.075995	0.035307	2.152390	0.0316
DISP_PEPSI	-0.158745	0.036031	-4.405776	0.0000

Keywords

@qfdist
@se
@sqrt
@sum
actual
add text
apply
Breusch-Pagan-Godfrey
coefficient diagnostics
confidence intervals
covariance matrix
custom test wizard
estimation settings
fitted
forecast
forecast name
F-test
generalized least squares
Goldfeld-Quandt test

graph object
Grouped data
heteroskedasticity tests
least squares line: plot
legend
line/shade
line/symbol
options: estimation
options: graph
outliers
plots
resid
residual diagnostics
residual graph
residual tests
residuals
sample
scaling
scatter

sort
sqr
standard errors: White
standardized residual graph
symbol size
symbol type
transformed variables
type: graph
variance function
variance function: testing
weight
weight type
weight series
weighted least squares
White cross terms
White test
XY line

CHAPTER **9**

Regression with Time-Series Data: Stationary Variables

CHAPTER OUTLINE

Chapter 9 is the first chapter in *POE4* devoted to some of the special issues that are considered when estimating relationships with **time-series data**. Time provides a natural ordering of the observations that is not present when using random cross-section observations, and it leads to dynamic features in regression equations. EViews has many options for handling such features. This chapter introduces some of those features.

9.1 FINITE DISTRIBUTED LAGS

The first dynamic regression model considered in the 4th edition of *Principles of Econometrics* (*POE4*) is a finite distributed lag model where the change in unemployment from one quarter to the next, DU_t, depends on current and past values of growth in GDP, G_t. It is assumed that, after

q quarters have elapsed, changes in G no longer have an influence on DU, and so the finite distributed lag model can be written as

$$DU_t = \alpha + \beta_0 G_t + \beta_1 G_{t-1} + \beta_2 G_{t-2} + \cdots + \beta_q G_{t-q} + e_t$$

The data for estimating this model is provided in the file **okun.wf1**. Before giving details of estimation, it is useful to examine some basic EViews tools for time-series data.

9.1.1 Structuring the workfile

When you open the file **okun.wf1**, you will discover there are 98 observations, but no information on the dates or time period covered by those observations. You can structure the workfile to include the dates and the frequency of the observations. The first of the following two screen shots shows the workfile range and sample before restructuring. The second shows how to locate the restructuring option: go to **Proc/Structure/Resize Current Page**.

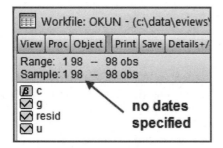 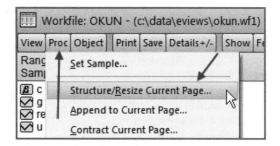

In the resulting dialog box, you choose **Dated – regular frequency** for the **structure**, **Quarterly** for the **Frequency**, and you insert the **Start** and **End dates** as **1985Q2** and **2009Q3**, respectively.

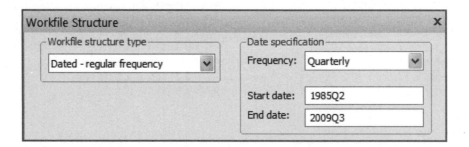

Notice how the workfile range and sample have changed to include the start and end dates.

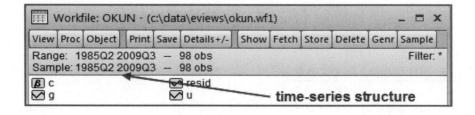

9.1.2 Lagging and differencing

The variables in our finite distributed lag model are the quarterly growth in GDP, G_t, and the change in quarterly unemployment DU_t. The EViews workfile contains GDP growth, but, instead of the change in unemployment, it contains the unemployment rate itself. The change in unemployment can be found by creating the differenced series $DU_t = \Delta U_t = U_t - U_{t-1}$. To do so we use the difference operator **D(u)**:

> **series du = D(u)**

To create the lagged variables $U_{t-1}, G_{t-1}, G_{t-2}, G_{t-3}$ that appear in Table 9.1 on page 345 of *POE4* and to name them *U1*, *G1*, *G2* and *G3*, we use the following commands:

> **series u1 = u(-1)**
> **series g1 = g(-1)**
> **series g2 = g(-2)**
> **series g3 = g(-3)**

Then, to display the spreadsheet in Table 9.1, we can construct a group containing the relevant variables as shown below. The arrows have been inserted to give examples of what happens to the positions of observations when variables are lagged. For example, in the row for 1986Q3,

$$U_t = U_{1986Q3} = 7.0 \qquad U_{t-1} = U_{1986Q2} = 7.2$$

$$G_t = G_{1986Q3} = 1.5 \qquad G_{t-1} = G_{1986Q2} = 0.9 \qquad G_{t-2} = G_{1986Q1} = 1.5 \qquad G_{t-3} = G_{1985Q4} = 1.4$$

Lagging or differencing means we lose the early observations; the number lost is equal to the number of lags. EViews inserts **NA** for "not available" for those observations that are lost. It omits these observations from any calculations involving these series.

obs	U	U1	DU	G	G1	G2	G3
1985Q2	7.3	NA	NA	1.4	NA	NA	NA
1985Q3	7.2	7.300000	-0.100000	2.0	1.400000	NA	NA
1985Q4	7.0	7.200000	-0.200000	1.4	2.000000	1.400000	NA
1986Q1	7.0	7.000000	0.000000	1.5	1.400000	2.000000	1.400000
1986Q2	7.2	7.000000	0.200000	0.9	1.500000	1.400000	2.000000
1986Q3	7.0	7.200000	-0.200000	1.5	0.900000	1.500000	1.400000
1986Q4	6.8	7.000000	-0.200000	1.2	1.500000	0.900000	1.500000

9.1.3 Line graphs

The starting point for any investigation using time-series data is graphing of the series. The two series of interest for estimating the Okun's Law equation are *G* and *DU*. To reproduce the graph in Figure 9.4(a) on page 345 of *POE4*, go to your workfile and open the series *DU*. Then select **View/Graph**.

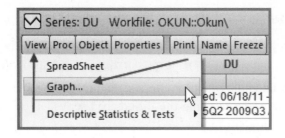

The **Graph Options** dialog box opens. The default settings displayed in the screen shot below are suitable for producing the typical line graph, which follows. If you are happy with this graph, you can save it by using **Freeze**. If you would first like to make some changes, go to **Options**.

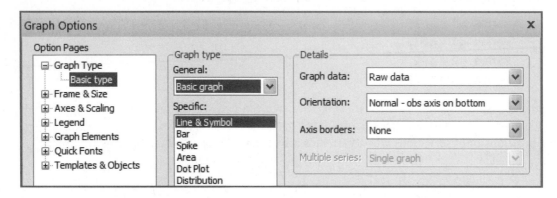

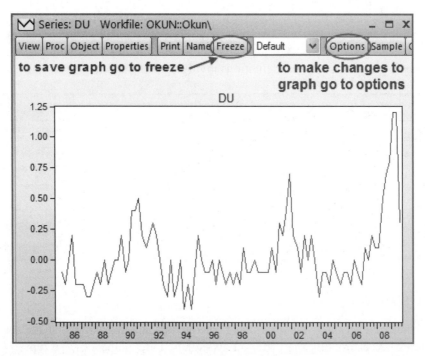

Before freezing the graph to save it, we will use **Options** to make one small change. The graph in *POE4* Figure 9.4(a) has symbols at each observation, as well being a line graph that joins those symbols. To insert the symbols, first go to the **Graph Options** dialog box. The left-hand inner box is **Option pages**. In that box, choose **Graph Elements/Lines & Symbols**. On the resulting option page the right-hand inner box is **Attributes**. In that box, from the drop-down menu for

Line/Symbol use, choose **Line & Symbol**. If you are comfortable with the color, the line pattern, the line width, the type of symbol, and the symbol size, you can click **Apply** and then **OK**. Otherwise, changes can be made accordingly.

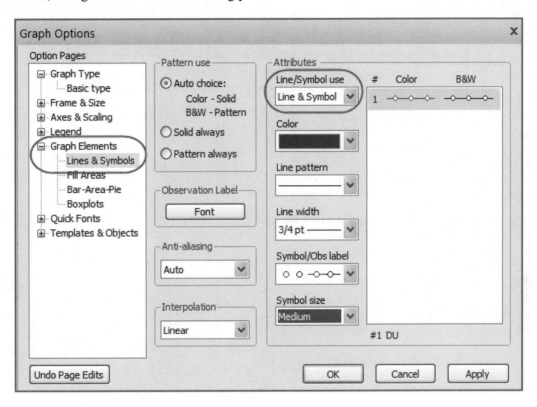

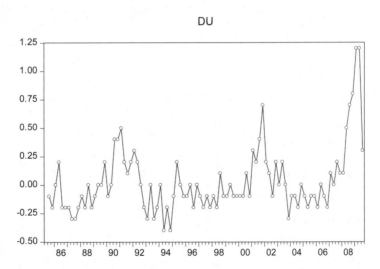

This graph resembles that in *POE4* Figure 9.4(a). Many other options are available; they include such things as labeling and setting up the axes. You should explore the various alternatives.

Having made any required changes to the graph, it can now be saved in your workfile. After you click on **Freeze**, the graph will reappear. The window will be different, however, because it will now be a "graph object" rather than a "series object". You can tell the difference because there will be a graph icon in the upper left of the window. Then, there is one remaining task; that is to name the graph. The following two screen shots show the graph icon and how the graph is named. In the first screen shot the graph has been cut off the bottom to economize on space. We call the graph **FIG_9_4A**.

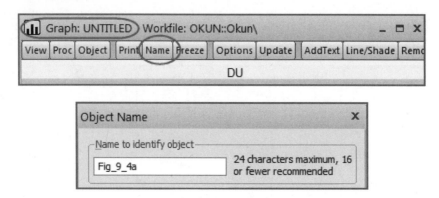

Similar steps can be followed to construct the line graph for GDP growth that appears in Figure 9.4(b) on page 345 of *POE4*.

9.1.4 Estimation

We now turn to estimation of the finite distributed lag model that relates the change in inflation to GDP growth. We first consider the model for $q = 3$:

$$DU_t = \alpha + \beta_0 G_t + \beta_1 G_{t-1} + \beta_2 G_{t-2} + \beta_3 G_{t-3} + e_t$$

We can specify the equation in the **Equation Estimation** window as follows:

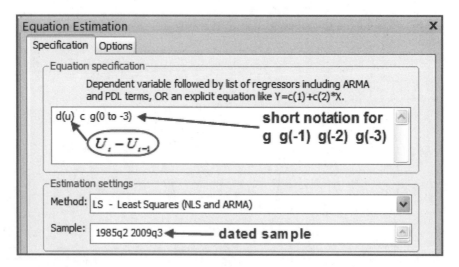

The dependent variable is $DU_t = \Delta U_t = U_t - U_{t-1}$. It can be inserted as **D(u)**, the difference of U. The current and lagged values of G could be inserted as **g g(-1) g(-2) g(-3)**, but a more convenient and equivalent way to write G and its lags is **g(0 to -3)**.

An alternative to using the **Equation specification** window is to use following command in the EViews Command window. Note that we have named the equation **OKUN_FDL3**.

```
equation okun_fdl3.ls D(u) c g(0 to -3)
```

The resulting output is that given in Table 9.2 on page 346 of *POE4*.

Dependent Variable: D(U)				
Method: Least Squares		**Fewer observations**		
Sample (adjusted): 1986Q1 2009Q3		**to accommodate lags**		
Included observations: 95 after adjustments				
Variable	Coefficient	Std. Error	t-Statistic	Prob.
C	0.580975	0.053889	10.78090	0.0000
G	-0.202053	0.033013	-6.120369	0.0000
G(-1)	-0.164535	0.035818	-4.593706	0.0000
G(-2)	-0.071556	0.035304	-2.026836	0.0456
G(-3)	0.003303	0.036260	0.091092	0.9276
R-squared	0.652406	Mean dependent var		0.027368
S.E. of regression	0.174329	Akaike info criterion		-0.604545

You may have noticed that we did not need the differenced and lagged variables *DU*, *G1*, *G2*, and *G3* that we created in Section 9.1.2. We could have used them. And we would obtain the same result. But it was not necessary. EViews will carry out the required differencing and lagging before estimating. Had we used the variables created in Section 9.1.2, the command would be

equation okun_fdl3.ls du c g g1 g2 g3

For the model with two lags of G_t, one can use **D(u) c g(0 to -2)** in the **Equation specification** window or use the command

equation okun_fdl2.ls D(u) c g(0 to -2)

The output in the lower part of Table 9.2 is as follows. Note that one more observation is used because there is one fewer lag.

Dependent Variable: D(U)				
Method: Least Squares				
Sample (adjusted): 1985Q4 2009Q3				
Included observations: 96 after adjustments				
Variable	Coefficient	Std. Error	t-Statistic	Prob.
C	0.583556	0.047212	12.36036	0.0000
G	-0.202022	0.032383	-6.238474	0.0000
G(-1)	-0.165327	0.033537	-4.929709	0.0000
G(-2)	-0.070013	0.033100	-2.115213	0.0371
R-squared	0.653946	Mean dependent var		0.025000
S.E. of regression	0.172600	Akaike info criterion		-0.634907

Once the equation has been estimated, the various multipliers are of interest. The impact, one-period delay, and two-period delay multipliers are given by $b_0 = -0.2020$, $b_1 = -0.1653$, and $b_2 = -0.0700$, respectively. The one-period and two-period interim multipliers are given by $b_0 + b_1 = -0.3673$, and $b_0 + b_1 + b_2 = -0.4374$. The natural growth rate is $\hat{\alpha}/(b_0 + b_1 + b_2) = 1.334$. These quantities can be found using the commands

scalar interim1 = c(2) +c(3)

```
scalar  interim2 = interim1 + c(4)
scalar  ngwth = -c(1)/interim2
```

9.2 SERIAL CORRELATION

In this section we are concerned with computing and displaying the autocorrelations of a series. The series could be a variable like GDP growth G, where the autocorrelations are the correlations between G_t and its lags $G_{t-1}, G_{t-2}, G_{t-3}, \cdots$, or it could be the residuals of an estimated regression, where the autocorrelations are the correlations between $\hat{e}_t$ and $\hat{e}_{t-1}, \hat{e}_{t-2}, \hat{e}_{t-2}, \cdots$. In the latter case the autocorrelations are used to assess whether the errors in the regression equation are serially correlated.

9.2.1 A scatter diagram

For a preliminary look at the possibility of correlation between G_t and G_{t-1}, we can examine a scatter diagram between these two variables, as depicted in Figure 9.5 on page 348 of *POE4*. To create this figure, go to **Object/New Object**, select **Graph**, and insert a name in the dialog box. When asked for the **Series List**, insert *G* and *G1*. After clicking **OK**, the graph icon fig_9_5 appears in your workfile. Opening the graph object **FIG_9_5** reveals two line graphs – not the scatter plot that you wanted! To change it to the scatter plot, go to **Options** and then select **Graph Type** and **Scatter.**

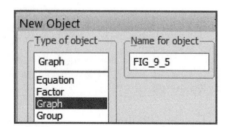
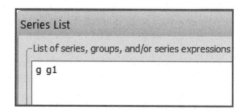

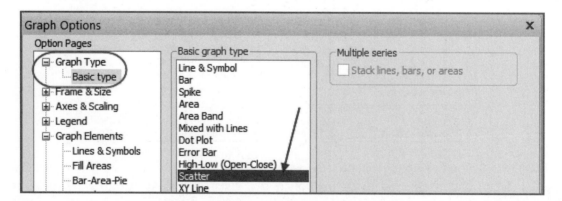

You will discover that the resulting scatter diagram has started to look like Figure 9.5, but the symbols for the scatter are hollow and small, and there are no lines drawn at the mean $\overline{G}$. First, to get larger, colored symbols, go to **Options/Graph Elements/Lines & Symbols** and fill in the **Attributes** box as shown below. Then, in the graph that follows after clicking **Apply** and **OK**, the only thing missing is the lines at $\overline{G}$. To add the lines, select Line/Shade. The **Lines_Shading** dialog box opens. We are interested in the **Orientation** and the **Data Value** that describes the **Position**. Choosing **Vertical – Bottom axis** and inserting $\overline{G} = 1.28$ as the **Data value** will give us the desired vertical line. Repeating the process but choosing **Horizontal – Left axis** gives us the horizontal line.

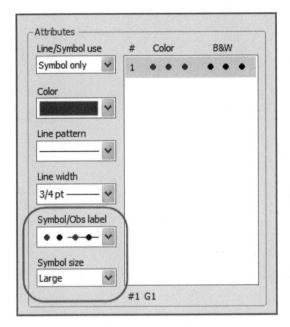
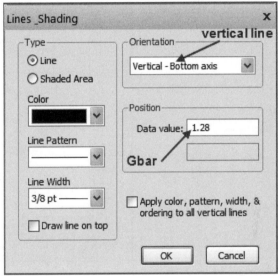

Now the graph will look like Figure 9.5. However, you might want to improve the figure even more by adding some labels or a title. For example, a suitable title might be **Scatter for *G* and its Lag**, and the values for $\overline{G}$ could be labeled as **Gbar**. For labeling of this type go to AddText. Then you can enter the desired heading or label in the text box. Notice the Font button; it can be used to set or change the font that you want. There are various other options that you could experiment with. However, the easiest way to position your text on the graph is to drag it from the EViews default position in the top left corner to wherever you want it.

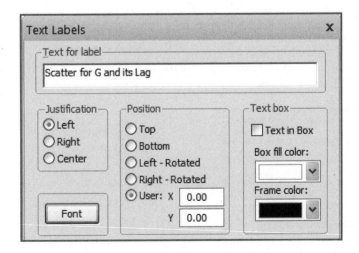

Let us review what we have done. We started by asking for a scatter graph between G_t and G_{t-1}. Then we enlarged and colored the symbols. The next step was to draw horizontal and vertical lines at the mean $\overline{G}$. Finally, we gave the graph a heading and labeled the lines drawn at the mean. The final result follows.

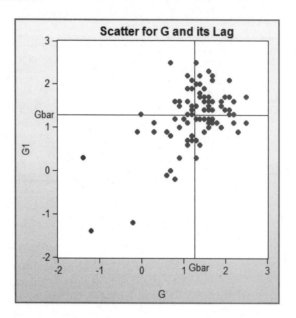

9.2.2 Correlogram for GDP growth

The scatter diagram for G_t and G_{t-1} shows a concentration of observations in the NE and SW quadrants, an indication that they are positively correlated. We now compute that correlation, along with that between G_t and its longer lags. The formula used for computing the correlations is

$$r_k = \frac{\sum\limits_{t=k+1}^{T} \left(G_t - \overline{G}\right)\left(G_{t-k} - \overline{G}\right)}{\sum\limits_{t=1}^{T}\left(G_t - \overline{G}\right)^2} \qquad k = 1, 2, \ldots$$

The sequence of correlations for $k = 1, 2, \ldots$, is called the **correlogram**. To compute and display the values for the correlogram, we open the series G, and choose **View/Correlogram**. For the **Correlogram Specification**, we are interested in the **Level** of the series and we include **12** lags.

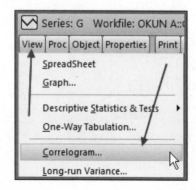
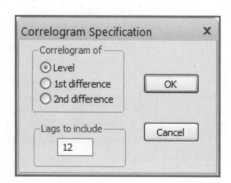

Information on the autocorrelations r_k is presented in two ways. The numerical values appear in the column **AC**. A bar chart with each bar reflecting the magnitude and sign of each r_k is given in the column headed **Autocorrelation**. Bars long enough to obscure one of the dotted lines signify autocorrelations that are significantly different from zero at a 5% significance level. We will not be concerned with the remaining information. **Partial Correlation (PAC)**, **Q-Stat** and their *p*-values, **Prob**, are covered in specialist time-series courses.

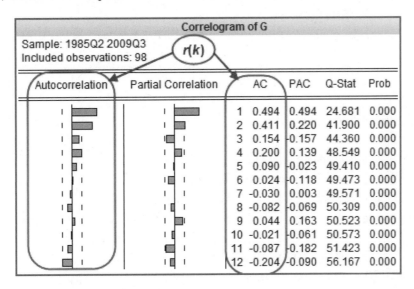

The first four autocorrelations $r_1 = 0.494$, $r_2 = 0.411$, $r_3 = 0.154$, and $r_4 = 0.200$ are those given in equation (9.16) on page 349 of *POE4*. The display is different from that in Figure 9.6 on page 350, where the bars are vertical rather than horizontal. We will investigate how to make a display like that in *POE4* Figure 9.6.

Creating a Correlogram Bar Chart

First, open a **New Page** in the workfile. Then choose **Specify by Frequency/Range**.

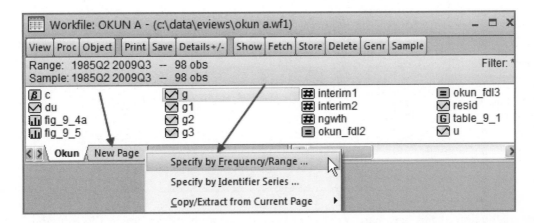

In the resulting **Workfile Create** dialog box, choose **Unstructured/Undated** for the **Workfile structure type**, insert **12 Observations** for the **Data range**, and name the page; we called it **correlogram**.

Workfile Create

Workfile structure type

Unstructured / Undated

Data range

Observations: 12

Workfile names (optional)

WF: OKUN A

Page: correlogram

When the new page is open, create a series called *R* using the command

series r

Then proceed with the following steps:

1. Open the series *R* and click **Edit**. At this time *R* will contain a column of **NA**'s.
2. Return to the page **Okun**, open *G*, and display the **correlogram**.
3. Highlight the values in the column **AC**.
4. Cut and paste those values into *R* and click **Edit**.
5. On the **correlogram** page, select **Object/New Object/Graph**, and name the figure, say **FIG_9_6**.
6. Insert *R* in the **Series List** dialog box.
7. Open **FIG_9_6** and select **Options/Graph Type/Bar**. Click **Apply** and **OK**.
8. Click **Line/Shade** to insert lines at the significance bounds $\pm 2/\sqrt{T} = 0.202$.
9. Label as required.

We will then have the following bar chart for the correlogram:

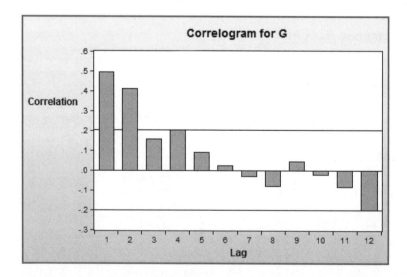

The orientation of this bar chart is different from the one created automatically by EViews, but the message is the same. The correlations for lags 1 and 2 are significantly different from zero at a 5% significance level. That at lag 4 is marginal.

9.2.3 Residual correlogram

To illustrate the correlogram for regression residuals, we introduce a new model that is a version of the Phillips curve, relating inflation *INF* to the change in unemployment *DU*:

$$INF_t = \beta_1 + \beta_2 DU_t + e_t$$

Quarterly data for this model are in the file ***phillips_aus.wf1***. They relate to the Australian economy for the period 1987Q1 to 2009Q3. To give the workfile a time-series structure that describes the dates and frequency of observations, one can follow the steps described in Section 9.1.1. Further, to create the line graphs that appear in Figures 9.7(a) and 9.7(b) on page 352 of *POE4*, the guidelines in Section 9.1.3 can be followed.

   We are now concerned with finding the correlogram for the least squares residuals

$$\hat{e}_t = INF_t - b_1 - b_2 DU_t$$

where b_1 and b_2 are the least squares estimates in the following output:

Dependent Variable: INF
Method: Least Squares
Sample (adjusted): 1987Q2 2009Q3
Included observations: 90 after adjustments

Variable	Coefficient	Std. Error	t-Statistic	Prob.
C	0.777621	0.065825	11.81347	0.0000
D(U)	-0.527864	0.229405	-2.301014	0.0238

From the output window, go to **View/Residual Diagnostics/Correlogram – Q-Statistics**.

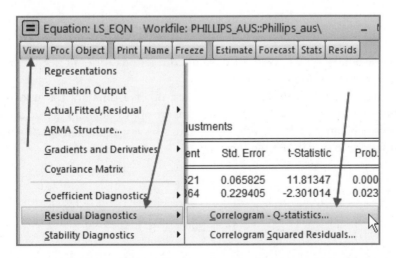

You will be asked to specify the number of lags – 12 have been entered in line with Figure 9.8 on page 353 of *POE4*.

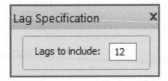

The correlogram follows. The circled portions of the output represent the autocorrelations. They correspond to the correlogram in Figure 9.8. If desired, we could construct vertical bars by following the steps described in Section 9.2.2. Since all correlations up to and including lag 6 are significantly different from zero, there is a strong indication of serially correlated errors.

Correlogram of Residuals					
Sample: 1987Q2 2009Q3					
Included observations: 90					

Autocorrelation	Partial Correlation		AC	PAC	Q-Stat	Prob
		1	0.549	0.549	28.006	0.000
		2	0.456	0.221	47.548	0.000
		3	0.433	0.176	65.409	0.000
		4	0.420	0.138	82.433	0.000
		5	0.339	-0.000	93.630	0.000
		6	0.271	-0.034	100.87	0.000
		7	0.191	-0.085	104.52	0.000
		8	0.251	0.116	110.86	0.000
		9	0.153	-0.078	113.27	0.000
		10	0.050	-0.125	113.53	0.000
		11	-0.016	-0.108	113.55	0.000
		12	-0.013	-0.022	113.57	0.000

9.2.4 Using the function @cor(•,•)

In the residual correlogram, the formula for the kth autocorrelation between the residuals is

$$r_k = \frac{\sum_{t=k+1}^{T} \hat{e}_t \hat{e}_{t-k}}{\sum_{t=1}^{T} \hat{e}_t^2} \qquad k = 1, 2, \ldots$$

This formula corresponds to that given for the autocorrelations for G in Section 9.2.2 because the mean of the least squares residuals is zero.

However, it is useful to be aware that there are other estimators for autocorrelations, with slightly different formulas, that lead to estimates that are approximately the same in large samples but can differ in small samples. For example, if we use EViews function **@cor(•,•)** to compute the kth autocorrelation for G, it will use the formula

$$r_k = \frac{\sum_{t=k+1}^{T} \left(G_t - \bar{G}_* \right) \left(G_{t-k} - \bar{G}_{**} \right)}{\sqrt{\sum_{t=k+1}^{T} \left(G_t - \bar{G}_* \right)^2 \sum_{t=1}^{T-k} \left(G_t - \bar{G}_{**} \right)^2}} \qquad k = 1, 2, \ldots$$

where $\bar{G}_* = (T-k)^{-1} \sum_{t=k+1}^{T} G_t$ and $\bar{G}_{**} = (T-k)^{-1} \sum_{t=1}^{T-k} G_t$. There are two differences between this formula and that in Section 9.2.2. In this formula, there are k fewer terms in the summations in the denominator and the means are no longer computed using all the observations. The following commands give us the alternative estimates of the first three autocorrelations:

```
scalar  rg1 = @cor(g,g1)
scalar  rg2 = @cor(g,g2)
```

```
scalar  rg3 = @cor(g,g3)
```

The values are $r_1 = 0.496$, $r_2 = 0.427$, and $r_3 = 0.177$, compared with the earlier estimates of $r_1 = 0.494$, $r_2 = 0.411$, and $r_3 = 0.154$.

A similar discrepancy can occur if one uses the **@cor(•,•)** function to get the autocorrelations for the least squares residuals. Fewer terms are included in the summations in the denominator, and when not all observations are used to compute the means of the residuals, those means will no longer be zero. Using this method to get the autocorrelations of the residuals from the Phillips curve, we write the following commands:

```
series  ehat = resid
scalar  re1 = @cor(ehat, ehat(-1))
scalar  re2 = @cor(ehat,ehat(-2))
scalar  re3 = @cor(ehat, ehat(-3))
```

The resulting correlations are $r_1 = 0.553$, $r_2 = 0.464$, and $r_3 = 0.448$, which are slightly larger than those from the correlogram, which were $r_1 = 0.549$, $r_2 = 0.456$, and $r_3 = 0.433$. Those from the correlogram are smaller in magnitude because they use more squared terms in the summation in the denominator.

9.3 TESTING FOR SERIAL CORRELATION

The residual correlogram is one way of testing for serially correlated errors. In this section we consider two more: a Lagrange multiplier test and the Durbin-Watson test.

9.3.1 Lagrange multiplier (*LM*) test

The null hypothesis for the Lagrange multiplier test is that the errors e_t are serially uncorrelated. The alternative hypothesis is that the errors are related in one of two possible ways:

$$H_1 : \begin{cases} e_t = \theta_1 e_{t-1} + \theta_2 e_{t-2} + \cdots + \theta_p e_{t-p} + v_t & \text{AR}(p) \\ e_t = v_t + \phi_1 v_{t-1} + \phi_2 v_{t-2} + \cdots + \phi_p v_{t-p} & \text{MA}(p) \end{cases}$$

where the v_t are uncorrelated random errors with zero mean and constant variance. The first process is called an autoregressive process of order p, shortened to AR(p), and the second is known as a moving-average process of order p, shortened to MA(p). The same *LM* test statistic is valid for both alternatives. In line with pages 354-355 of *POE4*, we focus on AR(1) errors as the alternative, but then indicate how EViews can be used to test for serial correlation at longer lags.

In the context of the Phillips curve example, the Lagrange multiplier test for an AR(1) error is a test of the significance of $\hat{\rho}$, where $\hat{\rho}$ is the least squares estimate from either of the following two equations:

$$INF_t = \beta_1 + \beta_2 DU_t + \rho \hat{e}_{t-1} + v_t$$

$$\hat{e}_t = \gamma_1 + \gamma_2 DU_t + \rho \hat{e}_{t-1} + v_t$$

In both cases the $\hat{e}_t$ are the least squares residuals. We will focus on the second equation. Both equations yield identical results for F- and t-tests on the significance of $\hat{\rho}$. The second equation has the advantage of producing a further test value of the form $LM = T \times R^2$. In both cases there are two different treatments depending on whether the pre-sample value $\hat{e}_0$ is set to zero or the first observation is omitted to accommodate the presence of the lag $\hat{e}_{t-1}$. EViews has an automatic command for the former – and so we call it "a short way". We also show how to do the latter using "a long way".

A short way

Reopen the least squares estimated Phillips curve and select **View/Residual Diagnostics/Serial Correlation LM Test**.

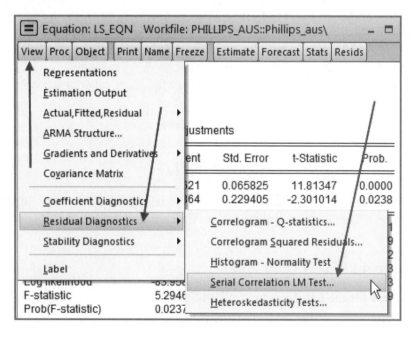

You will be asked how many lags to include. In this case we specify just 1. We are interested in testing for an AR(1) error and we only have one lag of $\hat{e}_t$ on the right side of the equation.

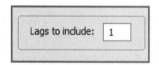

The output contains two parts – an upper part with the test results, and a lower part with the results of the estimated equation that produced the test results. The upper part follows. The values $F = 38.47$ and $LM = \chi^2 = 27.59$ are those reported as cases (ii) and (iv), respectively, in *POE4*.

Breusch-Godfrey Serial Correlation LM Test:			
F-statistic	38.46538	Prob. F(1,87)	0.0000
Obs*R-squared	27.59235	Prob. Chi-Square(1)	0.0000

To see where the test values come from, we consider the lower part of the output.

```
Test Equation:                  LM = 90x0.30658 = 27.59
Dependent Variable: RESID
Method: Least Squares
Sample: 1987Q2 2009Q3                          F = (6.202)^2 = 38.47
Included observations: 90
Presample missing value lagged residuals set to zero.
```

Variable	Coefficient	Std. Error	t-Statistic	Prob.
C	-0.002163	0.055129	-0.039237	0.9688
D(U)	-0.151494	0.193671	-0.782227	0.4362
RESID(-1)	0.558784	0.090097	6.202047	0.0000
R-squared	0.306582	Mean dependent var		1.89E-16

The value $F = 38.47$ is a test of the significance of $\hat{\rho}$, the coefficient of **RESID(-1)**. Because $F = 38.47 = t^2 = 6.202047^2$, the test can be performed as a t- or an F-test and the p-values will be the same in both cases. The other test is a χ^2- test with the test value being given by $LM = T \times R^2 = 90 \times 0.30658 = 27.59$. In both cases the p-value is 0.0000 and a null hypothesis of $H_0 : \rho = 0$ is rejected at a 5% significance level.

A long way

For testing the long way, we start by ensuring we have saved the least squares residuals

```
series  ehat = resid
```

Then we estimate the following equation, noting that an extra observation will be lost from $\hat{e}_{t-1}$:

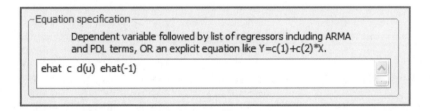

```
┌─Equation specification─────────────────────────────────
│      Dependent variable followed by list of regressors including ARMA
│      and PDL terms, OR an explicit equation like Y=c(1)+c(2)*X.
│  ehat c d(u) ehat(-1)
└────────────────────────────────────────────────────────
```

In the output below, the values $F = 38.67$ and $LM = \chi^2 = 27.61$ correspond to cases (i) and (iii), respectively, on pages 354 and 355 of *POE4*. There are 89 observations used in estimation.

```
Dependent Variable: EHAT    LM = 89x0.310211 = 27.61
Method: Least Squares
Sample (adjusted): 1987Q3 2009Q3
Included observations: 89 after adjustments    F = (6.2189)^2 = 38.67
```

Variable	Coefficient	Std. Error	t-Statistic	Prob.
C	-0.009373	0.055225	-0.169718	0.8656
D(U)	-0.144640	0.193060	-0.749196	0.4558
EHAT(-1)	0.558322	0.089778	6.218889	0.0000
R-squared	0.310211	Mean dependent var		-0.007524

Testing correlation at longer lags

If we wish to test for error correlation up to say four lags, where the correlation could be attributable to an AR(4) or an MA(4) process, the test equation is

$$\hat{e}_t = \gamma_1 + \gamma_2 DU_t + \theta_1 \hat{e}_{t-1} + \theta_2 \hat{e}_{t-2} + \theta_3 \hat{e}_{t-3} + \theta_4 \hat{e}_{t-4} + v_t$$

and the null hypothesis is $H_0 : \theta_1 = \theta_2 = \theta_3 = \theta_4 = 0$. To perform the test the short way, we again go to the *LM* test option under **Residual Diagnostics**, and choose four lags.

The complete output follows. The *F*-value is for a joint test that the coefficients of **RESID(-1)**, **RESID(-2)**, **RESID(-3)** and **RESID(-4)** are all zero. The χ^2-value comes from $LM = T \times R^2 = 90 \times 0.407466 = 36.67$.

Breusch-Godfrey Serial Correlation LM Test:

F-statistic	14.44098	Prob. F(4,84)	0.0000
Obs*R-squared	36.67190	Prob. Chi-Square(4)	0.0000

Test Equation:
Dependent Variable: RESID
Method: Least Squares
Sample: 1987Q2 2009Q3
Included observations: 90
Presample missing value lagged residuals set to zero.

Variable	Coefficient	Std. Error	t-Statistic	Prob.
C	-0.013002	0.051958	-0.250238	0.8030
D(U)	-0.473812	0.201371	-2.352931	0.0210
RESID(-1)	0.325470	0.106438	3.057826	0.0030
RESID(-2)	0.155441	0.111806	1.390275	0.1681
RESID(-3)	0.169392	0.112812	1.501547	0.1370
RESID(-4)	0.201361	0.109935	1.831631	0.0706

R-squared	0.407466	Mean dependent var	1.89E-16

9.3.2 Durbin-Watson test

You may have noticed a Durbin-Watson value that is automatically provided on the least squares output. The Durbin Watson test is a test for AR(1) errors. It is considered in Appendix 9A of *POE4*. Its critical values and *p*-values are less readily computed than those for other tests for AR(1) errors, and so its popularity as a test is declining. Although EViews computes the value of the test statistic, it does not have commands for computing corresponding critical or *p*-values. As a rough guide, values of the Durbin-Watson statistic of 1.3 or less are suggestive of autocorrelation. We can be more precise for the Phillips curve example. In this case where $T = 90$ and $K = 2$, we can find upper and lower 5% critical values from the web site http://principlesofeconometrics.com/poe4/poe4htm. We reject the null hypothesis of no serial correlation if the Durbin-Watson value d is less than $d_{Lc} = 1.653$, and we do not reject H_0 if d is greater than $d_{Uc} = 1.679$. The value from the least-squares estimated Phillips curve is 0.887. Since $0.887 < 1.635$, there is evidence of serially correlated errors.

Dependent Variable: INF
Method: Least Squares
Sample (adjusted): 1987Q2 2009Q3
Included observations: 90 after adjustments

Variable	Coefficient	Std. Error	t-Statistic	Prob.
C	0.777621	0.065825	11.81347	0.0000
D(U)	-0.527864	0.229405	-2.301014	0.0238

R-squared	0.056752	Mean dependent var		0.791111
F-statistic	5.294666	Durbin-Watson stat		0.887289
Prob(F-statistic)	0.023754			

9.4 HAC STANDARD ERRORS

In Chapter 8 when studying heteroskedasticity, we saw how least squares could be used instead of generalized least squares as long as we used White standard errors. A similar option exists for regression models with serially correlated errors. In this case the standard errors are called Newey-West or HAC standard errors, with HAC being an acronym for heteroskedasticity-autocorrelation consistent. To compute the Newey-West standard errors for the Phillips curve example, as reported on page 358 of *POE4*, we choose **Options** in the **Equation Estimation** window. Then, in the **Options** window, go to the **Coefficient covariance matrix** and select **HAC (Newey-West)**. There is a further window, accessed by clicking on **HAC options**, that gives numerous estimation options for finding HAC standard errors. We have chosen to use EViews' default setting with a degrees of freedom adjustment. Details of the other alternatives can be found in the EViews 7 User Guide II, pages 34-36 and 775-785.

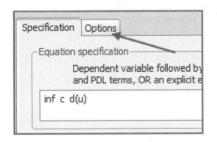
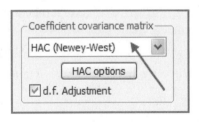

The least-squares output with the HAC standard errors follows. Notice that Eviews has a note to tell you that it has calculated HAC standard errors and indicate the estimation method that was used to obtain them. The values $se(b_1) = 0.1030$ and $se(b_2) = 0.3127$ are those given in equation (9.29) in *POE4*.

```
Dependent Variable: INF          Estimation method for
Method: Least Squares            HAC standard errors
Sample (adjusted): 1987Q2 2009Q3
Included observations: 90 after adjustments
HAC standard errors & covariance (Bartlett kernel, Newey-West fixed
   bandwidth = 4.0000)
```

Variable	Coefficient	Std. Error	t-Statistic	Prob.
C	0.777621	0.102999	7.549831	0.0000
D(U)	-0.527864	0.312719	-1.687982	0.0950

9.5 ESTIMATING AN AR(1) ERROR MODEL

Continuing with the Phillips curve example, we are interested in estimating the equation under the assumption that the errors follow an AR(1) model. These two components of the model can be written as

$$INF_t = \beta_1 + \beta_2 DU_t + e_t \qquad\qquad e_t = \rho e_{t-1} + v_t$$

Alternatively, as noted in equation (9.44) on page 362 of *POE4*, this model can be written in the nonlinear-in-the-parameters form

$$INF_t = \beta_1(1-\rho) + \beta_2 DU_t + \rho INF_{t-1} - \rho\beta_2 DU_{t-1} + v_t$$

Least squares estimation of this function requires minimization of

$$\sum_{t=2}^{T} v_t^2 = \sum_{t=2}^{T} \left(INF_t - \beta_1(1-\rho) - \beta_2 DU_t - \rho INF_{t-1} + \rho\beta_2 DU_{t-1} \right)^2$$

Because the parameters appear nonlinearly in this equation – we have the products $\beta_1(1-\rho)$ and $\rho\beta_2$ – the linear least squares formulas that we have been using so far in *POE4* are no longer appropriate. A numerical iterative procedure is needed. We will describe two ways of getting EViews to find estimates for β_1, β_2 and ρ that minimize $\sum_{t=2}^{T} v_t^2$, a short way and a long way. As its name suggests, the short way is easier, and it generalizes for AR errors of any order. The long way is instructive because it demonstrates how EViews can be used to estimate any function that is nonlinear in the parameters.

There are two error variances, σ_v^2 and σ_e^2. The procedures we describe provide an estimate for σ_v^2. Once we have estimated ρ and σ_v^2, we can always estimate σ_e^2 from the relationship $\sigma_e^2 = \sigma_v^2/(1-\rho^2)$.

9.5.1 A short way

To estimate a model with an AR(1) error we begin, as usual, by selecting **Object/New Object/ Equation**. After giving the equation object a name and clicking **OK**, the **Equation specification** box appears. Then, as before, you enter the names of the series that are in the equation, but this time you also add **AR(1)** to tell EViews the errors follow an AR(1) model.

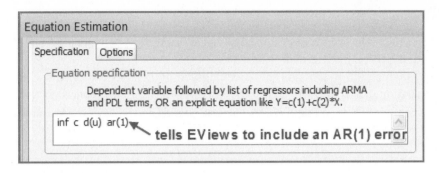

There are several features of the output worth noting.

1. An estimate $\hat{\rho} = 0.5574$ is provided next to the name **AR(1)**. It also appears at the bottom of the output as the **Inverted AR Root**.
2. The **S.E of regression** is the estimate $\hat{\sigma}_v = 0.5194$.
3. Two observations have been lost. One is lost through the creation of the variable $DU_t = U_t - U_{t-1}$. The other is lost because the nonlinear equation contains DU_{t-1} .
4. The note **Convergence achieved after 5 iterations** appears because of the nature of the nonlinear least squares estimator. This estimator is not a formula that calculates the required numbers. It is an iterative procedure that systematically tries different parameter values until it finds those that minimize the sum of squared residuals. The five iterations refer to the five different sets of parameters tried before it reached the minimum. If it fails to reach the minimum, the note will say **convergence not achieved**.

Dependent Variable: INF
Method: Least Squares
Sample (adjusted): 1987Q3 2009Q3
Included observations: 89 after adjustments
Convergence achieved after 5 iterations

Variable	Coefficient	Std. Error	t-Statistic	Prob.
C	0.760872	0.124531	6.109884	0.0000
D(U)	-0.694388	0.247894	-2.801148	0.0063
AR(1)	0.557392	0.090155	6.182630	0.0000

R-squared	0.348072	Mean dependent var	0.783146
Adjusted R-squared	0.332911	S.D. dependent var	0.635902
S.E. of regression	0.519377	Akaike info criterion	1.560752
Sum squared resid	23.19868	Schwarz criterion	1.644638

Inverted AR Roots	.56	

9.5.2 A long way

The long way for estimating the AR(1) error model is to write the equation

$$INF_t = \beta_1(1-\rho) + \beta_2 DU_t + \rho INF_{t-1} - \rho\beta_2 DU_{t-1} + v_t$$

directly into the **Equation specification** window. Before doing so, it is convenient to explicitly create the variable DU:

> **series du = D(u)**

It is convenient to create *DU* because it means we can write **DU(-1)** instead of **D(U(-1))**. Both are acceptable, but the former is less confusing.

The way in which the equation is specified is given in the screen shot below. Because we are writing the equation out in full, we need some notation for the coefficients. EViews assumes you will be using **C(•)** to describe a coefficient. Thus, we have $C(1)=\beta_1$, $C(2)=\beta_2$, and $C(3)=\rho$.

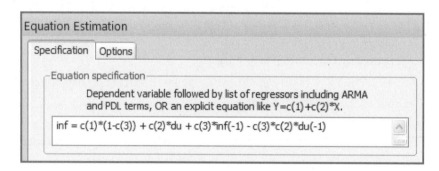

Can you see what is different? Instead of writing in the name of the dependent variable followed by the explanatory variables, we have written out the whole equation. Now check out the output that appears below. Instead of having the names of the variables, we have the coefficients C(1), C(2) and C(3). Satisfy yourself that the estimates are the same as those obtained using the short way. The equation being estimated is included in the output. And this time it took six iterations to reach convergence.

```
Dependent Variable: INF
Method: Least Squares
Sample (adjusted): 1987Q3 2009Q3
Included observations: 89 after adjustments
Convergence achieved after 6 iterations
INF = C(1)*(1-C(3)) + C(2)*DU + C(3)*INF(-1) - C(3)*C(2)*DU(-1)
```

	Coefficient	Std. Error	t-Statistic	Prob.
C(1)	0.760872	0.124531	6.109887	0.0000
C(3)	0.557392	0.090155	6.182630	0.0000
C(2)	-0.694388	0.247894	-2.801149	0.0063

R-squared	0.348072	Mean dependent var	0.783146
Adjusted R-squared	0.332911	S.D. dependent var	0.635902
S.E. of regression	0.519377	Akaike info criterion	1.560752
Sum squared resid	23.19868	Schwarz criterion	1.644638

9.5.3 A more general model

On pages 362 and 363 of *POE4*, we explain how the AR(1) error model can be viewed as a special case of an autoregressive distributed lag model with one lag of *y* and one lag of *x*. This ARDL(1,1) model can be written as

$$INF_t = \delta + \theta_1 INF_{t-1} + \delta_0 DU_t + \delta_1 DU_{t-1} + v_t$$

It is equivalent to the AR(1) error model if $\delta_1 = -\theta_1 \delta_0$. Thus, it is of interest to estimate the ARDL(1,1) model and to test $H_0 : \delta_1 = -\theta_1 \delta_0$ against the alternative $H_1 : \delta_1 \neq -\theta_1 \delta_0$. Since the ARDL model is a linear one, estimating it and testing the nonlinear restriction can be carried out using techniques described in Chapters 5 and 6. We briefly go through the necessary steps. The **Equation specification** is

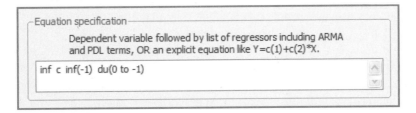

The output from this estimation, appearing in equation (9.49) of *POE4*, is

Dependent Variable: INF
Method: Least Squares
Sample (adjusted): 1987Q3 2009Q3
Included observations: 89 after adjustments

Variable	Coefficient	Std. Error	t-Statistic	Prob.
C	0.333633	0.089903	3.711037	0.0004
INF(-1)	0.559268	0.090796	6.159589	0.0000
DU	-0.688185	0.249870	-2.754169	0.0072
DU(-1)	0.319953	0.257504	1.242515	0.2175

To test the hypothesis $H_0 : \delta_1 = -\theta_1 \delta_0$, go to **View/Coefficient Diagnostics/Wald Test – Coefficient Restrictions** and fill in the dialog box as follows. The test result of $\chi^2 = 0.112$, with *p*-value of 0.738, suggests we cannot reject the restriction implied by the AR(1) error model.

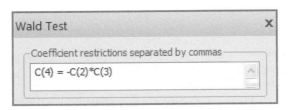

Wald Test:
Equation: ARDL11

Test Statistic	Value	df	Probability
t-statistic	-0.335068	85	0.7384
F-statistic	0.112270	(1, 85)	0.7384
Chi-square	0.112270	1	0.7376

Normalized Restriction (= 0)	Value	Std. Err.
C(2)*C(3) + C(4)	-0.064927	0.193773

9.6 AUTOREGRESSIVE DISTRIBUTED LAG MODELS

An ARDL(p,q) model has the general form

$$y_t = \delta + \theta_1 y_{t-1} + \cdots + \theta_p y_{t-p} + \delta_0 x_t + \delta_1 x_{t-1} + \cdots + \delta_q x_{t-q} + v_t$$

No new machinery is needed to estimate this model or to test for serial correlation in the errors. The equation can be estimated using least squares. The residual correlogram and *LM* tests can be used to test whether the errors are serially correlated.

Section 9.6 in *POE4* is devoted to experimenting with different lag lengths p and q for both the Okun's Law and Phillips curve equations, with a view to finding ARDL models with errors that are serially uncorrelated and coefficients that are significantly different from zero. The AIC and SC selection criteria are also used to help choose p and q. We present the equation specification and results for one pair (p,q) for each of the examples.

9.6.1 The Phillips curve

For the Phillips curve, we consider the ARDL(4,0) model

$$INF_t = \delta + \theta_1 INF_{t-1} + \theta_2 INF_{t-2} + \theta_3 INF_{t-3} + \theta_4 INF_{t-4} + \delta_0 DU_t + v_t$$

The **Equation specification** and output that follow are for the results reported in equation (9.57) on page 368 of *POE4*.

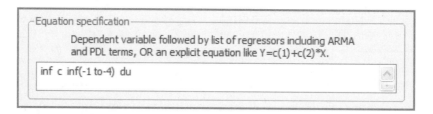

Dependent Variable: INF
Method: Least Squares
Sample (adjusted): 1988Q1 2009Q3
Included observations: 87 after adjustments

Variable	Coefficient	Std. Error	t-Statistic	Prob.
C	0.100100	0.098260	1.018726	0.3114
INF(-1)	0.235440	0.101556	2.318339	0.0230
INF(-2)	0.121328	0.103757	1.169347	0.2457
INF(-3)	0.167690	0.104960	1.597657	0.1140
INF(-4)	0.281916	0.101380	2.780779	0.0067
DU	-0.790172	0.188533	-4.191151	0.0001

To get the AIC and SC values for this model given in Table 9.4 of *POE4*, we need to change the sample starting point to 1988Q3 and run the same regression. Then, remembering that EViews definitions for the AIC and SC are in terms of the likelihood function rather than the sum of squared errors, we need to subtract $[1 + \ln(2\pi)]$ from the values produced by EViews. After estimating the model, we use the following commands:

```
scalar  aic = @aic – (1 + log(2*@acos(-1)))
scalar  sc = @sc – (1 + log(2*@acos(-1)))
```

Note that **@acos(-1)** is equal to π. In line with the entry in Table 9.4 for $p = 4$ and $q = 0$, these commands yield AIC $= -1.4020$ and SC $= -1.2296$.

9.6.2 Okun's law

The Okun's Law ARDL equation, estimated after experimenting with different lags, was

$$DU_t = \delta + \theta_1 DU_{t-1} + \delta_0 G_t + \delta_1 G_{t-1} + v_t$$

The **Equation specification** and output that follow are for the results reported in equation (9.59) on page 370 of *POE4*:

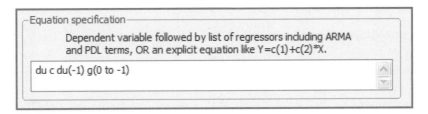

Dependent Variable: DU
Method: Least Squares
Sample (adjusted): 1985Q4 2009Q3
Included observations: 96 after adjustments

Variable	Coefficient	Std. Error	t-Statistic	Prob.
C	0.378010	0.057840	6.535473	0.0000
DU(-1)	0.350116	0.084573	4.139807	0.0001
G	-0.184084	0.030698	-5.996538	0.0000
G(-1)	-0.099155	0.036824	-2.692648	0.0084

9.6.3 Estimating an autoregressive model

In the section we are concerned with estimating a pure AR model with no distributed lag component. The example we use is GDP growth G from the workfile ***okun.wf1***. In a pure AR model, G_t is related to past values of itself and no other explanatory variables. There are no special features for estimation; least squares can be used as it has been throughout most of the book so far. However, where the AR model is particularly useful is in demonstrating how to forecast with a dynamic model. We devote this section to estimating the AR model and checking the residual correlogram to ensure enough residuals have been included to eliminate serial correlation. Then, in Section 9.7, we examine how to use the AR model for forecasting.

The AR model for GDP growth is the AR(2) model:

$$G_t = \delta + \theta_1 G_{t-1} + \theta_2 G_{t-2} + v_t$$

To find the estimates in equation (9.61) on page 371 of *POE4*, we use the **Equation specification**

┌─ Equation specification ─────────────────────────────────┐
│   Dependent variable followed by list of regressors including ARMA │
│   and PDL terms, OR an explicit equation like Y=c(1)+c(2)*X. │
│ ┌──┐ │
│ │ g c g(-1 to -2) │ │
│ └──┘ │
└──┘

leading to the following output:

Dependent Variable: G
Method: Least Squares
Sample (adjusted): 1985Q4 2009Q3
Included observations: 96 after adjustments

Variable	Coefficient	Std. Error	t-Statistic	Prob.
C	0.465726	0.143258	3.250970	0.0016
G(-1)	0.377001	0.100021	3.769225	0.0003
G(-2)	0.246239	0.102869	2.393723	0.0187

A check of the residuals yields a correlogram that is the equivalent of that in *POE4*'s Figure 9.11. There is no evidence of serially correlated residuals, except perhaps at lag 12, which is sufficiently distant not to be of great concern.

Correlogram of Residuals

Sample: 1985Q4 2009Q3
Included observations: 96

Autocorrelation	Partial Correlation		AC	PAC	Q-Stat	Prob
		1	0.033	0.033	0.1094	0.741
		2	0.015	0.014	0.1310	0.937
		3	-0.154	-0.155	2.5306	0.470
		4	0.135	0.149	4.3924	0.355
		5	0.042	0.036	4.5765	0.470
		6	-0.026	-0.062	4.6450	0.590
		7	-0.064	-0.017	5.0758	0.651
		8	-0.146	-0.154	7.3416	0.500
		9	0.138	0.141	9.4037	0.401
		10	0.088	0.084	10.248	0.419
		11	-0.040	-0.101	10.427	0.492
		12	-0.232	-0.159	16.470	0.171

9.7 FORECASTING

The first model that we use for forecasting is the AR(2) model for GDP growth whose estimates were presented in the previous section. Then we examine a second forecasting procedure, that of exponential smoothing.

9.7.1 Forecasting with an AR model

The last observation in the file *okun.wf1*, and the last observation used to estimate the AR(2) model $G_t = \delta + \theta_1 G_{t-1} + \theta_2 G_{t-2} + v_t$, was 2009Q3. Now suppose we are standing at the beginning of 2009Q4 and we would like to forecast growth for 2009Q4, 2010Q1 and 2010Q2. These forecasts, the standard errors of the forecast errors, and 95% forecast intervals are given in Table 9.7 on page 374 of *POE4*. Getting EViews to compute these quantities is our next task.

To make space for EViews to include the forecasts and standard errors, we extend the **Range** of the workfile by three observations. Select **Proc/Structure/Resize Current Page** from the workfile:

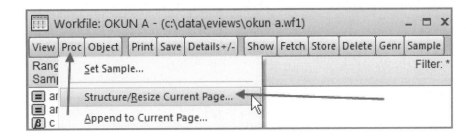

Change the **End date** of the **Date specification** to **2010Q2** and click **OK**. EViews will check whether you really want to make this change by asking **Resize involves inserting 3 observations. Continue?** Click **Yes.**

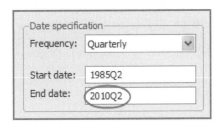

To compute the forecasts, you fill in the **Forecast** dialog box that is obtained by opening the estimated equation, and then select Forecast . Several pieces of information are required.

1. We have assigned *G_F* as the series name for the forecasts (**Forecast name**) and *SE_G_F* as the series name for the standard errors of the forecasts (**S.E. (optional)**).

2. The **Forecast sample** is 2009Q4 to 2010Q2, which we specify as **2009Q4 2010Q2**.

3. Ticking the box **Insert actuals for out-of-sample observations** means that actual values for *G* will be inserted in the series *G_F* for the period 1985Q2 to 2009Q3. (Out-of-sample means observations not in the forecast sample.)

4. **Dynamic forecast** is chosen for the **Method** because forecasts for future values will depend on earlier forecasts when actual values are not available.

5. Only error uncertainty, not coefficient uncertainty, is considered in the calculation of the forecast standard errors presented in Table 9.6 of *POE4* and so the box **Coef uncertainty in S.E. calc** is not ticked.

6. We have not worried about **Output** for **Forecast graph** and **Forecast evaluation**.

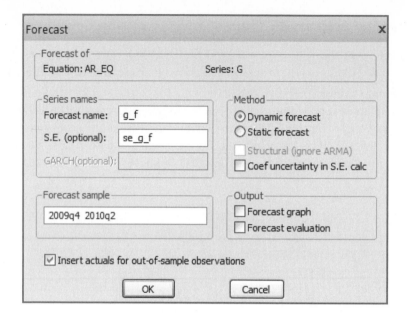

Clicking **OK** creates the series *G_F* and *SE_G_F*. The relevant values are given in the last three rows of their respective spreadsheets. To complete the information in Table 9.6 of the text we need the upper and lower values for the 95% forecast intervals. These values can be created using the commands below. Ask yourself where the 93 comes from.

```
scalar  tc = @qtdist(0.975, 93)
series  fint_low = g_f - tc*se_g_f
series  fint_up = g_f + tc*se_g_f
```

After collecting the relevant information into a group:

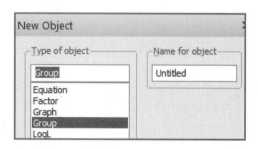

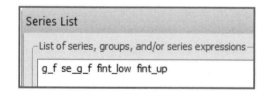

the values in Table 9.6 can be presented as follows:

obs	G_F	SE_G_F	FINT_LOW	FINT_UP
2009Q3	0.800000	NA	NA	NA
2009Q4	0.718079	0.552688	-0.379448	1.815607
2010Q1	0.933435	0.590660	-0.239499	2.106368
2010Q2	0.994452	0.628452	-0.253530	2.242434

9.7.2 Exponential smoothing

Exponential smoothing is a method for forecasting one period into the future and for smoothing a data series over the sample period. Using the series for GDP growth G in the file ***okun.wf1***, a forecast from exponential smoothing is given by

$$\hat{G}_t = \alpha G_{t-1} + (1-\alpha)\hat{G}_{t-1} \qquad t = 2,3,\ldots,T+1$$

The forecast is a weighted average of last period's value G_{t-1} and the forecast value for last period $\hat{G}_{t-1}$. Within the sample, the series $\hat{G}$ is a smoothed version of G; outside the sample, $\hat{G}_{T+1}$ is the forecast value for the next period. The degree of smoothing is controlled by the parameter α. Values of α close to one induce limited smoothing; values close to zero imply greater smoothing. The value of α can be set by the investigator or chosen to minimize the sum of squares of forecast errors that is given by

$$\sum_{t=2}^{T}\left(G_t - \hat{G}_t\right)^2 = \sum_{t=2}^{T}\left(G_t - \alpha G_{t-1} - (1-\alpha)\hat{G}_{t-1}\right)^2$$

The formula for exponential smoothing is a recursive one that requires the setting of some value for $\hat{G}_1$, the forecast of the first sample observation. EViews uses the average of the first $(T+1)/2$ observations.

To get EViews to produce an exponentially smoothed series for G and a forecast $\hat{G}_{T+1}$, open the series G, and go to **Proc/Exponential Smoothing**.

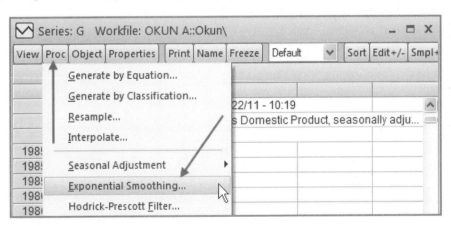

In the **Exponential Smoothing** dialog box that follows you will see a multitude of options. Let us consider each of the five boxes within the dialog box.

1. For **Smoothing method**, choose **Single**. We are not considering the other methods.
2. For the **Smoothed series**, we have given the name *G_SM*.
3. For **Smoothing parameters**, **E** has been inserted in the **Alpha** box, implying we are asking EViews to estimate α. The value that minimizes the sum of squares of the forecast errors is used. In *POE4* two values are used, the minimizing value that produces Figure 9.12(a) on page 377, and a value $\alpha = 0.8$ that gives Figure 9.12(b). We are not using the other parameters, **Beta** and **Gamma**.
4. The estimation sample is **1985Q2** to **2009Q3**.
5. Since we are not including a seasonal component, the **Cycle for seasonal** is irrelevant.

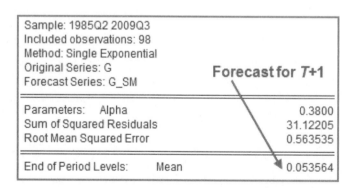

The following output appears. The parameter estimate is $\hat{\alpha} = 0.38$, and the forecast for the post-sample period is $\hat{G}_{T+1} = 0.05356$. The relationship between the sum of squared forecast errors and the root mean squared error (*RMSE*) is

$$RMSE = \sqrt{\frac{1}{T}\sum_{t=1}^{T}\left(G_t - \hat{G}_t\right)^2} = \sqrt{\frac{31.12205}{98}} = 0.563535$$

```
Sample: 1985Q2 2009Q3
Included observations: 98
Method: Single Exponential
Original Series: G                    Forecast for T+1
Forecast Series: G_SM

Parameters:   Alpha                            0.3800
Sum of Squared Residuals                       31.12205
Root Mean Squared Error                        0.563535

End of Period Levels:      Mean                0.053564
```

To reproduce the graph in Figure 9.12(a) on *POE4* page 377, we need to place two line graphs in the one figure. We create a graph object in the usual way, giving it a name of **FIG_9_12A**, and listing the two series *G* and *G_SM*.

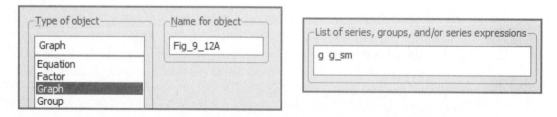

The line graph in Figure 9.12(a) will appear. It can be edited by using **Options** if a different presentation is required.

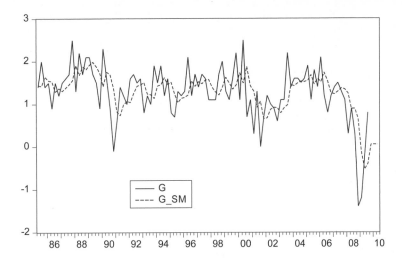

The process can be repeated with α set at 0.8 instead of being estimated. The only changes that are necessary are the **Alpha** box and a different name for the smoothed series. We chose *G_SM8*.

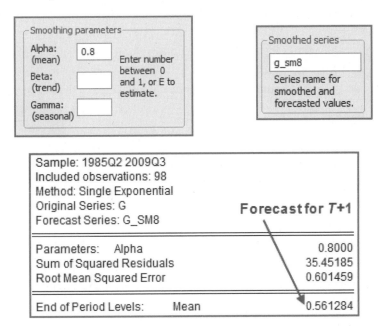

The different values for α lead to quite different forecasts because of the volatility of growth at the end of the sample period. See *POE4*, page 378 for an explanation.

Creating line graphs for *G* and *G_SM8* will reproduce Figure 9.12(b) in *POE4*.

9.8 MULTIPLIER ANALYSIS

Forecasting and multiplier analysis are the two main uses for ARDL models. We now turn to the second of these uses, multiplier analysis. In the context of the Okun's Law example, the problem is to find estimates of the β's in the infinite lag representation

$$DU_t = \alpha + \sum_{s=0}^{\infty} \beta_s G_{t-s} + e_t$$

from estimates of the coefficients in the ARDL model

$$DU_t = \delta + \theta_1 DU_{t-1} + \delta_0 G_t + \delta_1 G_{t-1} + v_t$$

In *POE4*, page 380, we show that the relationship between the two sets of coefficients is

$$\alpha = \frac{\delta}{1-\theta_1} \qquad \beta_0 = \delta_0 \qquad \beta_1 = \delta_1 + \beta_0\theta_1 \qquad \beta_s = \beta_{s-1}\theta_1 \ \text{ for } s \geq 2$$

If you are using a full version of EViews you can write a program to compute these values. If you have a student version, you will need to write a separate command for each coefficient. We will consider both approaches.

9.8.1 Using the student version

Assume you have just estimated the Okun's Law ARDL model so that the coefficients in the **C** vector are as follows:

$$C(1) = \hat{\delta} = 0.37801 \qquad C(2) = \hat{\theta}_1 = 0.350116 \qquad C(3) = \hat{\delta}_0 = -0.184084 \qquad C(4) = \hat{\delta}_1 = -0.099155$$

The first eight lag weights (for periods 0 to 7) can be calculated with the following commands:

```
series(8) beta
beta(1) = c(3)
beta(2) = c(4) + beta(1)*c(2)
beta(3) = beta(2)*c(2)
beta(4) = beta(3)*c(2)
beta(5) = beta(4)*c(2)
beta(6) = beta(5)*c(2)
beta(7) = beta(6)*c(2)
beta(8) = beta(7)*c(2)
```

To create the graph in Figure 9.13 in *POE4* we also need a series called *LAG*. A command that produces this series is

```
series  lag = @trend
```

The EViews function **@trend** defines a trend series beginning at zero and with each observation incremented by 1, giving the values $0, 1, 2, \ldots$. Now, since there are only eight values to graph, we need to restrict the sample to the first eight observations. The quarterly dates that EViews has attached to its sample observations are not really relevant in this case, but we can trick EViews by cutting the sample back to the first eight quarters. Select **Sample** from the workfile window and insert the following start and end dates:

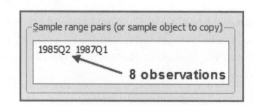

Then select **Object/New Object/Graph**. Name it **FIG_9_13**. Enter the two series for the graph, with the one on the *x*-axis first.

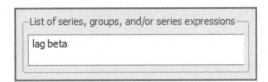

The graph **FIG_9_13** will appear in your workfile. However, it will need a bit of work before it is presentable. To ensure it is of the correct type, go to **Options/Graph Type/XY Line**. Click **Apply** and **OK**.

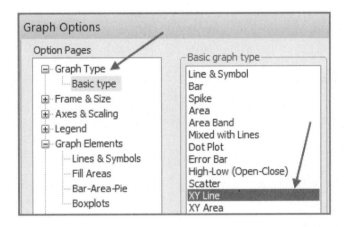

The following graph will then appear:

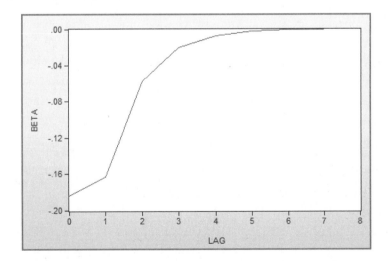

9.8.2 Writing a program

The commands used to compute the multipliers in the previous section were very repetitive. If you have the full version of EViews, you can avoid that repetition by creating a loop within a program. In this section, we describe how to write and run such a program.

First, go to **File/New/Program**:

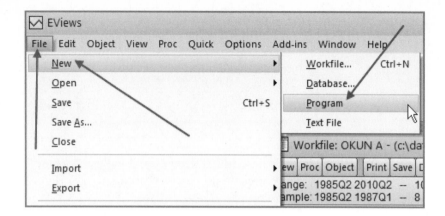

A window in which you can write a program will open. The program consists of a number of commands:

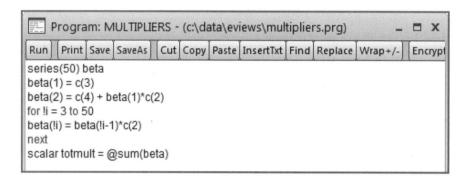

The first three commands are similar to those we used in the Command window in the previous section except that we have made *BETA* of dimension 50. Using a large number like 50, we can sum the multipliers to get the total multiplier, assuming values beyond 50 are negligible.

The next three commands define a loop:

> **for !i = 3 to 50**
> **beta(!i) = beta(!i-1)*c(2)**
> **next**

The index of the loop is **!i**. Eviews uses an exclamation mark followed by a letter to denote a loop index. In this case the index takes values from 3 to 50. It starts from 3; the third value in **beta** is computed, and then, at the command **next**, the index increments by 1 to 4 and returns to the start of the loop. This process continues until the index reaches 50, at which point we exit from the loop and the total multiplier is computed using the command

> **scalar totmult = @sum(beta)**

After the commands are entered into the Program window, the program can be saved by clicking Save. It is usually convenient to save it in the same folder as your workfile. We have named the program file *multipliers.prg*. To run the program you click Run. Then the multipliers can be found in the series *BETA* and the total multiplier can be found in the scalar **TOTMULT**.

Keywords

@aic
@cor
@sc
@sum
@trend
AC
AR(1)
AR(1) error
ARDL
autocorrelation
autoregressive models
bar graph
coefficient covariance
coefficient diagnostics
convergence
correlation
correlogram
date specification
delay multipliers
differencing
Durbin-Watson test
dynamic forecasting
end date
exponential smoothing

finite distributed lags
forecast name
forecast standard errors
forecasting
freeze
frequency
graph
graph attributes
graph elements
graph type
HAC standard errors
interim multipliers
lag specification
lag weights
lagging a series
Lagrange multiplier test
line & symbol
line/shade
loop
loop index
multipliers
NA
new page
Newey-West standard errors

nonlinear least squares
orientation
proc
programming
range
resid
residual correlogram
residual diagnostics
residual tests
residuals
resize
scatter
smoothed series
smoothing parameter
sample (adjusted)
serial correlation LM test
start date
time series data
unstructured/undated
Wald test
workfile structure
XY line

CHAPTER 10

Random Regressors and Moment-Based Estimation

CHAPTER OUTLINE

Chapter 10 introduces the violation of assumption SR5 (and MR5) of the linear regression model, which states that the regressors are nonrandom. When this assumption is relaxed, the explanatory variables are sometimes said to be **stochastic**, which is another word meaning random.

10.1 THE INCONSISTENCY OF THE LEAST SQUARES ESTIMATOR

To begin consideration of estimation in the simple linear regression framework in the presence of random regressors, open a new workfile, using **File/New/Workfile,** and in the dialog box enter

Assign a workfile name if you like, and click **OK**.

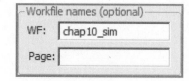

To produce a figure like Figure 10.2, showing the positive correlation between the x and e generated by the Monte Carlo experiment discussed in the text, first we "create" the values for the explanatory variable x and for the random errors e that are correlated. EViews has the capability of creating random numbers from many distributions. Random values from the standard normal distribution, $N(0,1)$ are generated by the function **nrnd**. Create the series x using

```
rndseed 1234567
series x = nrnd
```

The first command sets the "seed" for the sequence of random numbers generated. This statement is optional, but if it is omitted then different sequences of random values will be obtained. See *POE4* Appendix B.4 for a discussion of random numbers.

Double-click that series and examine the histogram and summary statistics:

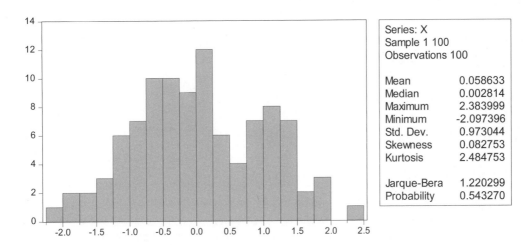

Clearly x has a normal-like distribution. Now create a series of random values e that is correlated with x. A simple method is to let e equal a linear function of x plus another random normal variable. For example,

```
series e = x + nrnd
```

The histogram shows

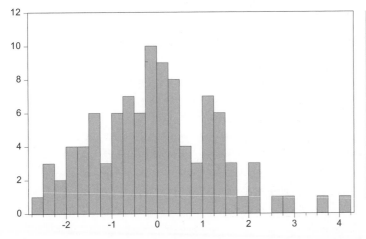

Open the x and e series and view the sample correlation, which is 0.67.

	X	E
		Correlati
X	1.000000	0.665729
E	0.665729	1.000000

As an exercise, determine the true variance of e and the true correlation between x and e.

In a Monte Carlo world we know the true parameters, and that y is created by

$$y = E(y) + e = \beta_1 + \beta_2 x + e = 1 + 1 \times x + e$$

To create the expected values $E(y)$ and the observed values y, use the EViews commands

> **series ey = 1 + x**
> **series y = 1 + x + e**

Using the series y and x, obtain the least squares estimates

> **equation ls.ls y c x**

Sample: 1 100
Included observations: 100

Variable	Coefficient	Std. Error	t-Statistic	Prob.
C	0.930425	0.099536	9.347639	0.0000
X	1.906344	0.102621	18.57663	0.0000

R-squared	0.778827	Mean dependent var		1.042199
Adjusted R-squared	0.776570	S.D. dependent var		2.101907
S.E. of regression	0.993538	Akaike info criterion		2.844708
Sum squared resid	96.73754	Schwarz criterion		2.896812

Note that the least squares estimate of the slope is 1.906 whereas we know the true data generating process specified a slope of 1.0.

In the regression window click **Forecast** and name the series *YHAT*.

Series names
Forecast name: yhat
S.E. (optional):
GARCH(optional):

From the main EViews menu select **Quick/Graph**. Enter into the **Series List** dialog box

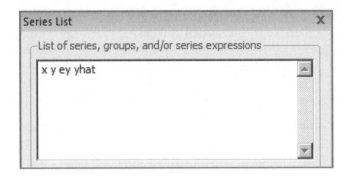

In the **Graph Options** box choose a basic **Scatter** diagram. Edit the graph so that the series *EY* is a line only with no symbols, and the series *YHAT* has both symbols and a line.

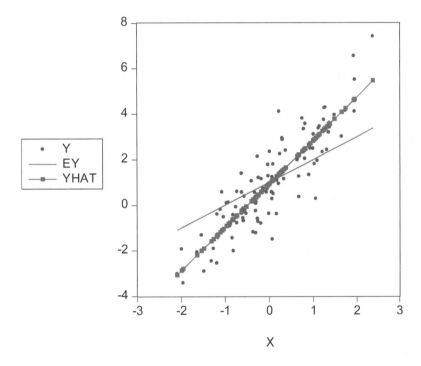

The data do not fall around the true regression function $E(y)$. However, the least squares estimator fits a line through the center of the data, and its slope is too large. The failure of least squares results from the correlation between *x* and *e*. Hence, least squares is invalid in cases where *x* and *e* are correlated. The variable *x* is said to be **endogenous**. The inconsistency of the least squares estimator is due to an **endogeneity problem**.

   The workfile ***chap10_sim.wf1*** can now be saved and closed.

10.2 IV/2SLS ESTIMATION

In Chapter 10 we introduced an important example, the estimation of the relationship between wages, specifically ln(*WAGE*), and years of education (*EDUC*). We will use the data on married women in the workfile ***mroz.wf1*** to examine this relationship. Open this workfile and **Save** the workfile under a new name, such as ***mroz_chap10.wf1***.

The first 428 women have wage data. The remainder have $WAGE = 0$ because they do not participate in the labor market. In the workfile window select the **Sample** button. Fill in the dialog box to include in the estimation sample only the first 428 observations.

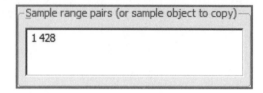

Now we can estimate the equation

$$\ln\left(WAGE\right) = \beta_1 + \beta_2 EDUC + \beta_3 EXPER + \beta_4 EXPER^2 + e$$

The command is

equation wage_eq.ls log(wage) c educ exper exper^2

Sample: 1 428
Included observations: 428

Variable	Coefficient	Std. Error	t-Statistic	Prob.
C	-0.522041	0.198632	-2.628179	0.0089
EDUC	0.107490	0.014146	7.598332	0.0000
EXPER	0.041567	0.013175	3.154906	0.0017
EXPER^2	-0.000811	0.000393	-2.062834	0.0397
R-squared	0.156820	Mean dependent var		1.190173

As noted in *POE4*, the concern is that the variable *EDUC* might be correlated with factors in the error term, such as ability. If that is the case, then the least squares estimator is biased and the bias will not disappear even if the sample size becomes very large.

Select **Quick/Estimate Equation**. In the **Estimation settings** choose **TSLS** from the pull-down menu.

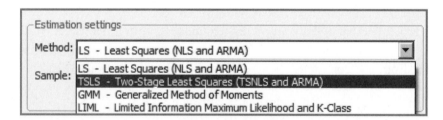

The Equation specification is

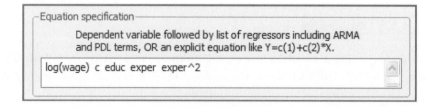

The **Instrument list** must include all the variables that are NOT correlated with the error term. These variables are said to be **exogenous**.

Click **OK**. The estimation results are

Dependent Variable: LOG(WAGE)
Method: Two-Stage Least Squares
Sample: 1 428
Included observations: 428
Instrument specification: EXPER EXPER^2 MOTHEREDUC
Constant added to instrument list

Variable	Coefficient	Std. Error	t-Statistic	Prob.
C	0.198186	0.472877	0.419107	0.6754
EDUC	0.049263	0.037436	1.315924	0.1889
EXPER	0.044856	0.013577	3.303856	0.0010
EXPER^2	-0.000922	0.000406	-2.268993	0.0238

R-squared	0.123130	Mean dependent var	1.190173
Adjusted R-squared	0.116926	S.D. dependent var	0.723198
S.E. of regression	0.679604	Sum squared resid	195.8291
F-statistic	7.347957	Durbin-Watson stat	1.941610
Prob(F-statistic)	0.000082	Second-Stage SSR	213.1462
J-statistic	6.21E-42	Instrument rank	4

Quite a few items are different here from in the usual least squares estimation results; however, the estimates and standard errors are in the usual format.

In the regression window select **View/Representations** to find the **Estimation Command**:

tsls log(wage) c educ exper exper^2 @ exper exper^2 mothereduc

The instruments are listed after the @ sign, and the estimation command itself is **tsls**.

The **minimum** number of instrumental variables required is the number of endogenous, or potentially endogenous, variables on the right-hand side of the equation. In this case the equation is said to be "just identified." If additional external instruments are available, we can use them as well. For example, if we use *FATHEREDUC* as an instrument in addition to *MOTHEREDUC,* the IV/2SLS estimates are obtained using

equation tsls_mom_dad.tsls log(wage) c educ exper exper^2 @ exper exper^2 mothereduc fathereduc

```
Sample: 1 428
Included observations: 428
Instrument specification: EXPER EXPER^2 MOTHEREDUC FATHEREDUC
Constant added to instrument list
```

Variable	Coefficient	Std. Error	t-Statistic	Prob.
C	0.048100	0.400328	0.120152	0.9044
EDUC	0.061397	0.031437	1.953024	0.0515
EXPER	0.044170	0.013432	3.288329	0.0011
EXPER^2	-0.000899	0.000402	-2.237993	0.0257

The equation is said to be "overidentified" because there is a surplus instrument. How many instruments to use is a difficult question to answer in general. Usually, it is desired to have some surplus instruments, but not a huge number.

In the equation estimation dialog box, the **Options** tab offers a choice of coefficient covariance matrices. If heteroskedasticity is a potential problem then choose **White**.

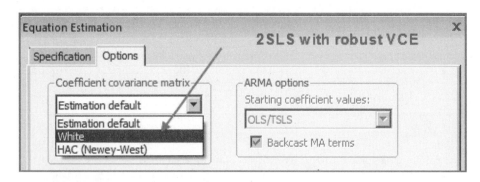

```
Sample: 1 428
Included observations: 428
White heteroskedasticity-consistent standard errors & covariance
Instrument specification: EXPER EXPER^2 MOTHEREDUC FATHEREDUC
Constant added to instrument list
```

Variable	Coefficient	Std. Error	t-Statistic	Prob.
C	0.048100	0.429798	0.111914	0.9109
EDUC	0.061397	0.033339	1.841609	0.0662
EXPER	0.044170	0.015546	2.841202	0.0047
EXPER^2	-0.000899	0.000430	-2.090220	0.0372
R-squared	0.135708	Mean dependent var		1.190173

10.3 TESTING INSTRUMENT STRENGTH

Instruments to be useful must be correlated with the endogenous right-hand-side variable after controlling for the effect of the exogenous regressors. The starting point is the **first stage** equation, with the endogenous variable on the left-hand side and all the exogenous and instrumental variables on the right-hand side. We seek instruments that are strongly significant in the first stage regression.

First, consider using only mother's education *MOTHEREDUC* as an instrumental variable:

equation stage1_mom.ls educ c exper exper^2 mothereduc

Variable	Coefficient	Std. Error	t-Statistic	Prob.
Sample: 1 428				
Included observations: 428				
C	9.775103	0.423889	23.06055	0.0000
EXPER	0.048862	0.041669	1.172603	0.2416
EXPER^2	-0.001281	0.001245	-1.029046	0.3040
MOTHEREDUC	0.267691	0.031130	8.599183	0.0000
R-squared	0.152694	Mean dependent var		12.65888

Note that the instrumental variable *MOTHEREDUC* is very significant, with a *t*-value of 8.6, indicating that this variable is strongly correlated with *EDUC*. With cross-sectional data, using a White robust VCE is often recommended:

equation stage1_mom_rob.ls(cov=white) educ c exper exper^2 mothereduc

Variable	Coefficient	Std. Error	t-Statistic	Prob.
White heteroskedasticity-consistent standard errors & covariance				
C	9.775103	0.413475	23.64135	0.0000
EXPER	0.048862	0.042627	1.146256	0.2523
EXPER^2	-0.001281	0.001342	-0.954546	0.3404
MOTHEREDUC	0.267691	0.031713	8.441155	0.0000

If we use both *MOTHEREDUC* and *FATHEREDUC* as instrumental variables, the estimated first stage is obtained using

equation stage1_mom_dad.ls educ c exper exper^2 mothereduc fathereduc

Variable	Coefficient	Std. Error	t-Statistic	Prob.
Sample: 1 428				
Included observations: 428				
C	9.102640	0.426561	21.33958	0.0000
EXPER	0.045225	0.040251	1.123593	0.2618
EXPER^2	-0.001009	0.001203	-0.838572	0.4022
MOTHEREDUC	0.157597	0.035894	4.390609	0.0000
FATHEREDUC	0.189548	0.033756	5.615173	0.0000

Both instruments are strongly related to the woman's education *EDUC*. To test their joint significance select **View/Coefficient Tests/Wald – Coefficient Restrictions**, or enter the command

stage1_mom_dad.wald c(4)=0, c(5)=0

Wald Test: Equation: STAGE1_DAD			
Test Statistic	Value	df	Probability
F-statistic	55.40030	(2, 423)	0.0000
Chi-square	110.8006	2	0.0000

The result shows an *F* value of 55.4, giving strong evidence that at least one of the instruments has a nonzero coefficient in the reduced form equation. A rule of thumb in this literature is that the *F*-value must be larger than 10. Again, this test can be made robust if desired.

10.3.1 Testing for weak instruments

Instrumental variables estimators can behave poorly if instruments are weak. Stock and Yogo (2005) have developed specific tests for weak instruments under two criteria. The **relative bias** criterion asks: what is the maximum acceptable IV bias for the coefficient of the endogenous variable, relative to the same bias using the least squares estimator? For the maximum relative biases of 5%, 10%, 20% and 30%, Stock and Yogo have developed critical values for a 5% test of the null hypothesis that the instruments are weak against the alternative that they are not weak. In order to use this test there must be at least three instrumental variables and model errors must be homoskedastic.

The **test size** criterion asks: if we test the coefficient at the 5% level of significance, what is the maximum acceptable rejection rate, 10%, 15%, 20% or 25%? Stock and Yogo have developed critical values for a 5% test of the null hypothesis that the instruments are weak against the alternative that they are not weak. In order to use this test model errors must be homoskedastic.

Examine the regression output for the IV estimation using *MOTHEREDUC* and *FATHEREDUC* as instruments. Select **View/IV Diagnostics & Tests/Weak Instruments Diagnostics**

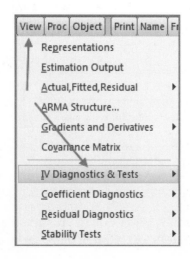

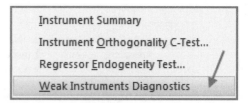

When there is a single endogenous variable, the test is based on the first stage joint F-test of significance. In this context it is called the Cragg-Donald F-statistic.

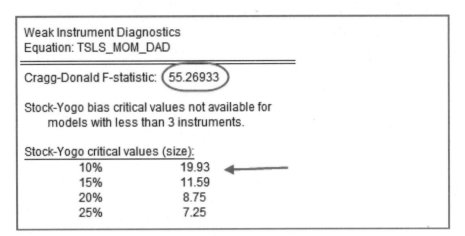

Because there are only two instruments, the **relative bias** criterion cannot be used. Using the **test size** criterion, first select the maximum acceptable test rejection rate of a true null hypothesis. Compare the Cragg-Donald F-statistic to the corresponding critical value. If the F-value is greater than the critical value, we reject the null hypothesis that the instruments are weak, and conclude that they are not weak. For more on this test, and other illustrations, see Appendix 10E in *Principles of Econometrics, 4th Edition*.

10.4 TEST OF ENDOGENEITY

If we have strong instruments we can test whether the variable we suspect to be endogenous actually is endogenous. There are several versions of this test, which is generally called the **Hausman test** in honor of test developer Jerry Hausman. The simplest and in our view most reliable test is called the **regression-based test**. To test the endogeneity of *EDUC* we obtain the first stage residuals and then include them in the wage equation as an extra explanatory variable. If the residual series is statistically significant then we conclude that *EDUC* is endogenous.

```
ls educ c exper exper^2 mothereduc fathereduc
series vhat = resid
equation hausman.ls log(wage) c educ exper exper^2 vhat
```

The estimation results show that the variable *VHAT* has a p-value of 0.0954, which is not strong evidence that *EDUC* is endogenous.

Variable	Coefficient	Std. Error	t-Statistic	Prob.
C	0.048100	0.394575	0.121904	0.9030
EDUC	0.061397	0.030985	1.981499	0.0482
EXPER	0.044170	0.013239	3.336272	0.0009
EXPER^2	-0.000899	0.000396	-2.270623	0.0237
VHAT	0.058167	0.034807	1.671105	0.0954

This test can be made robust to account for heteroskedasticity.

equation hausman_rob.ls(cov=white) log(wage) c educ exper exper^2 vhat

White heteroskedasticity-consistent standard errors & covariance				
Variable	Coefficient	Std. Error	t-Statistic	Prob.
C	0.048100	0.422102	0.113954	0.9093
EDUC	0.061397	0.032667	1.879485	0.0609
EXPER	0.044170	0.015122	2.920951	0.0037
EXPER^2	-0.000899	0.000415	-2.164931	0.0310
VHAT	0.058167	0.036413	1.597392	0.1109

EViews has a built-in test for endogeneity. Examine the regression output for the IV estimation using *MOTHEREDUC* and *FATHEREDUC* as instruments. Select **View/IV Diagnostics & Tests/Weak Instruments Diagnostics**

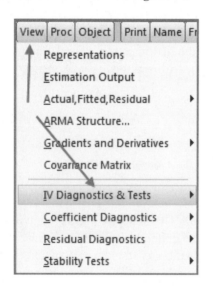

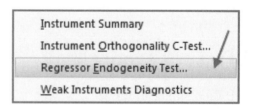

In the resulting dialog box, specify the endogenous variable for testing:

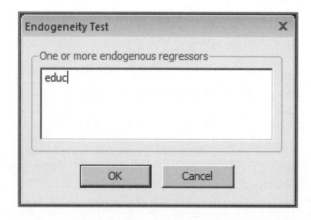

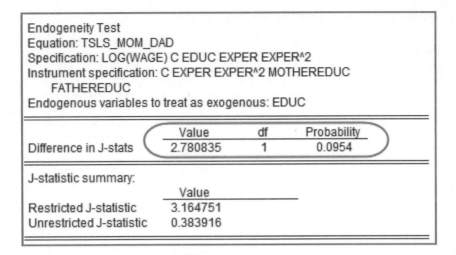

Endeneity Test
Equation: TSLS_MOM_DAD
Specification: LOG(WAGE) C EDUC EXPER EXPER^2
Instrument specification: C EXPER EXPER^2 MOTHEREDUC
    FATHEREDUC
Endogenous variables to treat as exogenous: EDUC

	Value	df	Probability
Difference in J-stats	2.780835	1	0.0954

J-statistic summary:	Value
Restricted J-statistic	3.164751
Unrestricted J-statistic	0.383916

The test statistic is computed as the difference between two statistics that are known as J statistics. It has an asymptotic chi-square distribution if the null hypothesis that the variable *EDUC* is exogenous is true. The degrees of freedom parameter (**df**) is the number of endogenous variables being tested, which in this case is one. The *p*-value is very close to that from the *t*-test in the regression-based test. We are hesitant to recommend this test as it relies on theory beyond the scope of this book, relating to the generalized method of moments estimator. It does have the advantage of being generalizable to other estimation problems. The interested reader can check the EViews 7 **User's Guide II**, page 79. Recall that full EViews documentation is available from **Help**, on the EViews menu.

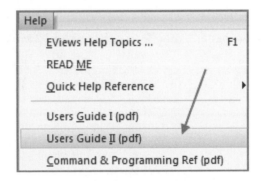

10.5 TESTING INSTRUMENT VALIDITY

A final diagnostic is for the validity of the proposed instruments. In order for instruments to be valid, they must be uncorrelated with the regression error. This test is sometimes called the Sargan test and it can be carried out only when there are surplus instruments. The idea is intuitive. First compute the 2SLS residuals:

**tsls log(wage) c educ exper exper^2 @ exper exper^2 mothereduc fathereduc
series ehat = resid**

Regress these residuals on all the exogenous variables and instruments:

ls ehat c exper exper^2 mothereduc fathereduc

Included observations: 428				
Variable	Coefficient	Std. Error	t-Statistic	Prob.
C	0.010964	0.141257	0.077618	0.9382
EXPER	-1.83E-05	0.013329	-0.001376	0.9989
EXPER^2	7.34E-07	0.000398	0.001842	0.9985
MOTHEREDUC	-0.006607	0.011886	-0.555804	0.5786
FATHEREDUC	0.005782	0.011179	0.517263	0.6052
R-squared	0.000883	Mean dependent var		-1.50E-16

If the instruments are valid, then we should find no relationship between the 2SLS residuals and the explanatory variables and instruments. The test statistic is $N \times R^2 \sim \chi^2_{(L-B)}$ where $L - B$ is the number of surplus instruments. For the artificial regression $R^2 = 0.000883$, and the test statistic value is

$$N \times R^2 = 428 \times 0.000883 = 0.3779$$

The 0.05 critical value for the chi-square distribution with one degree of freedom is 3.84, and thus we fail to reject the surplus instrument as valid. With this result we are reassured that our instrumental variables estimator for the wage equation is consistent.

EViews performs a slightly different version of this test as part of the routine output from IV estimation. It is called the *J*-test. Examine the lower part of the output from the command

tsls log(wage) c educ exper exper^2 @ exper exper^2 mothereduc fathereduc

R-squared	0.135708	Mean dependent var	1.190173
Adjusted R-squared	0.129593	S.D. dependent var	0.723198
S.E. of regression	0.674712	Sum squared resid	193.0200
F-statistic	8.140709	Durbin-Watson stat	1.945659
Prob(F-statistic)	0.000028	Second-Stage SSR	212.2096
J-statistic	0.374538	Instrument rank	5
Prob(J-statistic)	0.540541		

The *J*-statistic has a $\chi^2_{(L-B)}$ distribution under the null hypothesis that the surplus instruments are valid. In this case $L - B = 1$ and $J = 0.3745$, a value similar to that obtained using the statistic $N \times R^2$. With a *p*-value of 0.54, we have no evidence to suggest the instruments are invalid.

10.6 MONTE CARLO SIMULATION

In this section we show how to write an EViews program to run the Monte Carlo experiment that was performed in Appendix 10F on pages 440-444 of *POE4*. The objective is to examine the finite sample properties of the least squares and IV estimators and related tests under four scenarios: endogeneity and no endogeneity, combined with weak and strong instruments. When we have random regressors, our finite sample theory no longer holds. We must use large sample theory to derive the properties of estimators and tests. Monte Carlo experiments are used to examine the properties of estimators and tests in finite samples.

The model we use in the experiment is

$$y = \beta_1 + \beta_2 x + e \quad \text{with} \quad \beta_1 = 0 \quad \beta_2 = 1 \quad e \sim N(0,1)$$

$$x = \pi_0 + \pi_1 z_1 + \pi_2 z_2 + \pi_3 z_3 + v \quad \text{with} \quad \pi_0 = 0 \quad \text{and} \quad \pi_1 = \pi_2 = \pi_3 = \pi$$

$$v \sim N(0,1) \qquad E(ve) = \mathrm{cor}(e,v) = \rho \qquad N = 100$$

The degree of endogeneity was controlled by setting ρ. The strength of the instruments was controlled by setting π. Note that correlation between v and e implies correlation between x and e. The different settings investigated in the Monte Carlo experiment are given in the following table. For future reference we include values of the loop indexes **!i** and **!j** that denote the different settings in the program.

!i	!j	ρ (rho)	π (pi)
1	1	0.0	0.1
1	2	0.0	0.5
2	1	0.8	0.1
2	2	0.8	0.5

Open a workfile, make it unstructured with 100 observations, and save it as ***appendix_10f.wf1***. Open a new Program window and save it as ***appendix_10f.prg***. If necessary, go back and read Section 5.10 in this manual to see how a program is created. We begin by introducing blocks of commands that will form part of the complete program that we list at the end of this section:

```
vector(2) rho
vector(2) pi
rho(1)=0
rho(2)=0.8
pi(1)=0.1
pi(2)=0.5
```

These commands define the 2×1 vectors **rho** and **pi** and set the values for ρ and π to be used in the Monte Carlo experiment.

```
for !i=1 to 2
for !j=1 to 2
    matrix(10000,3) ests{!i}{!j}
next
next
```

This double loop defines four 10000×3 matrices **ESTS11**, **ESTS12**, **ESTS21** and **ESTS22**. These are the matrices we are going to use to store (i) the F-values for testing the significance of the instruments in the first stage regression, (ii) the least squares estimates for β_2, and (iii) the IV estimates for β_2. There are 10,000 rows because we are considering 10,000 samples in the Monte Carlo experiment. The three columns will contain the values for $\left(F, b_2, \hat{\beta}_2\right)$ where b_2 is the least squares estimate and $\hat{\beta}_2$ is the IV estimate. There are four different matrices because we are obtaining estimates for four different combinations of ρ and π. Note the correspondence between the two digits at the end of each matrix name and the settings in the above table. Using curly brackets with a loop index, as in **ests{!i}{!j}**, is EViews' way of appending a number or numbers to a name. It is also used to refer to a name with number(s) at the end of that name. It will be convenient later when we are storing the estimates for different settings of ρ and π.

```
series z1
series z2
series z3
series x
series v
series vhat
series e
series y
scalar check
scalar tee
scalar tc=@qtdist(0.975,98)
```

This sequence of commands defines a number of series and scalars that will be used later within the loop used for the Monte Carlo experiment. The variables **z1**, **z2**, **z3**, **x**, **v**, **e** and **y** are those specified in the model, **vhat** will be the residuals from the first stage regression, **check** will be an indicator variable equal to 1 when a hypothesis is rejected, **tee** is used to denote a t-value, and **tc** is the critical t-value used for hypothesis tests. We could define these variables within the loop when they first take on values, but doing it outside makes our later statements less burdensome.

```
for !i=1 to 2                              Outer loop for different values of rho
for !j=1 to 2                              Outer loop for different values of pi
    scalar tb_ls=0
    scalar tb_iv=0
    scalar th=0
    for !k=1 to 10000
    ......... Inner loop commands go here
    next
    scalar tb_ls{!i}{!j}=tb_ls/10000
    scalar tb_iv{!i}{!j}=tb_iv/10000
    scalar th{!i}{!j}=th/10000
next                                       End of loop for different values of pi
next                                       End of loop for different values of rho
```

We now have a sequence of three nested loops – somewhat more complicated than the single loop we had for the experiment in Appendix 5B. Consider the inner loop first. It is governed by the index **!k** that takes values 1 to 10,000. For each value of **!k** a new sample is generated, new least squares and IV estimates are obtained, and new test values are computed. We will consider these inner loop commands shortly. The outer loops, which are of interest now, are needed because we are repeating the experiment four times, once for each (ρ, π) combination. Having **!i** and **!j** each go from 1 to 2 repeats the experiment four times.

The scalars **tb_ls**, **tb_iv** and **th** are used to count the number of test rejections. The tests are (i) using the least squares estimator to test $\beta_2 = 1$, (ii) using the IV estimator to test $\beta_2 = 1$, and

(iii) using the Hausman test to test the endogeneity of x via the significance of the first stage residuals. Within the inner loop the scalars are incremented by 1 each time there is a test rejection. They are initialed to zero outside the inner loop but inside the outer loops, because the same scalars are used to count rejections for each (ρ, π) setting. The final counts for each (ρ, π) setting are saved and turned into proportions of rejections at the end of the inner loop, using the commands **tb_ls{!i}{!j}=tb_ls/10000**, **tb_iv{!i}{!j}=tb_iv/10000** and **th{!i}{!j}=th/10000**. These commands create the scalars **tb_ls11**, **tb_ls12**, **tb_ls21**, **tb_ls22**, **tb_iv11**, **tb_iv12**, **tb_iv21**, **tb_iv22**, **th11**, **th12**, **th21**, and **th22**. They contain the proportions of rejections for each setting; the two digits at the end of each name indicate the (ρ, π) setting.

We are now in a position to examine the commands inside the inner loop. These commands are repeated 40,000 times $(10000 \times 2 \times 2)$. We consider them in blocks:

```
z1=@rnorm
z2=@rnorm
z3=@rnorm
v=@rnorm
e=rho(!i)*v + (@sqrt(1-rho(!i)^2))*@rnorm
x=pi(!j)*(z1+z2+z3)+v
y=x+e
```

This group of commands generates samples of size 100 on the required variables. The function **@rnorm** generates a normal random variate with mean 0 and variance 1. An alternative that does the same thing is **nrnd**. The experiment uses each z and v generated as independent $N(0,1)$ random variates. We generate e as

$$e = \rho v + \sqrt{1-\rho^2}\, u \quad \text{where} \quad u \sim N(0,1)$$

This gives an e with the desired properties of unit variance and a correlation with v equal to ρ:

$$\text{var}(e) = \rho^2 \,\text{var}(v) + \left(1-\rho^2\right)\text{var}(u) = \rho^2 + \left(1-\rho^2\right) = 1$$

$$\text{cor}(e,v) = \text{cov}(e,v) = E(ev) = \rho E\left(v^2\right) + \sqrt{1-\rho^2}\, E(uv) = \rho$$

The series x and y are generated in line with our original model specification:

```
equation stage1.ls x c z1 z2 z3
ests{!i}{!j}(!k,1)=@f
vhat=resid
```

These three commands estimate the first stage regression, store the F-value in the first column of the matrix **ESTSij**, and save the residuals as **vhat**. The index **!k** is used to denote the row of the matrix in which F is stored.

```
equation ls.ls y c x
ests{!i}{!j}(!k,2)=c(2)
tee=(c(2)-1)/@stderrs(2)
check=(tee>tc or tee<-tc)
tb_ls=tb_ls+check
```

This block of commands is concerned with least squares estimation of the main equation. The least squares estimate b_2 is stored in the second column of **ESTSij**. A t-value called **tee** is calculated for testing $\beta_2 = 1$. If this value is in the rejection region, then **check** = 1; otherwise **check** = 0. If $\beta_2 = 1$ is rejected, **tb_ls** increases by 1, otherwise it remains unchanged.

```
equation haus.ls y c x vhat
tee=@tstats(3)
check=(tee>tc or tee<-tc)
th=th+check
```

These commands perform the Hausman test. If the *t*-value for **vhat**, called **tee**, is in the rejection region, then **check** = 1; otherwise **check** = 0. If exogeneity is rejected, **th** increases by 1, otherwise it remains unchanged.

```
equation iv.tsls y c x @ z1 z2 z3
ests{!i}{!j}(!k,3)=c(2)
tee=(c(2)-1)/@stderrs(2)
check=(tee>tc or tee<-tc)
tb_iv=tb_iv+check
```

This block of commands is concerned with IV estimation of the main equation. The IV estimate $\hat{\beta}_2$ is stored in the third column of **ESTS*ij***. A *t*-value called **tee** is calculated for testing $\beta_2 = 1$. If this value is in the rejection region, then **check** = 1; otherwise **check** = 0. If $\beta_2 = 1$ is rejected, **tb_iv** increases by 1, otherwise it remains unchanged.

We are now in a position to list the complete program that must be entered in the Program window:

```
vector(2) rho
vector(2) pi
rho(1)=0
rho(2)=0.8
pi(1)=0.1
pi(2)=0.5
for !i=1 to 2
for !j=1 to 2
    matrix(10000,3) ests{!i}{!j}
next
next
series z1
series z2
series z3
series x
series v
series vhat
series e
series y
scalar check
scalar tee
scalar tc=@qtdist(0.975,98)
for !i=1 to 2
for !j=1 to 2
    scalar tb_ls=0
```

```
scalar tb_iv=0
scalar th=0
for !k=1 to 10000
    z1=@rnorm
    z2=@rnorm
    z3=@rnorm
    v=@rnorm
    e=rho(!i)*v + (@sqrt(1-rho(!i)^2))*@rnorm
    x=pi(!j)*(z1+z2+z3)+v
    y=x+e
    equation stage1.ls x c z1 z2 z3
    ests{!i}{!j}(!k,1)=@f
    vhat=resid
    equation ls.ls y c x
    ests{!i}{!j}(!k,2)=c(2)
    tee=(c(2)-1)/@stderrs(2)
    check=(tee>tc or tee<-tc)
    tb_ls=tb_ls+check
    equation haus.ls y c x vhat
    tee=@tstats(3)
    check=(tee>tc or tee<-tc)
    th=th+check
    equation iv.tsls y c x @ z1 z2 z3
    ests{!i}{!j}(!k,3)=c(2)
    tee=(c(2)-1)/@stderrs(2)
    check=(tee>tc or tee<-tc)
    tb_iv=tb_iv+check
next
scalar tb_ls{!i}{!j}=tb_ls/10000
scalar tb_iv{!i}{!j}=tb_iv/10000
scalar th{!i}{!j}=th/10000
next
next
```

After entering all the commands into your program, click **Save** and then **Run**. Your workfile should also be open at this time.

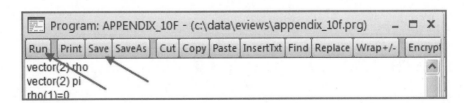

EViews will respond with the following window:

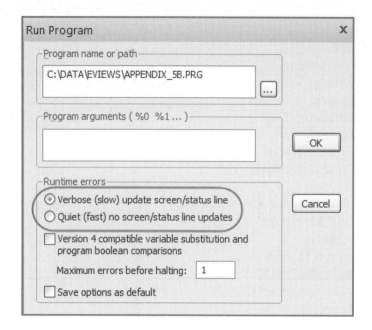

You can simply click **OK**, but first it is good to choose between **Verbose** mode and **Quiet** mode. **Verbose** mode is a good choice if you are uncertain about whether your program has errors, or if you want the reassurance that something is being computed. In this mode EViews keeps updating a "status line" with the most recent quantity calculated. **Verbose** mode is much, much slower than **Quiet** mode, however.

After the program has run, your workfile will contain several extra items. Those that we are interested in are the **ESTS*ij*** matrices and the scalars **TB_LS*ij***, **TB_IV*ij*** and **TH*ij***. The equation and series objects will contain estimates and values from the last of the 40,000 samples. To clean up your workfile you could delete these items, leaving the following workfil:.

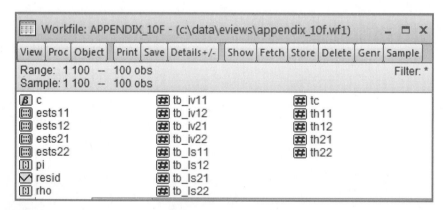

As an example of the test results, we consider the case where $\rho = 0.8$ and $\pi = 0.5$. Opening the relevant values yields

	Value
TB_LS22	1.000000

	Value
TB_IV22	0.064500

	Value
TH22	1.000000

This is a setup with strong endogeneity and strong instruments. The least squares based test rejects a true null hypothesis 100% of the time! The IVbased test rejects the true null hypothesis

6% of the time, which is sufficiently close to the 5% significance level to be acceptable. The strong instruments and strong endogeneity lead to a good result for the Hausman test; it picks up the endogeneity 100% of the time.

Now, we check the means and standard deviations of the least squares and IV estimates and the average of the F-value used to test for strong instruments. Again, using the case where $\rho = 0.8$ and $\pi = 0.5$ as an example, open the matrix **ESTS22**, and go to **View/Descriptive Stats by Column:**

Matrix: ESTS22 Workfile: APPENDIX_10F::Untitled\			
View Proc Object Print Name Freeze Edit+/- Label+/- Shee			
ESTS22			
	C1	C2	C3
Mean	26.31755	1.456900	1.010373
Median	25.50666	1.457367	1.020335
Maximum	73.50054	1.685947	1.368339
Minimum	6.105276	1.242230	0.383533
Std. Dev.	8.037162	0.061275	0.117830

The average F-value of 26.32 indicates that the test for strong instruments has worked well. The mean of the least squares estimates is 1.457, showing a bias of 0.457, whereas the IV estimator shows negligible bias, with a mean of 1.010. The standard deviation of the IV estimator is nearly double that of the least squares estimator, however.

In the table below, we report the complete set of results from our Monte Carlo experiment. This table is comparable to Table 10F.1 on page 443 of *POE4*. It is not identical, of course, because our random numbers will be different. But it does tell the same story. If you try the same program, you should get similar but not identical results. Note that for the case with $\rho = 0.8$ (strong endogeneity) and with $\pi = 0.1$ (weak instruments), the standard deviation of the IV estimator is 0.5392 in our experiment, while in *POE4* it is reported to be 0.9483. This serves as another warning of how poor IV estimation can be with weak instruments, especially with strong endogeneity.

					Monte Carlo Simulation Results				
ρ	π	$\overline{F}$	$\overline{b}_2$	$s.d.(b_2)$	$t(b_2)$	$t(H)$	$\overline{\hat{\beta}}_2$	$s.d.(\hat{\beta}_2)$	$t(\hat{\beta}_2)$
0.0	0.1	2.03	1.0005	0.1002	0.0516	0.0474	1.0030	0.5987	0.0052
0.0	0.5	26.40	1.0007	0.0769	0.0545	0.0463	1.0016	0.1171	0.0428
0.8	0.1	2.02	1.7766	0.0611	1.0000	0.3910	1.3370	0.5392	0.2822
0.8	0.5	26.32	1.4569	0.0613	1.0000	1.0000	1.0104	0.1178	0.0645

Keywords

@f

@rnorm

@tstats

chi-square test

Cragg-Donald F-test

C-test

endogeneity problem

endogenous regressor

for

Hausman test

identified

inconsistent estimator

instrument list

instrumental variables

instruments

J-test

just-identified

least squares

loop

loop index

matrix

Monte Carlo

Mroz data

next

nrnd

over-identified

program

program window

quiet mode

random regressors

reduced form

relative bias criteria

rndseed

run

Sargan statistic

scatter plot

simulation

stochastic

Stock-Yogo critical value

surplus instruments

test for weak instruments

test size criteria

TSLS

two-stage least squares

validity of surplus instruments

vector

verbose mode

wage equation

Wald test

CHAPTER **11**

Simultaneous Equations Models

CHAPTER OUTLINE

11.1 Examining the Data
11.2 Estimating the Reduced Form
11.3 TSLS Estimation of an Equation

11.4 TSLS Estimation of a System of Equations
11.5 Supply and Demand at Fulton Fish Market
11.6 LIML and *k*-class Estimation
KEYWORDS

Until now, we have considered estimation and hypothesis testing in a variety of single equation models. Here we introduce models for the joint estimation of two or more equations. While there are countless applications for simultaneous equations models in economics, some applications with which you will be familiar include market demand and supply models and the multi-equation Keynesian models that we analyze in macroeconomics.

11.1 EXAMINING THE DATA

In this section, *POE4* introduces a two-equation demand and supply model for truffles, a French gourmet mushroom delicacy. To estimate the truffles model in EViews, open the workfile *truffles.wf1*. Open a **Group** containing the data. While holding down the **Ctrl**-key, select *P*, *Q*, *PS*, *DI* and *PF*. The first few observations look like

obs	P	Q	PS	DI	PF
1	29.64000	19.89000	19.97000	2.103000	10.52000
2	40.23000	13.04000	18.04000	2.043000	19.67000
3	34.71000	19.61000	22.36000	1.870000	13.74000
4	41.43000	17.13000	20.87000	1.525000	17.95000
5	53.37000	22.55000	19.79000	2.709000	13.71000

The summary statistics for the variables are obtained from the spreadsheet by selecting **View/Descriptive Stats/Common Sample.**

	P	Q	PS	DI	PF
Mean	62.72400	18.45833	22.02200	3.526967	22.75333
Median	63.07500	19.27000	22.68500	3.708000	24.14500
Maximum	105.4500	26.27000	28.98000	5.125000	34.01000
Minimum	29.64000	6.370000	15.21000	1.525000	10.52000
Std. Dev.	18.72346	4.613088	4.077237	1.040803	5.329654

11.2 ESTIMATING THE REDUCED FORM

We first estimate the reduced form equations of *POE4* Section 11.6.2 by regressing each endogenous variable, *Q*, and *P*, on the exogenous variables, *PS, DI,* and *PF*. We can quickly accomplish this task with the following statements typed in the EViews Command window. The results match those in *POE4* Table 11.2, page 456.

equation redform_q.ls q c ps di pf

Dependent Variable: Q
Method: Least Squares
Sample: 1 30

	Coefficient	Std. Error	t-Statistic	Prob.
C	7.895099	3.243422	2.434188	0.0221
PS	0.656402	0.142538	4.605115	0.0001
DI	2.167156	0.700474	3.093842	0.0047
PF	-0.506982	0.121262	-4.180896	0.0003
R-squared	0.697386	Mean dependent var		18.45833

equation redform_p.ls p c ps di pf

Dependent Variable: P
Method: Least Squares
Sample: 1 30

	Coefficient	Std. Error	t-Statistic	Prob.
C	-32.51242	7.984235	-4.072077	0.0004
PS	1.708147	0.350881	4.868172	0.0000
DI	7.602491	1.724336	4.408939	0.0002
PF	1.353906	0.298506	4.535603	0.0001
R-squared	0.888683	Mean dependent var		62.72400

11.3 TSLS ESTIMATION OF AN EQUATION

Any identified equation within a system of simultaneous equations can be estimated by two-stage least squares (2SLS/TSLS). Click on **Quick/Estimate Equation**.

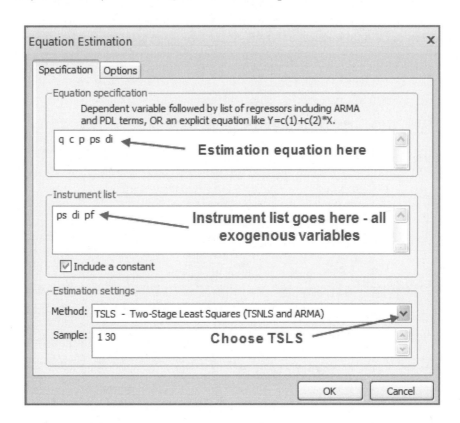

To estimate the demand equation by *2SLS,* select the method to be **TSLS**, fill in the demand equation variables in **Equation specification,** the upper area of the dialog box, and list <u>all</u> the exogenous variables in the system in the **Instrument list**. Click **OK**. Name the resulting equation **DEMAND**.

Alternatively, to estimate the supply equation we illustrate the use of the command line:

equation supply.tsls q c p pf @ ps di pf

Instrument specification: PS DI PF
Constant added to instrument list

Variable	Coefficient	Std. Error	t-Statistic	Prob.
C	20.03280	1.223115	16.37851	0.0000
P	0.337982	0.024920	13.56290	0.0000
PF	-1.000909	0.082528	-12.12813	0.0000

In this command we name the estimation **SUPPLY** and choose the estimation technique TSLS by using **equation supply.tsls**. The specification of the equation is followed by the instrumental variables, which follow **@**.

11.4 TSLS ESTIMATION OF A SYSTEM OF EQUATIONS

As noted in Section 11.3, we can apply TSLS equation by equation for all the identified equations within a system of equations. If all the equations in the system are identified, then all the equations can be estimated in one step.

We introduce a new EViews object here: the **SYSTEM**. From the EViews menubar, click on **Objects/New Object**, select **System**, name the system object **TRUFFLE**, and click **OK**.

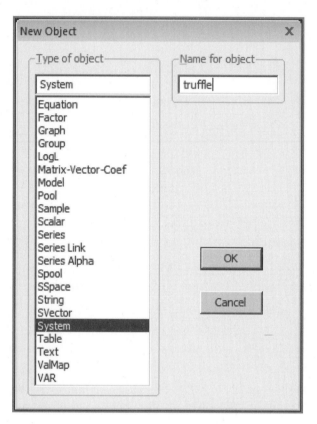

Next, enter the system equation specification given in *POE4* equations (11.11) and (11.12) on page 454. Note that you must enter a line that contains the exogenous (determined outside the model) variables in the system, *PS*, *DI*, and *PF*. In the context of two-stage least squares estimation of our truffles system, EViews refers to these exogenous variables as "instruments." Enter the line **inst ps di pf** directly below the supply equation, and click **Estimate** on the system's toolbar.

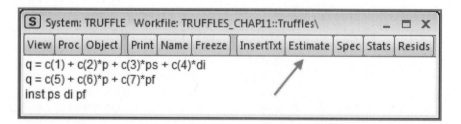

To reproduce the results found in Tables 11.3a and 11.3b in *POE4*, under **Estimation Method**, check the **Two-Stage Least Squares** checkbox and click **OK**.

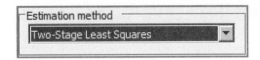

The results are identical to the equation-by-equation approach of estimating demand and then supply, but this system estimation approach opens the door to many advanced procedures that you may learn about in subsequent econometrics courses.

System: TRUFFLE
Estimation Method: Two-Stage Least Squares
Sample: 1 30
Total system (balanced) observations 60

	Coefficient	Std. Error	t-Statistic	Prob.
C(1)	-4.279471	5.543884	-0.771926	0.4436
C(2)	-0.374459	0.164752	-2.272869	0.0271
C(3)	1.296033	0.355193	3.648812	0.0006
C(4)	5.013977	2.283556	2.195688	0.0325
C(5)	20.03280	1.223115	16.37851	0.0000
C(6)	0.337982	0.024920	13.56290	0.0000
C(7)	-1.000909	0.082528	-12.12813	0.0000

At the bottom of the **System Table** we find each equation represented and summarized:

Equation: Q = C(1) + C(2)*P + C(3)*PS + C(4)*DI
Instruments: PS DI PF C
Observations: 30

R-squared	-0.023950	Mean dependent var	18.45833
Adjusted R-squared	-0.142098	S.D. dependent var	4.613088
S.E. of regression	4.929960	Sum squared resid	631.9171
Prob(F-statistic)	1.962370		

Note in these results that R^2 and adjusted-R^2 are negative. This is not uncommon when using generalized least squares, instrumental variables, or two-stage least squares. For any estimator but least squares, the identity $SST = SSR + SSE$ does not hold, so the usual $R^2 = 1 - SSE/SST$ can produce negative numbers. This just shows that the goodness-of-fit measure is not appropriate in this context and should be ignored.

11.5 SUPPLY AND DEMAND AT FULTON FISH MARKET

A second example of a simultaneous equations model is given by the Fulton Fish Market discussed in *POE* Section 11.7, page 457. Open the workfile *fultonfish.wf1*. Let us specify the demand equation for this market as

$$\ln(QUAN_t) = \alpha_1 + \alpha_2 \ln(PRICE_t) + \alpha_3 MON_t + \alpha_4 TUE_t + \alpha_5 WED_t + \alpha_6 THU_t + e_{dt}$$

where $QUAN_t$ is the quantity sold, in pounds, and $PRICE_t$ the average daily price per pound. Note that we are using the subscript "t" to index observations for this relationship because of the time series nature of the data. The remaining variables are dummy variables for the days of the week, with Friday being omitted. The coefficient α_2 is the price elasticity of demand, which we expect to be negative. The daily dummy variables capture day-to-day shifts in demand. The supply equation is

$$\ln(QUAN_t) = \beta_1 + \beta_2 \ln(PRICE_t) + \beta_3 STORMY_t + e_{st}$$

The coefficient β_2 is the price elasticity of supply. The variable *STORMY* is a dummy variable indicating stormy weather during the previous three days. This variable is important in the supply equation because stormy weather makes fishing more difficult, reducing the supply of fish brought to market.

The reduced form equations specify each endogenous variable as a function of all exogenous variables

$$\ln(QUAN_t) = \pi_{11} + \pi_{21} MON_t + \pi_{31} TUE_t + \pi_{41} WED_t + \pi_{51} THU_t + \pi_{61} STORMY_t + v_{t1}$$

$$\ln(PRICE_t) = \pi_{12} + \pi_{22} MON_t + \pi_{32} TUE_t + \pi_{42} WED_t + \pi_{52} THU_t + \pi_{62} STORMY_t + v_{t2}$$

The least squares estimates of the reduced forms are given by

ls lquan c mon tue wed thu stormy
ls lprice c mon tue wed thu stormy

The key reduced form equation is the second, for ln(*PRICE*). For the supply equation to be reliably estimated, the daily indicator variables must be jointly significant. For the demand equation to be reliably estimated, *STORMY* must be significant. See *POE4*, pages 459-460 for a discussion.

Dependent Variable: LPRICE				
	Coefficient	Std. Error	t-Statistic	Prob.
C	-0.271705	0.076389	-3.556867	0.0006
MON	-0.112922	0.107292	-1.052480	0.2950
TUE	-0.041149	0.104509	-0.393740	0.6946
WED	-0.011825	0.106930	-0.110587	0.9122
THU	0.049646	0.104458	0.475268	0.6356
STORMY	0.346406	0.074678	4.638681	0.0000

We find that *STORMY* is strongly significant but, individually, the daily indicator variables are not. To check the joint significance of the daily indicator variables, we use the Wald test:

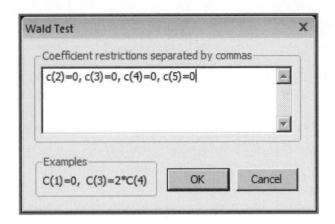

or, in the Command window,

redform_price.wald c(2)=0, c(3)=0, c(4)=0, c(5)=0

Wald Test:
Equation: REDFORM_PRICE

Test Statistic	Value	df	Probability
F-statistic	0.618762	(4, 105)	0.6501
Chi-square	2.475049	4	0.6491

Null Hypothesis: C(2)=0, C(3)=0, C(4)=0, C(5)=0

The joint insignificance of the daily indicator variables suggests that the supply equation cannot be reliably estimated. However, because *STORMY* was significant, we proceed to estimate the demand equation. The 2SLS estimates of the demand equation in *POE4* Table 11.5, page 460, are obtained using

equation demand.tsls lquan c lprice mon tue wed thu @ mon tue wed thu stormy

Dependent Variable: LQUAN
Method: Two-Stage Least Squares
Sample: 12/02/1991 5/08/1992
Included observations: 111
Instrument specification: MON TUE WED THU STORMY
Constant added to instrument list

Variable	Coefficient	Std. Error	t-Statistic	Prob.
C	8.505911	0.166167	51.18896	0.0000
LPRICE	-1.119417	0.428645	-2.611524	0.0103
MON	-0.025402	0.214774	-0.118274	0.9061
TUE	-0.530769	0.208000	-2.551775	0.0122
WED	-0.566351	0.212755	-2.661989	0.0090
THU	0.109267	0.208787	0.523345	0.6018

10.6 LIML AND K-CLASS ESTIMATION

Appendix 11B in *POE4* discusses alternatives to TSLS/2SLS estimation. The limited information maximum likelihood (LIML) estimator has been found to have desirable properties when there are weak instruments and/or a large number of instruments. The modifications known as Fuller's *k*-class estimators can have smaller bias and mean squared error than the 2SLS/TSLS estimator. The implementation of these estimators, use the **Quick/Estimate Equation** dialog box.

To illustrate we estimate the *HOURS* supply equation for married women using ***mroz.wf1***. Open that workfile. Change the sample to include only the 428 observations on married women in the labor force. Create the series $NWIFEINC = (FAMINC - WAGE \times HOURS)/1000$. This variable represents household income that comes from sources other than the wife's earnings:

> **smpl 1 428**
> **series nwifeinc =(faminc - wage*hours)/1000**

The equation of interest is

$$HOURS = \beta_1 + \beta_2 MTR + \beta_3 EDUC + \beta_4 KIDSL6 + \beta_5 NWIFEINC + e$$

The specifications we consider are discussed on page 471 of *POE4*. Here we consider only

> Model 2: endogenous: *MTR*; instruments: $EXPER, EXPER^2, LARGECITY$
> Model 4: endogenous: *MTR, EDUC*; instruments: *MOTHEREDUC, FATHEREDUC, EXPER*

On the EViews menu select **Quick/Estimate Equation**. Under **Estimation settings**, choose the method **LIML**.

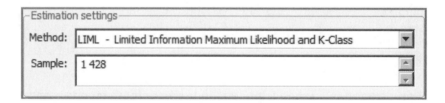

Enter the **Equation specification**

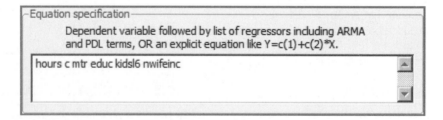

and **Instrument list**. Note that the box labeled **K** is blank for LIML.

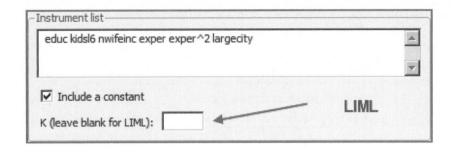

On the **Options** tab select the **K-Class based** coefficient covariance matrix.

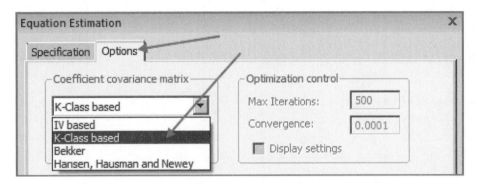

The results match those from specification (2) in Table 11B.3. Note that (1) the R-squared is negative, again reminding us that this measure is unreliable once we leave the world of least squares estimation, and (2) the EViews output includes the LIML min. eigenvalue, 1.01540, which is the calculated value of ℓ in Equation (11B.6). When the k-class approach is used, called $k = \hat{\ell}$, we obtain LIML estimates.

Dependent Variable: HOURS
Method: LIML / K-Class
Sample: 1 428
Included observations: 428
Covariance type: K-Class
Instrument specification: EDUC KIDSL6 NWIFEINC EXPER EXPER^2
    LARGECITY
Constant added to instrument list

Variable	Coefficient	Std. Error	t-Statistic	Prob.
C	16191.33	2996.790	5.402892	0.0000
MTR	-17023.82	3474.779	-4.899252	0.0000
EDUC	-134.5504	31.59192	-4.259014	0.0000
KIDSL6	113.5034	135.1545	0.839805	0.4015
NWIFEINC	-96.28949	18.84513	-5.109516	0.0000

R-squared	-0.053980	Mean dependent var	1302.930
Adjusted R-squared	-0.063947	S.D. dependent var	776.2744
S.E. of regression	800.7098	Sum squared resid	2.71E+08
Durbin-Watson stat	1.903246	LIML min. eigenvalue	1.019540

Select **View/Representations**. The command for the estimation above is

**liml(se=kclass) hours c mtr educ kidsl6 nwifeinc @ educ
kidsl6 nwifeinc exper exper^2 largecity**

Select **View/IV Diagnostics & Tests/Weak Instruments Diagnostics:**

```
Weak Instrument Diagnostics
Equation: LIML2

Cragg-Donald F-statistic:   13.18941

Stock-Yogo K-class critical values (relative bias):
                5%              9.61
                10%             7.90
                20%             6.61
                30%             5.60

Stock-Yogo critical values (size):
                10%             6.46
                15%             4.36
                20%             3.69
                25%             3.32
```

There we find the **Cragg-Donald F-statistic,** which can be compared to the critical value in Table 11B.1. For $B = 1$ and $L = 3$ the critical value is 6.46 for the 10% Test Size criterion, and thus we can reject the null hypothesis that the instruments are weak for this LIML estimation.

The model (4) in Table 11B.3 is estimated using

**equation liml4.liml(se=kclass) hours c mtr educ kidsl6 nwifeinc @ kidsl6
nwifeinc exper mothereduc fathereduc**

The estimates match those in *POE4*. Select **View/IV Diagnostics & Tests/Weak Instruments Diagnostics**.

```
Weak Instrument Diagnostics
Equation: LIML4

Cragg-Donald F-statistic:   8.560615

Stock-Yogo K-class critical values (relative bias):
                5%              10.83
                10%             8.96
                20%             7.18
                30%             6.15

Stock-Yogo critical values (size):
                10%             5.44
                15%             3.81
                20%             3.32
                25%             3.09
```

Now $B = 2$ and $L = 3$, and the critical value for the weak instrument test is 5.44 for the 10% Test Size criterion, and again we can reject the hypothesis of weak instruments.

The Fuller k-class estimators are based on the value

$$k = \hat{\ell} - \frac{a}{N - K}$$

Fuller determined that the choice $a = 1$ should be used when one is interested in minimizing bias. In our example $N = 428$ and $K = 5$. For model (2) in Table 11B.3 in *POE4*, $\hat{\ell} = 1.0195$. The corresponding value for k is $k = 1.01713593308$, or approximately 1.0171. Use **Quick/ Estimate Equation**:

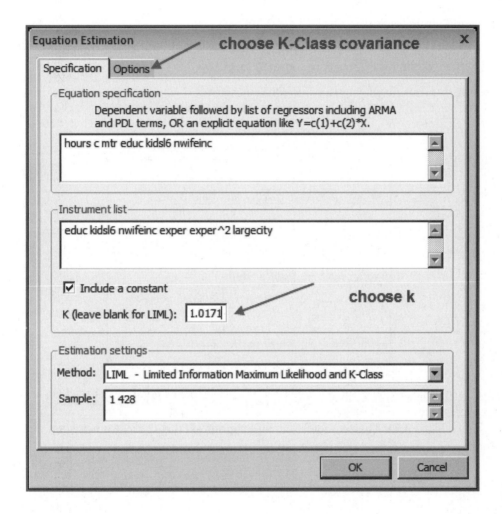

The estimation results are very close to those in *POE4*, Table 11B.4 for model (2). The estimates in the book were generated using alternative software, which yielded a slightly different value for $\hat{\ell}$, thus a slightly different value of k, and thus slightly different estimates. This will happen when using complicated estimators like LIML and the k-class.

```
Included observations: 428
K-Class estimation, K = 1.0171
Covariance type: K-Class
Instrument specification: EDUC KIDSL6 NWIFEINC EXPER EXPER^2
      LARGECITY
Constant added to instrument list
```

Variable	Coefficient	Std. Error	t-Statistic	Prob.
C	15917.14	2924.254	5.443144	0.0000
MTR	-16705.04	3390.379	-4.927189	0.0000
EDUC	-132.1603	30.98529	-4.265261	0.0000
KIDSL6	105.1557	133.0445	0.790380	0.4297
NWIFEINC	-94.59661	18.39977	-5.141185	0.0000

The command for this estimation is

liml(kclass=1.0171,se=kclass) hours c mtr educ kidsl6 nwifeinc @ educ kidsl6 nwifeinc exper exper^2 largecity

The weak instruments diagnostics for this equation show

```
Weak Instrument Diagnostics
Equation: KCLASS2

Cragg-Donald F-statistic:   13.18941

Stock-Yogo K-class critical values (relative bias):
      5%            9.61
      10%           7.90
      20%           6.61
      30%           5.60

Stock-Yogo critical values (size):
      10%           6.46
      15%           4.36
      20%           3.69
      25%           3.32
```

Compare this value to the critical values for the weak instruments test based on the Fuller-k relative bias in Table 11B.2, page 470 in *POE4*. For $B = 1$ and $L = 3$, the 0.05 maximum relative bias critical value is 9.61. Thus we reject the null hypothesis that the instruments are weak for this estimation.

Keywords

Cragg-Donald F-test	instrumental variables	Stock-Yogo Weak IV tests
demand equation	k-class	supply equation
endogenous variables	k-class covariance	system of equations
exogenous variables	liml	test size criterion
Fuller k-class	reduced form equation	Wald test
instrument list	relative bias criterion	weak instruments

CHAPTER 12

Regression with Time-Series Data: Nonstationary Variables

CHAPTER OUTLINE

12.1 Stationary and Nonstationary Variables
12.2 Spurious Regressions

12.3 Unit Root Tests for Stationarity
12.4 Cointegration
KEYWORDS

12.1 STATIONARY AND NONSTATIONARY VARIABLES

Time-series data display a variety of behavior. The data shown in Figure 12.1 are stored in the EViews workfile ***usa.wf1***. They are real gross domestic product (*GDP*), inflation rate (*INF*), Federal funds rate (*F*) and the Three-year Bond rate (*B*). The changes for real gross domestic product (*DG*), inflation (*DI*), Federal funds rate (*DF*), and the Three-year Bond rate (*DB*) are computed by typing the following commands in the Command window and pressing **Enter:**

> **series dg = D(gdp)**
> **series di = D(inf)**
> **series df = D(f)**
> **series db = D(b)**

where **D** is the first-difference operator.

To plot the graphs, select the eight variables, open the **Group**, then select **View/ Graph** and pick the **Line & Symbol/ Multiple graphs** options as shown below:

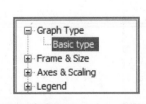
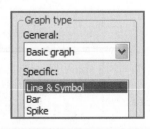
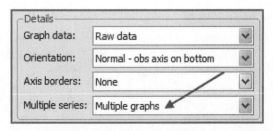

Clicking on **OK** produces the EViews ouput below. This set of graphs illustrates the variety of behavior observed with time series data, such as 'trending' (see *GDP*), 'wandering around a trend' (see *F* and *B*), 'fluctuating around a trend', until the financial crisis (see *DG*) and fluctuating around a constant (see *DB*). In general, nonstationary variables display wandering behavior (around constant and/or trend) while stationary data display fluctuating behavior (around constant and/or trend).

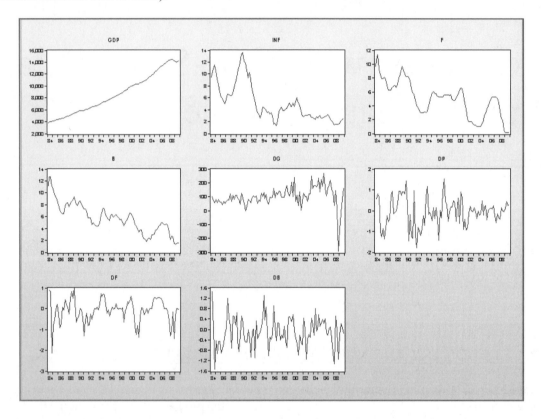

12.2 SPURIOUS REGRESSIONS

The main reason why it is important to know whether a time series is stationary or nonstationary before one embarks on a regression analysis is that there is a danger of obtaining apparently significant regression results from unrelated data when nonstationary series are used in regression analysis. Such regressions are said to be **spurious**.

   The EViews workfile *spurious.wf1* contains the two random variables (*RW1* and *RW2*) shown in Figure 12.3(a). To plot the scatter graph, select the two variables, open **Group, View / Graph/** and select **Scatter** as shown below:

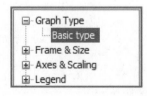
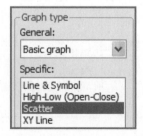

Clicking **OK** will produce the EViews output below:

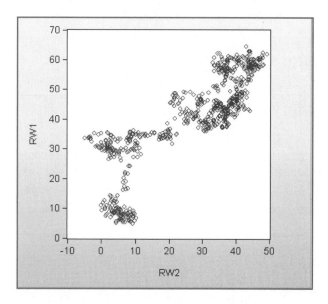

Although the series (*RW1* and *RW2*) were generated independently and, in truth, have no relation to each other, the scatter plot suggests a positive relationship between them. The **spurious regression** of series one (*RW1*) on series two (*RW2*) is shown in the EViews ouput below.

Dependent Variable: RW1
Method: Least Squares

Sample: 1 700
Included observations: 700

Variable	Coefficient	Std. Error	t-Statistic	Prob.
C	17.81804	0.620478	28.71665	0.0000
RW2	0.842041	0.020620	40.83684	0.0000

R-squared	0.704943	Mean dependent var	39.44163
Adjusted R-squared	0.704521	S.D. dependent var	15.74242
S.E. of regression	8.557268	Akaike info criterion	7.134292
Sum squared resid	51112.33	Schwarz criterion	7.147295
Log likelihood	-2495.002	Hannan-Quinn criter.	7.139319
F-statistic	1667.648	Durbin-Watson stat	0.022136
Prob(F-statistic)	0.000000		

12.3 UNIT ROOT TESTS FOR STATIONARITY

To obtain the unit root test for the variable *F*, select the variable then click on **View /Unit Root Test/** and select the options shown below.

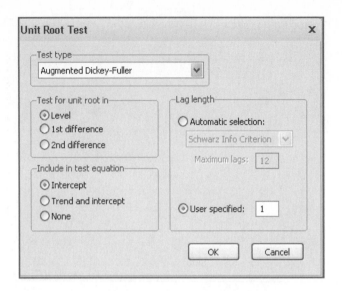

Clicking on **OK** will produce the Dickey-Fuller test with an intercept and with one lag term.

Augmented Dickey-Fuller Unit Root Test on F			

Null Hypothesis: F has a unit root
Exogenous: Constant
Lag Length: 1 (Fixed)

		t-Statistic	Prob.*
Augmented Dickey-Fuller test statistic		-2.504819	0.1173
Test critical values:	1% level	-3.495677	
	5% level	-2.890037	
	10% level	-2.582041	

*MacKinnon (1996) one-sided p-values.

Augmented Dickey-Fuller Test Equation
Dependent Variable: D(F)
Method: Least Squares

Sample (adjusted): 1984Q3 2009Q4
Included observations: 102 after adjustments

Variable	Coefficient	Std. Error	t-Statistic	Prob.
F(-1)	-0.044621	0.017814	-2.504819	0.0139
D(F(-1))	0.561058	0.080983	6.928120	0.0000
C	0.172522	0.100233	1.721206	0.0883

R-squared	0.339568	Mean dependent var	-0.102353
Adjusted R-squared	0.326226	S.D. dependent var	0.542556
S.E. of regression	0.445350	Akaike info criterion	1.249058
Sum squared resid	19.63532	Schwarz criterion	1.326263
Log likelihood	-60.70194	Hannan-Quinn criter.	1.280321
F-statistic	25.45097	Durbin-Watson stat	2.079507
Prob(F-statistic)	0.000000		

Since the calculated Dickey-Fuller test statistic (-2.505) is greater than the 5% critical value of (-2.890), do not reject the null of nonstationarity. In other words, the variable F is a nonstationary series.

To perform the test for the first-difference of *F*, select the options shown below:

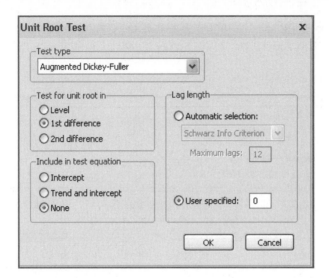

Clicking on **OK** gives the output below.

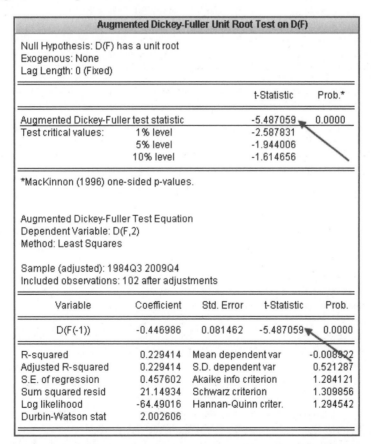

Since the calculated Dickey-Fuller test statistic (−5.487) is less than the 5% critical value of (−1.944), we reject the null of nonstationarity. In other words, the variable **D(f)** $= \Delta F$ is a stationary series. It follows that since *F* has to be differenced once to obtain stationarity, it is integrated of order 1.

12.4 COINTEGRATION

To test whether the nonstationary variables, *B* and *F*, are cointegrated or spuriously related, we need to examine the properties of the regression residuals. The first step is to estimate the least squares regression:

```
Dependent Variable: B
Method: Least Squares

Sample: 1984Q1 2009Q4
Included observations: 104
```

Variable	Coefficient	Std. Error	t-Statistic	Prob.
C	1.139830	0.174083	6.547610	0.0000
F	0.914411	0.031080	29.42111	0.0000

R-squared	0.894585	Mean dependent var	5.697115
Adjusted R-squared	0.893551	S.D. dependent var	2.483198
S.E. of regression	0.810180	Akaike info criterion	2.435923
Sum squared resid	66.95197	Schwarz criterion	2.486777
Log likelihood	-124.6680	Hannan-Quinn criter.	2.456526
F-statistic	865.6017	Durbin-Watson stat	0.319330
Prob(F-statistic)	0.000000		

Next, to save the residuals from the regression equation, type the following command in the command window and press **Enter**:

> **series e = resid**

Next perform a Dickey-Fuller test by regressing the change of *E* (namely, **D(E)**) on lagged *E* (namely **E(-1)**) and the lagged term **D(E(-1))**.

```
Dependent Variable: D(E)
Method: Least Squares

Sample (adjusted): 1984Q3 2009Q4
Included observations: 102 after adjustments
```

Variable	Coefficient	Std. Error	t-Statistic	Prob.
E(-1)	-0.224509	0.053504	-4.196133	0.0001
D(E(-1))	0.254045	0.093701	2.711239	0.0079

R-squared	0.167788	Mean dependent var	-0.016701
Adjusted R-squared	0.159466	S.D. dependent var	0.455146
S.E. of regression	0.417281	Akaike info criterion	1.109301
Sum squared resid	17.41237	Schwarz criterion	1.160771
Log likelihood	-54.57433	Hannan-Quinn criter.	1.130143
Durbin-Watson stat	1.929403		

Since the calculated Dickey-Fuller test statistic (−4.196) is less than the 5% critical value of (−3.37), we reject the null of no cointegration. Recall that the critical values are those from Table 12.4 and it is for the case where the regression model includes an intercept term.

Another way to test for cointegration, allowing more explicitly for lags, is to use the error correction model. In this approach, the first step is to estimate the nonlinear model that combines stationary and non-stationary variables. Click **Quick /Estimate Equation** and type in the following equation:

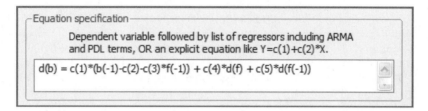

Clicking **OK**, yields the following results:

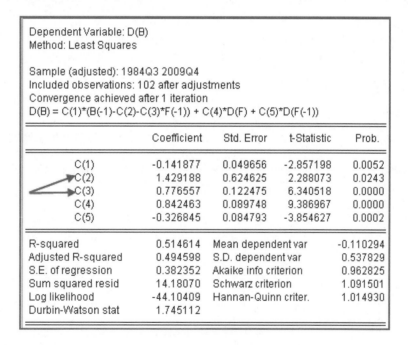

The residuals are generated using the **Genr** option:

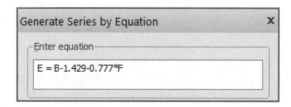

where C(2) = 1.429 and C(3) = 0.777 are the coefficients in the cointegrating equation. Next perform a Dickey-Fuller test by regressing the change of E (namely, **D(E)**) on lagged E (namely **E(-1)**) and the lagged term **D(E(-1))**.

```
Dependent Variable: D(E)
Method: Least Squares

Sample (adjusted): 1984Q3 2009Q4
Included observations: 102 after adjustments
```

Variable	Coefficient	Std. Error	t-Statistic	Prob.
E(-1)	-0.168835	0.042967	-3.929421	0.0002
D(E(-1))	0.179768	0.092447	1.944539	0.0546

R-squared	0.141572	Mean dependent var		-0.030706
Adjusted R-squared	0.132987	S.D. dependent var		0.433667
S.E. of regression	0.403802	Akaike info criterion		1.043631
Sum squared resid	16.30563	Schwarz criterion		1.095101
Log likelihood	-51.22516	Hannan-Quinn criter.		1.064473
Durbin-Watson stat	1.920324			

Since the calculated Dickey-Fuller test statistic (-3.929) is less than the 5% critical value of (-3.37), we reject the null of no cointegration.

Keywords

cointegration
D: difference operator
Dickey-Fuller tests
multiple graphs

nonstationary variables
order of Integration
spurious regression
stationary variables

stationarity tests
unit root test of residuals
unit root tests of variables

CHAPTER **13**

Vector Error Correction and Vector Autoregressive Models

CHAPTER OUTLINE

13.1 Estimating a VEC Model

13.2 Estimating a VAR Model

13.3 Impulse Responses and Variance Decompositions

KEYWORDS

13.1 ESTIMATING A VEC MODEL

A VAR model describes a system of equations in which each variable is a function of its own lag and the lag of the other variables in the system. A VEC model is a special form of the VAR for I(1) variables that are cointegrated.

The results in *POE4* are based on data contained in the EViews workfile *gdp.wf1*. The variables are *AUS* (real GDP for Australia) and *USA* (real GDP for US). To check whether the variables *AUS* and *USA* are cointegrated or spuriously related, we need to test the regression residuals for stationarity. To do this, first estimate the following least squares equation:

```
Dependent Variable: AUS
Method: Least Squares

Sample: 1970Q1 2000Q4
Included observations: 124
```

Variable	Coefficient	Std. Error	t-Statistic	Prob.
USA	0.985350	0.001657	594.7872	0.0000

R-squared	0.995228	Mean dependent var	62.72528
Adjusted R-squared	0.995228	S.D. dependent var	17.65155
S.E. of regression	1.219375	Akaike info criterion	3.242585
Sum squared resid	182.8855	Schwarz criterion	3.265329
Log likelihood	-200.0403	Hannan-Quinn criter.	3.251824
Durbin-Watson stat	0.255302		

Next, generate the residuals by typing the following command in the Command window:

series e = resid

Next, perform the unit root test by regressing the change of the residual **D(E)** on the lagged residual **E(-1).** Do this by typing the following command in the Command window:

ls D(e) e(-1)

```
Dependent Variable: D(E)
Method: Least Squares

Sample (adjusted): 1970Q2 2000Q4
Included observations: 123 after adjustments
```

Variable	Coefficient	Std. Error	t-Statistic	Prob.
E(-1)	-0.127937	0.044279	-2.889318	0.0046

R-squared	0.064044	Mean dependent var		-0.000490
Adjusted R-squared	0.064044	S.D. dependent var		0.618638
S.E. of regression	0.598500	Akaike info criterion		1.819315
Sum squared resid	43.70063	Schwarz criterion		1.842179
Log likelihood	-110.8879	Hannan-Quinn criter.		1.828602
Durbin-Watson stat	1.978150			

Since the calculated unit root test value (−2.889) is less than the critical value (−2.76, see Table 12.4), the null of no cointegration is rejected.

As an aside, extra lags of the dependent variable (for example **D(E(-1))**) were not introduced in the test equation above, as they were insignificant. See for example the case below, which is obtained by typing the following command in the Command window:

ls D(e) e(-1) D(e(-1))

```
Dependent Variable: D(E)
Method: Least Squares

Sample (adjusted): 1970Q3 2000Q4
Included observations: 122 after adjustments
```

Variable	Coefficient	Std. Error	t-Statistic	Prob.
E(-1)	-0.128207	0.046197	-2.775232	0.0064
D(E(-1))	-0.008532	0.093408	-0.091341	0.9274

R-squared	0.065661	Mean dependent var		-0.004169
Adjusted R-squared	0.057875	S.D. dependent var		0.619836
S.E. of regression	0.601632	Akaike info criterion		1.837917
Sum squared resid	43.43537	Schwarz criterion		1.883884
Log likelihood	-110.1129	Hannan-Quinn criter.		1.856588
Durbin-Watson stat	1.960758			

The estimated error-correction equations are shown below. The error-correction coefficients are the parameters of the lagged residual term, namely **E(-1)**.

Dependent Variable: D(AUS)
Method: Least Squares

Sample (adjusted): 1970Q2 2000Q4
Included observations: 123 after adjustments

Variable	Coefficient	Std. Error	t-Statistic	Prob.
C	0.491706	0.057909	8.490936	0.0000
E(-1)	-0.098703	0.047516	-2.077267	0.0399
R-squared	0.034434	Mean dependent var		0.499554
Adjusted R-squared	0.026454	S.D. dependent var		0.649528
S.E. of regression	0.640879	Akaike info criterion		1.964174
Sum squared resid	49.69782	Schwarz criterion		2.009901
Log likelihood	-118.7967	Hannan-Quinn criter.		1.982748
F-statistic	4.315037	Durbin-Watson stat		1.640143
Prob(F-statistic)	0.039893			

Dependent Variable: D(USA)
Method: Least Squares

Sample (adjusted): 1970Q2 2000Q4
Included observations: 123 after adjustments

Variable	Coefficient	Std. Error	t-Statistic	Prob.
C	0.509884	0.046677	10.92372	0.0000
E(-1)	0.030250	0.038299	0.789837	0.4312
R-squared	0.005129	Mean dependent var		0.507479
Adjusted R-squared	-0.003093	S.D. dependent var		0.515771
S.E. of regression	0.516568	Akaike info criterion		1.532907
Sum squared resid	32.28793	Schwarz criterion		1.578633
Log likelihood	-92.27376	Hannan-Quinn criter.		1.551481
F-statistic	0.623843	Durbin-Watson stat		1.367645
Prob(F-statistic)	0.431168			

13.2 ESTIMATING A VAR MODEL

The results in *POE4* are based on data contained in the EViews workfile *fred.wf1*. The variables are *LC* (log of real personal consumption expenditure) and *LY* (log of real personal disposable income). (Note that *C* is a reserved object in EViews.) To check whether the variables are cointegrated or spuriously related, we need to test the regression residuals for stationarity. To do this, first estimate the following least squares equation:

```
Dependent Variable: LC
Method: Least Squares

Sample: 1960Q1 2009Q4
Included observations: 200
```

Variable	Coefficient	Std. Error	t-Statistic	Prob.
LY	1.035288	0.002947	351.3046	0.0000
C	-0.404164	0.025053	-16.13206	0.0000

R-squared	0.998398	Mean dependent var	8.383637
Adjusted R-squared	0.998390	S.D. dependent var	0.490502
S.E. of regression	0.019680	Akaike info criterion	-5.008432
Sum squared resid	0.076689	Schwarz criterion	-4.975449
Log likelihood	502.8432	Hannan-Quinn criter.	-4.995084
F-statistic	123414.9	Durbin-Watson stat	0.202576
Prob(F-statistic)	0.000000		

Next, generate the residuals by typing the following command in the Command window:

series e = resid

Next, perform the unit root test by regressing the change of the residual **D(E)** on the lagged residual **E(-1)** by typing the following command in the Command window:

ls D(e) e(-1) D(e(-1))

```
Dependent Variable: D(E)
Method: Least Squares

Sample (adjusted): 1960Q3 2009Q4
Included observations: 198 after adjustments
```

Variable	Coefficient	Std. Error	t-Statistic	Prob.
E(-1)	-0.087650	0.030509	-2.872923	0.0045
D(E(-1))	-0.299404	0.067161	-4.458021	0.0000

R-squared	0.150787	Mean dependent var	-0.000201
Adjusted R-squared	0.146454	S.D. dependent var	0.008864
S.E. of regression	0.008189	Akaike info criterion	-6.761920
Sum squared resid	0.013145	Schwarz criterion	-6.728705
Log likelihood	671.4301	Hannan-Quinn criter.	-6.748476
Durbin-Watson stat	1.940353		

Since the calculated tau statistic (−2.873) is greater than the 5% critical value (−3.37, see Table 12.4), we accept the null of no cointegration. In other words, the variables are spuriously related.

The estimated VAR equations are estimated by least squares as shown below.

```
Dependent Variable: DC
Method: Least Squares

Sample (adjusted): 1960Q3 2009Q4
Included observations: 198 after adjustments
```

Variable	Coefficient	Std. Error	t-Statistic	Prob.
C	0.005278	0.000757	6.968764	0.0000
DC(-1)	0.215603	0.074748	2.884383	0.0044
DY(-1)	0.149377	0.057734	2.587327	0.0104

R-squared	0.120482	Mean dependent var	0.008308
Adjusted R-squared	0.111461	S.D. dependent var	0.006976
S.E. of regression	0.006575	Akaike info criterion	-7.195903
Sum squared resid	0.008431	Schwarz criterion	-7.146081
Log likelihood	715.3944	Hannan-Quinn criter.	-7.175736
F-statistic	13.35615	Durbin-Watson stat	2.085702
Prob(F-statistic)	0.000004		

```
Dependent Variable: DY
Method: Least Squares

Sample (adjusted): 1960Q3 2009Q4
Included observations: 198 after adjustments
```

Variable	Coefficient	Std. Error	t-Statistic	Prob.
C	0.006037	0.000986	6.121874	0.0000
DC(-1)	0.475428	0.097326	4.884920	0.0000
DY(-1)	-0.217167	0.075173	-2.888918	0.0043

R-squared	0.111817	Mean dependent var	0.008219
Adjusted R-squared	0.102708	S.D. dependent var	0.009038
S.E. of regression	0.008562	Akaike info criterion	-6.668031
Sum squared resid	0.014294	Schwarz criterion	-6.618209
Log likelihood	663.1351	Hannan-Quinn criter.	-6.647865
F-statistic	12.27468	Durbin-Watson stat	1.993482
Prob(F-statistic)	0.000010		

13.3 IMPULSE RESPONSES AND VARIANCE DECOMPOSITION

In POE4, we discuss the interpretation of impulse responses and variance decomposition for the special case where the shocks are uncorrelated. This is not usually the case; EViews is set up for the more general cases when identification is an issue. See EViews 7 User Guide II, p.467-470.

Keywords

error correction	impulse responses	variance decomposition
identification	VAR	VEC

CHAPTER **14**

Time-Varying Volatility and ARCH Models

CHAPTER OUTLINE

14.1 Time-Varying Volatility
14.2 Testing for ARCH Effects
14.3 Estimating an ARCH Model

14.4 Generalized ARCH
14.5 Asymmetric GARCH
14.6 GARCH-in-Mean Model
KEYWORDS

14.1 TIME-VARYING VOLATILITY

In this chapter we are concerned with **variances that change over time,** i.e., time-varying variance processes. The model we focus on is called the **AutoRegressive Conditional Heteroskedastic (ARCH)** model:

$$y_t = \beta_0 + e_t$$

$$e_t \mid I_{t-1} \sim N(0, h_t)$$

$$h_t = \alpha_0 + \alpha_1 e_{t-1}^2, \quad \alpha_0 > 0, \quad 0 \le \alpha_1 < 1$$

This is an example of an ARCH(1) model since the time-varying variance h_t is a function of a constant term (α_0) plus a term lagged once, the square of the error in the previous period ($\alpha_1 e_{t-1}^2$). The coefficients, α_0 and α_1, have to be positive to ensure a positive variance. The coefficient α_1 must be less than 1, otherwise h_t will continue to increase over time, eventually exploding. Conditional normality means that the distribution is a function of known information at time $t-1$; i.e., when $t = 2$, $(e_2 \mid I_1) \sim N(0, \alpha_0 + \alpha_1 e_1^2)$ and so on.

The EViews workfile **byd.wf1** contains the returns to BrightenYourDayLighting. To plot the times series, double-click the variable, select **View/Graph/** and pick the option **Line & Symbol**.

338

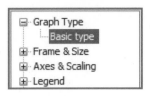

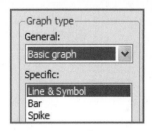

Click **OK** to produce the figure below:

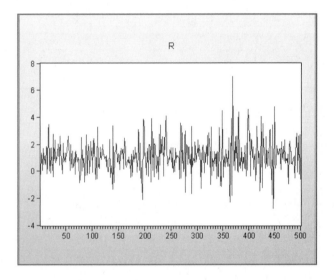

To generate the histogram, select **View/ Descriptive Statistics & Tests/ Histogram and Stats.**

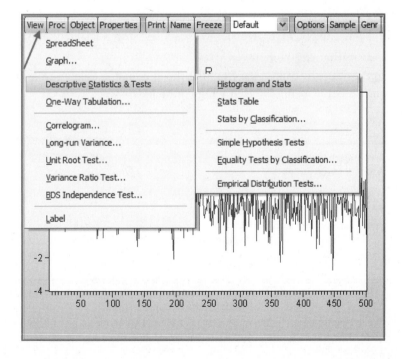

Clicking this option gives the distribution below:

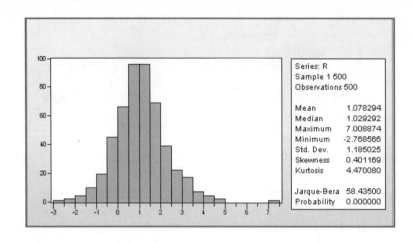

14.2 TESTING FOR ARCH EFFECTS

To test for first-order ARCH, regress the squared regression residuals $\hat{e}_t^2$ on their lags $\hat{e}_{t-1}^2$:

$$\hat{e}_t^2 = \gamma_0 + \gamma_1 \hat{e}_{t-1}^2 + v_t$$

where v_t is a random term. The null and alternative hypotheses are:

$$H_0 : \gamma_1 = 0$$

$$H_1 : \gamma_1 \neq 0$$

If there are no ARCH effects, then $\gamma_1 = 0$ and the fit of the testing equation will be poor with a low R^2. If there are ARCH effects, we expect the magnitude of $\hat{e}_t^2$ to depend on its lagged values and the R^2 will be relatively high. Hence, we can test for ARCH effects by checking the significance of γ_1 as well as applying the LM test based on R^2.

The regression residuals are obtained from the mean equation. The regression of returns on a constant term is shown below using the following command:

ls r c

Dependent Variable: R
Method: Least Squares

Sample: 1 500
Included observations: 500

Variable	Coefficient	Std. Error	t-Statistic	Prob.
C	1.078294	0.052996	20.34675	0.0000

R-squared	0.000000	Mean dependent var	1.078294
Adjusted R-squared	0.000000	S.D. dependent var	1.185025
S.E. of regression	1.185025	Akaike info criterion	3.179402
Sum squared resid	700.7373	Schwarz criterion	3.187831
Log likelihood	-793.8505	Hannan-Quinn criter.	3.182710
Durbin-Watson stat	1.918974		

To test the regression residuals for ARCH effects, select **View/Residual Diagnostics/ Heteroskedasticity Tests** from the drop-down menus.

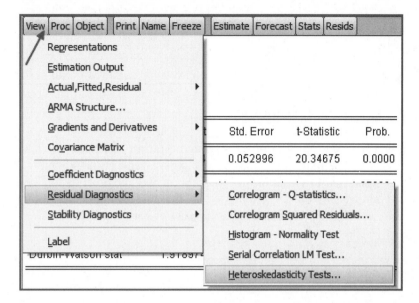

Then select the **ARCH** option. Inserting **1** in the **Number of lags** box means that we are testing for ARCH(1) effects.

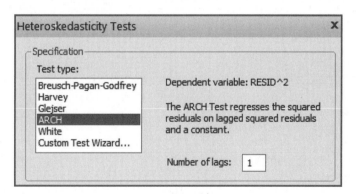

Clicking on **OK** gives the ARCH test results below:

Heteroskedasticity Test: ARCH				
F-statistic	70.71980	Prob. F(1,497)		0.0000
Obs*R-squared	62.15950	Prob. Chi-Square(1)		0.0000

Test Equation:
Dependent Variable: RESID^2
Method: Least Squares
Sample (adjusted): 2 500
Included observations: 499 after adjustments

Variable	Coefficient	Std. Error	t-Statistic	Prob.
C	0.908262	0.124401	7.301068	0.0000
RESID^2(-1)	0.353071	0.041985	8.409506	0.0000
R-squared	0.124568	Mean dependent var		1.401953

Since the *LM* statistic (62.159) is significant, we reject the null hypothesis that there is no first-order ARCH effect. Note that the *LM* statistic in EViews is calculated as $LM = T \times R^2 = 499 \times 0.124568 = 62.16$. Furthermore, the *F*- and *t*-statistics ($62.16 = 8.4095^2$) corroborate the presence of first-order ARCH effects. (The *LM* statistic in *POE4* is calculated as $499 \times 0.124 = 61.876$.)

14.3 ESTIMATING AN ARCH MODEL

To estimate an ARCH model, click **Quick/Estimate equation** and select the ARCH option from the drop-down menu in **Method**. A screen with an upper **Mean equation** and a lower **Variance and distribution specification** section will open. In the mean equation section, enter the regression of the returns, *R*, on a constant, *C*. In the variance and distribution specification section, to estimate an ARCH model of order 1, type a **1** against **ARCH**.

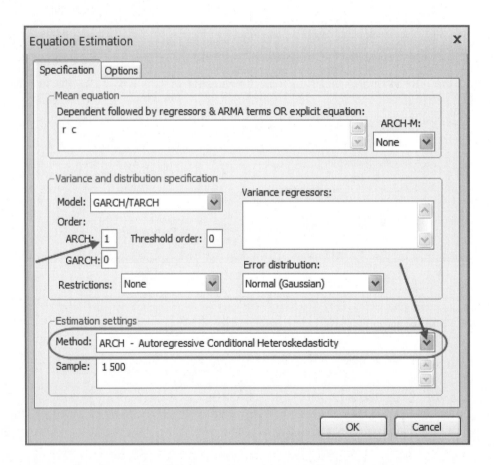

To obtain the standard errors reported in *POE4*, click on **Options** (top left-hand corner) and then pick the options noted below. As discussed in *POE4*, time series models require an initial starting value, in this case the initial variance h_0. The options suggested here set the initial variance to the unconditional sample variance.

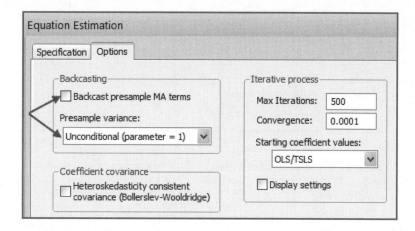

Clicking on **OK** will give the EViews output below:

```
Dependent Variable: R
Method: ML - ARCH (Marquardt) - Normal distribution

Sample: 1 500
Included observations: 500
Convergence achieved after 10 iterations
Presample variance: unconditional
GARCH = C(2) + C(3)*RESID(-1)^2
```

Variable	Coefficient	Std. Error	z-Statistic	Prob.
C	1.063940	0.039442	26.97458	0.0000
Variance Equation				
C	0.642140	0.063214	10.15827	0.0000
RESID(-1)^2	0.569343	0.102845	5.535933	0.0000

R-squared	-0.000147	Mean dependent var	1.078294
Adjusted R-squared	-0.000147	S.D. dependent var	1.185025
S.E. of regression	1.185112	Akaike info criterion	2.975173
Sum squared resid	700.8403	Schwarz criterion	3.000460
Log likelihood	-740.7932	Hannan-Quinn criter.	2.985096
Durbin-Watson stat	1.918692		

The top section is the mean equation. It shows that the average return is 1.063940. The lower section is the variance equation, which gives the result of the ARCH model, namely, that the time varying volatility h_t includes a constant component (0.642140) plus a component that depends on past errors ($0.569343\hat{e}_{t-1}^2$). Note the significance of the ARCH effects.

To generate the conditional variance series shown in the text, click on **Proc** and select **Make GARCH Variance Series** from the drop-down menu.

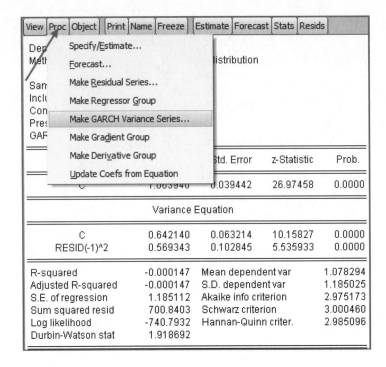

		td. Error	z-Statistic	Prob.
C	1.003940	0.039442	26.97458	0.0000

Variance Equation				
C	0.642140	0.063214	10.15827	0.0000
RESID(-1)^2	0.569343	0.102845	5.535933	0.0000

R-squared	-0.000147	Mean dependent var	1.078294
Adjusted R-squared	-0.000147	S.D. dependent var	1.185025
S.E. of regression	1.185112	Akaike info criterion	2.975173
Sum squared resid	700.8403	Schwarz criterion	3.000460
Log likelihood	-740.7932	Hannan-Quinn criter.	2.985096
Durbin-Watson stat	1.918692		

Clicking opens the window below. We have used **H** to label the conditional variance.

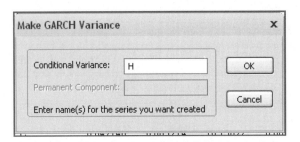

Clicking on **OK** creates the series that you can then graph by selecting **View/Graph/Line & Symbol/** .

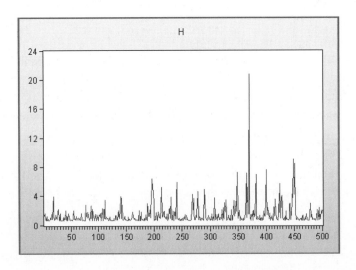

14.4 GENERALIZED ARCH

To estimate a GARCH(1,1) model, select the option shown below:

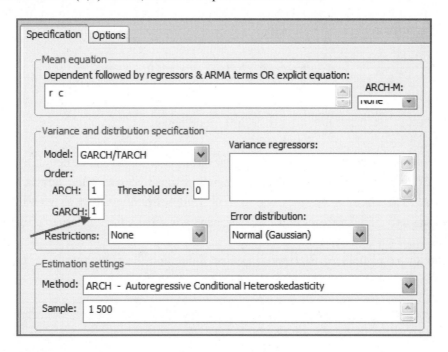

Clicking on **OK** produces the EViews results below:

```
Dependent Variable: R
Method: ML - ARCH (Marquardt) - Normal distribution
Sample: 1 500
Included observations: 500
Convergence achieved after 17 iterations
Presample variance: unconditional
GARCH = C(2) + C(3)*RESID(-1)^2 + C(4)*GARCH(-1)
```

Variable	Coefficient	Std. Error	z-Statistic	Prob.
C	1.049869	0.040465	25.94522	0.0000
Variance Equation				
C	0.401046	0.089940	4.459029	0.0000
RESID(-1)^2	0.491025	0.101570	4.834362	0.0000
GARCH(-1)	0.238005	0.111500	2.134574	0.0328

Recall that the generalized GARCH(1,1) model is of the form:

$$h_t = \delta + \alpha_1 e_{t-1}^2 + \beta_1 h_{t-1}$$

We also note that we need $\alpha_1 + \beta_1 < 1$ for stationarity; if $\alpha_1 + \beta_1 \geq 1$ we have a so-called "integrated GARCH" process, or IGARCH. The EViews output shows the significance of the GARCH term. These results indicate that the volatility coefficients, the one in front of the ARCH effect (0.491025) and the one in front of the GARCH effect (0.238005) are both positive and their sum is between zero and one, as required by theory.

14.5 ASYMMETRIC GARCH

The threshold ARCH model, or T-ARCH, is one example where positive and negative news is treated asymmetrically. In the T-GARCH version of the model, the specification of the conditional variance is:

$$h_t = \delta + \alpha_1 e_{t-1}^2 + \gamma d_{t-1} e_{t-1}^2 + \beta_1 h_{t-1}$$

$$d_t = \begin{cases} 1 & e_t < 0 \text{ (bad news)} \\ 0 & e_t \geq 0 \text{ (good news)} \end{cases}$$

where γ is known as the asymmetry or leverage term. When $\gamma = 0$, the model collapses to the standard GARCH form. Otherwise, when the shock is positive (i.e. good news), the effect on volatility is α_1, but when the news is negative (i.e. bad news), the effect on volatility is $\alpha_1 + \gamma$. Hence, so long as γ is significant and positive, negative shocks have a larger effect on h_t than positive shocks.

To estimate a threshold GARCH model, select the option shown below:

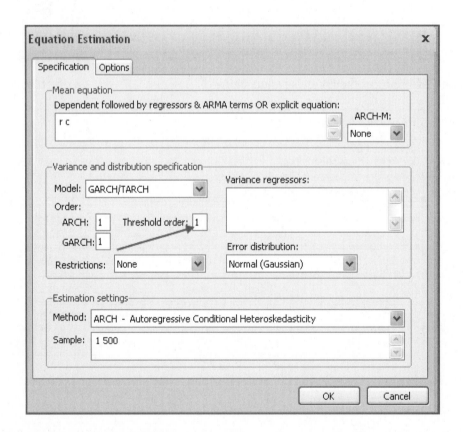

Clicking **OK** gives the EViews output

```
Dependent Variable: R
Method: ML - ARCH (Marquardt) - Normal distribution

Sample: 1 500
Included observations: 500
Convergence achieved after 34 iterations
Presample variance: unconditional
GARCH = C(2) + C(3)*RESID(-1)^2 + C(4)*RESID(-1)^2*(RESID(-1)<0) +
    C(5)*GARCH(-1)
```

Variable	Coefficient	Std. Error	z-Statistic	Prob.
C	0.994828	0.042918	23.17966	0.0000

Variance Equation				
C	0.355671	0.090048	3.949779	0.0001
RESID(-1)^2	0.262577	0.080374	3.266923	0.0011
RESID(-1)^2*(RESID(-1)<0)	0.491882	0.204560	2.404580	0.0162
GARCH(-1)	0.287359	0.115485	2.488291	0.0128

R-squared	-0.004971	Mean dependent var	1.078294
Adjusted R-squared	-0.004971	S.D. dependent var	1.185025
S.E. of regression	1.187966	Akaike info criterion	2.942216
Sum squared resid	704.2206	Schwarz criterion	2.984362
Log likelihood	-730.5540	Hannan-Quinn criter.	2.958754
Durbin-Watson stat	1.909482		

Since the coefficient on the asymmetric term (0.492) is significant, we infer that there is evidence that positive and negative shocks have different effects. In particular, when the shock is positive, the estimate of the time-varying volatility is

$$h_t = 0.355671 + 0.262577e_{t-1}^2 + 0.287359h_{t-1}$$

and when the shock is negative, the estimate of the time-varying volatility is

$$h_t = 0.355671 + (0.262577 + 0.491882)e_{t-1}^2 + 0.287359h_{t-1}$$

14.6 GARCH-IN-MEAN MODEL

The equations of a GARCH-in-mean model are:

$$y_t = \beta_0 + \theta h_t + e_t$$

$$e_t \mid I_{t-1} \sim N(0, h_t)$$

$$h_t = \delta + \alpha_1 e_{t-1}^2 + \beta_1 h_{t-1}, \quad \delta > 0,\ 0 \le \alpha_1 < 1,\ 0 \le \beta_1 < 1$$

The first equation is the mean equation; it now shows the effect of the conditional variance on the dependent variable. In particular, note that the model postulates that the conditional variance h_t affects y_t by a factor θ. The other two equations are as before.

To estimate a GARCH-in-mean model, select the option shown below:

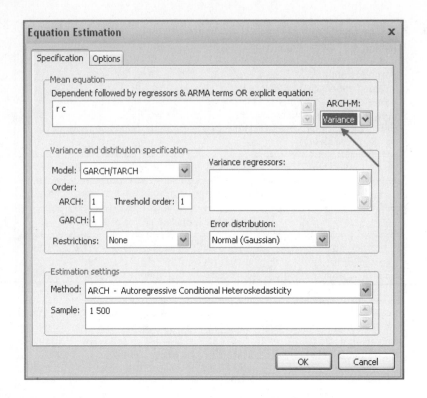

Clicking on **OK** produces the EViews output below:

```
Dependent Variable: R
Method: ML - ARCH (Marquardt) - Normal distribution

Sample: 1 500
Included observations: 500
Convergence achieved after 144 iterations
Presample variance: unconditional
GARCH = C(3) + C(4)*RESID(-1)^2 + C(5)*RESID(-1)^2*(RESID(-1)<0) +
     C(6)*GARCH(-1)
```

Variable	Coefficient	Std. Error	z-Statistic	Prob.
GARCH	0.195866	0.067165	2.916190	0.0035
C	0.818168	0.071163	11.49715	0.0000
Variance Equation				
C	0.370578	0.081873	4.526257	0.0000
RESID(-1)^2	0.294985	0.086098	3.426166	0.0006
RESID(-1)^2*(RESID(-1)<0)	0.321103	0.162222	1.979407	0.0478
GARCH(-1)	0.278285	0.103903	2.678322	0.0074

R-squared	0.043887	Mean dependent var		1.078294
Adjusted R-squared	0.041967	S.D. dependent var		1.185025
S.E. of regression	1.159892	Akaike info criterion		2.922631
Sum squared resid	669.9841	Schwarz criterion		2.973206
Log likelihood	-724.6576	Hannan-Quinn criter.		2.942476
Durbin-Watson stat	1.822255			

Since the coefficient on the GARCH in mean term (0.196) is significant, we infer that there is evidence that volatility affects returns.

To finish, we list the commands that one can use to estimate ARCH models. The general form of the EViews command is

arch(p, q, options) y x

where p is the order of the ARCH term, q is the order of the GARCH term, and **options** allows you to introduce variations such as asymmetric and in-mean effects. **y** is the dependent variable and **x** is an explanatory variable. The commands for the 4 models discussed here are:

Model	EViews Command
ARCH (1)	**arch(1,0,z) byd c**
GARCH (1,1)	**arch(1,1,z) byd c**
TARCH (1,1)	**arch(thrsh=1,1,z) byd c**
TARCH (1,1)-in-mean	**arch(thrsh=1,1,archm=var,z) byd c**

The option '**z**' sets the initial variance to the unconditional sample variance.

Keywords

ARCH test	GARCH	time-varying volatility
asymmetric GARCH	GARCH-in-mean	threshold GARCH

CHAPTER **15**

Panel Data Models

15.1 A MICROECONOMIC PANEL

Panel data are data with two dimensions, a time dimension and a cross-section dimension. They typically comprise observations on a number of economic units, such as individuals or firms, over a number of time periods. The use of panel data involves new models, new econometric techniques and new ways of handling the data. EViews has the capacity to estimate a vast array of models, using many different estimation techniques. Also, the user has various options for handling the data and proceeding to estimation. Some but not all of those options will be introduced as we lead you through the examples in Chapter 15 of *POE4*. The first example involves $T = 5$ time series observations on $N = 716$ women, stored in the file *nls_panel.wf1*. This file is from the National Longitudinal Surveys conducted by the U.S. Department of Labor. It is a large file that, in its current form, cannot be saved by the Student Version of EViews. We can nevertheless use the Student Version to analyze the data. After you have finished estimation, if you wish to save your results, you will need to reduce the **range** of the **workfile structure** and delete some of the series until the file is small enough to be saved by EViews Student Version.

When saving it, name it differently, say ***nls_results.wf1***. You will then have two files, the original one with the data and another one with your results. This is an inconvenient state of affairs, but not an impossible scenario. The other alternative is to pay more for convenience and buy the EViews full version.

Opening the file ***nls_panel.wf1*** reveals 3580 observations with a panel structure comprising 5 time series observations (1982, 1983, 1987, 1988) on 716 individuals:

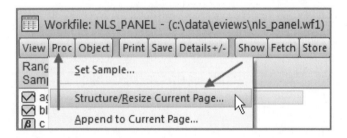

Normally, a range of **1982 1988** would imply seven time series observations. However, because we have no observations for the years 1984 and 1986, there are only five. The file has already been set up with a panel data structure, and so no extra work is required to make it suitable to use for panel data estimation techniques. Nevertheless, it is instructive to examine what is needed to create a panel data structure. Go to **Proc/Structure/Resize Current Page**:

The **Workfile Structure** dialog box follows. The type is a **Dated Panel**. The series *ID* is used to identify each woman in the sample. The **Date series** has been created by EViews as *DATEID*. One could equally well use *YEAR* for this identifying series. The frequency of the observations is **Annual**. The **Start** and **End** dates are 1982 and 1988, but we can also use **@first** and **@last**, in which case EViews will figure it out. The panel is a balanced one – we have the same number of time-series observations on each woman – and so the boxes asking about how to balance the data are not needed in this case.

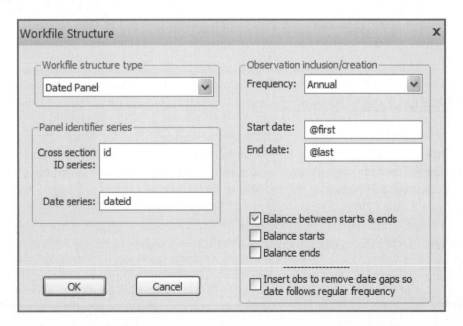

To reproduce Table 15.1 on page 540 of *POE4*, we create a group containing the variables in that table. Highlight the variables in the workfile that you wish to include in the group, and highlight them in the same order as they appear in Table 15.1. Then right-click on any of the highlighted variables, and select **Open/as Group**.

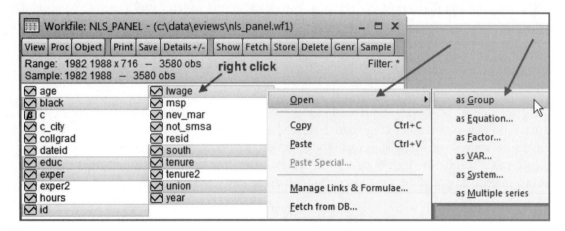

The following group appears. We present the first 15 observations, as shown in Table 15.1:

ID	YEAR	LWAGE	EDUC	SOUTH	BLACK	UNION	EXPER	TENURE
1	82	1.808289	12	0	1	1	7.666667	7.666667
1	83	1.863417	12	0	1	1	8.583333	8.583333
1	85	1.789367	12	0	1	1	10.17949	1.833333
1	87	1.846530	12	0	1	1	12.17949	3.750000
1	88	1.856449	12	0	1	1	13.62179	5.250000
2	82	1.280933	17	0	0	0	7.576923	2.416667
2	83	1.515855	17	0	0	0	8.384615	3.416667
2	85	1.930170	17	0	0	0	10.38461	5.416667
2	87	1.919034	17	0	0	1	12.03846	0.333333
2	88	2.200974	17	0	0	1	13.21154	1.750000
3	82	1.814825	12	0	0	0	11.41667	11.41667
3	83	1.919913	12	0	0	1	12.41667	12.41667
3	85	1.958377	12	0	0	0	14.41667	14.41667
3	87	2.007068	12	0	0	0	16.41667	16.41667
3	88	2.089854	12	0	0	0	17.82051	17.75000

15.2 POOLED LEAST SQUARES

The easiest, but also the least realistic, estimation procedure to use for panel data is pooled least squares. With pooled least squares the panel nature of the data is ignored, and the error is assumed to have constant variance and to be uncorrelated over time and individuals. In a model with just two explanatory variables, the model can be written as

$$y_{it} = \beta_1 + \beta_2 x_{2it} + \beta_3 x_{3it} + e_{it}$$

The subscripts *i* and *t* refer to the individual and the time period, respectively. The coefficients are the same for all individuals (and over time), and we assume $\text{var}(e_{it}) = \sigma^2$ and $E(e_{it}e_{js}) = 0$ for $i \neq j$ or $t \neq s$. The pooled least squares estimates of the wage equation for women are given in the first four columns of Table 15.2 on page 543 of *POE4*. To find these estimates, we set up the **Equation specification** in the usual way.

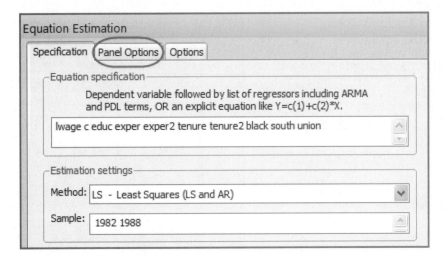

There is one difference in the **Equation Estimation** window: a new tab called **Panel Options** has appeared. Pooled least squares is the panel option default, so no changes to the options are necessary. We can proceed directly to estimation and obtain the following results. Notice that EViews includes information on the number of cross sections and the number of time periods.

Dependent Variable: LWAGE
Method: Panel Least Squares
Sample: 1982 1988
Periods included: 5
Cross-sections included: 716
Total panel (balanced) observations: 3580

Variable	Coefficient	Std. Error	t-Statistic	Prob.
C	0.476600	0.056156	8.487095	0.0000
EDUC	0.071449	0.002689	26.56689	0.0000
EXPER	0.055685	0.008607	6.469621	0.0000
EXPER2	-0.001148	0.000361	-3.176251	0.0015
TENURE	0.014960	0.004407	3.394390	0.0007
TENURE2	-0.000486	0.000258	-1.886046	0.0594
BLACK	-0.116714	0.015716	-7.426485	0.0000
SOUTH	-0.106003	0.014201	-7.464534	0.0000
UNION	0.132243	0.014962	8.838836	0.0000

15.2.1 Cluster-robust standard errors

One way to make pooled least squares estimation more realistic is to relax the assumption that the errors for the same individual in different time periods are correlated, and to allow heteroskedasticity (different variances) across individuals, assumptions that can be written as $E(e_{it}, e_{is}) = \psi_{i,ts}$. We continue to assume that $E(e_{it}, e_{js}) = 0$ for $i \neq j$. Cluster-robust standard errors are standard errors for estimates computed under these assumptions. They can be used not just for pooled least squares but also for fixed and random effects estimation that we consider shortly. To obtain pooled least squares estimates with cluster-robust standard errors, we modify the **Panel Options** window as follows:

**Pooled Least Squares
Traditional Standard Errors**

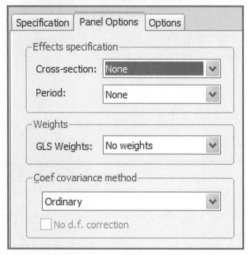

**Pooled Least Squares
Cluster-Robust Standard Errors**

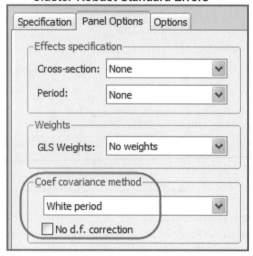

The type of standard errors depends on the choice of **Coef covariance method**. We choose **White period,** which allows for correlation over periods for each individual. It is equivalent to treating the individuals as the "clusters" and having correlation within each cluster. We obtain the following output, which agrees with that in the last three columns of Table 15.2. Note that the coefficient estimates have not changed, but the standard errors, *t*-values, and *p*-values are different. EViews provides a message on the output indicating that "White period" standard errors have been used.

Dependent Variable: LWAGE
Method: Panel Least Squares
Sample: 1982 1988
Periods included: 5
Cross-sections included: 716
Total panel (balanced) observations: 3580
White period standard errors & covariance (d.f. corrected)

Variable	Coefficient	Std. Error	t-Statistic	Prob.
C	0.476600	0.084516	5.639192	0.0000
EDUC	0.071449	0.005496	12.99913	0.0000
EXPER	0.055685	0.011304	4.926220	0.0000
EXPER2	-0.001148	0.000492	-2.331463	0.0198
TENURE	0.014960	0.007119	2.101364	0.0357
TENURE2	-0.000486	0.000410	-1.185476	0.2359
BLACK	-0.116714	0.028118	-4.150793	0.0000
SOUTH	-0.106003	0.027046	-3.919281	0.0001
UNION	0.132243	0.027060	4.887120	0.0000

15.3 FIXED EFFECTS ESTIMATION

The fixed effects model allows for different intercepts for each individual and so can be written with an i subscript on the intercept as

$$y_{it} = \beta_{1i} + \beta_2 x_{2it} + \beta_3 x_{3it} + e_{it}$$

The β_{1i} are treated as fixed unknown parameters that can be estimated, in contrast to the random effects model where they are treated as random draws from a bigger population and where they form part of the error term. Estimates for the fixed effects model can be obtained in one of two ways – by including dummy (indicator) variables for each individual, or by "subtracting out" the intercepts prior to estimation. The first is called the least squares dummy variable estimator; the second is called the fixed effects estimator. We consider each in turn.

15.3.1 Least squares dummy variable estimator

Including a dummy variable for each individual, and dropping the intercept, means estimation of an extra 715 coefficients. EViews can handle a model this big, but it becomes susceptible to rounding error, it produces an enormous amount of output, and, even on a fast computer, it pauses slightly before giving you the output. Thus, to illustrate the dummy variable model we restrict ourselves to the first 10 individuals in the sample. For convenience, we have placed those observations in a new file called *nls_panel10.wf1*. We use this file to illustrate the dummy variable estimator.

EViews can automatically create the required dummy variables by including as part of the equation specification

@expand(id)

Because this command creates one dummy variable for each individual (for each value of *ID*), the constant needs to be omitted. Thus, to estimate the wage equation that we set up previously, we would write the **Equation specification** as follows:

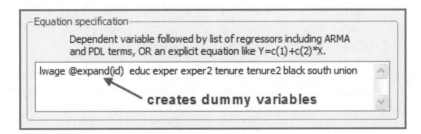

Something is wrong, however! EViews returns the following error message:

This message occurs if the explanatory variables in the model are perfectly collinear. In fact, EViews is being kind. The relevant matrix is singular (there is exact collinearity), not just "nearly" singular. Collinearity occurs because some of our variables are time invariant and time-invariant variables are collinear with the dummy variables. In our case, we cannot separate the individual effect from the effects of *BLACK*, *EDUC*, and *SOUTH*. Some women changed their location (moved into or out of the *SOUTH*) in the large sample, but none of the first 10 individuals had ever lived in the *SOUTH*. After dropping the three offending variables, the specification is

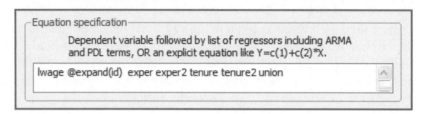

This specification yields the output in Table 15.3 on page 545 of *POE4*. Since we are using least squares and traditional standard errors, and we inserted the dummy variables ourselves, there are no special **Panel Options** that we need to consider.

Dependent Variable: LWAGE
Method: Panel Least Squares
Sample: 1982 1988
Periods included: 5
Cross-sections included: 10
Total panel (balanced) observations: 50

Variable	Coefficient	Std. Error	t-Statistic	Prob.
ID=1	0.151905	1.096745	0.138506	0.8906
ID=2	0.186894	1.071485	0.174426	0.8625
ID=3	-0.063042	1.350917	-0.046666	0.9630
ID=4	0.185626	1.343498	0.138166	0.8909
ID=5	0.938987	1.097780	0.855351	0.3982
ID=6	0.794485	1.111771	0.714612	0.4796
ID=7	0.581199	1.235914	0.470258	0.6411
ID=8	0.537925	1.097498	0.490138	0.6271
ID=9	0.418334	1.084049	0.385900	0.7019
ID=10	0.614558	1.090176	0.563724	0.5765
EXPER	0.237999	0.187757	1.267591	0.2133
EXPER2	-0.008188	0.007905	-1.035845	0.3074
TENURE	-0.012350	0.034143	-0.361712	0.7197
TENURE2	0.002296	0.002688	0.854077	0.3989
UNION	0.113543	0.150863	0.752627	0.4567

Testing the Fixed Effects

If the intercepts are equal for all individuals, then there are no fixed effects. There is no individual heterogeneity to be captured by those effects. We can test for equality of all the intercepts using the Wald test. Noting that the first 10 coefficients are those of the dummy variables, we set up the Wald test as follows. From the estimated equation, go to **View/ Coefficient Diagnostics/Wald – Coefficient Restrictions**, and enter the restrictions:

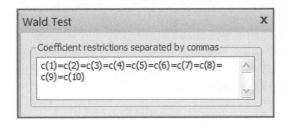

The test results are presented below. The null hypothesis of equal intercepts is rejected at the 1% level of significance. The *F*-value corresponds to that given on page 546 of *POE4*. In *POE4* the *F*-value was computed using restricted and unrestricted sums of squared errors. We suggest that you try using pooled least squares to estimate the restricted model in Table 15.4, and then confirm that the same *F*-value is obtained.

Wald Test:
Equation: DV_EST

Test Statistic	Value	df	Probability
F-statistic	4.133967	(9, 35)	0.0011
Chi-square	37.20570	9	0.0000

15.3.2 Fixed effects estimator

The fixed effects estimator that subtracts out the intercepts prior to estimation is the least squares estimator applied to the model

$$\tilde{y}_{it} = \beta_2 \tilde{x}_{2it} + \beta_3 \tilde{x}_{3it} + \tilde{e}_{it}$$

where $\tilde{y}_{it} = y_{it} - \bar{y}_i$, $\tilde{x}_{2it} = x_{2it} - \bar{x}_{2i}$, and $\tilde{x}_{3it} = x_{3it} - \bar{x}_{3i}$ are observations in terms of deviations from individual means and $\bar{y}_i$, $\bar{x}_{2i}$, and $\bar{x}_{3i}$ are the individual means (averages over time for each individual). Note that there is no intercept in this model. It is instructive to illustrate how to obtain the estimates a long way and a short way. In any practical research problem, you would only do it the short way, using EViews' automatic fixed effects command. Doing it the long way now helps you appreciate the nature of the fixed effects estimator, and also shows you how to create the deviation variables.

A long way

The file *nls_panel_devn.wf1* has all the required series in deviation form. Simply applying least squares to these variables will yield the estimates in the first two columns of Table 15.6. However, we continue to use the file *nls_panel10.wf1* to demonstrate how to construct the series in terms of deviations from their individual means. The first step is to create series containing the individual means. We give an example for *LWAGE*. The others can be created in a similar way.

To obtain a series that contains the individual means for *LWAGE* and to create from that a series containing deviations from the individual means, we use the following commands:

```
series  lwage_means = @meansby(lwage, id, "@all")
series  lwage_dev = lwage – lwage_means
```

The function **@meansby(lwage, id, "@all")** finds the group means for observations *LWAGE*, grouped according to the identifying series *ID*. The last argument is optional and specifies the sample. Here we have used **"@all"** to describe the whole sample. Collecting *LWAGE*, *LWAGE_MEANS* and *LWAGE_DEV* into a group, we can display the columns that are labeled y_{it}, $\bar{y}_i$ and $(y_{it} - \bar{y}_i)$ in *POE4* Table 15.5.

LWAGE	LWAGE_MEANS	LWAGE_DEV
1.808289	1.832810	-0.024521
1.863417	1.832810	0.030607
1.789367	1.832810	-0.043443
1.846530	1.832810	0.013720
1.856449	1.832810	0.023639
1.280933	1.769393	-0.488460
1.515855	1.769393	-0.253538
1.930170	1.769393	0.160777
1.919034	1.769393	0.149641
2.200974	1.769393	0.431581
1.814825	1.958007	-0.143182
1.919913	1.958007	-0.038094
1.958377	1.958007	0.000370
2.007068	1.958007	0.049061

Repeating this process with *EXPER, EXPER2, TENURE, TENURE2,* and *UNION* puts us in a position to obtain the estimates in the first two columns of Table 15.6. The required **Equation specification** and the output follow. The coefficient estimates are identical to those obtained using the dummy variable estimator, but the standard errors are not. The dummy variable estimator and the fixed effects estimator are two different ways of computing the same estimator. The standard errors are wrong because the dummy variable coefficients have not been counted in the degrees of freedom correction. See *POE4*, page 549 for details. This oversight is corrected when you use EViews' fixed effects command.

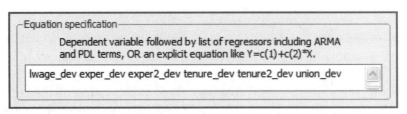

Dependent Variable: LWAGE_DEV
Method: Least Squares
Sample: 1 50
Included observations: 50

Variable	Coefficient	Std. Error	t-Statistic	Prob.
EXPER_DEV	0.237999	0.165586	1.437313	0.1575
EXPER2_DEV	-0.008188	0.006971	-1.174538	0.2464
TENURE_DEV	-0.012350	0.030112	-0.410143	0.6836
TENURE2_DEV	0.002296	0.002371	0.968433	0.3380
UNION_DEV	0.113543	0.133049	0.853399	0.3980
Sum squared resid	2.667190			

A short way

Computing the fixed effects estimator the long way was instructive, but laborious. In practice, we use the fixed effects command that is in the **Panel Options** window. It does all the transforming of the series into deviation form automatically. Returning to the original variables, the **Equation specification** and the **Panel Options** are:

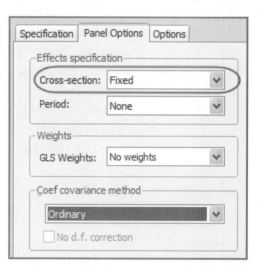

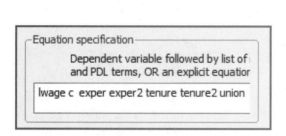

You might be surprised that we have included a constant C in the **Equation specification**. The fixed effects estimator subtracts out all the intercepts prior to estimation. It actually does not matter whether you include a constant or not. EViews can tolerate this little bit of ignorance. In the **Panel Options** window we select **Fixed** for the **Cross-section Effects specification**:

Dependent Variable: LWAGE
Method: Panel Least Squares
Average of fixed effects
Sample: 1982 1988
Periods included: 5
Cross-sections included: 10
Total panel (balanced) observations: 50

Variable	Coefficient	Std. Error	t-Statistic	Prob.
C	0.434687	1.145180	0.379580	0.7066
EXPER	0.237999	0.187757	1.267591	0.2133
EXPER2	-0.008188	0.007905	-1.035845	0.3074
TENURE	-0.012350	0.034143	-0.361712	0.7197
TENURE2	0.002296	0.002688	0.854077	0.3989
UNION	0.113543	0.150863	0.752627	0.4567

Effects Specification				
Cross-section fixed (dummy variables)				

| Sum squared resid | 2.667190 | Schwarz criterion | | 1.080486 |

The results are identical to those in the last two columns of *POE4*, Table 15.6 and are self-explanatory except perhaps the estimate of 0.4347 for the constant. This value is the average of the fixed effects. Specifically, if $b_{i,1}$ are the estimates of the fixed effects (intercepts) $\beta_{1,i}$, then

$$\sum_{i=1}^{10} b_{1,i} = 0.4347 .$$

Retrieving the fixed effects

Sometimes the fixed effects (intercept estimates) are of special interest. They can be used to analyze the extent of individual heterogeneity and to examine any particular individuals that may be of interest. For many examples the number of fixed effects is enormous and so rather than print them on the output, Eviews puts them in a special spreadsheet. To locate this spreadsheet, go to **View/Fixed/Random Effects/Cross-section Effects**.

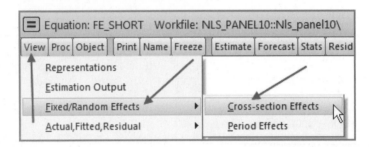

The spreadsheet for the fixed effects for each of the 10 firms is given in the left-hand side of the panel below. A comparison with the dummy variable coefficients from Table 15.3 reveals that they are not the same. The difference is that EViews has expressed them in terms of deviations from the mean of 0.434687 that was reported on the output. To get the original fixed effects, you add the mean as done on the right-hand side of the panel below:

Cross-section Fixed Effects		fixed effects not mean corrected
ID	**Effect**	
1	-0.282782	0.151905
2	-0.247793	0.186894
3	-0.497729	-0.063042
4	-0.249061	0.185626
5	0.504300	0.938987
6	0.359798	0.794485
7	0.146512	0.581199
8	0.103238	0.537925
9	-0.016353	0.418334
10	0.179871	0.614558

Testing the fixed effects

Can we use the fixed effects output to test for equality of the fixed effects (dummy variable coefficients) a we did earlier using the dummy variable specification? The answer is yes. Go to **View/Fixed/Random Effects Testing/Redundant Fixed Effects – Likelihood Ratio**.

Two versions of the likelihood ratio test appear in the output, an F-test and a χ^2-test. The F-test is identical to the one we considered earlier and gives the same test results. The χ^2-test has a different origin and so leads to a different test value. The details are beyond the level of our current description, but you can get a feel for where it comes from by checking equation (C.25) on page 728 of *POE4*. The test equation that appears below the test results is the restricted estimation obtained by assuming there are no fixed effects, just a single intercept that is relevant for all individuals. The results are identical to those given in Table 15.4 on page 546 of *POE4*.

Redundant Fixed Effects Tests
Equation: FE_SHORT
Test cross-section fixed effects

Effects Test	Statistic	d.f.	Prob.
Cross-section F	4.133967	(9,35)	0.0011
Cross-section Chi-square	36.208547	9	0.0000

Cross-section fixed effects test equation:
Dependent Variable: LWAGE
Method: Panel Least Squares
Sample: 1982 1988
Periods included: 5
Cross-sections included: 10
Total panel (balanced) observations: 50

Variable	Coefficient	Std. Error	t-Statistic	Prob.
C	0.620852	1.017209	0.610348	0.5448
EXPER	0.194749	0.173044	1.125433	0.2665
EXPER2	-0.004865	0.007074	-0.687683	0.4953
TENURE	0.001367	0.037501	0.036443	0.9711
TENURE2	-0.000869	0.002343	-0.370993	0.7124
UNION	-0.017542	0.102435	-0.171246	0.8648
Sum squared resid	5.502466			

15.3.3 Fixed effects estimation of complete panel

We complete this section on fixed effects estimation by obtaining fixed effects estimates for the complete panel of 716 individuals, with both traditional and cluster-robust standard errors. The variable *SOUTH* can be included because the complete panel contains women who moved into or out of the South during the sample period; *BLACK* and *EDUC* continue to be omitted because of their collinearity with the dummy variables.

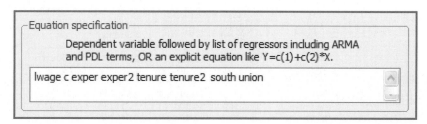

Equation specification

Dependent variable followed by list of regressors including ARMA
and PDL terms, OR an explicit equation like Y=c(1)+c(2)*X.

lwage c exper exper2 tenure tenure2 south union

We present two **Panel Options** windows, one that computes traditional standard errors and one that computes cluster-robust standard errors:

Fixed Effects with Traditional Standard Errors

Fixed Effects with Cluster-Robust Standard Errors

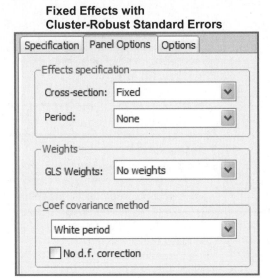

The output from each of these alternatives is given in Table 15.7 on page 550 of *POE4*. It corresponds to what is presented below:

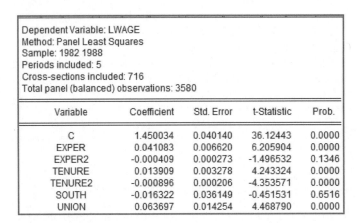

Dependent Variable: LWAGE
Method: Panel Least Squares
Sample: 1982 1988
Periods included: 5
Cross-sections included: 716
Total panel (balanced) observations: 3580

Variable	Coefficient	Std. Error	t-Statistic	Prob.
C	1.450034	0.040140	36.12443	0.0000
EXPER	0.041083	0.006620	6.205904	0.0000
EXPER2	-0.000409	0.000273	-1.496532	0.1346
TENURE	0.013909	0.003278	4.243324	0.0000
TENURE2	-0.000896	0.000206	-4.353571	0.0000
SOUTH	-0.016322	0.036149	-0.451531	0.6516
UNION	0.063697	0.014254	4.468790	0.0000

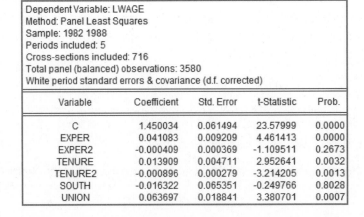

Dependent Variable: LWAGE
Method: Panel Least Squares
Sample: 1982 1988
Periods included: 5
Cross-sections included: 716
Total panel (balanced) observations: 3580
White period standard errors & covariance (d.f. corrected)

Variable	Coefficient	Std. Error	t-Statistic	Prob.
C	1.450034	0.061494	23.57999	0.0000
EXPER	0.041083	0.009209	4.461413	0.0000
EXPER2	-0.000409	0.000369	-1.109511	0.2673
TENURE	0.013909	0.004711	2.952641	0.0032
TENURE2	-0.000896	0.000279	-3.214205	0.0013
SOUTH	-0.016322	0.065351	-0.249766	0.8028
UNION	0.063697	0.018841	3.380701	0.0007

Computing marginal effects

Table 15.8 of *POE4* contains the approximate percentage marginal effects on *WAGE* from a change in *EXPER*, *TENURE*, *SOUTH*, and *UNION*. Obtaining these effects is straightforward for *SOUTH* and *UNION*: they can be obtained directly from the coefficients by multiplying by 100. However, because *EXPER* and *TENURE* have both linear and quadratic terms, some calculations are needed to obtain their marginal effects. For example, if β_2 and β_3 are the coefficients of *EXPER* and *EXPER*^{2}, respectively, then the approximate percentage marginal effect from a change in experience is

$$100 \times \frac{\partial LWAGE}{\partial EXPER} = 100 \times (b_2 + 2b_3 EXPER)$$

The commands for computing this effect and its counterpart for *TENURE* at the means *EXPER* $= 12$ and *TENURE* $= 7$ are

> scalar me_exp = 100*(c(2) + 2*c(3)*12)
> scalar me_ten = 100*(c(4) + 2*c(5)*7)

The results concur with those in the last column of Table 15.8.

	Value
ME_EXP	3.126593

	Value
ME_TEN	0.136177

15.4 RANDOM EFFECTS

In the random effects model we continue to assume that individual differences are captured by differences in the intercept parameter, but we recognize that the individuals in our sample were randomly selected, and we treat the individual differences as random rather than fixed. Each intercept β_{1i} is written as $\beta_{1i} = \bar{\beta}_1 + u_i$, where $\bar{\beta}_1$ is the population mean intercept and u_i is a random effect that now forms part of the error term. With two explanatory variables, the model can be written as

$$y_{it} = \bar{\beta}_1 + \beta_2 x_{2it} + \beta_3 x_{3it} + v_{it}$$

where $v_{it} = u_i + e_{it}$ is composed of the random individual effect u_i and the usual regression random error e_{it}. We assume the e_{it} have zero mean and constant variance σ_e^2, and are uncorrelated over time and individuals. Further, we assume the individual effects u_i have zero mean and constant variance σ_u^2, are uncorrelated over individuals, and are not correlated with the regression error e_{it}. We assume both e_{it} and u_i are uncorrelated with the explanatory variables. Under these assumptions, the properties of the combined error term v_{it} are:

$$E(v_{it}) = 0 \quad \text{var}(v_{it}) = \sigma_v^2 = \sigma_u^2 + \sigma_e^2 \quad \text{cov}(v_{it}, v_{is}) = \sigma_u^2 \text{ for } t \neq s \quad \text{cov}(v_{it}, v_{js}) = 0 \text{ for } i \neq j$$

The correlation between two errors for the same individual in different time periods is

$$\rho = \text{corr}(v_{it}, v_{is}) = \frac{\text{cov}(v_{it}, v_{is})}{\sqrt{\text{var}(v_{it}) \text{var}(v_{is})}} = \frac{\sigma_u^2}{\sigma_u^2 + \sigma_e^2}$$

The random effects estimator is a generalized least squares estimator that uses the covariance structure to weight the observations. Unlike the fixed effects estimator, it takes into account variation between individuals as well as variation within individuals. For our data set, this means it is possible to include *EDUC* and *BLACK* in the model. The EViews commands are similar to those for the fixed effects estimator, except that this time we choose **Random** for the **Cross-section Effects specification**. The **Equation specification** and the **Panel Options** with and without cluster-robust standard errors are as follows:

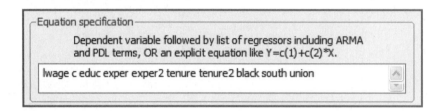

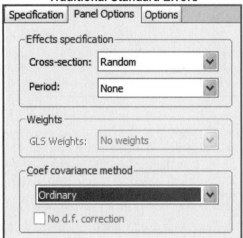

The output that follows relates to the results in Table 15.9 on page 556 of *POE4*. You will notice that the standard errors on Table 15.9 are slightly different from those reported by EViews. Different software can estimate these quantities slightly differently; those in the table were not computed using EViews. In the lower part of the output, **cross section random** refers to the estimate $\hat{\sigma}_u = 0.3291$ and **idiosyncratic random** refers to the estimate $\hat{\sigma}_e = 0.1951$. The values in the column **rho** are the proportions of total error variance attributable to each of the components. Thus,

$$\hat{\rho}_u = \frac{\hat{\sigma}_u^2}{\hat{\sigma}_u^2 + \hat{\sigma}_e^2} = \frac{(0.3291)^2}{(0.3291)^2 + (0.1951)^2} = 0.7399$$

and

$$\hat{\rho}_e = 1 - \hat{\rho}_u = 0.2601$$

Dependent Variable: LWAGE
Method: Panel EGLS (Cross-section random effects)
Sample: 1982 1988
Periods included: 5
Cross-sections included: 716
Total panel (balanced) observations: 3580
Swamy and Arora estimator of component variances

Variable	Coefficient	Std. Error	t-Statistic	Prob.
C	0.533929	0.079722	6.697408	0.0000
EDUC	0.073254	0.005320	13.76943	0.0000
EXPER	0.043617	0.006345	6.874478	0.0000
EXPER2	-0.000561	0.000262	-2.140427	0.0324
TENURE	0.014154	0.003160	4.478901	0.0000
TENURE2	-0.000755	0.000194	-3.886833	0.0001
BLACK	-0.116737	0.030148	-3.872140	0.0001
SOUTH	-0.081812	0.022366	-3.657897	0.0003
UNION	0.080235	0.013187	6.084619	0.0000

Effects Specification			S.D.	Rho
Cross-section random			0.329050	0.7399
Idiosyncratic random			0.195110	0.2601

Dependent Variable: LWAGE
Method: Panel EGLS (Cross-section random effects)
Sample: 1982 1988
Periods included: 5
Cross-sections included: 716
Total panel (balanced) observations: 3580
Swamy and Arora estimator of component variances
White period standard errors & covariance (d.f. corrected)

Variable	Coefficient	Std. Error	t-Statistic	Prob.
C	0.533929	0.082044	6.507825	0.0000
EDUC	0.073254	0.005395	13.57733	0.0000
EXPER	0.043617	0.007542	5.783468	0.0000
EXPER2	-0.000561	0.000307	-1.829246	0.0674
TENURE	0.014154	0.003995	3.542975	0.0004
TENURE2	-0.000755	0.000235	-3.209400	0.0013
BLACK	-0.116737	0.029267	-3.988673	0.0001
SOUTH	-0.081812	0.028313	-2.889526	0.0039
UNION	0.080235	0.015457	5.190842	0.0000

15.5 THE HAUSMAN TEST

The ability of the random effects model to take into account variation between individuals as well as variation within individuals makes it an attractive alternative to fixed effects estimation. However, for the random effects estimator to be unbiased in large samples, the effects must be uncorrelated with the explanatory variables, an assumption that is often unrealistic. This assumption can be tested using a Hausman test. The Hausman test is a test of the significance of the difference between the fixed effects estimates and the random effects estimates. Correlation between the random effects and the explanatory variables will cause these estimates to diverge; their difference will be significant. If the difference is not significant, there is no evidence of the offending correlation. The differences between the two sets of estimates can be tested separately using t-tests, or as a block using a χ^2-test.

You can ask EViews to perform a Hausman test by opening the random-effects estimated equation and going to **View/Fixed/Random Effects Testing/Correlated Random Effects – Hausman Test**.

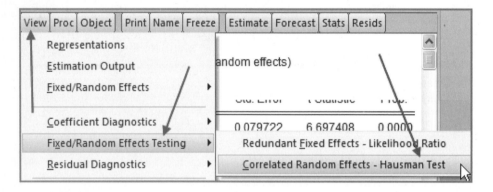

For the wage equation we get the following results:

```
Correlated Random Effects - Hausman Test
Equation: RE
Test cross-section random effects
```

Test Summary	Chi-Sq. Statistic	Chi-Sq. d.f.	Prob.
Cross-section random	20.437076	6	0.0023

Cross-section random effects test comparisons:

Variable	Fixed	Random	Var(Diff.)	Prob.
EXPER	0.041083	0.043617	0.000004	0.1798
EXPER2	-0.000409	-0.000561	0.000000	0.0504
TENURE	0.013909	0.014154	0.000001	0.7782
TENURE2	-0.000896	-0.000755	0.000000	0.0380
SOUTH	-0.016322	-0.081812	0.000807	0.0211
UNION	0.063697	0.080235	0.000029	0.0022

The value of the $\chi^2_{(6)}$-statistic for testing differences between all coefficients is $\chi^2 = 20.437$. Its corresponding p-value of 0.0023 suggests the null hypothesis of no correlation between the explanatory variables and the random effects should be rejected. The p-values for separate tests on the differences between each pair of coefficients are given in the column **Prob**. The results here are mixed. At a 5% significance level, the null hypothesis is rejected for *TENURE2*, *SOUTH* and *UNION*, but not for *EXPER*, *EXPER2* and *TENURE*. The variables *BLACK*, *EDUC*, and the constant are not included because we do not have coefficient estimates for them in the fixed effects model.

To see how the output for *SOUTH* relates to the calculation of the *t*-value on page 559 of *POE4*, note that this *t*-value can be written as

$$t = \frac{b_{FE,k} - b_{RE,k}}{\left[\widehat{\text{var}\left(b_{FE,k} - b_{RE,k}\right)} \right]^{1/2}} = \frac{-0.01632 - (-0.08181)}{[0.000807]^{1/2}} = 2.31$$

15.6 THE HAUSMAN-TAYLOR ESTIMATOR

The Hausman-Taylor estimator is an instrumental variables estimator applied to the random effects model in order to overcome the problem of inconsistency caused by correlation between the random effects and some of the explanatory variables. It is an alternative to fixed effects estimation when we have time-invariant variables whose effects we wish to measure. The model can contain four different types of variables:

$x_{it,exog}$: exogenous variables that vary over time and individuals

$x_{it,endog}$: endogenous variables that vary over time and individuals

$w_{i,exog}$: time-invariant exogenous variables

$w_{i,endog}$: time-invariant endogenous variables

The number of exogenous time-varying variables $\left(x_{it,exog}\right)$ must be at least as great as the number of endogenous time-invariant variables $\left(w_{i,endog}\right)$. With these variables we write the model as

$$y_{it} = \beta_1 + \beta_2 x_{it,exog} + \beta_3 x_{it,endog} + \delta_1 w_{i,exog} + \delta_2 w_{i,endog} + u_i + e_{it}$$

Comparing the notation in this equation with that in equation (15.38) on page 560 of *POE4*, you will discover that we have labeled the coefficients of the time-invariant variables as δ s instead of β s. This change will prove convenient in our description of the estimation technique. Also, although we have written the model in terms of one variable of each type, in practice there can be more than one of each type. For the wage equation, we make the following assumptions:

$x_{it,exog} = \{EXPER, EXPER2, TENURE, TENURE2, UNION\}$

$x_{it,endog} = \{SOUTH\}$

$w_{i,exog} = \{BLACK\}$

$w_{i,endog} = \{EDUC\}$

There is no automatic command in EViews for computing the Hausman-Taylor estimates. However, we can construct a series of commands that will do the job for us. We give a list of those commands, explaining their purpose as we go. These commands can be executed one by one by placing them in the Command window. Or, alternatively, they can be written into an

EViews program and executed all at once. Details of the estimation procedure can be found in Greene, W. (2012), *Econometric Analysis*, 7th edition, Prentice Hall, Chapter 11.8.1.

The first step is to find an estimate for σ_e^2, which is the variance of e_{it}. To do so we use the residuals from fixed effects estimation. Commands that create the variables

$$\tilde{y}_{it} = y_{it} - \overline{y}_i \qquad \tilde{x}_{it,exog} = x_{it,exog} - \overline{x}_{i,exog} \qquad \tilde{x}_{it,endog} = x_{it,endog} - \overline{x}_{i,endog}$$

and then get fixed effects estimates are:

```
series  lwage_means = @meansby(lwage,id,"@all")
series  exper_means = @meansby(exper,id,"@all")
series  exper2_means = @meansby(exper2,id,"@all")
series  tenure_means = @meansby(tenure,id,"@all")
series  tenure2_means = @meansby(tenure2,id,"@all")
series  union_means = @meansby(union,id,"@all")
series  south_means = @meansby(south,id,"@all")
series  lwage_dev = lwage - lwage_means
series  exper_dev = exper - exper_means
series  exper2_dev = exper2 - exper2_means
series  tenure_dev = tenure - tenure_means
series  tenure2_dev = tenure2 - tenure2_means
series  union_dev = union - union_means
series  south_dev = south - south_means
equation fe.ls  lwage_dev  exper_dev  exper2_dev  tenure_dev  tenure2_dev
                union_dev  south_dev
```

Notice the extensions used to denote the individual means of a variable and the deviations from those means; for example, **lwage_means** and **lwage_dev**.

The variance estimate is given by

$$\hat{\sigma}_e^2 = \frac{1}{NT - N} \sum_{i=1}^{N} \sum_{t=1}^{T} \hat{e}_{it}$$

To compute this estimate as **sige2** and to save the coefficients from fixed effects estimation as **b**, we use the following commands:

```
scalar  sige2 = @ssr/(3580-716)
vector(6) b
b=c
```

Now we work towards an estimate for σ_u^2. The first step is to compute estimates of the fixed effects d_i, which we refer to as **dee**. The series **dee** will contain each of the d_i repeated T times:

```
series dee = lwage_means - b(1)*exper_means - b(2)*exper2_means -
             b(3)*tenure_means - b(4)*tenure2_means - b(5)*union_means -
             b(6)*south_means
```

Instrumental variables estimates of δ_1 and δ_2 can be found by regressing the d_i on the time invariant variables $w_{i,exog}$ and $w_{i,endog}$ using as instruments $w_{i,exog}$ and $x_{it,exog}$:

```
equation iv.tsls  dee  c  black  educ @ black  exper  exper2  tenure  tenure2  union
```

Having obtained consistent estimates for β_2, β_3, δ_1 and δ_2, we find residuals $\hat{v}_{it}$ corresponding to $v_{it} = u_i + e_{it}$. From those residuals that we call **v**, we estimate the variance $\sigma_B^2 = T\sigma_u^2 + \sigma_e^2$ using

$$\hat{\sigma}_B^2 = \frac{1}{N} \sum_{i=1}^{N} \sum_{t=1}^{T} \left(\frac{1}{T} \sum_{t=1}^{T} \hat{v}_{it} \right)^2$$

Then, an estimate for σ_u^2 can be found from

$$\hat{\sigma}_u^2 = \frac{\hat{\sigma}_B^2 - \hat{\sigma}_e^2}{T}$$

We refer to $\hat{\sigma}_B^2$ and $\hat{\sigma}_u^2$ as **sb2** and **su2**, respectively.

```
series v=lwage - b(1)*exper - b(2)*exper2 - b(3)*tenure - b(4)*tenure2 - b(5)*union -
        b(6)*south - c(1) - c(2)*black - c(3)*educ
series vbar=@meansby(v,id,"@all")
series vbar2=vbar^2
scalar sb2=@sum(vbar2)/716
scalar su2=(sb2-sige2)/5
```

Using $\hat{\sigma}_B^2$ and $\hat{\sigma}_u^2$ we compute the transformation parameter **alpha** as

$$\alpha = 1 - \left(\frac{\hat{\sigma}_e^2}{T\hat{\sigma}_u^2 + \hat{\sigma}_e^2} \right)^{1/2}$$

This transformation parameter is used to transform all the variables in the model in the same way as we do for the random effects model. See *POE4*, page 555. Variables such as $y_{it}^* = y_{it} - \alpha \bar{y}_i$ are called **lwage_star**. Other transformed variables have similar names. The transformed constant is called **cstar**.

```
scalar  alpha = 1-@sqrt(sige2/(sige2+5*su2))
series  lwage_star = lwage - alpha*lwage_means
series  exper_star = exper - alpha*exper_means
series  exper2_star = exper2 - alpha*exper2_means
series  tenure_star = tenure - alpha*tenure_means
series  tenure2_star = tenure2 - alpha*tenure2_means
series  union_star = union - alpha*union_means
series  south_star = south - alpha*south_means
series  educ_star = (1-alpha)*educ
series  black_star = (1-alpha)*black
series  cstar = 1-alpha
```

In the final step we estimate the original equation by applying instrumental variables estimation to the transformed variables, using as instruments $\tilde{x}_{it,exog}$, $\tilde{x}_{it,endog}$, $\bar{x}_{i,exog}$ and $w_{i,exog}$:

```
equation ht.tsls lwage_star cstar educ_star exper_star exper2_star tenure_star
        tenure2_star black_star south_star union_star @ exper_dev
        exper2_dev tenure_dev tenure2_dev union_dev south_dev
        exper_means exper2_means tenure_means tenure2_means
        union_means black
```

We can now examine the results. Estimates of the standard deviations of the two error components are $\hat{\sigma}_e = \sqrt{0.037988} = 0.1949$ and $\hat{\sigma}_u = \sqrt{0.202383} = 0.4499$. The transformation parameter is $\alpha = 0.8098$.

	Value
SIGE2	0.037988

	Value
SU2	0.202383

	Value
ALPHA	0.809783

The coefficient estimates given in the following output corresponds to that in Table 15.10 on page 562 of *POE4*.

Dependent Variable: LWAGE_STAR
Method: Panel Two-Stage Least Squares
Sample: 1982 1988
Periods included: 5
Cross-sections included: 716
Total panel (balanced) observations: 3580
Instrument specification: C EXPER_DEV EXPER2_DEV TENURE_DEV
    TENURE2_DEV UNION_DEV SOUTH_DEV EXPER_MEANS
    EXPER2_MEANS TENURE_MEANS TENURE2_MEANS
    UNION_MEANS BLACK
Constant added to instrument list

Variable	Coefficient	Std. Error	t-Statistic	Prob.
CSTAR	-0.750769	0.586236	-1.280661	0.2004
EDUC_STAR	0.170508	0.044463	3.834851	0.0001
EXPER_STAR	0.039908	0.006475	6.163824	0.0000
EXPER2_STAR	-0.000391	0.000268	-1.462223	0.1438
TENURE_STAR	0.014326	0.003160	4.533882	0.0000
TENURE2_STAR	-0.000853	0.000197	-4.318852	0.0000
BLACK_STAR	-0.035914	0.060068	-0.597881	0.5500
SOUTH_STAR	-0.031712	0.034847	-0.910031	0.3629
UNION_STAR	0.071969	0.013454	5.349097	0.0000

15.7 SETS OF REGRESSION EQUATIONS

We now consider an example of panel data where N is small relative to T. It involves $T = 20$ time series observations on just $N = 2$ cross-sectional units, the firms General Electric and Westinghouse. The data can be found in the file *grunfeld2.wf1*. We are interested in estimating the two equations

$$INV_{GE} = \beta_{1,GE} + \beta_{2,GE}V_{GE} + \beta_{3,GE}K_{GE} + e_{GE}$$

$$INV_{WE} = \beta_{1,WE} + \beta_{2,WE}V_{WE} + \beta_{3,WE}K_{WE} + e_{WE}$$

where *INV* denotes investment, *V* denotes market value of stock, and *K* denotes capital stock, with the subscripts *GE* and *WE* referring to General Electric and Westinghouse, respectively. There are various ways of estimating these two equations depending on what further assumptions are made about the coefficients and the error terms in each of the equations. We first consider pooled least squares.

15.7.1 Equal coefficients, equal error variances

When the two equations are assumed to have the same coefficients and the same variances, we can proceed with least squares estimation without changing the structure of the workfile. We can simply regress *INV* on *V* and *K* without distinguishing between what values belong to Westinghouse and what values belong to General Electric:

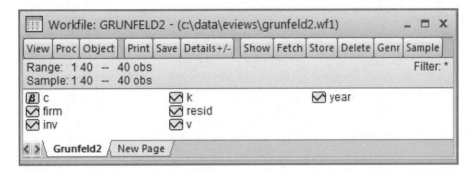

The **Equation specification** and the resulting output follow. See Table 15.11 on page 564 of *POE4*.

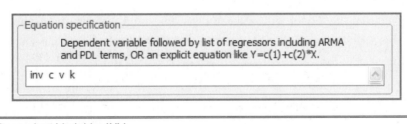

Dependent Variable: INV
Method: Least Squares
Sample: 1 40
Included observations: 40

Variable	Coefficient	Std. Error	t-Statistic	Prob.
C	17.87200	7.024081	2.544390	0.0153
V	0.015193	0.006196	2.451913	0.0191
K	0.143579	0.018601	7.718900	0.0000

15.7.2 Different coefficients, equal error variances

To relax the assumption of identical coefficients for the two firms, we introduce an indicator (dummy) variable *DUM* that is equal to 1 for the Westinghouse observations and zero for the General Electric observations. Recognizing that *FIRM* = 2 denotes Westinghouse observations, we use the command

```
series  dum = (firm=2)
```

Then equation (15.44) on page 564 of *POE4* can be specified as follows, giving the output in Table 15.12:

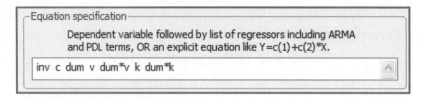

Dependent Variable: INV
Method: Least Squares
Sample: 1 40
Included observations: 40

Variable	Coefficient	Std. Error	t-Statistic	Prob.
C	-9.956306	23.62636	-0.421407	0.6761
DUM	9.446916	28.80535	0.327957	0.7450
V	0.026551	0.011722	2.265064	0.0300
DUM*V	0.026343	0.034353	0.766838	0.4485
K	0.151694	0.019356	7.836865	0.0000
DUM*K	-0.059287	0.116946	-0.506962	0.6155

Testing the equality of the coefficients

Using the output from the model with indicator variables and different coefficients, we can test for equality of the coefficients using the following Wald test:

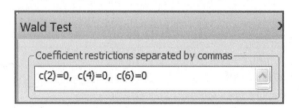

Wald Test:
Equation: TABLE_15_12

Test Statistic	Value	df	Probability
F-statistic	1.189433	(3, 34)	0.3284
Chi-square	3.568300	3	0.3120

The *F*-value of 1.189 is that obtained in equation (15.45) in *POE4*. We could have also done the calculation using the sums of squared errors.

From Table 15.11,

Sum squared resid	16563.00

From Table 15.12,

Sum squared resid	14989.82

15.7.3 Different coefficients, different error variances

If we assume the equations have both different coefficients and different error variances, then estimation is equivalent to running two separate regressions, one for each firm. Both sets of results in *POE4* Table 15.13 can be obtained using the following **Equation specification**:

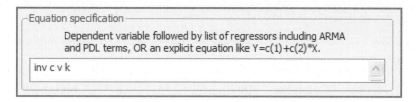

However, a different **Sample** is needed for each equation. For the General Electric equation, we have

and, for the Westinghouse equation, we have

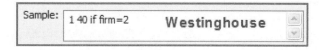

Estimation after restructuring the workfile

Alternatively, we can use another option in a restructured workfile. To restructure the workfile in panel format, go to **Proc/Structure/Resize Current Page**, and fill in the resulting dialog box as indicated.

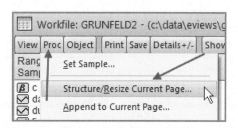

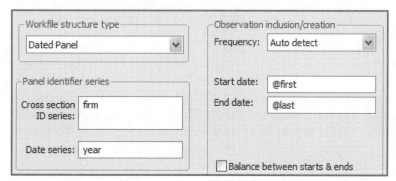

The new structure is displayed with a sample time period going from 1935 to 1954, for two cross-sectional units and a total of 40 observations.

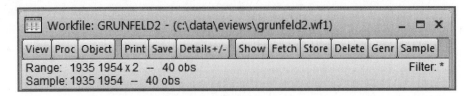

The alternative way of estimating the two equations with different coefficients and different error variances is to include the dummy variable and to use EViews **Panel Option** for different variances. The **Equation Specification** and **Panel Options** are:

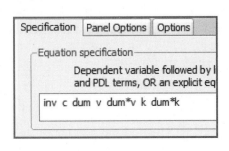

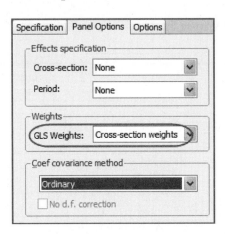

Dependent Variable: INV
Method: Panel EGLS (Cross-section weights)
Sample: 1935 1954
Periods included: 20
Cross-sections included: 2
Total panel (balanced) observations: 40
Linear estimation after one-step weighting matrix

Variable	Coefficient	Std. Error	t-Statistic	Prob.
C	-9.956306	31.37425	-0.317340	0.7529
DUM	9.446916	32.38191	0.291734	0.7723
V	0.026551	0.015566	1.705705	0.0972
DUM*V	0.026343	0.022113	1.191271	0.2418
K	0.151694	0.025704	5.901548	0.0000
DUM*K	-0.059287	0.061707	-0.960783	0.3434

Comparing these estimates with those in Table 15.13, you will notice that the coefficients of C, *V,* and *K* are those for General Electric and the coefficients for Westinghouse are obtained by adding the General Electric coefficients to the corresponding dummy variable coefficients. Specifically,

$$\hat{\beta}_{1,WE} = \hat{\beta}_{1,GE} + \hat{\delta}_1 = -9.9563 + 9.4469 = -0.5094$$

$$\hat{\beta}_{2,WE} = \hat{\beta}_{2,GE} + \hat{\delta}_2 = 0.02655 + 0.02634 = 0.0529$$

$$\hat{\beta}_{3,WE} = \hat{\beta}_{3,GE} + \hat{\delta}_3 = 0.15169 - 0.05929 = 0.0924$$

To obtain standard errors for the Westinghouse coefficient estimates, we can use a Wald test command. For example, to obtain the standard error for $\hat{\beta}_{3,WE}$, go to **View/Coefficient Diagnostics/Wald -Coefficient Restrictions** and insert the following:

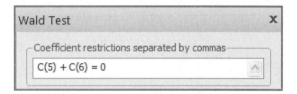

The lower part of the Wald test output contains the standard error:

Normalized Restriction (= 0)	Value	Std. Err.
C(5) + C(6)	0.092406	0.056099

15.7.4 Seemingly unrelated regressions

The seemingly unrelated regression framework is the same as that in the previous section except that we relax the assumption that the General Electric and Westinghouse errors for the same year are uncorrelated. The new assumption is known as contemporaneous correlation. To obtain estimates for this model using the dummy variable format, we proceed as before except that we select **Cross-section SUR** for the **GLS weights**.

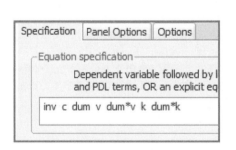 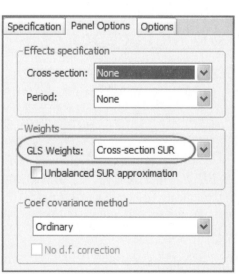

The EGLS estimation method referred to in the output that follows is shorthand for estimated generalized least squares. It is a generalized least squares method that uses estimates of the variances and covariance. The coefficient estimates for corresponding coefficients agree with those in Table 15.14 on page 568 of *POE4*, but the standard errors are slightly different. First, to reconcile the coefficient estimates, we have

$$\hat{\beta}_{1,WE} = \hat{\beta}_{1,GE} + \hat{\delta}_1 = -27.7193 + 26.4673 = -1.2520$$

$$\hat{\beta}_{2,WE} = \hat{\beta}_{2,GE} + \hat{\delta}_2 = 0.03831 + 0.01932 = 0.0576$$

$$\hat{\beta}_{3,WE} = \hat{\beta}_{3,GE} + \hat{\delta}_3 = 0.13904 - 0.07506 = 0.0640$$

The standard errors differ because those in Table 15.14 have used a degrees-of-freedom correction and those in the EViews output have not. To obtain the standard errors in Table 15.14 from those in the EViews output, you need to multiply by $\sqrt{T/(T-K)} = \sqrt{20/17}$. To obtain standard errors of the Westinghouse coefficients instead of those for the $\hat{\delta}_k$, the Wald test can be used as before.

Dependent Variable: INV
Method: Panel EGLS (Cross-section SUR)
Sample: 1935 1954
Periods included: 20
Cross-sections included: 2
Total panel (balanced) observations: 40
Linear estimation after one-step weighting matrix

Variable	Coefficient	Std. Error	t-Statistic	Prob.
C	-27.71932	27.03283	-1.025395	0.3124
DUM	26.46733	22.91810	1.154866	0.2562
V	0.038310	0.013290	2.882609	0.0068
DUM*V	0.019320	0.010793	1.789947	0.0824
K	0.139036	0.023036	6.035716	0.0000
DUM*K	-0.075058	0.041621	-1.803384	0.0802

15.8 USING THE POOL OBJECT

One of the disadvantages of the estimations in the previous section was the need to use indicator (dummy) variables to model coefficients that were different in different equations. It would be more convenient if the coefficients estimates and their standard errors could be obtained directly. We can achieve this goal by unstacking the data and using a **Pool** object.

Before proceeding in this direction, we create an **alpha** series so that we can label the General Electric and Westinghouse observations as **GE** and **WE**, respectively. We could continue to use the series *FIRM*, which is equal to 1 for **GE** and 2 for **WE**, but **GE** and **WE** are more explicit and easier to remember. To create a series *FIRMID* with the labels **GE** and **WE**, we use the following commands. A few observations confirming the contents of *FIRMID* are on the right of the commands. They are for General Electric in 1953 and 1954 and Westinghouse in 1935 and 1936.

```
smpl  if firm = 1
alpha  firmid = "ge"
smpl  if firm = 2
alpha  firmid = "we"
smpl  @first  @last
```

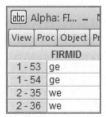

15.8.1 Unstacking the data

To unstack the data so that there are 20 observations on each variable and so that we distinguish between those for each firm, we proceed as follows. Go to **Proc/Reshape Current Page /Unstack in New Page**.

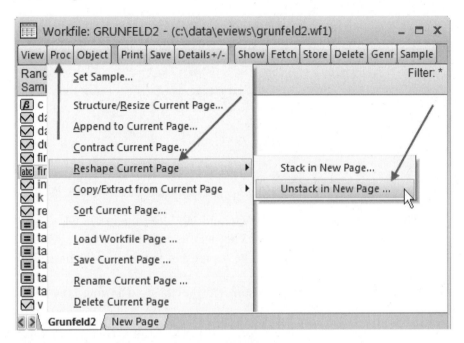

In the **Workfile Unstack** window, there are two tabs, one labeled **Unstack Workfile** and another labeled **Page Destination**. For **Page Destination**, we retain the same workfile and we name the new page **unstack**. For **Unstack Workfile**, we make the following entries:

1. The **Series name** for **unstacking the identifiers** is *FIRMID*.
2. The series that **identifies observations** is *YEAR*.

3. The **name pattern for unstacked series** is *_?. This entry has the effect of retaining the current names for *INV*, *V* and *K*, but adding a suffix _*GE* or _*WE* to indicate the firm.

4. The **series to unstack** are *INV*, *V* and *K*.

The new page of the workfile then has the following form:

The series *INV* has been unstacked into *INV_GE* and *INV_WE*; then *INV_GE* and *INV_WE* have been placed in a group that is labeled **INV**. The same is true for *V* and *K*. Also, a **pool** object called **FIRMID** has been created. The **Range** and **Sample** for the unstacked data are 20 observations.

We can now revisit the equations we estimated previously, showing how to estimate them using the pool object.

15.8.2 Equal coefficients, equal error variances

Opening the pool object **FIRMID** reveals the following window:

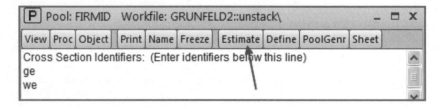

Then click on **Estimate**. Wow! Look at all the boxes you have to fill in. Don't be scared. At the moment we are only concerned with two of them.

1. For the **Dependent variable** we have written **INV_?**. Writing it this way, with the question mark, tells EViews to consider all values on investment. Remember that you have already told EViews about the cross-section identifiers. It won't forget.

2. The other box that is filled in is the **Common coefficients** box. We chose this one because we are assuming the General Electric coefficients are identical to the Westinghouse coefficients. If you wanted them to be different, you would choose the **Cross-section specific coefficients** box. If you wanted the coefficients for some variables to be the same and some to be different, you can write some of the explanatory variable names in one box and some in the other.

3. Because we are estimating the equation by straightforward least squares, we do not need to change the default settings in the **Estimation method** box. Assuming equal variances

means we leave **None** in the **Weights** box. Also, we are not assuming **Fixed** or **Random Effects**.

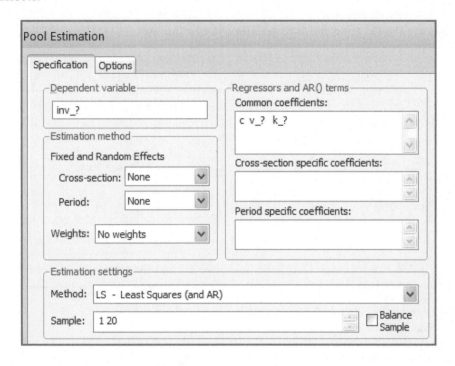

The results are those given in Table 15.11 on page 564 of *POE4*.

Dependent Variable: INV_?
Method: Pooled Least Squares
Sample: 1 20
Included observations: 20
Cross-sections included: 2
Total pool (balanced) observations: 40

Variable	Coefficient	Std. Error	t-Statistic	Prob.
C	17.87200	7.024081	2.544390	0.0153
V_?	0.015193	0.006196	2.451913	0.0191
K_?	0.143579	0.018601	7.718900	0.0000

Since we are going to use the same pool object for other estimations, it is a good idea to click Freeze and name your output, as we have done in the following screen shot:

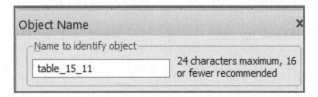

15.8.3 Different coefficients, equal error variances

If we relax the assumption that the coefficients are equal, but continue to assume the variances are the same, the **Pool Estimation Specification** and results are:

```
┌─────────────────────────────────────────────────────────────────────┐
│ Specification │ Options                                               │
│  ┌─Dependent variable──────────┐  ┌─Regressors and AR() terms───────┐│
│  │                             │  │ Common coefficients:            ││
│  │  inv_?                      │  │ ┌─────────────────────────────┐ ││
│  │                             │  │ │                           ▲ │ ││
│  └─────────────────────────────┘  │ │                           ▼ │ ││
│  ┌─Estimation method───────────┐  │ └─────────────────────────────┘ ││
│  │ Fixed and Random Effects    │  │ Cross-section specific          ││
│  │                             │  │ coefficients:                   ││
│  │ Cross-section: None      ▼  │  │ ┌─────────────────────────────┐ ││
│  │                             │  │ │ c v_? k_?                 ▲ │ ││
│  │ Period:        None      ▼  │  │ │                           ▼ │ ││
│  │                             │  │ └─────────────────────────────┘ ││
│  │ Weights:  No weights     ▼  │  │ Period specific coefficients:   ││
│  │                             │  │ ┌─────────────────────────────┐ ││
│  │                             │  │ │                           ▲ │ ││
│  │                             │  │ │                           ▼ │ ││
│  └─────────────────────────────┘  └─────────────────────────────────┘│
└─────────────────────────────────────────────────────────────────────┘
```

Dependent Variable: INV_?
Method: Pooled Least Squares
Sample: 1 20
Included observations: 20
Cross-sections included: 2
Total pool (balanced) observations: 40

Variable	Coefficient	Std. Error	t-Statistic	Prob.
GE--C	-9.956306	23.62636	-0.421407	0.6761
WE--C	-0.509390	16.47857	-0.030912	0.9755
GE--V_GE	0.026551	0.011722	2.265064	0.0300
WE--V_WE	0.052894	0.032291	1.638052	0.1106
GE--K_GE	0.151694	0.019356	7.836865	0.0000
WE--K_WE	0.092406	0.115333	0.801212	0.4286

These results are equivalent to those in Table 15.12, although at first glance you might not think so. We can see the equivalence by noting that

$$\hat{\delta}_1 = -0.5094 - (-9.9563) = 9.4469 \qquad \hat{\delta}_2 = 0.052894 - 0.026551 = 0.026343$$

$$\hat{\delta}_3 = 0.09241 - 0.15169 = -0.05928$$

15.8.4 Different coefficients, different error variances

If we assume the equations have both different coefficients and different error variances, then estimation is equivalent to running two separate regressions, one for each firm. We can do so using the usual single equation commands or by using the pool object. We will consider both. The results are those in *POE4* Table 15.13. The single equation commands follow. We have included commands to save the residuals, and to save estimates of the error standard deviations; they are used to find (a) an estimate of the covariance between the two errors, and (b) an estimate of the contemporaneous correlation between the errors. Look through the following commands and make sure you appreciate their purpose.

```
equation ge.ls  inv_ge  c  v_ge  k_ge
series  ehat_ge = resid
scalar  sig_ge = @se
equation we.ls  inv_we  c  v_we  k_we
series  ehat_we = resid
scalar  sig_we = @se
series  ee=ehat_ge*ehat_we
scalar  cov = @sum(ee)/17
scalar  r = cov/(sig_ge*sig_we)
```

The standard deviations, covariance, and correlation for the residuals are

	Value
SIG_GE	27.88272

	Value
SIG_WE	10.21312

	Value
COV	207.5871

	Value
R	0.728965

The contemporaneous correlation is $r = 0.729$. In the first printing of *POE4*, this was incorrectly recorded as $r^2 = 0.729$ on page 569. The other quantities on that page agree with our calculations: $\hat{\sigma}_{GE,WE} = 207.587$, and $\hat{\sigma}_{WE}^2 = (10.2131)^2 = 104.308$. The outputs for each of the equations – see *POE4* Table 15.4 – are

Dependent Variable: INV_GE
Method: Least Squares
Sample: 1 20
Included observations: 20

Variable	Coefficient	Std. Error	t-Statistic	Prob.
C	-9.956306	31.37425	-0.317340	0.7548
V_GE	0.026551	0.015566	1.705705	0.1063
K_GE	0.151694	0.025704	5.901548	0.0000

S.E. of regression	27.88272	Akaike info criterion		9.631373

Dependent Variable: INV_WE
Method: Least Squares
Sample: 1 20
Included observations: 20

Variable	Coefficient	Std. Error	t-Statistic	Prob.
C	-0.509390	8.015289	-0.063552	0.9501
V_WE	0.052894	0.015707	3.367658	0.0037
K_WE	0.092406	0.056099	1.647205	0.1179

S.E. of regression	10.21312	Akaike info criterion		7.622705

To find the same estimates using the pool object, we use the following **Pool Estimation Specification.** What differs from last time where the error variances were assumed equal is that we are now using **Cross-section weights.** In the results the coefficients are ordered according to variable rather than according to equation:

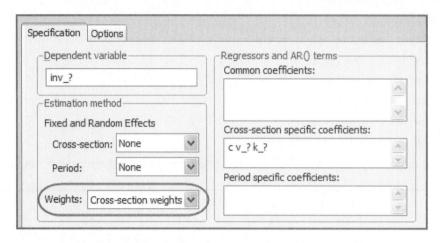

Dependent Variable: INV_?
Method: Pooled EGLS (Cross-section weights)
Sample: 1 20
Included observations: 20
Cross-sections included: 2
Total pool (balanced) observations: 40
Linear estimation after one-step weighting matrix

Variable	Coefficient	Std. Error	t-Statistic	Prob.
GE--C	-9.956306	31.37425	-0.317340	0.7529
WE--C	-0.509390	8.015289	-0.063552	0.9497
GE--V_GE	0.026551	0.015566	1.705705	0.0972
WE--V_WE	0.052894	0.015707	3.367658	0.0019
GE--K_GE	0.151694	0.025704	5.901548	0.0000
WE--K_WE	0.092406	0.056099	1.647205	0.1087

To find the covariance and correlation matrices for the residuals, go to **View/Residual/Covariance Matrix** and **View/Residual/Correlation Matrix**.

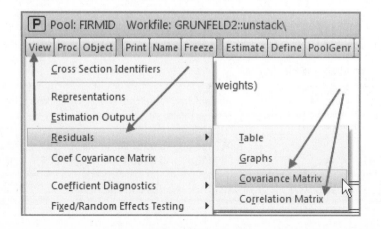

Residual Covariance Matrix		
	GE	WE
GE	660.8294	176.4491
WE	176.4491	88.66170

Residual Correlation Matrix		
	GE	WE
GE	1.000000	0.728965
WE	0.728965	1.000000

The correlation of $r = 0.729$ agrees with what we calculated previously, but the covariance matrix does not. The different covariance matrix arises because EViews uses T as the divisor instead of $(T - K)$ when computing the variances and covariance. Multiplying the EViews values by $20/17$ eliminates the differences: $660.8294 \times 20/17 = 777.446$, $88.6617 \times 20/17 = 104.308$, and $176.4491 \times 20/17 = 204.587$.

Testing for contemporaneous correlation

In the context of the two-equation SUR model, a test for contemporaneous correlation is a test of $H_0 : \text{cov}(e_{GE,t}, e_{WE,t}) = 0$. The relevant test statistic, described on page 569 of *POE4*, is $LM = T \times r_{GE,WE}^2$ where $r_{GE,WE}^2$ is the squared correlation between the least squares residuals from the two equations. From the results above, we have $r_{GE,WE}^2 = (0.728965)^2 = 0.53139$, giving a test statistic value of $LM = 20 \times 0.53139 = 10.628$. The command

```
scalar pval = 1 - @cchisq(10.6278,1)
```

yields a *p*-value of 0.0011. We reject H_0 and conclude that contemporaneous correlation between the equation errors exists.

15.8.5 Seemingly unrelated regressions

The final set of estimates that we obtain using the pool object is the seemingly unrelated regression estimates. We assume $\sigma_{GE}^2 \neq \sigma_{WE}^2$ and, in line with the outcome for the test for contemporaneous correlation, $\text{cov}(e_{GE,t}, e_{WE,t}) \neq 0$. The change from the previous section is that we now use **Cross-section SUR** for the **Weights**. The results are those given in Table 15.14 on page 568 of *POE4*. To get the standard errors in Table 15.14, we multiply those in the output by the degrees of freedom correction $\sqrt{20/17}$:

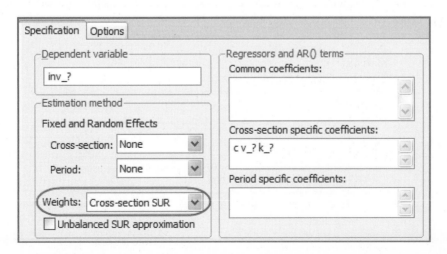

Dependent Variable: INV_?
Method: Pooled EGLS (Cross-section SUR)
Sample: 1 20
Included observations: 20
Cross-sections included: 2
Total pool (balanced) observations: 40
Linear estimation after one-step weighting matrix

Variable	Coefficient	Std. Error	t-Statistic	Prob.
GE--C	-27.71932	27.03283	-1.025395	0.3124
WE--C	-1.251988	6.956347	-0.179978	0.8582
GE--V_GE	0.038310	0.013290	2.882609	0.0068
WE--V_WE	0.057630	0.013411	4.297200	0.0001
GE--K_GE	0.139036	0.023036	6.035716	0.0000
WE--K_WE	0.063978	0.048901	1.308318	0.1995

Testing the equality of the coefficients

To test the equality of the coefficients, we test the hypothesis

$$H_0 : \beta_{1,GE} = \beta_{1,WE}, \quad \beta_{2,GE} = \beta_{2,WE}, \quad \beta_{3,GE} = \beta_{3,WE}$$

This hypothesis can be tested using the **Wald test** option from SUR estimation. To carry out the test we can follow the same steps as described in Chapter 6, although in this case the formulas for the test statistics are more complicated than we have divulged. Also, special care must be exercised to make sure we are testing the coefficients that we want to test. Return to the SUR output. Note the order of the coefficients. This is the order in which EViews stores them in the **C** vector. Consequently, writing the null hypothesis in terms of EViews coefficients, we have

$$H_0 : C(1)=C(2), \quad C(3)=C(4), \quad C(5)=C(6)$$

Select **View/Coefficient Diagnostics/Wald - Coefficient Restrictions**. Entering the following restrictions in the **Wald test** box yields the output that follows:

Coefficient restrictions separated by commas

c(1) = c(2), c(3) = c(4), c(5) = c(6)

Wald Test:
Equation: TABLE_15_14

Test Statistic	Value	df	Probability
F-statistic	3.437931	(3, 34)	0.0275
Chi-square	10.31379	3	0.0161

Null Hypothesis: C(2)=C(4)=C(6)=0

The F- and χ^2-values for the test are given in the upper part of the output, along with their corresponding p-values. The hypothesis of equal coefficients is rejected.

There is a discrepancy between the values in *POE4* on page 570 and those in the above output. Those in the text are $F = 2.92$ and $\chi^2 = 8.77$. The difference is again attributable to the treatment of a degrees of freedom correction when estimating the error variances and covariance. To convert the EViews values to the *POE4* values, we multiply by $(17/20)$:

$$3.4379 \times \frac{17}{20} = 2.92 \qquad 10.3138 \times \frac{17}{20} = 8.77$$

Keywords

@expand	EGLS	random effects
@first	effects specification	redundant fixed effects
@last	endogenous variables	reshape page
@meansby	exogenous variables	residual correlation matrix
alpha	fixed effects	resize current page
coef covariance method	fixed effects estimator	seemingly unrelated regression
cluster robust standard errors	fixed effects: testing	singular matrix
common coefficients	Hausman test	stacked data
contemporaneous correlation	Hausman-Taylor estimator	stacking identifiers
correlated random effects	identifier series	SUR
cross-section coefficients	idiosyncratic random	transformed variables
cross-section effects	instruments	unstack in new page
cross section identifiers	page destination	unstacked data
cross-section random	panel options	Wald test
cross-section SUR	panel structure	White period
date series	pool object	workfile unstack
dated panel	pooled least squares	workfile structure
dummy variable estimator	pooling	

CHAPTER **16**

Qualitative and Limited Dependent Variables

CHAPTER OUTLINE

Microeconomics is a general theory of choice, and many of the choices that individuals and firms make cannot be measured by a continuous outcome variable. In this chapter we examine some fascinating models that are used to describe choice behavior, and that do not have the usual continuous dependent variable. Our descriptions will be brief, since we will not go into all the theory, but we will reveal to you a rich area of economic applications.

We also introduce a class of models with dependent variables that are *limited*. By that, we mean that they are continuous, but their range of values is constrained in some way and their values are not completely observable. Alternatives to least squares estimation must be considered for such cases, since the least squares estimator is both biased and inconsistent.

16.1 MODELS WITH BINARY DEPENDENT VARIABLES

We will illustrate **binary choice models** using an important problem from transportation economics. How can we explain an individual's choice between driving (private transportation) and taking the bus (public transportation) when commuting to work, assuming, for simplicity, that these are the only two alternatives? We represent an individual's choice by the dummy variable

$$y = \begin{cases} 1 & \text{individual drives to work} \\ 0 & \text{individual takes bus to work} \end{cases}$$

If we collect a random sample of workers who commute to work, then the outcome y will be unknown to us until the sample is drawn. Thus, y is a random variable. If the probability that an individual drives to work is p, then $P[y=1]=p$. It follows that the probability that a person uses public transportation is $P[y=0]=1-p$. The probability function for such a binary random variable is

$$f(y) = p^y (1-p)^{1-y}, \quad y = 0,1$$

where p is the probability that y takes the value 1. This discrete random variable has expected value $E(y)=p$ and variance $\text{var}(y)=p(1-p)$.

What factors might affect the probability that an individual chooses one transportation mode over the other? One factor will certainly be how long it takes to get to work one way or the other. Define the explanatory variable

$$x = (\text{commuting time by bus} - \text{commuting time by car})$$

There are other factors that affect the decision, but let us focus on this single explanatory variable. *A priori* we expect that as x increases, and commuting time by bus increases relative to commuting time by car, an individual would be more inclined to drive. That is, we expect a positive relationship between x and p, the probability that an individual will drive to work.

16.1.1 Examine the data

Open the workfile *transport.wf1*. Save the workfile with a new name to *transport_chap16.wf1* so that the original workfile will not be changed. The variables included are

AUTOTIME	commute time via auto, minutes
BUSTIME	commute time via bus, minutes
DTIME	= (bus time - auto time)/10, 10 minute units
AUTO	= 1 if auto chosen

Highlight the series *AUTOTIME, BUSTIME, DTIME* and *AUTO* in order. Double-click in the blue to open the **Group**. The data are shown on the next page.

G	Group: UNTITLED Workfile: TRANSPORT_CHAP16::Transport\				_ ▢ X	

| View | Proc | Object | Print | Name | Freeze | Default ▼ | Sort | Transpose | E |

obs	AUTOTIME	BUSTIME	DTIME	AUTO	
1	52.9	4.4	-4.85	0	▲
2	4.1	28.5	2.44	0	▬
3	4.1	86.9	8.28	1	
4	56.2	31.6	-2.46	0	
5	51.8	20.2	-3.16	0	
6	0.2	91.2	9.10	1	▼
7	◀			▶	

The key point is that *AUTO*, which is to be the dependent variable in the model, only takes the values 0 and 1.

Obtain the descriptive statistics from the spreadsheet view: Select **View/Descriptive Stats/ Common Sample**.

	AUTOTIME	BUSTIME	DTIME	AUTO
Mean	49.34762	48.12381	-0.122381	0.476190
Median	51.40000	38.00000	-0.700000	0.000000
Maximum	99.10000	91.50000	9.100000	1.000000
Minimum	0.200000	1.600000	-9.070000	0.000000
Std. Dev.	32.43491	34.63082	5.691037	0.511766
Skewness	0.027350	0.062843	-0.021945	0.095346
Kurtosis	1.819548	1.332525	1.724165	1.009091
Jarque-Bera	1.221902	2.446737	1.425971	3.500072
Probability	0.542834	0.294237	0.490179	0.173768
Sum	1036.300	1010.600	-2.570000	10.00000
Sum Sq. Dev.	21040.47	23985.88	647.7580	5.238095
Observations	21	21	21	21

The summary statistics will be useful later, but for now notice that the **SUM** of the *AUTO* series is 10, meaning that of the 21 individuals in the sample, 10 take their automobile to work and 11 take public transportation (the bus).

16.1.2 The linear probability model

Our objective is to estimate a model explaining why some choose *AUTO* and some choose *BUS* transportation. Because the outcome variable is binary, its expected value is the probability of observing *AUTO* = 1,

$$E(y) = p = \beta_1 + \beta_2 x$$

The model

$$y = E(y) + e = \beta_1 + \beta_2 x + e$$

is called the **linear probability model**. It looks like a regression, but as noted in *POE4*, page 588, there are some problems. Nevertheless, apply least squares using $y = AUTO$ and $x = DTIME$:

equation linprob.ls auto c dtime

Variable	Coefficient	Std. Error	t-Statistic	Prob.
C	0.484795	0.071449	6.785151	0.0000
DTIME	0.070310	0.012862	5.466635	0.0000

Included observations: 21

The problems with this estimation procedure can be observed by examining the predicted values, which we call *PHAT*. In the regression window select the **Forecast** button. Fill in the dialog box with a **Forecast name**.

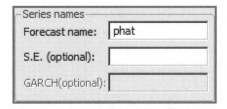

A series object *PHAT* appears in the workfile. Double-click to open. Examining just a few observations shows the unfortunate outcome that the linear probability model has predicted some probabilities to be greater than 1 or less than 0.

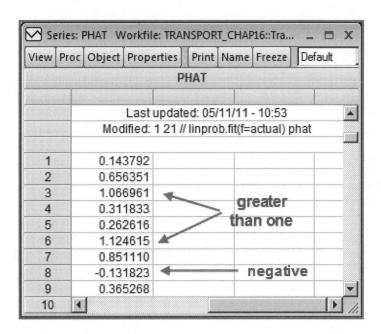

Now, examine the summary statistics for *PHAT* from the spreadsheet view, by selecting **View/Descriptive Statistics & Tests/Stats Table**.

Series: PHAT Workfile: TRANSPORT_CH... _ □ X		
View Proc Object Properties	Print Name Freeze	Sa
		PHAT
Mean	Mean	0.476190 ▲
Median	Median	0.435578
Maximum	Maximum	1.124615
Minimum	Minimum	-0.152916
Std. Dev.	Std. Dev.	0.400136 ▼
Skewness	◄	►

Note that the average value of the predicted probability is 0.476, which is exactly equal to the fraction (10/21) of riders who choose *AUTO* in the sample. But also note that the minimum and maximum values are outside the feasible range.

Because the linear probability model regression error term is heteroskedastic, a generalized least squares estimator is feasible. See Chapter 8 in this manual, and in *POE4*, for a discussion.

16.1.3 The probit model

The probit statistical model expresses the probability p that y takes the value 1 as

$$p = P[Z \leq \beta_1 + \beta_2 x] = \Phi(\beta_1 + \beta_2 x)$$

where $\Phi(z)$ is the probit function, which is the standard normal cumulative distribution function (CDF). This is a **nonlinear model** because the parameters β_1 and β_2 are inside the very nonlinear function $\Phi(\cdot)$. Using numerical optimization procedures that are discussed in EViews 7, User Guide II, Appendix B, we can obtain **maximum likelihood** estimates. From the EViews menubar select **Quick/Estimate Equation**. In the resulting dialog box, click the pull-down list in the **Method** section of **Estimation settings.** A long list of options appears. Choose **Binary Choice**.

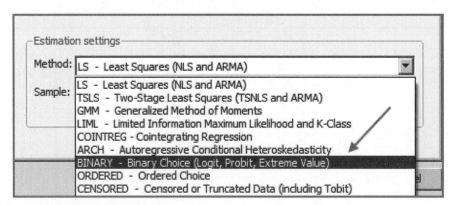

The estimation settings should look like

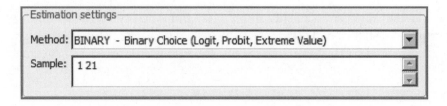

In the **Equation specification** box enter the equation as usual, but select the radio button for **Probit**.

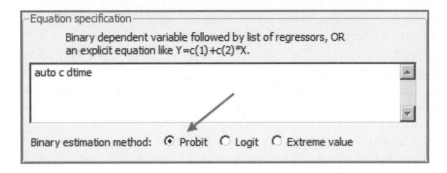

Click **OK**. The estimation results appear below. The command version is

binary(d=n) auto c dtime

In most ways the output looks similar to the regression output we have seen many times. The **Coefficients**, **Std. Error** and **Prob**. columns are familiar.

Dependent Variable: AUTO
Method: ML - Binary Probit (Quadratic hill climbing)
Sample: 1 21
Included observations: 21
Convergence achieved after 5 iterations
Covariance matrix computed using second derivatives

Variable	Coefficient	Std. Error	z-Statistic	Prob.
C	-0.064434	0.399244	-0.161390	0.8718
DTIME	0.299990	0.102867	2.916279	0.0035

McFadden R-squared	0.575761	Mean dependent var	0.476190
S.D. dependent var	0.511766	S.E. of regression	0.310890
Akaike info criterion	0.777634	Sum squared resid	1.836405
Schwarz criterion	0.877112	Log likelihood	-6.165158
Hannan-Quinn criter.	0.799223	Deviance	12.33032
Restr. deviance	29.06454	Restr. log likelihood	-14.53227
LR statistic	16.73423	Avg. log likelihood	-0.293579
Prob(LR statistic)	0.000043		

Obs with Dep=0	11	Total obs	21
Obs with Dep=1	10		

There are many items included in the output that you will not understand, and we are just omitting them. However, we note the following:

- The **Method: ML** means that the model was estimated by maximum likelihood. Quadratic hill climbing is the numerical optimization algorithm used.

- The usual t-Statistic has been replaced by **z-Statistic**. The reason for this change is that the standard errors given are only valid in **large samples**. As we know, the t-distribution converges to the standard normal distribution in large samples, so using "**z**" rather than "**t**" recognizes this fact. The p-values **Prob.** are calculated using the $N(0,1)$ distribution rather than the t-distribution.

- In the bottom portion of the output we see an R^2 value called **McFadden R-squared**. This is not a typical R^2 and cannot be interpreted like an R^2. When you were a child, your mother pointed to a pan of boiling water on the stove and said **Hot! Don't touch!** We have a similar attitude about this value. We don't want you to "get burned," so please disregard this number until you know much more.

- The **LR statistic** is comparable to the overall F-test of model significance in regression. It is a test statistic for the null hypothesis that all the model coefficients are zero <u>except</u> the intercept, against the alternative that at least one of the coefficients is not zero. The **LR** statistic has a chi-square distribution if the null hypothesis is true, with degrees of freedom equal to the number of explanatory variables, here 1. **Prob(LR statistic)** is the p-value for this test, and it is used in the standard way. If $p \leq \alpha$ then we reject the null hypothesis at the α level of significance.

16.1.4 Predicting probabilities

The "prediction" problem in probit is to predict the choice by an individual. We can predict the probability that individuals in the sample choose *AUTO*. In order to predict the probability that an individual chooses the alternative *AUTO* (y) = 1, we use the probability model $p = \Phi(\beta_1 + \beta_2 x)$, with estimates $\tilde{\beta}_1 = -0.0644$ and $\tilde{\beta}_2 = 0.29999$ of the unknown parameters obtained in the previous section. Using these estimates, we estimate the probability p to be

$$\hat{p} = \Phi(\tilde{\beta}_1 + \tilde{\beta}_2 x)$$

By comparing to a threshold value, like 0.5, we can predict choice using the rule

$$\hat{y} = \begin{cases} 1 & \hat{p} > 0.5 \\ 0 & \hat{p} \leq 0.5 \end{cases}$$

In the probit regression result, select **View/Expectation-Prediction Evaluation**.

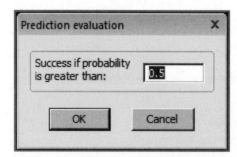

The result is a detailed analysis of the predictions, using the cutoff value 0.5.

Expectation-Prediction Evaluation for Binary Specification
Equation: PROBIT
Success cutoff: C = 0.5

	Estimated Equation			Constant Probability		
	Dep=0	Dep=1	Total	Dep=0	Dep=1	Total
P(Dep=1)<=C	10	1	11	11	10	21
P(Dep=1)>C	1	9	10	0	0	0
Total	11	10	21	11	10	21
Correct	10	9	19	11	0	11
% Correct	90.91	90.00	90.48	100.00	0.00	52.38
% Incorrect	9.09	10.00	9.52	0.00	100.00	47.62
Total Gain*	-9.09	90.00	38.10			
Percent Gain**	NA	90.00	80.00			

	Estimated Equation			Constant Probability		
	Dep=0	Dep=1	Total	Dep=0	Dep=1	Total
E(# of Dep=0)	9.05	1.74	10.79	5.76	5.24	11.00
E(# of Dep=1)	1.95	8.26	10.21	5.24	4.76	10.00
Total	11.00	10.00	21.00	11.00	10.00	21.00
Correct	9.05	8.26	17.31	5.76	4.76	10.52
% Correct	82.24	82.59	82.41	52.38	47.62	50.11
% Incorrect	17.76	17.41	17.59	47.62	52.38	49.89
Total Gain*	29.86	34.97	32.30			
Percent Gain**	62.71	66.77	64.74			

*Change in "% Correct" from default (constant probability) specification
**Percent of incorrect (default) prediction corrected by equation

The predicted probabilities are easily obtained in EViews. Within the probit estimation window, select **Forecast**. In the resulting **Forecast** dialog box, choose the **Series to forecast** to be the **Probability**, and assign the **Forecast name** *PHAT_PROBIT*. Click **OK**.

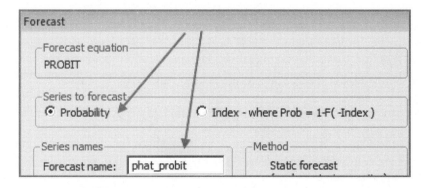

Open the series *PHAT_PROBIT* by double-clicking the series icon in the workfile window. The values of the predicted probabilities are given for each individual in the sample, based on their actual *DTIME*.

It is useful to see that these predicted probabilities can be computed directly using the EViews function **@cnorm**, which is the CDF of a standard normal random variable, what we have called "Φ". Noting that EViews places the estimates of the unknown parameters in the coefficient vector **C**,

$$\boxed{\beta}\ \mathsf{c}$$

With $C(1) = \tilde{\beta}_1 = -0.0644$ and $C(2) = \tilde{\beta}_2 = 0.29999$, we can create a series of predicted probabilities using the command

series phat_probit_calc = @cnorm(c(1)+c(2)*dtime)

The predicted probabilities from the linear probability model and probit methods are

obs	DTIME	PHAT	PHAT_PROBIT	PHAT_PROBIT_CALC
1	-4.85	0.143792	0.064333	0.064333
2	2.44	0.656351	0.747787	0.747787
3	8.28	1.066961	0.992229	0.992229
4	-2.46	0.311833	0.211158	0.211158
5	-3.16	0.262616	0.155673	0.155673
6	9.10	1.124615	0.996156	0.996156
7	5.21	0.851110	0.933000	0.933000
8	-8.77	-0.131823	0.003516	0.003516

Note that the probit predictions do not fall outside the $[0,1]$ interval.

16.1.5 Marginal effects in the probit model

In this model we can examine the effect of a one-unit change in x on the probability that $y = 1$ by considering the derivative, which is often called the **marginal effect** by economists:

$$\frac{dp}{dx} = \phi(\beta_1 + \beta_2 x)\beta_2$$

This quantity can be computed using the EViews function **@dnorm**, which gives the standard normal density function value that we have represented by ϕ. To generate the series of marginal effects for each individual in the sample, enter the command

series mfx_probit = @dnorm(c(1)+c(2)*dtime)*c(2)

Rather than evaluate the marginal effect at a specific value, or the mean value, the **average marginal effect (_AME_)** is often considered. It is the average of the marginal effects evaluated at each sample data point. That is,

$$\widehat{AME} = \frac{1}{N}\sum_{i=1}^{N}\phi(\tilde{\beta}_1 + \tilde{\beta}_2 DTIME_i)\tilde{\beta}_2$$

The average marginal effect has become a popular alternative to computing the marginal effect at the mean as it summarizes the response of individuals in the sample to a change in the value of an explanatory variable. For the current example the average marginal effect and its standard deviation are

	MFX_PROBIT
Mean	0.048407
Std. Dev.	0.036457

The marginal effect at a particular point uses the same calculation for a particular value of *DTIME*, such as 2, which represents a 20-minute differential.

scalar mfx_probit_20 = @dnorm(c(1)+c(2)*2)*c(2)

This value is 0.10369. EViews is very powerful; one of its features is the calculation of complicated nonlinear expressions involving parameters as well as their standard errors, computed using the "Delta" method. In the **PROBIT** estimation window, select **View/ Coefficient Diagnostics/Wald – Coefficient Restrictions**. In the dialog window enter the expression for the marginal effect, assuming *DTIME* = 2, setting it equal to zero as if it were a hypothesis test.

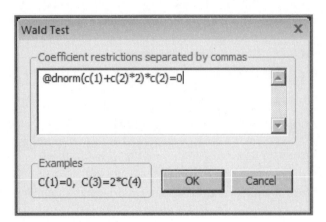

This returns the test statistics for the null hypothesis that the marginal effect is zero. The *p*-value is 0.005 leading us to reject the null hypothesis that additional *BUSTIME* has no effect on the probability of *AUTO* travel when *DTIME* = 2. Furthermore, the **Value** and the **Std. Err.** are computed. The value matches the scalar **MFX_PROBIT_20** computed earlier, and we now have a standard error that can be used to construct a confidence interval. Very cool.

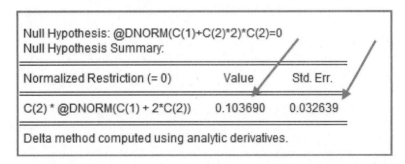

To make the estimations using the **Logit** model, simply change the **Equation Estimation** entries to

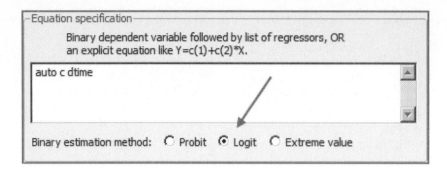

The corresponding command is

        binary(d=l) auto c dtime

16.2 BINARY CHOICE EXTENSIONS

To illustrate a bit more about the logit model and also other features of both probit and logit models, open the workfine *coke.wf1*, naming it *coke_chap16.wf1*. As an example we consider the variables

COKE	=1 if coke chosen, =0 if pepsi chosen
PR_PEPSI	price of 2 liter bottle of pepsi
PR_COKE	price of 2 liter bottle of coke
DISP_PEPSI	= 1 if pepsi is displayed at time of purchase, otherwise = 0
DISP_COKE	= 1 if coke is displayed at time of purchase, otherwise = 0
PRATIO	price of coke relative to price of pepsi

First, compare the linear probability model estimates, with robust standard errors, with probit and logit parameter estimates:

        equation coke_linprob.ls(cov=white) coke c pratio disp_coke disp_pepsi

Included observations: 1140
White heteroskedasticity-consistent standard errors & covariance

Variable	Coefficient	Std. Error	t-Statistic	Prob.
C	0.890215	0.065301	13.63240	0.0000
PRATIO	-0.400861	0.060373	-6.639779	0.0000
DISP_COKE	0.077174	0.033932	2.274393	0.0231
DISP_PEPSI	-0.165664	0.034365	-4.820738	0.0000

        equation coke_probit.probit coke c pratio disp_coke disp_pepsi
        coef b_probit = @coefs

The second command saves the estimated coefficients from the probit estimation.

Included observations: 1140
Convergence achieved after 3 iterations
Covariance matrix computed using second derivatives

Variable	Coefficient	Std. Error	z-Statistic	Prob.
C	1.108060	0.189959	5.833142	0.0000
PRATIO	-1.145963	0.180883	-6.335369	0.0000
DISP_COKE	0.217187	0.096608	2.248117	0.0246
DISP_PEPSI	-0.447297	0.101403	-4.411068	0.0000

equation coke_logit.logit coke c pratio disp_coke disp_pepsi
coef b_logit = @coefs

Included observations: 1140
Convergence achieved after 4 iterations
Covariance matrix computed using second derivatives

Variable	Coefficient	Std. Error	z-Statistic	Prob.
C	1.922972	0.325833	5.901715	0.0000
PRATIO	-1.995742	0.314587	-6.344000	0.0000
DISP_COKE	0.351599	0.158540	2.217736	0.0266
DISP_PEPSI	-0.730986	0.167838	-4.355318	0.0000

The numerical values of the estimates are quite different and should not be compared. However, marginal effects and average marginal effects can be compared. The average marginal effect of a change in *PRATIO* for the probit model is

$$\widehat{AME} = \frac{1}{N}\sum_{i=1}^{N}\phi(\tilde{\beta}_1 + \tilde{\beta}_2 PRATIO_i + \tilde{\beta}_3 DISP\_COKE_i + \tilde{\beta}_4 DISP\_PEPSI_i)\tilde{\beta}_2$$

For probit, this is calculated using

series mfx_probit = @dnorm(b_probit(1) + b_probit(2)*pratio+_probit(3)*disp_coke
+b_probit(4)*disp_pepsi)*b_probit(2)

For the logit calculation, use

series mfx_logit = @dlogistic(b_logit(1) + b_logit(2)*pratio+b_logit(3)*disp_coke
+b_logit(4)*disp_pepsi)*b_logit(2)

The average and standard deviation (not the standard error) of these series are

	MFX_PROBIT			MFX_LOGIT
Mean	-0.409695		Mean	-0.433263
Std. Dev.	0.066724		Std. Dev.	0.085458

To compute the marginal effect of a change in the price ratio for the probit and logit models, when the price ratio is 1.1 and the display variables equal to zero, we use the Wald test using the function **@dnorm** for probit and **@dlogisitic** for logit.

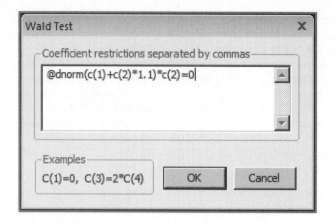

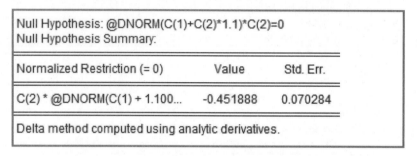

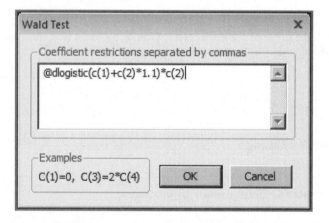

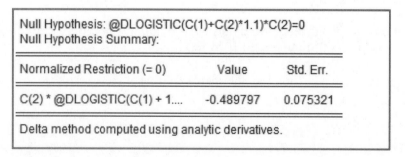

To compare successful predictions from the probit and logit estimations, in the estimation window, select **View/Expectation-Prediction Evaluation**.

16.2.1 Wald hypothesis tests

Consider the two hypotheses

$$\text{Hypothesis (1)} \quad H_0 : \beta_3 = -\beta_4, \quad H_1 : \beta_3 \neq -\beta_4$$

$$\text{Hypothesis (2)} \quad H_0 : \beta_3 = 0, \beta_4 = 0, \quad H_1 : \text{either } \beta_3 \text{ or } \beta_4 \text{ is not zero}$$

In the probit estimation window, select **View/Coefficient Diagnostics/Wald-Coefficient Restrictions.** To test the first hypothesis, enter

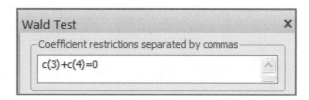

Wald Test:
Equation: COKE_PROBIT

Test Statistic	Value	df	Probability
t-statistic	-2.324653	1136	0.0203
F-statistic	5.404011	(1, 1136)	0.0203
Chi-square	5.404011	1	0.0201

For the second hypothesis, enter

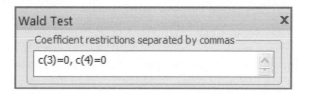

Wald Test:
Equation: COKE_PROBIT

Test Statistic	Value	df	Probability
F-statistic	9.729716	(2, 1136)	0.0001
Chi-square	19.45943	2	0.0001

16.2.2 Likelihood ratio tests

These tests are based on the difference between the log-likelihood values for the model and the model upon which the hypothesis has been imposed. The former is called the unrestricted model, and the latter the restricted model. The likelihood ratio test statistic is $LR = 2(\ln L_U - \ln L_R)$, where $\ln L_U$ is the log-likelihood from the unrestricted model and $\ln L_R$ is the log-likelihood from the restricted model. If the null hypothesis is true, the statistic has an asymptotic chi-square distribution with degrees of freedom equal to the number of hypotheses being tested. The null hypothesis is rejected if the value LR is larger than the chi-square distribution critical value.

Using the probit estimates as an example, the log-likelihood for the unrestricted model is given in the estimation results:

McFadden R-squared	0.093016	Mean dependent var	0.447368
S.D. dependent var	0.497440	S.E. of regression	0.465137
Akaike info criterion	1.254296	Sum squared resid	245.7764
Schwarz criterion	1.271976	Log likelihood	-710.9486

This value is saved as a scalar after a probit estimation and can be retrieved using **@logl**.

The restricted model, for the first hypothesis listed in the previous section, is

$$p_{COKE} = \Phi\big(\beta_1 + \beta_2 PRATIO + \beta_4 \big(DISP\_PEPSI - DISP\_COKE\big)\big)$$

Estimate this model using

> **equation coke_probit_r1.probit coke c pratio (disp_pepsi-disp_coke)**

Estimating this model by maximum likelihood probit, we obtain $\ln L_R = -713.6595$. The likelihood ratio test statistic value is then

$$LR = 2\big(\ln L_U - \ln L_R\big) = 2\big(-710.9486 - (-713.6595)\big) = 5.4218$$

This value is larger than the 0.95 percentile from the $\chi^2_{(1)}$ distribution, 3.84, and thus we reject the null hypothesis (1).

16.3 MULTINOMIAL AND CONDITIONAL LOGIT

At this time EViews does not have built-in estimation for multinomial choice models such as **Multinomial Logit** and **Conditional Logit**. However, EViews does provide sample programs for some applications. See **Help/Quick Help Reference:**

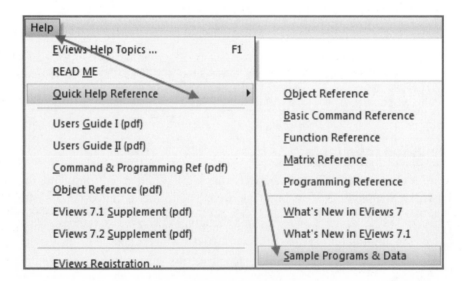

The **logl** subdirectory contains sample program files for the **logl** objects.

logl ← Sample programs for the log-likelihood object as listed in Chapter 29 of the *EViews 7 User's Guide*.

EViews documentation says about the **logl** object:

EViews contains customized procedures which help solve the majority of the estimation problems that you might encounter. On occasion, however, you may come across an estimation specification which is not included among these specialized routines. This specification may be an extension of an existing procedure, or it could be an entirely new class of problem.

Fortunately, EViews provides you with tools to estimate a wide variety of specifications through the *log likelihood (logl)* object. The logl object provides you with a general, open-ended tool for estimating a broad class of specifications by maximizing a likelihood function with respect to parameters.

The examples provided include:

- Multinomial logit (mlogit1.prg) ←
- AR(1) (ar1.prg)
- Conditional logit (clogit1.prg) ←
- Box-Cox transformation (boxcox1.prg)
- Disequilibrium switching model (diseq1.prg)
- Multiplicative heteroskedasticity (hetero1.prg)
- Probit with heteroskedasticity (hprobit1.prg)
- Probit with grouped data (gprobit1.prg)
- Nested logit (nlogit1.prg)
- Zero-altered Poisson model (zpoiss1.prg)
- Heckman sample selection model (heckman1.prg)
- Weibull hazard model (weibull1.prg)

The use of these programs requires an understanding of EViews programming. See **Help/EViews 7 Command and Programming Reference** for a complete discussion. The **logl** object is also discussed in Appendix C of this manual.

16.4 ORDERED CHOICE MODELS

In *POE4* Chapter 16.3 we considered the problem of choosing what type of college to attend after graduating from high school as an illustration of a choice among unordered alternatives. However, in this particular case there may in fact be natural ordering. We might rank the possibilities as

$$y = \begin{cases} 3 & \text{4-year college (the full college experience)} \\ 2 & \text{2-year college (a partial college experience)} \\ 1 & \text{no college} \end{cases}$$

The usual linear regression model is not appropriate for such data, because in regression we would treat the y values as having some numerical meaning when they do not. When faced with a ranking problem, we develop a "sentiment" about how we feel concerning the alternative choices; the higher the sentiment, the more likely a higher ranked alternative will be chosen. This sentiment is, of course, unobservable to the econometrician. Unobservable variables that enter decisions are called **latent variables**, and we will denote our sentiment towards the ranked alternatives by y_i^*, with the "star" reminding us that this variable is unobserved.

As a concrete example, let us think about what factors might lead a high school graduate to choose among the alternatives "no college," "2-year college" and "4-year college" as described by the ordered choices above. For simplicity, let us focus on the single explanatory variable *GRADES*. The model is then

$$y_i^* = \beta \times GRADES_i + e_i$$

This model is not a regression model because the dependent variable is unobservable. Consequently it is sometimes called an **index model**.

Because there are $M = 3$ alternatives, there are $M-1 = 2$ thresholds μ_1 and μ_2, with $\mu_1 < \mu_2$. The index model does not contain an intercept because it would be exactly collinear with the threshold variables. If sentiment towards higher education is in the lowest category, then $y_i^* \leq \mu_1$ and the alternative "no college" is chosen, if $\mu_1 < y_i^* \leq \mu_2$ then the alternative "2-year college" is chosen, and if sentiment towards higher education is in the highest category, then $y_i^* > \mu_2$ and "4-year college" is chosen. That is,

$$y = \begin{cases} 3 \text{ (4-year college)} & \text{if} \quad y_i^* > \mu_2 \\ 2 \text{ (2-year college)} & \text{if} \quad \mu_1 < y_i^* \leq \mu_2 \\ 1 \text{ (no college)} & \text{if} \quad y_i^* \leq \mu_1 \end{cases}$$

We are able to represent the probabilities of these outcomes if we assume a particular probability distribution for y_i^*, or equivalently for the random error e_i. If we assume that the errors have the standard normal distribution, $N(0,1)$, and the CDF is denoted Φ, an assumption that defines the ordered probit model, then we can calculate the following:

$$P[y=1] = \Phi(\mu_1 - \beta GRADES_i)$$

$$P[y=2] = \Phi(\mu_2 - \beta GRADES_i) - \Phi(\mu_1 - \beta GRADES_i)$$

$$P[y=3] = 1 - \Phi(\mu_2 - \beta GRADES_i)$$

In this model we wish to estimate the parameter β, and the two threshold values μ_1 and μ_2. These parameters are estimated by maximum likelihood.

In EViews open the workfile *nels_small.wf1*. Save it under the name *nels_small_oprobit.wf1*. The dependent variable of interest is *PSECHOICE* and the explanatory variable is *GRADES*. Select **Quick/Estimate Equation**. In the drop-down menu of estimation methods choose **Ordered Choice**.

```
LS  - Least Squares (NLS and ARMA)
TSLS  - Two-Stage Least Squares (TSNLS and ARMA)
GMM  - Generalized Method of Moments
LIML  - Limited Information Maximum Likelihood and K-Class
COINTREG - Cointegrating Regression
ARCH  - Autoregressive Conditional Heteroskedasticity
BINARY  - Binary Choice (Logit, Probit, Extreme Value)
ORDERED  - Ordered Choice
CENSORED  - Censored or Truncated Data (including Tobit)
```

The **Estimation settings** should be

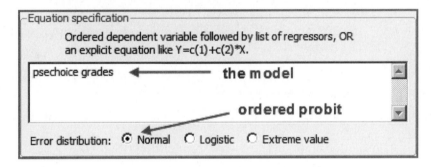

Enter the estimation equation with <u>NO INTERCEPT</u>. Make sure the **Normal** radio button is selected so that the model is **Ordered Probit**.

The results are

```
Dependent Variable: PSECHOICE
Method: ML - Ordered Probit (Quadratic hill climbing)
Sample: 1 1000
Included observations: 1000
Number of ordered indicator values: 3
Convergence achieved after 4 iterations
Covariance matrix computed using second derivatives
```

Variable	Coefficient	Std. Error	z-Statistic	Prob.
GRADES	-0.306625	0.019173	-15.99217	0.0000
Limit Points				
LIMIT_2:C(2)	-2.945600	0.146828	-20.06154	0.0000
LIMIT_3:C(3)	-2.089993	0.135768	-15.39385	0.0000

The coefficient of *GRADES* is the maximum likelihood estimate $\tilde{\beta}$. The values labeled **LIMIT_2:C(2)** and **LIMIT_3:C(3)** are the maximum likelihood estimates of μ_1 and μ_2. The notation points out that the these parameter estimates are saved into the coefficient vector as C(2) and C(3). C(1) contains $\tilde{\beta}$. Name this equation **OPROBIT**.

16.4.1 Ordered probit predictions

To predict the probabilities of various outcomes, as shown on page 609 of *POE4*, we can again use the computing abilities of EViews. In the **OPROBIT** estimation window select **View/Coefficient Diagnostics/Wald – Coefficient Restrictions**. To compute the probability that a student with *GRADES* = 2.5 will attend a 2-year college we calculate

$$\overline{P\big[y=2\,|\,GRADES=2.5\big]} = \Phi\big(\tilde{\mu}_2 - \tilde{\beta} \times 2.5\big) - \Phi\big(\tilde{\mu}_1 - \tilde{\beta} \times 2.5\big)$$

Enter into the **Wald Test** dialog box

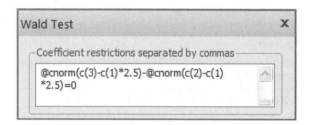

Equivalently, enter into the Command window

oprobit.wald @cnorm(c(3)-c(1)*2.5)-@cnorm(c(2)-c(1)*2.5)=0

The predicted probability is the relatively low 0.078, which makes sense because *GRADES* =2.5 is very high on the 13-point scale.

Normalized Restriction (= 0)	Value	Std. Err.
-@CNORM(-2.5*C(1) + C(2)) + @CNORM(-2.5*C(1) + C(3))	0.078182	0.011972

Delta method computed using analytic derivatives.

We can use the same general approach to compute the probabilities for each option for all the individuals in the sample. Recall that the maximum likelihood estimates of μ_1 and μ_2 are saved into the coefficient vector as C(2) and C(3). C(1) contains $\tilde{\beta}$.

```
series phat_y1 = @cnorm(c(2) - c(1)*grades)
series phat_y2 = @cnorm(c(3) - c(1)*grades) -@cnorm(c(2) - c(1)*grades)
series phat_y3 = 1 - phat_y1 - phat_y2
```

Open a **Group** showing the *GRADES*, *PSECHOICE* and the predicted probabilities.

obs	GRADES	PSECHOICE	PHAT_Y1	PHAT_Y2	PHAT_Y3
1	9.08	2	0.435872	0.320338	0.243790
2	8.31	2	0.345483	0.331063	0.323454
3	7.42	3	0.251288	0.322162	0.426550
4	7.42	3	0.251288	0.322162	0.426550
5	7.42	3	0.251288	0.322162	0.426550
6	7.46	3	0.255213	0.323042	0.421745
7	9.67	2	0.507765	0.301467	0.190767
8	11.77	1	0.746456	0.189161	0.064383
9	8.81	3	0.403526	0.325999	0.270476
10	6.44	3	0.165791	0.288302	0.545907

A standard procedure is to predict the actual choice using the highest probability. Thus we would predict that person 1 would attend no college, and the same with person 2. Both of these predictions are in fact incorrect because they choose a 2-year college. Individual 3 we predict will attend a 4-year college, and they did.

In the EViews window containing the estimated model **OPROBIT**, select **View/Dependent Variable Frequencies:**

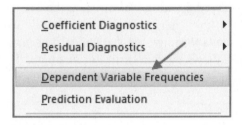

We see the choices made in the data

Dependent Variable Frequencies
Equation: OPROBIT

			Cumulative	
Dep. Value	Count	Percent	Count	Percent
1	222	22.00	222	22.20
2	251	25.00	473	47.30
3	527	52.00	1000	100.00

Now select **View/Prediction Evaluation**.

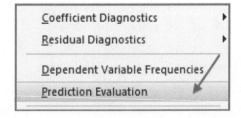

Using the "highest probability" prediction rule, EViews calculates

Prediction Evaluation for Ordered Specification
Equation: OPROBIT

		Estimated Equation			
Dep. Value	Obs.	Correct	Incorrect	% Correct	% Incorrect
1	222	116	106	52.252	47.748
2	251	0	251	0.000	100.000
3	527	471	56	89.374	10.626
Total	1000	587	413	58.700	41.300

This model, being a very simple one, has a difficult time predicting who will attend 2-year colleges, being incorrect 100% of the time.

16.4.2 Ordered probit marginal effects

The marginal effects in the ordered probit model measure the change in probability of choosing a particular category given a 1-unit change in an explanatory variable. The calculations are different by category. The calculations involve the standard normal probability density function, denoted ϕ and calculated in EViews by **@dnorm**. For example, the marginal effect of *GRADES* on the probability that a student attends no college is

$$\frac{\partial P[y=1]}{\partial GRADES} = -\phi(\mu_1 - \beta GRADES) \times \beta$$

In the **OPROBIT** window select **View/Coefficient Tests/Wald – Coefficient Restrictions**. Or in the Command window, enter

oprobit.wald (-@dnorm(c(2)-c(1)*5)*c(1))=0

Recalling that a higher value of *GRADES* indicates a poorer academic performance, we see that the probability of attending no college increases by 0.045 for a student with *GRADES* =5.

Null Hypothesis Summary:		
Normalized Restriction (= 0)	Value	Std. Err.
-C(1) * @DNORM(-5*C(1) + C(2))	0.045112	0.003058

The marginal effect calculation can be carried out for each person in the sample using the command

series mfx_y1 = - @dnorm(c(2) - c(1)*grades)*c(1)

Open a **Group** showing *PSECHOICE*, *GRADES*, and this marginal effect. Note that increasing *GRADES* by 1 point (worse grades) increases the probabilities of attending no college, but for students with better grades (*GRADES* lower) the effect is smaller.

obs	PSECHOICE	GRADES	MFX_Y1
1	2	9.08	0.120742
2	2	8.31	0.113032
3	3	7.42	0.097704
4	3	7.42	0.097704
5	3	7.42	0.097704
6	3	7.46	0.098503
7	2	9.67	0.122303
8	1	11.77	0.098165

Find the summary statistics for *MFX_Y1* for the average marginal effect and its standard deviation:

	MFX_Y1
Mean	0.075187
Std. Dev.	0.037340

16.5 MODELS FOR COUNT DATA

If Y is a Poisson random variable, then its probability function is

$$f(y) = P(Y = y) = \frac{e^{-\lambda}\lambda^{y}}{y!}, \quad y = 0,1,2,\ldots$$

The factorial (!) term $y! = y \times (y-1) \times (y-2) \times \cdots \times 1$. This probability function has one parameter, λ, which is the mean (and variance) of Y. In a regression model we try to explain the behavior of $E(Y)$ as a function of some explanatory variables. We do the same here, keeping the value of $E(Y) \geq 0$ by defining

$$E(Y) = \lambda = \exp(\beta_1 + \beta_2 x)$$

This choice defines the **Poisson regression model** for count data.

Prediction of the conditional mean of y is straightforward. Given the maximum likelihood estimates $\tilde{\beta}_1$ and $\tilde{\beta}_2$ and given a value of the explanatory variable x_0, then

$$\widehat{E(y_0)} = \tilde{\lambda}_0 = \exp(\tilde{\beta}_1 + \tilde{\beta}_2 x_0)$$

This value is an estimate of the expected number of occurrences observed, if x takes the value x_0. The probability of a particular number of occurrences can be estimated by inserting the estimated conditional mean into the probability function, as

$$\widehat{\Pr(Y = y)} = \frac{\exp(-\tilde{\lambda}_0)\tilde{\lambda}_0^{y}}{y!}, \quad y = 0,1,2,\ldots$$

The marginal effect of a change in a continuous variable x in the Poisson regression model is not simply given by the parameter, because the conditional mean model is a nonlinear function of the parameters. Using our specification that the conditional mean is given by

$$E(y_i) = \lambda_i = \exp(\beta_1 + \beta_2 x_i)$$

and using rules for derivatives of exponential functions, we obtain the marginal effect

$$\frac{\partial E(y_i)}{\partial x_i} = \lambda_i \beta_2$$

To estimate this marginal effect, replace the parameters by their maximum likelihood estimates and select a value for x. The marginal effect is different depending on the value of x chosen.

To illustrate, open the workfile *olympics.wf1* and save it as *Olympics_chap16.wf1*. Keep only the observations for the year 1988 by modifying the **Sample**.

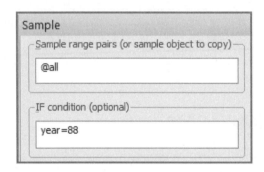

Equivalently, use the command

    smpl if year=88

16.5.1 Examine the data

Open a group consisting of *MEDALTOT*, *POP* and *GDP*. Obtain summary statistics for the individual samples:

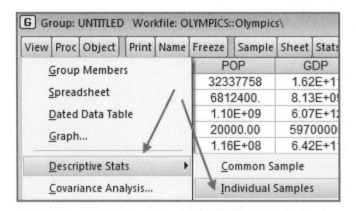

Finding the summary statistics for individual samples is important when some observations are missing, or NA.

Note that there are 152 observations for *MEDALTOT*, 176 for *POP*, and 179 for *GDP*.

	MEDALTOT	POP	GDP
Mean	4.855263	28866147	1.38E+11
Median	0.000000	5921270.	5.51E+09
Maximum	132.0000	1.10E+09	6.07E+12
Minimum	0.000000	20000.00	41700000
Std. Dev.	16.57630	1.08E+08	5.92E+11
Skewness	5.543308	8.023542	7.908054
Kurtosis	36.84647	72.99436	71.93663
Jarque-Bera	8033.810	37815.94	37309.63
Probability	0.000000	0.000000	0.000000
Sum	738.0000	5.08E+09	2.46E+13
Sum Sq. Dev.	41490.82	2.03E+18	6.23E+25
Observations	152	176	179

Obtaining summary statistics for the **Common Sample**, we find that 151 observations are available on all three variables:

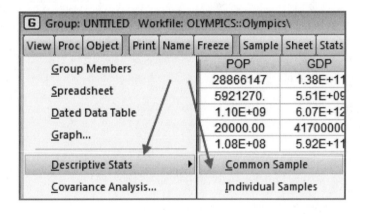

	MEDALTOT	POP	GDP
Mean	4.887417	32337758	1.62E+11
Median	0.000000	6812400.	8.13E+09
Maximum	132.0000	1.10E+09	6.07E+12
Minimum	0.000000	20000.00	59700000
Std. Dev.	16.62670	1.16E+08	6.42E+11
Skewness	5.524132	7.437776	7.253078
Kurtosis	36.60302	62.78908	60.71151
Jarque-Bera	7872.302	23883.27	22279.09
Probability	0.000000	0.000000	0.000000
Sum	738.0000	4.88E+09	2.44E+13
Sum Sq. Dev.	41467.09	2.01E+18	6.17E+25
Observations	151	151	151

16.5.2 Estimating a Poisson model

To estimate the model by maximum likelihood, choose **Quick/Estimate Equation**. In the **Estimation settings,** choose **COUNT**.

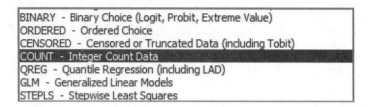

```
BINARY - Binary Choice (Logit, Probit, Extreme Value)
ORDERED - Ordered Choice
CENSORED - Censored or Truncated Data (including Tobit)
COUNT - Integer Count Data
QREG - Quantile Regression (including LAD)
GLM - Generalized Linear Models
STEPLS - Stepwise Least Squares
```

In the Equation specification, choose the radio button **Poisson** and enter the equation.

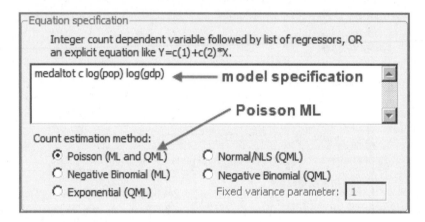

The estimated model is

Dependent Variable: MEDALTOT
Method: ML/QML - Poisson Count (Quadratic hill climbing)
Sample: 1 1610 IF YEAR=88
Included observations: 151
Convergence achieved after 6 iterations
Covariance matrix computed using second derivatives

Variable	Coefficient	Std. Error	z-Statistic	Prob.
C	-15.88746	0.511805	-31.04203	0.0000
LOG(POP)	0.180038	0.032280	5.577348	0.0000
LOG(GDP)	0.576603	0.024722	23.32376	0.0000

Note that the number of observations used in the estimation is only 151, which is the number of observations common to all variables. Save these estimation results as an object named **POISSON_REG**.

16.5.3 Predicting with a Poisson model

In the estimation window click **Forecast**. Choose the **Series to forecast** as **Expected dependent var.** and assign a name:

Recall that the expected value of the dependent variable, in a simple model, is given by

$$E(y_i) = \lambda_i = \exp(\beta_1 + \beta_2 x_i)$$

The forecast can be replicated using the following command:

series lam = exp(c(1) + c(2)*log(pop) + c(3)*log(gdp))

obs	POP	GDP	MEDALTOT	MEDALTOTF	LAM
5	3138000.	2.80E+09	NA	0.521277	0.521277
20	7004000.	1.17E+10	NA	1.373831	1.373831
69	NA	1.61E+08	0.000000	NA	NA
89	5158420.	1.06E+09	NA	0.325605	0.325605
91	8115690.	2.09E+09	NA	0.522552	0.522552
99	327970.0	3.33E+08	NA	0.101693	0.101693

We have shown a few values.

To compute the predicted mean for specific values of the explanatory variables, we again use the trick of applying the "Wald test." Select **View/Coefficient Tests/Wald – Coefficient Restrictions**. We must choose some values for *POP* and *GDP* at which to evaluate the prediction. Enter the **median values from the individual samples** for *POP* and *GDP*. The command is

poisson_reg.wald exp(c(1) + c(2)*log(5921270) + c(3)*log(5.51e9))=0

The result shows that for these population and *GDP* values we predict that 0.8634 medals will be won.

Null Hypothesis: EXP(C(1) + C(2)*LOG(5921270) + C(3) *LOG(5.51E9))=0 Null Hypothesis Summary:		
Normalized Restriction (= 0)	Value	Std. Err.
EXP(C(1) + 22.429830460111234*C(3) + C(2)*LOG(5921270))	0.863443	0.075976

Delta method computed using analytic derivatives.

16.5.4 Poisson model marginal effects

As shown in *POE4* equation (16.29), the marginal effects in the simple Poisson model

$$E(y_i) = \lambda_i = \exp(\beta_1 + \beta_2 x_i)$$

are

$$\frac{\partial E(y_i)}{\partial x_i} = \exp(\beta_1 + \beta_2 x_i)\beta_2 = \lambda_i \beta_2$$

This marginal effect is correct if the values of the explanatory variable x are not transformed. In the Olympics medal example, the explanatory variables are in logarithms, so the model is

$$E(y_i) = \lambda_i = \exp(\beta_1 + \beta_2 \ln(x_i))$$

and the marginal effect is, using the chain rule of differentiation,

$$\frac{\partial E(y_i)}{\partial x_i} = \exp(\beta_1 + \beta_2 \ln(x_i))\frac{\beta_2}{x_i} = \lambda_i \frac{\beta_2}{x_i}$$

While this does not necessarily look very pretty, it has a rather nice interpretation. Rearrange it as

$$\frac{\partial E(y_i)}{100(\partial x_i / x_i)} = \exp(\beta_1 + \beta_2 \ln(x_i))\frac{\beta_2}{100} = \lambda_i \frac{\beta_2}{100}$$

Are you still not finding this attractive? This quantity can be called a **semi-elasticity**, because it expresses the change in $E(y)$ given a 1% change in x. Recalling that $E(y_i) = \lambda_i$, we can make one further enhancement that will leave you speechless with joy. Divide both sides by $E(y)$ to obtain

$$\frac{\partial E(y_i)/E(y_i)}{(\partial x_i / x_i)} = \beta_2 = \varepsilon$$

The parameter β_2 is the **elasticity** of the output y with respect to x. A 1% change in x is estimated to change $E(y)$ by $\beta_2 \%$.

In the Olympics example, based on the estimation results, we conclude that a 1% increase in population increases the expected medal count by 0.18%, and a 1% increase in GDP increases the expected medal count by 0.5766%.

16.6 LIMITED DEPENDENT VARIABLES

The idea of censored data is well illustrated by the Mroz data on labor force participation of married women. Open the workfile *mroz.wf1*. Save the workfile as *mroz_tobit.wf1* so as to keep the original file intact.

A **Histogram** of the variable *HOURS* shows the problem with the full sample. There are 753 observations on the wages of married women, but 325 of these women did not engage in market work and thus their *HOURS* = 0, leaving 428 observations with positive *HOURS*.

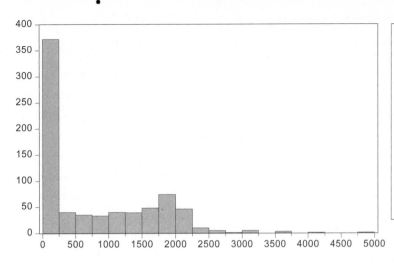

16.6.1 Least squares estimation

We are interested in the equation

$$HOURS = \beta_1 + \beta_2 EDUC + \beta_3 EXPER + \beta_4 AGE + \beta_4 KIDSL6 + e$$

The question is, "How shall we treat the observations with $HOURS = 0$"?

A first solution is to apply least squares to all the observations. Select **Quick/Estimate Equation** and fill in the **Equation Estimation** dialog box, or enter the command

equation hours_all.ls hours c educ exper age kidsl6

The estimation results are:

Dependent Variable: HOURS
Method: Least Squares
Sample: 1 753
Included observations: 753

	Coefficient	Std. Error	t-Statistic	Prob.
C	1335.306	235.6487	5.666511	0.0000
EDUC	27.08568	12.23989	2.212902	0.0272
EXPER	48.03981	3.641804	13.19121	0.0000
AGE	-31.30782	3.960990	-7.904040	0.0000
KIDSL6	-447.8547	58.41252	-7.667100	0.0000

Repeat the estimation using only those women who "participated in the labor force." Those women who worked are indicated by a dummy variable *LFP* that is 1 for working women but zero otherwise.

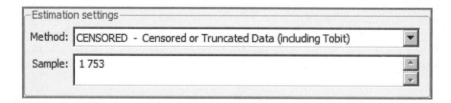

The estimation results are shown below. Note that the included observations are 428. The estimation results now show the effect of education (*EDUC*) to have a negative, but insignificant, effect on *HOURS*. In the estimation using all the observations *EDUC* had a positive and significant effect on *HOURS*.

Dependent Variable: HOURS
Method: Least Squares
Sample: 1 753 IF LFP = 1
Included observations: 428

	Coefficient	Std. Error	t-Statistic	Prob.
C	1829.746	292.5356	6.254781	0.0000
EDUC	-16.46211	15.58083	-1.056562	0.2913
EXPER	33.93637	5.009185	6.774829	0.0000
AGE	-17.10821	5.457674	-3.134708	0.0018
KIDSL6	-305.3090	96.44904	-3.165495	0.0017

The least squares estimator is biased and inconsistent for models using censored data.

16.6.2 Tobit estimation and interpretation

An appropriate estimation procedure is **Tobit**, which uses maximum likelihood principles. Select **Quick/Estimate Equation**. The **Estimation settings** show the method to include **Tobit**:

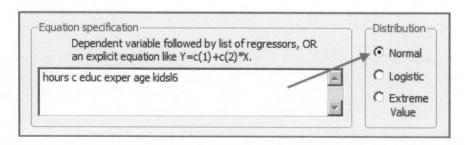

In the **Equation Estimation** window fill in the options as shown below. Tobit estimation is predicated upon the regression errors being **Normal**, so tick that radio button.

In our cases the observations that are "censored" take the actual value 0, and the dependent variable is said to be **Left censored** because 0 is a minimum value and all relevant values of *HOURS* are positive.

```
┌─Dependent variable censoring points──────────────────────────────┐
│         Enter a number, a series, a series      Left & right points entered as: │
│         expression, or blank for no censoring    ⊙ Actual censoring value      │
│   Left: │0 ◄─────────────────────┘          ○ Zero/one censoring indicator   │
│                                                                    │
│   Right:│                              │        □ Truncated sample             │
└──────────────────────────────────────────────────────────────────┘
```

Dependent Variable: HOURS
Method: ML - Censored Normal (TOBIT) (Quadratic hill climbing)
Sample: 1 753
Included observations: 753
Left censoring (value) at zero
Convergence achieved after 5 iterations
Covariance matrix computed using second derivatives

Variable	Coefficient	Std. Error	z-Statistic	Prob.
C	1349.876	386.2991	3.494381	0.0005
EDUC	73.29099	20.47459	3.579607	0.0003
EXPER	80.53527	6.287808	12.80816	0.0000
AGE	-60.76780	6.888193	-8.822022	0.0000
KIDSL6	-918.9181	111.6607	-8.229558	0.0000

Error Distribution				
SCALE:C(6)	1133.697	42.06239	26.95275	0.0000

Mean dependent var	740.5764	S.D. dependent var	871.3142
S.E. of regression	754.0561	Akaike info criterion	10.18099
Sum squared resid	4.25E+08	Schwarz criterion	10.21784
Log likelihood	-3827.143	Hannan-Quinn criter.	10.19519
Avg. log likelihood	-5.082528		

Left censored obs	325	Right censored obs	0
Uncensored obs	428	Total obs	753

The estimation command is

equation tobit.censored(d=n) hours c educ exper age kidsl6

The estimation output shows the usual **Coefficient** and **Std. Error** columns. Instead of a **t-Statistic** EViews reports a **z-Statistic** because the standard errors are only valid in large samples, making the test statistic only valid in large samples, and in large samples a *t*-statistic converges to the standard normal distribution. The *p*-value **Prob.** is based on the standard normal distribution.

The parameter called **SCALE:C(6)** is the estimate of σ, the square root of the error variance. This value is an important ingredient in Tobit model interpretation. As noted in *POE*, equation (16.35), the marginal effect of an explanatory variable in a simple model, is

$$\frac{\partial E(y \mid x)}{\partial x} = \beta_2 \Phi\left(\frac{\beta_1 + \beta_2 x}{\sigma}\right)$$

where as usual Φ is the CDF of a standard normal variable. To evaluate the marginal effect of *EDUC* on *HOURS*, given that *HOURS* > 0, we can use **Wald** test dialog box. Select **View/Coefficient Diagnostics/Wald – Coefficient Restrictions**. Enter the expression for the marginal effect of *EDUC* at the sample means, as shown on page 620 of *POE4*. The command is

tobit.wald c(2)*@cnorm((c(1) +c(2)*12.29+c(3)*10.63+c(4)*42.54+c(5))/c(6))=0

The obtained value is slightly different from the value in the text. Slight differences in results are inevitable when carrying out complicated nonlinear estimations and calculations. The maximum likelihood routines are all slightly different and they stop when "convergence" is achieved. These stopping rules are different from one software package to another.

Null Hypothesis: C(2)*@CNORM((C(1) +C(2)*12.29+C(3)
    *10.63+C(4)*42.54+C(5))/C(6))=0
Null Hypothesis Summary:

Normalized Restriction (= 0)	Value	Std. Err.
C(2) * @CNORM((C(1) + 12.29*C(2) + 10.63*C(3) + 42.54*C(4) + C(5)) / C(6))	26.60555	7.548908

Delta method computed using analytic derivatives.

16.6.3 The Heckit selection bias model

If you consult an econometrician concerning an estimation problem, the first question you will usually hear is, "How were the data obtained?" If the data are obtained by random sampling, then classic regression methods, such as least squares, work well. However, if the data are obtained by a sampling procedure that is not random, then standard procedures do not work well. Economists regularly face such data problems. A famous illustration comes from labor economics. If we wish to study the determinants of the wages of married women we face a **sample selection** problem. If we collect data on married women and ask them what wage rate they earn, many will respond that the question is not relevant since they are homemakers. We only observe data on market wages when the woman chooses to enter the workforce. One strategy is to ignore the women who are homemakers, omit them from the sample, then use least squares to estimate a wage equation for those who work. This strategy fails, the reason for the failure being that our sample is not a random sample. The data we observe are "selected" by a systematic process for which we do not account.

A solution to this problem is a technique called **Heckit**, named after its developer, Nobel Prize-winning econometrician James Heckman. This simple procedure uses two estimation steps. In the context of the problem of estimating the wage equation for married women, a probit model is first estimated explaining why a woman is in the labor force or not. In the second stage, a least squares regression is estimated relating the wage of a working woman to education, experience, etc., and a variable called the "Inverse Mills Ratio," or IMR. The IMR is created from the first-step probit estimation, and takes into account the fact that the observed sample of working women is not random.

The econometric model describing the situation is composed of two equations. The first, is the **selection equation** that determines whether the variable of interest is observed. The sample consists of N observations; however, the variable of interest is observed only for $n < N$ of these. The selection equation is expressed in terms of a latent variable z_i^* that depends on one or more explanatory variables w_i and is given by

$$z_i^* = \gamma_1 + \gamma_2 w_i + u_i \quad i = 1, \ldots, N$$

For simplicity we will include only one explanatory variable in the selection equation. The latent variable is not observed, but we do observe the binary variable

$$z_i = \begin{cases} 1 & z_i^* > 0 \\ 0 & \text{otherwise} \end{cases}$$

The second equation is the linear model of interest. It is

$$y_i = \beta_1 + \beta_2 x_i + e_i \quad i = 1, \ldots, n \quad N > n$$

A **selectivity problem** arises when y_i is observed only when $z_i = 1$, and if the errors of the two equations are correlated. In such a situation the usual least squares estimators of β_1 and β_2 are biased and inconsistent.

Consistent estimators are based on the conditional regression function

$$E\left[y_i \mid z_i^* > 0 \right] = \beta_1 + \beta_2 x_i + \beta_\lambda \lambda_i \quad i = 1, \ldots, n$$

where the additional variable λ_i is the "Inverse Mills Ratio." It is equal to

$$\lambda_i = \frac{\phi\left(\gamma_1 + \gamma_2 w_i \right)}{\Phi\left(\gamma_1 + \gamma_2 w_i \right)}$$

where, as usual, $\phi(\cdot)$ denotes the standard normal probability density function, and $\Phi(\cdot)$ denotes the cumulative distribution function for a standard normal random variable. While the value of λ_i is not known, the parameters γ_1 and γ_2 can be estimated using a probit model, based on the observed binary outcome z_i. Then the estimated IMR,

$$\tilde{\lambda}_i = \frac{\phi\left(\tilde{\gamma}_1 + \tilde{\gamma}_2 w_i \right)}{\Phi\left(\tilde{\gamma}_1 + \tilde{\gamma}_2 w_i \right)}$$

is inserted into the regression equation as an extra explanatory variable, yielding the estimating equation

$$y_i = \beta_1 + \beta_2 x_i + \beta_\lambda \tilde{\lambda}_i + v_i \quad i = 1, \dots, n$$

First, let us estimate a simple wage equation, explaining $\ln(WAGE)$ as a function of the woman's education, *EDUC*, and years of market work experience (*EXPER*), and using the 428 women who have positive wages. Select **Quick/Estimate Equation**. Under Estimation settings, set

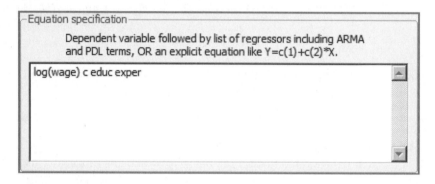

The equation specification is

Dependent variable followed by list of regressors including ARMA and PDL terms, OR an explicit equation like Y=c(1)+c(2)*X.

```
log(wage) c educ exper
```

Dependent Variable: LOG(WAGE)
Method: Least Squares
Sample: 1 753 IF WAGE>0
Included observations: 428

	Coefficient	Std. Error	t-Statistic	Prob.
C	-0.400174	0.190368	-2.102107	0.0361
EDUC	0.109489	0.014167	7.728334	0.0000
EXPER	0.015674	0.004019	3.899798	0.0001

Heckit estimation begins with a probit model estimation of the "participation equation," in which *LFP* is taken to be a function of *AGE*, *EDUC*, a dummy variable for whether or not the woman has children (*KIDS*), and her marginal tax rate *MTR*. Create the dummy variable *KIDS* using

series kids = (kidsl6 + kids618 > 0)

Estimate the probit equation (see Section 16.1 of this manual)

equation working.binary(d=n) lfp c age educ kids mtr

Using all the sample data, we obtain

Dependent Variable: LFP
Method: ML - Binary Probit
Sample: 1 753
Included observations: 753

	Coefficient	Std. Error	z-Statistic	Prob.
C	1.192296	0.720544	1.654717	0.0980
AGE	-0.020616	0.007045	-2.926390	0.0034
EDUC	0.083775	0.023205	3.610225	0.0003
KIDS	-0.313885	0.123711	-2.537248	0.0112
MTR	-1.393853	0.616575	-2.260638	0.0238

The inverse Mills ratio *IMR* requires computation of the fitted **index model**. In the probit estimation window, select **Forecast**. In the **Forecast** dialog box choose the radio button for **Index** and give this variable a name.

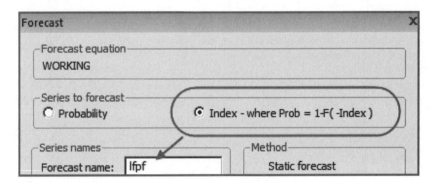

The inverse Mills ratio is then calculated using the EViews functions for the standard normal pdf **@dnorm** and the standard normal CDF **@cnorm**:

series imr = @dnorm(lfpf)/@cnorm(lfpf)

Include *IMR* in the wage equation as an explanatory variable, using only those women who were in the labor force and had positive wages. In the **Estimation settings** choose

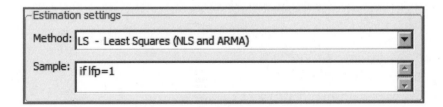

In the **Equation specification** use

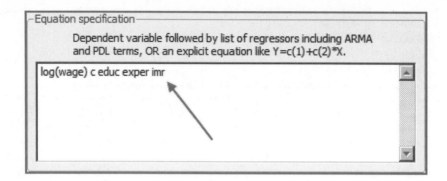

This two-step estimation process is a consistent estimator, but the standard errors **Std. Error** do not account for the fact the *IMR* is in fact estimated. However, if the errors are homoskedastic, we <u>can</u> carry out a test of the significance of the *IMR* variable based on the *t*-statistic that is reported by EViews. This is because under the null hypothesis that there is <u>no selection bias</u> the coefficient of *IMR* is zero, and thus under the null hypothesis the usual *t*-test is valid. Here we reject the null hypothesis of no selection bias and conclude that using the two-step Heckit estimation process is needed:

Dependent Variable: LOG(WAGE)
Method: Least Squares
Sample: 1 753 IF LFP=1
Included observations: 428

Variable	Coefficient	Std. Error	t-Statistic	Prob.
C	0.810542	0.494472	1.639206	0.1019
EDUC	0.058458	0.023849	2.451122	0.0146
EXPER	0.016320	0.003998	4.081732	0.0001
IMR	-0.866439	0.326986	-2.649777	0.0084

If the regression errors may be heteroskedastic, as they might be for this microeconomic example, a robust standard error can be used. On the **Options** tab of the **Equation Estimation** dialog box, select **White** as the **Coefficient covariance matrix**.

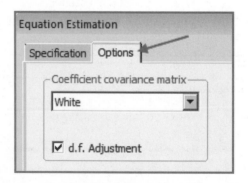

The resulting *t*-statistic is still significant at the .05 level.

Dependent Variable: LOG(WAGE)
Method: Least Squares
Sample: 1 753 IF LFP=1
Included observations: 428
White heteroskedasticity-consistent standard errors & covariance

Variable	Coefficient	Std. Error	t-Statistic	Prob.
C	0.810542	0.498852	1.624816	0.1049
EDUC	0.058458	0.024143	2.421369	0.0159
EXPER	0.016320	0.004101	3.979199	0.0001
IMR	-0.866439	0.340561	-2.544154	0.0113

Correct standard errors for the two-step estimation procedure are difficult to obtain without specially designed software. Maximum likelihood estimation of the Heckit model will provide the correct standard errors. EViews does not have an automatic command for maximum likelihood estimation of the Heckit model, but it does provide an example program of how to use the **logl** object to do so.

- Multinomial logit (mlogit1.prg)
- AR(1) (ar1.prg)
- Conditional logit (clogit1.prg)
- Box-Cox transformation (boxcox1.prg)
- Disequilibrium switching model (diseq1.prg)
- Multiplicative heteroskedasticity (hetero1.prg)
- Probit with heteroskedasticity (hprobit1.prg)
- Probit with grouped data (gprobit1.prg)
- Nested logit (nlogit1.prg)
- Zero-altered Poisson model (zpoiss1.prg)
- Heckman sample selection model (heckman1.prg) ←
- Weibull hazard model (weibull1.prg)

Keywords

@cnorm	individual samples	ordered choice models
@dnorm	inverse Mills ratio	ordered probit
binary choice models	latent variables	Poisson regression
censored data	limit values	prediction evaluation
common sample	linear probability model	probability forecast
count data models	logit	probit
elasticity	LR statistic	sample
EViews size limitations	marginal effect	semi-elasticity
Heckit	maximum likelihood	threshold values
IMR	McFadden R-squared	Tobit
index model	NA	

APPENDIX A

Review of Math Essentials

CHAPTER OUTLINE
A.1 Mathematical Operations
A.2 Logarithms and Exponentials

A.3 Graphing Functions
KEYWORDS

A.1 MATHEMATICAL OPERATIONS

EViews has many mathematical functions. Click on **Help/Help Reference/Function Reference**. Choose **Basic Mathematical Functions**. Some of these are:

Name	Function
@abs(x), abs(x)	*absolute value*
@ceiling(x)	*smallest integer not less than*
@exp(x), exp(x)	*exponential*
@fact(x)	*factorial*
@floor(x)	*largest integer not greater than*
@inv(x)	*reciprocal*
@log(x), log(x)	*natural logarithm*
@round(x)	*round to the nearest integer*
@sqrt(x), sqr(x)	*square root*

Some of these functions require the "**@**" sign in front, and some do not. Also recall the basic mathematical operators:

Expression	Operator	Description
+	*add*	*x+y adds the contents of X and Y.*
-	*subtract*	*x-y subtracts the contents of Y from X.*
*****	*multiply*	*x*y multiplies the contents of X by Y.*
/	*divide*	*x/y divides the contents of X by Y.*
^	*raise to the power*	*x^y raises X to the power of Y.*

To illustrate these operations, create a workfile with 101 undated observations. Name it *appendix_a.wf1*. Select **File/New/Workfile** from the EViews menu, or use the key stroke combination **Ctrl+N**.

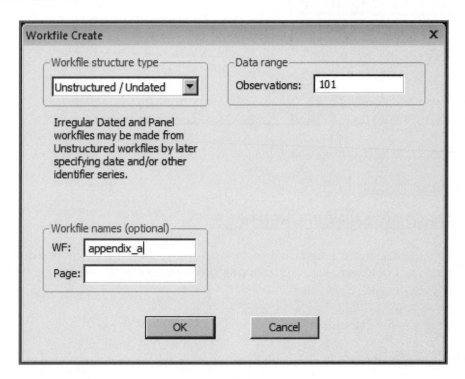

Create a scalar $a = 3$, and carry out some basic operations on this scalar by entering the following lines in the command window:

```
scalar a = 3
scalar acube = a^3
scalar roota = sqr(a)
scalar lna = log(a)
scalar expa = exp(a)
```

All of the results are scalars because we have defined **a** to be a scalar and declared the outcome a scalar as well. EViews uses **Scientific Notation** when reporting extremely large numbers. On the command line enter

```
scalar b = 510000/.00000034
```

EViews reports the value of **B** as

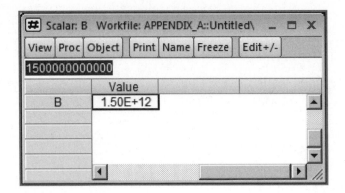

This means $\mathbf{B} = 1.5 \times 10^{12}$ or 1500000000000.

A.2 LOGARITHMS AND EXPONENTIALS

For practice purposes, create a variable X that ranges from −5 to +5 in increments of 0.1. To do this, we create a **Trend** variable. The command **@trend** creates a variable starting at 0 and increasing by one for each observation:

> **series x = -5 + @trend/10**

Alternatively, we could have clicked on the **Genr** tab on the EViews menubar and entered

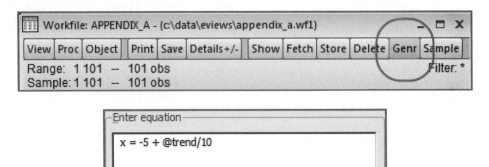

Now we can create new variables using the mathematical functions. Note that since we are using the command **series** we are in fact creating new series containing 101 observations.

> **series absx = @abs(x)**
> **series expx = @exp(x)**

Click on each series to open it. For example, the first few values of *EXPX* are

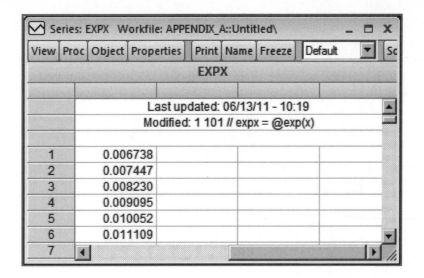

In this spreadsheet window click on **View/Graph**. Select the default **Line & Symbol** plot:

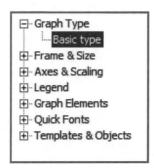

The resulting graph is

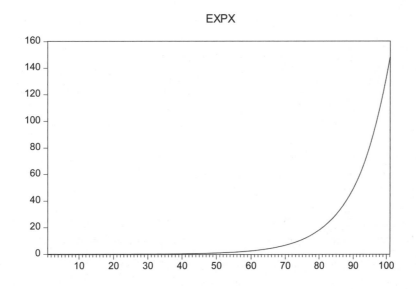

On the horizontal axis is the observation number. Observation 51 corresponds to $X = 0$ and **exp(0) = 1**. As X increases in value the value of **exp(x)** becomes very large, and thus on the graph the values below observation 51, which are less than one, actually do not show up.

Logarithms are only defined for positive numbers. Thus to illustrate its use we first change the sample to include only positive values of X. Click the **Sample** button on the EViews menubar:

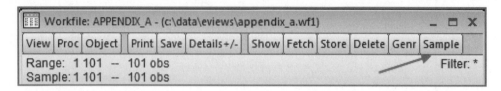

In the dialog box that appears, add an **IF condition** that ensures that $X > 0$. Click **OK**. All operations now will only take place on the positive values of X. This is important not only for the logarithm, but also for square roots.

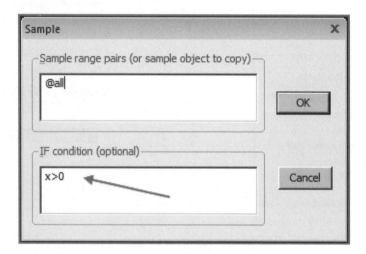

Note that in the EViews workfile the header now indicates that the sample has a condition.

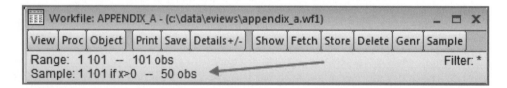

Now we may safely generate the natural logarithms of X:

series lnx = log(x)

Examine the values of *LNX*. You will find "NA" for the nonpositive values of X. If you graph *LNX* it will not show values for observations 51 (where $X = 0$) and below.

A.3 GRAPHING FUNCTIONS

Let us use the *X* variable we created in Section A.2 (**series x = -5 + @trend/10**) to explore the shapes of some functional forms. First, change the sample back to the full 101 observations, not just the positive values. Click on **Sample** in the main menubar and remove the condition that *X* > 0. It should look like

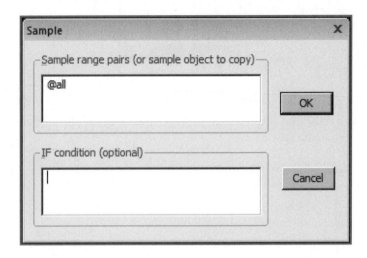

Then click **OK**.

We will create the values of the quadratic function $ysq = 1 + 2x + x^2$ by typing into the Command window

series ysq = 1 + 2*x + x^2

Plot the resulting series against *X* by selecting **Quick/Graph** from the EViews menu.

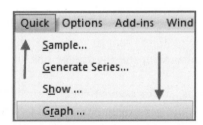

In the dialog box enter the *x*-axis variable first:

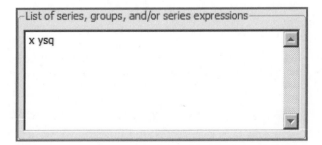

In the **Graph Options** dialog box select **XY Line,** then **OK**.

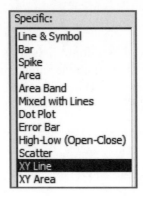

The resulting graph shows the parabolic shape that we expected, with *YSQ* taking the value 1 when *X* = 0.

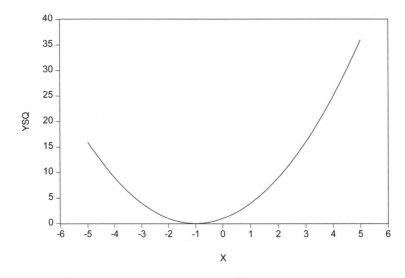

As you are examining the various functions described in Appendix A of *POE4*, there is no better way to grasp their nature than by plotting them for some specific values. Using EViews makes it easy. Because you are less familiar with the **log-linear** and **log-log** functions, let us plot some examples.

We will be working with logs, so for convenience let us again work with sample values for which *X* > 0. Click on **Sample** on the main menubar, and add the **IF** condition *X* > 0.

A **log-log** function is

$$\ln(y) = \beta_1 + \beta_2 \ln(x)$$

which can be solved for *y* as

$$y = \exp\left[\beta_1 + \beta_2 \ln(x)\right]$$

We must use this expression because we want to plot *y* values against *x* values. As an illustration, let us select the values $\beta_1 = 1$ and $\beta_2 = -.5$, so that the function we wish to graph is

$$y = \exp\left[1 - .5\ln(x)\right]$$

The negative value of β_2 will create an inverse relationship. This is a **constant elasticity** relationship and the elasticity is $\beta_2 = -.5$. That is, a 1% increase in X leads to a ½% reduction in Y. Into the EViews command line, type

series lny2 = exp(1 - .5*log(x))

Using **Quick/Graph/XY Line** plot the values *LNY2* against *X*, to produce

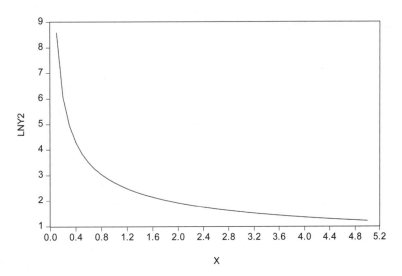

The **log-linear** function is

$$\ln(y) = \beta_1 + \beta_2 x$$

To plot this function we make use of the fact that taking antilogarithms we can express the dependent variable as

$$y = \exp(\beta_1 + \beta_2 x)$$

For illustration let us plot $y = \exp(1 + 1x)$. Into the EViews command line type:

series lny = exp(1 + 1* x)

Using **Quick/Graph/XY Line** plot the values *LNY* against *X*, to produce

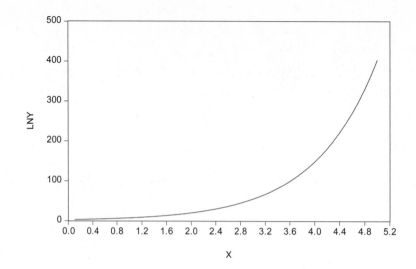

Keywords

@abs	exponential	scientific notation
@exp	logarithm	sqr
@trend	sample: if condition	XY line graph
exp		

APPENDIX B

Statistical Distribution Functions

CHAPTER OUTLINE

EViews has several types of functions for working with probability distributions. These are:

Function Type	Beginning of Name
Cumulative distribution (CDF)	**@c**
Density or probability	**@d**
Quantile (inverse CDF)	**@q**
Random number generator	**@r**

Of these four functions we are at the moment interested in the **Cumulative distribution (CDF)** and the **Quantile (inverse CDF)**.

If $f(x)$ is some probability density function, then its cumulative distribution function is

$$F(x) = P[X \leq x]$$

That is, **the CDF gives the probability that the random variable X takes a value less than, or equal to, the specified value, x.**

The quantile function works just the reverse. You provide a probability, say .10, and **the quantile function tells you the value of x such that** $F(x) = .10$. This answer is exact for continuous distributions. For discrete random variables there may not be an exact x value corresponding to any probability value that you select. The EViews help file says, "*The quantile functions will return the smallest value where the CDF evaluated at the value equals or exceeds the probability of interest.*"

The list of probability distributions that EViews can work with is extensive. Click **Help/Quick Help Reference/Function Reference**.

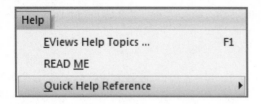

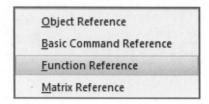

The links to different types of functions are listed. Select **Statistical distribution functions**.

Operator and Function Reference

This material is divided into several topics:

- Operators.
- Basic mathematical functions.
- Time series functions.
- Financial functions.
- Descriptive statistics.
- Cumulative statistics functions.
- Moving statistics functions.
- Group row functions.
- By-group statistics.
- Additional and special functions.
- Trigonometric functions.
- Statistical distribution functions.

B.1 CUMULATIVE NORMAL PROBABILITIES

The EViews function **@cnorm(z)** returns the cumulative probability that a standard normal random variable falls to the left of the given value **z**, as shown below.

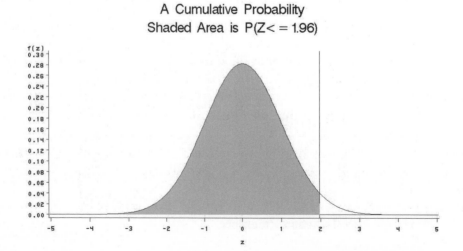

A Cumulative Probability
Shaded Area is P(Z< = 1.96)

We will illustrate how to use EViews to compute cumulative probabilities However, as always, you must begin by creating a workfile:

- Click on **File/New/Workfile** (or **Ctrl + N**)
- Click on **Unstructured/Undated**. Enter some number for observations, say 101, though it doesn't matter here since we will not be entering data. The reason for the odd choice will become clear later. Click **OK**.

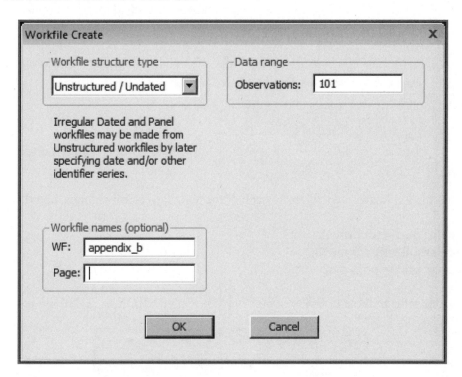

Entering the **Name** for the workfile is optional, but doing it now, before we forget, saves time later. Name this workfile *appendix_b.wf1*.

To compute the probability that a standard normal random variable takes a value less than or equal to 1.96, type into the Command window

      scalar p1 = @cnorm(1.96)

The scalar **P1** is added to the workfile. Scalars are indicted by # symbols. Highlight **P1** and double-click. The value of the scalar appears in a spreadsheet:

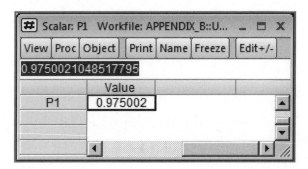

That is, the probability that a standard normal random variable falls to the left of, or equals, 1.96 is .975. For a continuous random variable, the probability of any one point is zero. We can also say that the probability that the standard normal random variable falls to the right of 1.96 is .025.

These cumulative probabilities for the standard normal distribution are provided in Table 1 at the back of *POE4*. This cumulative probability is used so often it is given its own symbol, Φ. Thus we can write

$$P[Z \leq 1.96] = \Phi(1.96) = .9750$$

Using the CDF, we can compute any probability we might be given. For example, suppose $X \sim N(3,9)$, that is, X is normally distributed with mean $\mu = 3$ and variance $\sigma^2 = 9$. We can compute the probability that X falls in the interval [4,6] as

$$P[4 \leq X \leq 6] = P\left[\frac{4-\mu}{\sigma} \leq \frac{X-\mu}{\sigma} \leq \frac{6-\mu}{\sigma}\right] = P[.33 \leq Z \leq 1] = \Phi(1) - \Phi(.33)$$

To compute this in EViews we will create each of the cumulative probabilities, and then subtract:

```
scalar phi1=@cnorm(1)
scalar phi2=@cnorm(.33)
scalar prob = phi1-phi2
```

The calculated value of the probability, which we have called **PROB,** is .2120.

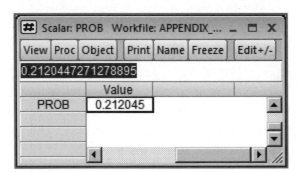

> **Remark**: When writing EViews commands, try to make the names somewhat relevant to the algebraic form or the context of the problem. This will help you recall what you were doing when looking back at it later.

B.2 USING VECTORS

The approach above obviously works, but if you wish to have the results in a convenient form for a paper, using **coefficient vectors** is an option. Click on **Object/New Object** on the EViews menubar:

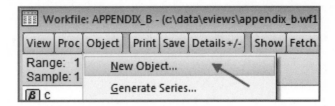

Click on **Matrix-Vector-Coef**, giving the new object the name **P**:

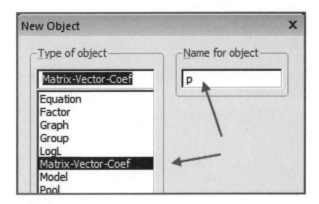

Make this object a vector, which is just a single column of numbers, with three rows. Click **OK**.

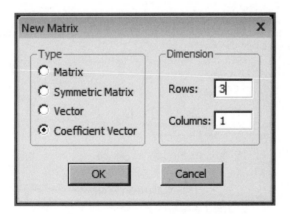

Instead of pointing and clicking, you can simply type **coef(3) p** into the Command window and press **Enter**.

Type into the Command window the following series of statements:

p(1) =(6-3)/3
p(2)=(4-3)/3
p(3)=@cnorm(p(1))-@cnorm(p(2))

With each command you will see an entry appear in the vector **P**, with the final entry being the probability you seek.

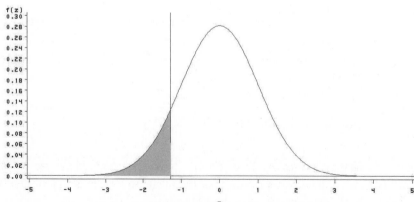

The advantage of this approach is that now we can **Freeze** this screen, then **Name** it (**P_TABLE**), and it will appear in our workfile. Furthermore, the contents of this table can be copied (highlight, then **Ctrl+C**) and pasted (**Ctrl+V**) into a document:

R1	1.000000
R2	0.333333
R3	0.210786

The result is a table that can be formatted, edited, etc.

B.3 COMPUTING NORMAL DISTRIBUTION PERCENTILES

The function **@qnorm(p)** returns the percentile value **z** from a standard normal probability density, such that

$$P[Z \leq z] = \Phi(z) = p$$

For example, a probability of .10 falls to the **left** of -1.28.

The 10th percentile
Shaded Area is $P(Z < = -1.28) = .10$

Percentiles that identify regions containing a certain probability are often called **critical values**. To illustrate, type in the command

scalar z10 = @qnorm(.10)

That is, we are asking what is the value z from a standard normal distribution such that

$$P[Z \le z] = \Phi(z) = .10$$

The value of the scalar **Z10** is

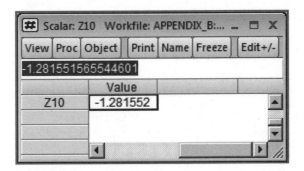

EViews will compute similar probabilities for many types of random variables. Click on **Help/Function Reference**. Scroll down to the section entitled *Statistical Distribution Functions*. There you will find a long list of probability distributions for which EViews can compute cumulative probabilities and percentiles. You have heard of some, like the **Binomial**. Many others will not be familiar. We use several of these distributions throughout *POE4*, such as the **Chi-square**, the **F-distribution**, and the **Student's *t*-distribution**.

B.4 PLOTTING SOME NORMAL DISTRIBUTIONS

It is useful to plot some normal distributions to see their shapes and locations. Recall that we set the sample size of the workfile to 101. Create a variable X that covers the $[-5, 5]$ interval in increments of 1/10. Type into the Command window (or use the **Genr** button):

series x = -5 + @trend/10

Double-click on the generated series to verify.

The formula for the normal probability density function is given in Equation (P.25) in the Probability Primer of *POE4*. It is

$$f(x) = \frac{1}{\sqrt{2\pi\sigma^2}} \exp\left[\frac{-(x-\mu)^2}{2\sigma^2}\right]$$

where μ is the mean of the random variable and σ^2 is its variance. We are simply going to type this formula into EViews and substitute values for the mean and variance. First we plot the $N(0,1)$ density. On the Command window type, pressing **Enter** after each line,

```
scalar mu0 = 0
scalar var1 = 1
series n01 = exp( -(x-mu0)^2/(2*var1) )/sqr(2*3.14159*var1)
```

Using **Quick/Graph/XY line**, we can plot *N01* against *X*. Create the density functions of a N(0,2) and a N(2,1). To do so we can simply edit the items on the Command window and press **Enter**. The commands are

```
scalar mu2 = 2
scalar var2 = 2
series n02 = exp( -(x-mu0)^2/(2*var2) )/sqr(2*3.14159*var2)
series n21 = exp( -(x-mu2)^2/(2*var1) )/sqr(2*3.14159*var1)
```

Using **Quick/Graph**, we can plot all the graphs in the same picture. In the dialog box enter

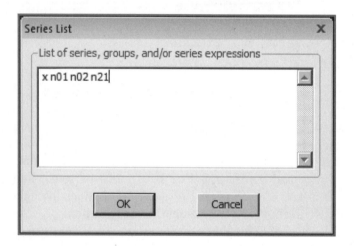

In the **Graph Options** dialog box choose

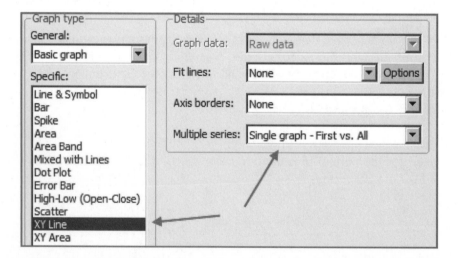

This will cause the three densities to be plotted against *X* in color, which looks good on the screen, and printed in a color document. In a black and white document the lines will all look the same. However, the smart programmers at EViews have figured this out. Click inside the figure

(the border will darken) and enter **Ctrl+C** to copy. The default is to copy the graph in color. **Remove** the tick in the box and click **OK**.

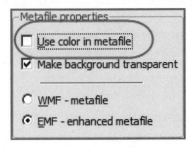

Go to an open document and enter **Ctrl+V** to paste. The figure will be

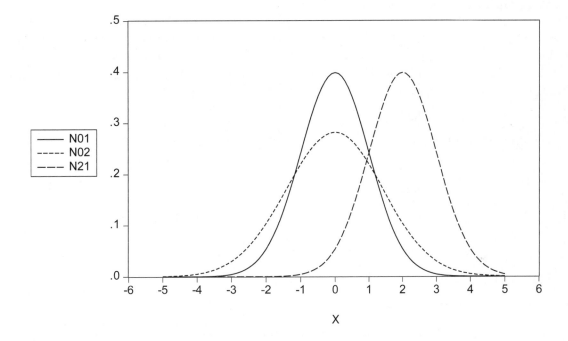

Using the **Options/Line & Symbols** feature in the graph, we can also apply different symbols to the curves so that they can be distinguished in black and white. For more on graphics options, on the main EViews menu select **Help/Users Guide I**.

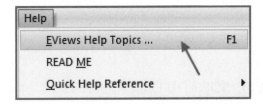

Open the sequence of help links shown on the next page to find help on graphics.

- "Object View and Procedure Reference" lists all of the views and procedures associated with each object.

- "Object Command Summary" provides the reverse listing of the objects associated with each view and procedure.

- "Graph Creation Commands" documents the specialized object view commands for producing graph views from various EViews data objects. Commands for customizing graphs are outlined in the graph object reference (see "Graph").

- "Command Reference" lists basic EViews auxiliary (generally commands not associated with specific objects) and interactive commands.

B.5 PLOTTING THE *T*-DISTRIBUTION

The distribution that you will be using perhaps the most is the *t*-distribution. It is discussed in Section B.3.7 in *POE4*. The formula is very complicated, and we will not report it, but EViews allows us to plot the distribution easily. The function **@dtdist(x,v)** returns the value of the density function of a *t*-random variable with **v** degrees of freedom for the value **x**. To generate the density values for a *t*-distribution with three degrees of freedom, the command is

  series t3 = @dtdist(x,3)

Using **Quick/Graph/XY line** plot the N(0,1) density *N01* and the $t_{(3)}$ density on the same graph.

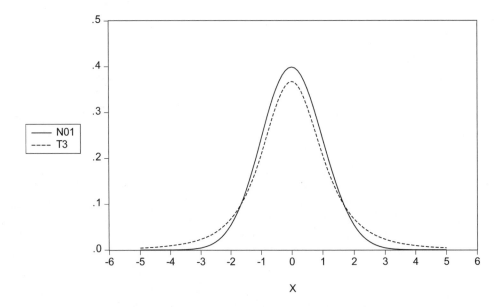

B.6 PLOTTING THE CHI-SQUARE DISTRIBUTION

The *F* and chi-square distributions are only defined for positive values. Let's create a new variable *W* that takes values in the interval [.1, 25.1] in increments of 0.25. These are simply positive values that can be used to construct the graphs.

  series w = .1 + @trend/4

For the chi-square density we need to specify the value of one parameter, its degrees of freedom, *m*, which is also its mean:

> **series chi4 = @dchisq(w,4)**
> **series chi8 = @dchisq(w,8)**

Plot these values against *W*.

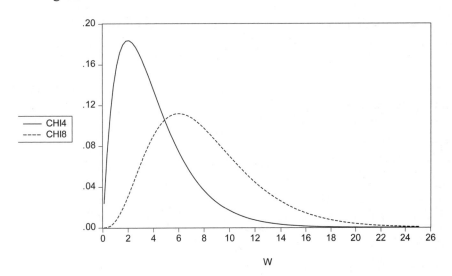

B.7 PLOTTING THE *F* DISTRIBUTION

The *F*-distribution depends on two degrees of freedom parameters: The numerator degrees of freedom m_1 and the denominator degrees of freedom m_2. Let's choose $m_1 = 7$ and $m_2 = 30$. Define *WF* for these plots so that it ranges from [.1, 5.1]. In the Command window, type

> **series wf = .1 + @trend/20**

Then generate the *F*- distribution values and plot:

> **series F = @dfdist(wf,7,30)**

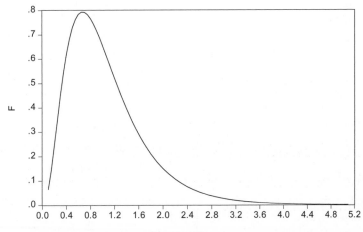

B.8 PROBABILITY CALCULATIONS FOR THE *T, F,* AND CHI-SQUARE

Probability calculations for distributions other than the normal are set up the same way using functions beginning with **@c**. Thus we can compute, for some specified value *x*:

The probability that $t_{(m)} \leq x$ uses the command **scalar pt = @ctdist(x,m)**.

The probability that $\chi^2_{(m)} \leq x$ uses the command **scalar pc = @cchisq(x,m)**.

The probability that $F_{(m_1, m_2)} \leq x$ uses the command **scalar pf = @cfdist(x,m1,m2)**.

We can compute critical values such that a probability **p** falls to the left of the critical value by using quantile functions that begin with **@q**. The commands for the three distributions are:

```
scalar tc = @qtdist(p,m)
scalar cc = @qchisq(p,m)
scalar fc = @qfdist(p,m1,m2)
```

The names we have assigned can be changed, of course, and specific values must be used for **m** and **p**. For example, for a *t*-distribution with 20 degrees of freedom, the value t_c such that

$$P\left[t_{(20)} \leq t_c \right] = 0.95$$

uses the command

```
scalar tc = @qtdist(.95,20)
```

The resulting value is 1.724718, which you may compare with the value in Table 2 of *POE4*.

B.9 RANDOM NUMBERS

At the basis of Monte Carlo simulations is the ability to draw samples of random numbers from specific distributions. EViews has a full complement of random number generators. Go to the Function Reference Help:

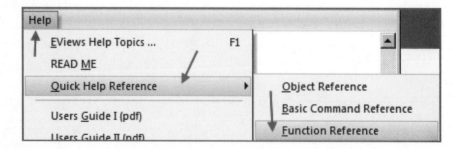

Select **Statistical Distribution Functions**.

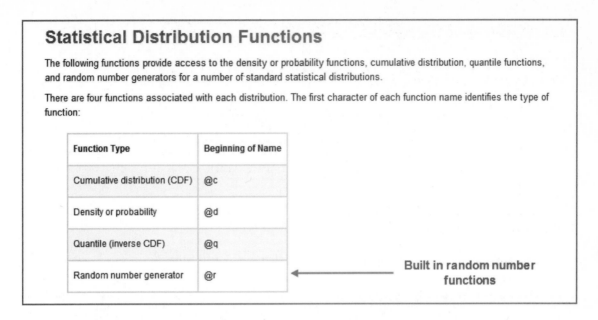

Statistical Distribution Functions

The following functions provide access to the density or probability functions, cumulative distribution, quantile functions, and random number generators for a number of standard statistical distributions.

There are four functions associated with each distribution. The first character of each function name identifies the type of function:

Function Type	Beginning of Name
Cumulative distribution (CDF)	@c
Density or probability	@d
Quantile (inverse CDF)	@q
Random number generator	@r

Built in random number functions

For the long list of statistical distributions that follows, each has these four types of functions. In particular, for the uniform we have

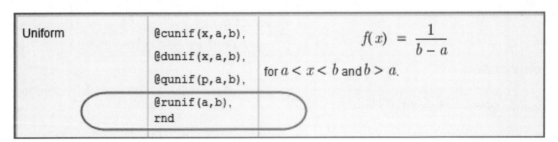

Uniform	`@cunif(x,a,b),`	
	`@dunif(x,a,b),`	$f(x) = \dfrac{1}{b-a}$
	`@qunif(p,a,b),`	for $a < x < b$ and $b > a$.
	`@runif(a,b),` `rnd`	

The function **@runif(a,b)** generates a random value on the interval (a, b). The function **rnd** creates a random value in the $(0, 1)$ interval.

To illustrate, in the workfile *appendix_b.wf1* change the range of observations to 1000. Double-click on **Range** and change the number of observations.

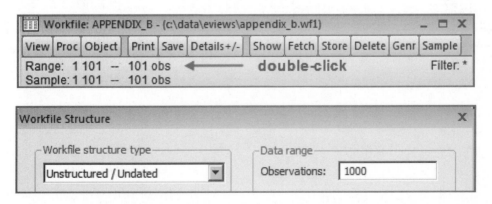

You will be asked if this is **OK**. Select **Yes**.

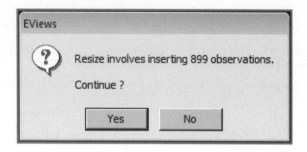

Enter the command

    series u12 = @runif(1,2)

Open this series by double-clicking and obtain the **Histogram and Stats**.

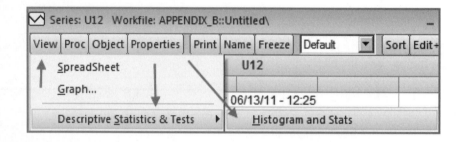

As you can see, all the values fall between 1 and 2 with mean value 1.4789, which is close to the theoretically true value of 1.5.

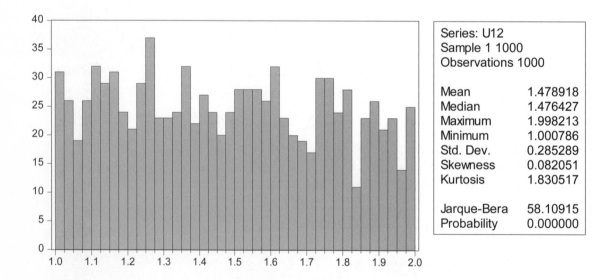

The uniformity of the values is made clearer by using 10,000 observations.

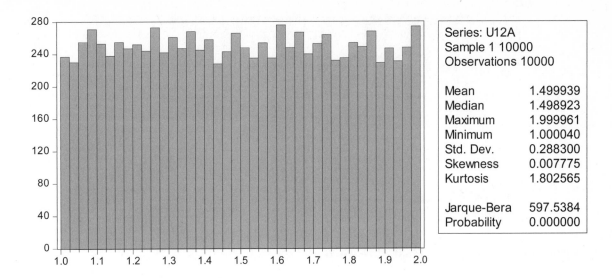

Similarly, for the normal distribution the function **@rnorm**, or simply **nrnd**, generates random values from the standard normal distribution:

Normal (Gaussian)	@cnorm(x), @dnorm(x), @qnorm(p), @rnorm, nrnd	$f(x) = (2\pi)^{-1/2} e^{-x^2/2}$ for $-\infty < x < \infty$. $\longleftarrow$ **N(0, 1)**

The command is

> **series rnormal01 = nrnd**

Double-click the series to open it, and choose **View/Graph**.

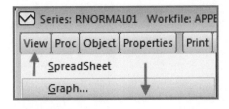

Choose the **Histogram** and click **Options.**

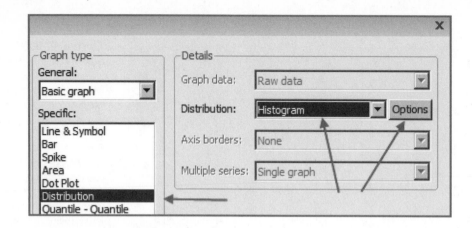

Select **Add**, then choose **Theoretical Density.**

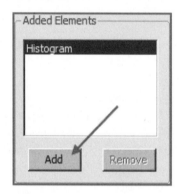

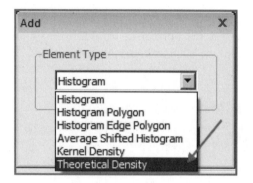

The dialog box now shows

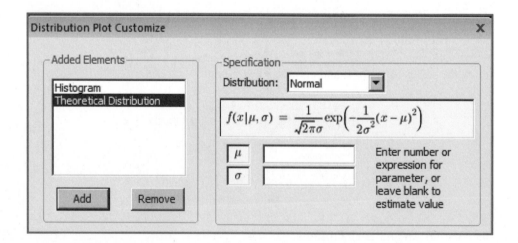

Select **OK** and then **OK** again. The resulting graph is the histogram of the values and the superimposed **Theoretical Distribution** using the sample mean −0.0090 and sample standard deviation 0.9956:

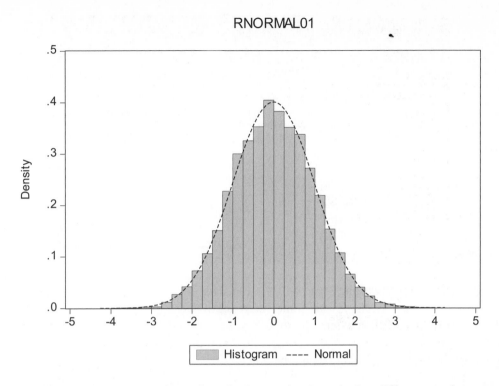

RNORMAL01

The only problem with what we have done is that each of us obtains different random numbers. As explain in *POE4*, Appendix B.4.1, random number generators are actually functions that have a starting value called a **seed**. In EViews press F1, find and display Random number seed in the index:

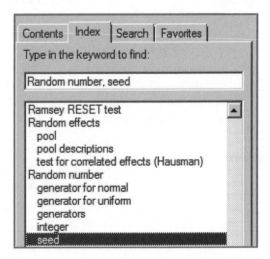

There you find that the command to set a random number seed is **rndseed**. Give it a try. Issue the commands

```
rndseed 1234567
series rnormal01_seeded = nrnd
```

The first few values we obtain are

Below the syntax for **rndseed** you will find discussions of the types of random number generators EViews has available and some references. There is a huge literature in numerical analysis on this topic. Do <u>not</u> attempt to use your own random number generators in your research. Leave it to the professionals, though when you do simulations the software used, and its version, plus the type of generator, should be noted.

Keywords

@cchisq	@qnorm	nrnd
@cfdist	@rnorm	probability density function
@cnorm	@runif	quantile functions
@ctdist	@trend	random number
@dchisq	chi-square distribution	rnd
@dfdist	cumulative distribution	scalar
@dtdist	F distribution	t distribution
@qchisq	histogram	vector
@qfdist	normal distribution	XY line graph

APPENDIX **C**

Review of Statistical Inference

CHAPTER OUTLINE

C.1 A HISTOGRAM

Open the EViews workfile *hip.wf1*. Double-click on Y, which is hip width, to open the series into a spreadsheet view. Select **View/Descriptive Statistics & Tests/Stats Table.**

	Y
Mean	17.15820
Median	17.08500
Maximum	20.40000
Minimum	13.53000
Std. Dev.	1.807013
Skewness	-0.013825
Kurtosis	2.331534
Jarque-Bera	0.932523
Probability	0.627343
Sum	857.9100
Sum Sq. Dev.	159.9995
Observations	50

To construct a histogram, from the spreadsheet select **View/Graph,** then choose **Distribution.**

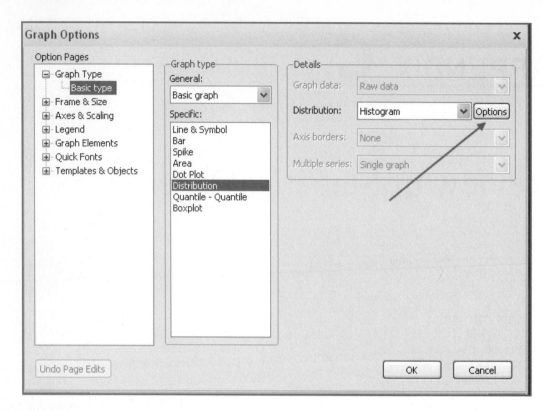

To have the figure closely resemble Figure C.1, select **Options,** then choose **Relative Frequency** for **Scaling** and choose the **User-specified Bin width** of 0.9814. This seemingly odd choice is the maximum value (20.4) minus the minimum value (13.53) divided by 7, which will be the number of bins (or figure bars). Click **OK**.

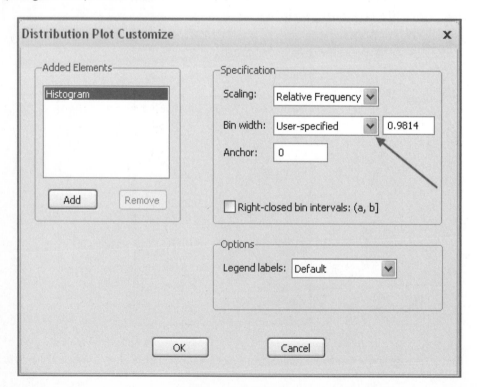

On the **Axes & Scaling** tab select the **Bottom Axis,** and for the **Bottom axis scale endpoints** select **User specified.** Type in the minimum and maximum values suggested below.

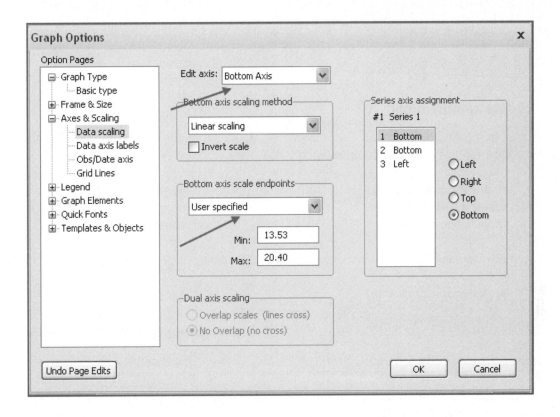

Select **OK** and the resulting figure is

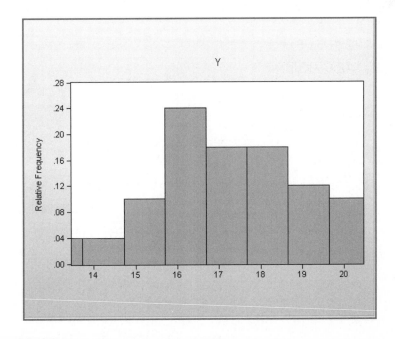

C.2 SUMMARY STATISTICS

The sample mean $\bar{y} = \sum y_i / N = 17.1582$ is shown in the descriptive statistics table, along with several other summary measures. In this section we illustrate how to create a wide range of summary statistics with EViews functions. There are several ways to do these calculations; we suggest one set of commands.

C.2.1 The sample mean

The sample mean is discussed in *POE4* Section C.3. To generate the sample mean for the hip data, use the following Eviews commands:

scalar ysum = @sum(y)	*sum of y values*
scalar n = @obs(y)	*number of observations*
scalar ybar = ysum/n	*sample mean*

There is also an inbuilt Eviews command to compute the mean:

scalar ybar = @mean(y)	*sample mean*

Your workfile will now look like this; double-clicking on a scalar item will reveal the computed values.

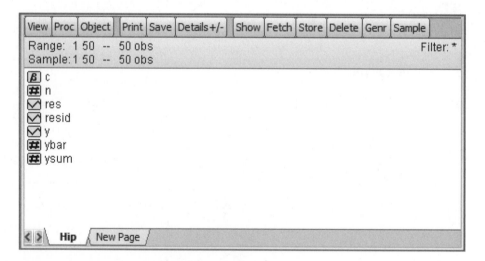

The scalar values created are:

	Value
YSUM	857.9100

	Value
N	50.00000

	Value
YBAR	17.15820

C.2.2 Estimating higher moments

In *POE4* Section C.4.2, higher moments for the hip data are also estimated. The formulas for computing these higher moments, as well as the mean, variance and standard deviation, are shown in the table below:

Descriptive Statistics	Formula	EViews commands
Sample Mean	$\bar{Y} = \dfrac{1}{N}\sum Y_i$	scalar ybar = @mean(y) or scalar mu1 = @sum(y)/n
Sample Variance	$\hat{\sigma}^2 = \dfrac{1}{N-1}\sum\left(Y_i - \bar{Y}\right)^2$	scalar sig2 = @vars(y) or scalar mu2 = @sumsq(y-ybar)/(n-1)
Standard Deviation	$\hat{\sigma} = \sqrt{\hat{\sigma}^2}$	scalar sig1 = @sqrt(sig2)
Standard Error of the Mean	$se(\bar{Y}) = \dfrac{\hat{\sigma}}{\sqrt{N}}$	scalar sem = sig1/@sqrt(n)
3rd Moment About Mean	$\tilde{\mu}_3 = \dfrac{1}{N}\sum\left(Y_i - \bar{Y}\right)^3$	series yy3 = (y-ybar)^3 scalar mu3 = @sum(yy3)/n
4th Moment About Mean	$\tilde{\mu}_4 = \dfrac{1}{N}\sum\left(Y_i - \bar{Y}\right)^4$	series yy4 = (y-ybar)^4 scalar mu4 = @sum(yy4)/n
Skewness	$S = \dfrac{\tilde{\mu}_3}{\tilde{\sigma}^3}$	scalar sk1 = @skew(y) or scalar sk2 = mu3/sig1^3
Kurtosis	$K = \dfrac{\tilde{\mu}_4}{\tilde{\sigma}^4}$	scalar ku1 = @kurt(y) or scalar ku2 = mu4/sig1^4

The hip data are slightly negatively skewed ($S = -0.0138$) and slightly less peaked ($K = 2.3315$) than would be expected for a normal distribution.

C.3 HYPOTHESIS TESTING AND INTERVAL ESTIMATION

In *POE4* Sections C.5-7, various hypothesis tests are discussed. In this section we show how to extract probability values from EViews. Eviews offers four functions associated with each distribution and the type of function is identified by the first character. For details, see Appendix B. Or, for an overview of what EViews offers, click **Help** on the EViews main menu, then select **Quick Help Reference/Function Reference** and click on **Statistical Distribution Functions**.

Function Type	Beginning of Name
Cumulative distribution (CDF)	@c
Density or probability	@d
Quantile (inverse CDF)	@q
Random number generator	@r

The following examples are based on data in the EViews workfile *hip.wf1*.

1. What is the probability that a randomly drawn person will have hips larger than 18 inches?

$$\widehat{P(Y > 18)} \cong P\left(\frac{Y - \bar{y}}{\hat{\sigma}} > \frac{18 - 17.158}{1.8070}\right) = P(Z > .4659) = .3207$$

Use **@cnorm** to compute the cumulative normal probability that Z is greater than .4659.

scalar pygt18 = 1 - @cnorm(.4659)

	Value
PYGT18	0.320644

2. How wide would an airplane seat have to be to fit 95% of the population? Let $y*$ denote the required seat size; then

$$\widehat{P(Y \leq y*)} \cong P\left(\frac{Y - \bar{y}}{\hat{\sigma}} \leq \frac{y* - 17.1582}{1.8070}\right) = P\left(Z \leq \frac{y* - 17.1582}{1.8070}\right) = .95$$

The value of Z such that $P(Z \leq z*) = .95$ is $z* = 1.645$. It is computed using **@qnorm**.

scalar z95 = @qnorm(.95)

	Value
Z95	1.644854

Then $y*$ can be calculated as

$$\frac{y*-17.1582}{1.8070} = 1.645 \Rightarrow y* = 20.1305$$

This value can be computed using the EViews command

scalar ystar = ybar + sig1*z95

	Value
YSTAR	20.13047

3. The $100(1-\alpha)\%$ interval estimator for μ for the hip data is:

$$\bar{y} \pm t_c \frac{\hat{\sigma}}{\sqrt{N}} = 17.1582 \pm 2.01 \frac{1.807}{\sqrt{50}} = [16.6447, \ 17.6717]$$

The critical value for interval estimation comes from a t-distribution with $N-1 = 49$ degrees of freedom. This value is found using the EViews command **@qtdist(p,v)**, which calculates the **p -quantile**, or **percentile**, of the t-distribution with **v** degrees of freedom. Thus the 97.5 percentile of the t-distribution with 49 degrees of freedom is obtained using

scalar t975 = @qtdist(.975,49)

	Value
T975	2.009575

The upper and lower bounds of the interval estimate are given by

scalar lb = ybar - t975*sem
scalar ub = ybar + t975*sem

	Value
LB	16.64465

	Value
UB	17.67175

4. Consider a one-tail test:

$$H_0 : \mu = 16.5, \quad H_1 : \mu > 16.5$$

The test statistic is

$$t = \frac{\bar{Y} - 16.5}{\hat{\sigma}/\sqrt{N}} \sim t_{(N-1)}$$

The value of the test statistic is calculated using

scalar t1 = (ybar - 16.5)/sem

	Value
T1	2.575619

The right tail $\alpha = 0.05$ critical value of the t-distribution with 49 degrees of freedom is

scalar t95 = @qtdist(.95,49)

	Value
T95	1.676551

The *p*-value is the probability that a *t*-statistic with 49 degrees of freedom is greater than **T1** = 2.5756. Recalling the definition of a **cumulative distribution function**, this value is given by

scalar p1 = 1 - @ctdist(t1,49)

	Value
P1	0.006537

5. Consider a two-tail test:

$$H_0 : \mu = 17, \qquad H_1 : \mu \neq 17$$

The test statistic is

$$t = \frac{\overline{Y} - 17}{\hat{\sigma}/\sqrt{N}} \sim t_{(N-1)}$$

For a test at the α = 0.05 level, the critical value is the 97.5 percentile of the $t_{(49)}$ distribution. This value was calculated and called **T975** when we found an interval estimate. The value of the test statistic is calculated using

scalar t2 = (ybar - 17)/sem

	Value
T2	0.619056

The *p*-value is the probability that a *t*-statistic with 49 degrees of freedom is greater than **T2** = 0.6191, or less than −0.6191. This value is given by

scalar p2 = 2*(1 - @ctdist(abs(t2),49))

	Value
P2	0.538747

The complicated formula for the *p*-value is useful because its general setup will work for any two-tail test. It is twice the area in the right tail of the *t*-distribution beyond the **absolute value** of the *t*-statistic.

C.4 MAXIMUM LIKELIHOOD ESTIMATION

POE4 also contains an introduction to maximum likelihood estimation. In this section, we show how to apply the maximum likelihood method to obtain estimates of a mean and a variance. We shall use the hip data, for which we have already established that the sample mean is 17.1582 and the sample standard deviation is 1.8070.

The method is based on the assumption that an observation (in this case the width of hips) is a drawing from a specified form of probability distribution. We will assume that hip width is a drawing from a normal distribution with unknown mean μ and unknown variance σ^2:

$$y_i \sim N(\mu, \sigma^2)$$

The probability density function for y is:

$$f(y \mid \mu, \sigma^2) = (2\pi\sigma^2)^{-1/2} \exp\left\{\frac{1}{2}\left(\frac{y-\mu}{\sigma}\right)^2\right\}$$

The log-likelihood function, obtained by taking logs of the density function and then summing over all observations, is:

$$\ln L(\mu, \sigma) = \sum_{i=1}^{N} \ln f(y_i \mid \mu, \sigma^2)$$

$$= -\frac{N}{2}(\log(2\pi) + \log\sigma^2) - \frac{1}{2}\sum_{i=1}^{N}\left(\frac{y_i - \mu}{\sigma}\right)^2$$

$$= \sum_{i=1}^{N}\left\{\log\left[\phi\left(\frac{y_i - \mu}{\sigma}\right)\right] - \frac{1}{2}\log(\sigma^2)\right\}$$

where

$$\phi(z) = (2\pi)^{-1/2} \exp\left\{-z^2/2\right\}$$

is the density function of a standard normal random variable.

To get EViews to find the values for μ and σ^2 that maximize the log-likelihood function, open the Eviews workfile *hip.wf1*, then select **Object/New Object/LogL**:

Click OK and type in the following commands:

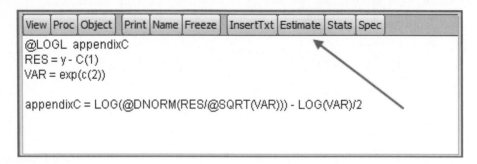

In this window:
1. The first line assigns a name to the log-likelihood to be calculated. We have called it **appendixC**.
2. The parameter μ to be estimated is denoted by C(1).
3. The second parameter to be estimated is given as $c(2) = \log(\sigma^2)$. This specification is convenient because it means that $\sigma^2 = \exp(c(2))$, guaranteeing that we will obtain a positive estimate for σ^2.
4. The variables **RES** and **VAR** are convenient intermediate steps.
5. The last line computes a value for the log-likelihood for a single observation. EViews sums these values to give the log-likelihood that we specified above.

Clicking on **Estimate** yields the following results:

Method: Maximum Likelihood (Marquardt)

Sample: 1 50
Included observations: 50
Evaluation order: By equation
Convergence achieved after 1 iteration

	Coefficient	Std. Error	z-Statistic	Prob.
C(1)	17.15820	0.252999	67.81912	0.0000
C(2)	1.163149	0.245131	4.745000	0.0000

Log likelihood	-100.0256	Akaike info criterion	4.081025
Avg. log likelihood	-2.000512	Schwarz criterion	4.157506
Number of Coefs.	2	Hannan-Quinn criter.	4.110149

The results show that the maximum likelihood estimate of the mean is identical to the sample mean calculated earlier. The maximum likelihood estimate of the standard deviation can be computed as follows:

scalar sdml = @sqrt(exp(1.163149))

	Value
SDML	1.788853

This value is different from the sample variance because the divisor for the maximum likelihood estimate of the variance is N, not $N-1$:

$$\tilde{\sigma}^2_{ML} = \sum\left(Y_i - \overline{Y}\right)^2 \Big/ N$$

As a check, compute this value as

scalar check = @sqrt(@vars(y)*49/50)

	Value
CHECK	1.788852

C.5 KERNEL DENSITY ESTIMATOR

Section C.10 in *POE4* contains a brief description of the kernel density estimator. In this section, we show how to use Eviews to superimpose a kernel distribution on top of a histogram.

Double-click the variable y and select **View/Graph/Distribution**, and from the drop-down menu in **Options** select 'Kernel Density':

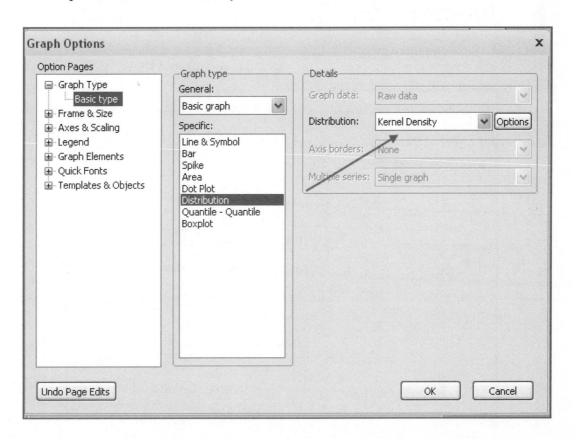

Click **Options** and from the drop-down menu select '**Normal**':

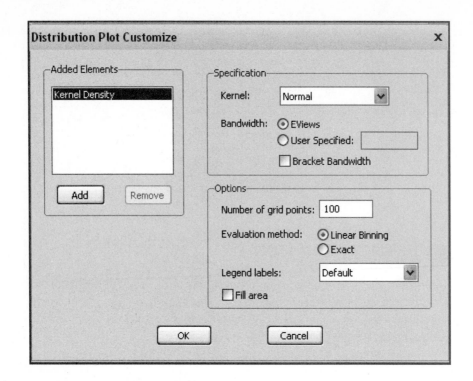

Then click on "**Add**" and select 'Histogram':

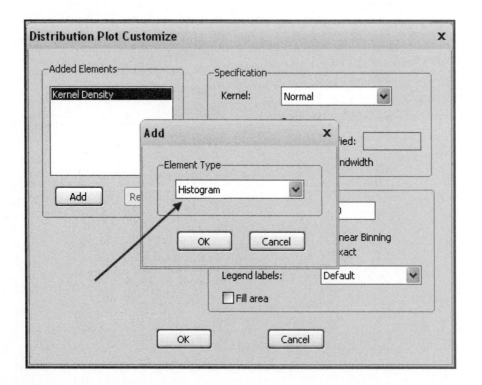

Click **OK**.

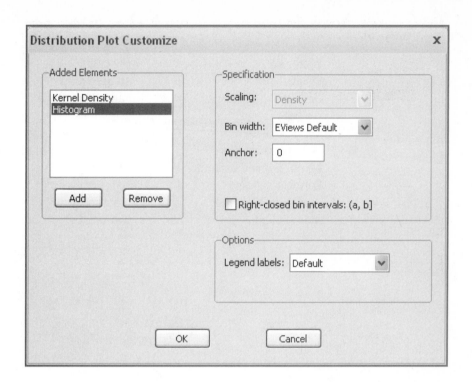

Eviews allows many options to manipulate the kernel, but for now, click **OK** to yield an example of the type of figures shown in Appendix C of *POE4*.

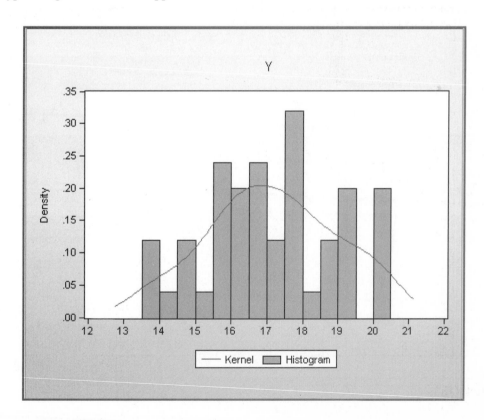

Keywords

@cnorm	@sumsq	p-value
@ctdist	@vars	sample mean
@kurt	descriptive statistics	sample variance
@mean	histogram	skewness
@obs	hypothesis test	standard deviation
@qnorm	interval estimates	standard error of mean
@qtdist	kernel density estimator	Std. Dev.
@skew	kurtosis	Std. Err.
@stdev	maximum likelihood	t-distribution
@sum	one-tail test	two-tail test

INDEX

463